Photoshop® Elements 3 For Dummies®

W9-AND-182

Cheat Sheet

Shortcuts for Mac and Editor Component of Windows

Toolbox Shortcuts

Note: To access the tools, press the key(s) listed. If the Use Shift Key for Tool Switch option is unchecked in your Preferences, you don't need to press the Shift key to change tools.

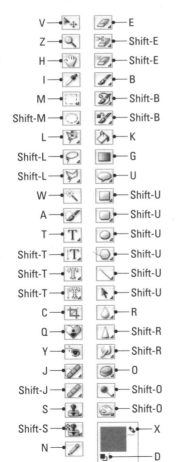

Daily Activities

Function	Windows	Mac
Cancel operation	Ctrl+period or Esc	⌘+period or Esc
Close image	Ctrl+W	⌘+W
General preferences	Ctrl+K	⌘+K
Hide selection outlines	Ctrl+H	⌘+H
Open image	Ctrl+O	⌘+O
Print image	Ctrl+P	⌘+P
Page setup	Ctrl+Shift+P	⌘+Shift+P
Quit Elements	Ctrl+Q	⌘+Q
Save image to disk	Ctrl+S	⌘+S
Save As	Ctrl+Shift+S	⌘+Shift+S
Save for Web	Ctrl+Alt+Shift+S	⌘+Option+Shift+S
Undo last operation	Ctrl+Z	⌘+Z

Selection Tricks

Note: All selection tricks are performed with the lasso, marquee, and wand tools.

Trick	Windows	Mac
Draw straight lines	Alt+click with lasso tool	Option+click with lasso tool
Add to selection outline	Shift+drag	Shift+drag
Deselect specific area	Alt+drag	Option+drag
Deselect all but intersected area	Shift+Alt+drag	Shift+Option+drag
Deselect entire image	Ctrl+D	⌘+D
Reselect last selection	Ctrl+Shift+D	⌘+Shift+D
Select everything	Ctrl+A	⌘+A

Photoshop® Elements 3 For Dummies®

Shortcuts for Mac and Editor Component of Windows

Navigation Tricks

Trick	Windows	Mac
Scroll image	spacebar+drag	spacebar+drag
Zoom in	Ctrl+spacebar+click	⌘+spacebar+click
Zoom in and change window size	Ctrl+plus	⌘+plus
Zoom out	Alt+spacebar+click	Option+spacebar+click
Zoom out and change window size	Ctrl+minus	⌘+minus
Scroll up or down one screen	Page Up/Page Down	Page Up/Page Down
Scroll left or right	Ctrl+Page Up/Page Down	⌘+Page Up/Page Down
Move to upper-left corner of image	Home	Home
Move to lower-right corner of image	End	End
Zoom to 100%	Double-click zoom tool	Double-click zoom tool
Fit on screen	Ctrl+0	⌘+0

Shortcuts for Organizer Component of Windows

Function	Shortcut	Function	Shortcut
Get photos from camera or card reader	Ctrl+G	Clear set date range	Ctrl+Shift+F
Get photos from files and folders	Ctrl+Shift+G	Find by caption or note	Ctrl+Shift+J
Burn or Backup dialog box	Ctrl+B	Find by filename	Ctrl+Shift+K
Rename photo	Ctrl+Shift+N	Open Photo Review	F11
Attach photo to e-mail	Ctrl+Shift+E	Open Photo Compare	F12
Rotate photo 90 degrees left	Ctrl+left arrow	Show details	Ctrl+D
Rotate photo 90 degrees right	Ctrl+right arrow	Show timeline	Ctrl+L
Auto fix photo	Ctrl+Shift+I	Collapse all tags	Ctrl+Alt+T
Go to Standard Edit mode in Editor	Ctrl+I	Expand all tags	Ctrl+Alt+X
Adjust date and time of photos	Ctrl+J	Expand all stacks	Ctrl+Alt+Y
Add caption to photos	Ctrl+Shift+T	Show Photo Browser	Ctrl+Alt+O
Update selected thumbnail	Ctrl+Shift+U	Show Date View	Ctrl+Alt+C
Stack selected photos	Ctrl+Alt+S	Show tags	Ctrl+T
Reveal photos in selected stack	Ctrl+Alt+R	Show collections	Ctrl+Alt+L
Set date range in timeline	Ctrl+Alt+F	Show properties	Alt+Enter

For Dummies: Bestselling Book Series for Beginners

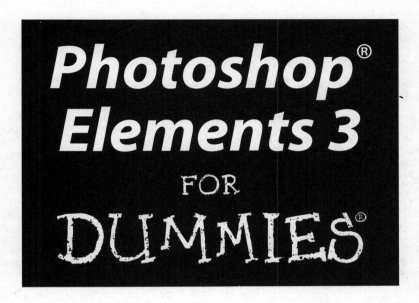

Photoshop® Elements 3 FOR DUMMIES®

by Deke McClelland and Galen Fott

WILEY

Wiley Publishing, Inc.

Photoshop® Elements 3 For Dummies®

Published by
Wiley Publishing, Inc.
111 River Street
Hoboken, NJ 07030-5774
www.wiley.com

Copyright © 2005 by Wiley Publishing, Inc., Indianapolis, Indiana

Published by Wiley Publishing, Inc., Indianapolis, Indiana

Published simultaneously in Canada

For general information on our other products and services, please contact our Customer Care Department within the U.S. at 800-762-2974, outside the U.S. at 317-572-3993, or fax 317-572-4002.

For technical support, please visit www.wiley.com/techsupport.

Wiley also publishes its books in a variety of electronic formats. Some content that appears in print may not be available in electronic books.

Library of Congress Control Number: 2004111024

ISBN: 0-7645-7062-5

Manufactured in the United States of America

10 9 8 7 6 5 4 3 2 1

1O/QT/RR/QU/IN

WILEY

About the Authors

Deke McClelland wrote the *Photoshop Bible* and *Photoshop Bible, Professional Edition* (both published by Wiley), bestselling guides on digital imaging. He has written 76 titles in 25 languages with 3 million copies in print, including *Photoshop For Dummies* (published by Wiley) and the tutorial-based *Adobe Photoshop One-on-One* (published by O'Reilly/Deke Press). In addition to his books, Deke hosts the video training series *Total Training for Adobe Photoshop* and *Total Training Presents: Adobe Photoshop Elements* (published by Total Training). One of the most award-winning writers in the business, Deke has received seven honors from the Computer Press Association. In 2002, he was inducted into the Photoshop Hall of Fame.

Galen Fott contributed to two editions of Deke's *Photoshop Bible* and to *Adobe InDesign CS One-on-One* (O'Reilly/Deke Press). He has also written for *Macworld* and *PC Magazine*. Galen created and hosted *Total Training for Mac OS X*, co-hosted *Total Training for Adobe Premiere 6*, and presented more than two hours of Photoshop training for the Apple Web site (all published by Total Training). In his theoretical spare time, Galen is involved in a number of other pursuits. As an animator, he has worked for AT&T and Paramount. As a performer, he has played leading roles in musicals across the country. As a puppeteer, he has performed with the Jim Henson Company. Those with piqued interest can visit his Web site at www.grundoon.com.

Dedication

To Max, Sam, and Burton: The future of digital imaging is in good (if grubby) hands.

And to Elle and Laura: Whose good hands we're glad to be in.

Authors' Acknowledgments

The authors would like to thank Matt Wagner at Waterside Productions, Susan Pink, Brian Maffitt, the Corbis Corporation, Barbara Obermeier, Linda Bigbee, Veronica Langley, and especially Laura Bigbee-Fott for many wonderful photos.

Publisher's Acknowledgments

We're proud of this book; please send us your comments through our online registration form located at www.dummies.com/register/.

Some of the people who helped bring this book to market include the following:

Acquisitions, Editorial, and Media Development

Project Editor: Susan Pink

Acquisitions Editor: Bob Woerner

Technical Editor: Allen L. Wyatt, Discovery Computing Inc.

Editorial Manager: Carol Sheehan

Media Development Manager: Laura VanWinkle

Media Development Supervisor: Richard Graves

Editorial Assistant: Amanda Foxworth

Cartoons: Rich Tennant, www.the5thwave.com

Composition

Project Coordinator: Maridee Ennis

Layout and Graphics: Lauren Goddard, Joyce Haughey, Stephanie D. Jumper, Barry Offringa, Jacque Roth, Ron Terry

Proofreaders: John Greenough, Brian H. Walls TECHBOOKS Production Services

Indexer: TECHBOOKS Production Services

Publishing and Editorial for Technology Dummies

Richard Swadley, Vice President and Executive Group Publisher

Andy Cummings, Vice President and Publisher

Mary Bednarek, Executive Acquisitions Director

Mary C. Corder, Editorial Director

Publishing for Consumer Dummies

Diane Graves Steele, Vice President and Publisher

Joyce Pepple, Acquisitions Director

Composition Services

Gerry Fahey, Vice President of Production Services

Debbie Stailey, Director of Composition Services

Contents at a Glance

Table of Contents

Introduction

Well, Photoshop Elements 3.0 is here, and we have good news and — for some, at least — bad news to report. But gee, let's start with the good news. Adobe, once again, did an outstanding job updating Photoshop Elements, their popular image editor for Windows and Macintosh. They've packed in an amazingly generous assortment of new tools from the latest version of Photoshop, including the healing brush. (The healing brush! Infirm and sickly photos, rejoice!) Adobe has also thrown in a few new Elements-exclusive goodies for your delectation and delight.

And now for the bad news (Mac users, brace yourselves). The Windows version of Elements gets another big addition to the program's arsenal of tools — and that's good — but the Mac version doesn't get it, and that's too bad. Windows users get not only the updated image editor, but also Photoshop Album, Adobe's powerful image-organizing program. And Album isn't just tagging along for the ride; it's been integrated into Elements, so much so that it's not even referred to as "Album," but as the "Organizer" component of Elements. So what you used to think of as Photoshop Elements, the image editor, is now just one half of Photoshop Elements 3.0 — the "Editor" component. The other half is The Organizer Formerly Known As Photoshop Album.

Now, to be fair, Photoshop Album was always a Windows-only application, and Adobe would have had to do a huge amount of work to turn it into an Organizer component for the Mac. And truthfully, it would have been somewhat redundant because the Mac already has a powerful built-in image organizer in iPhoto. But as a consolation, Adobe stuck some great organizing and photo-searching features into Elements' File Browser — for the Mac only.

So we've added a lengthy new Chapter 6, giving Windows users the lowdown on how Organizer works. (In truth, organizing photos is nowhere near as complicated as editing them can be.) But by and large, 19 chapters in this 20-chapter book apply equally to all, regardless of what flavor of computer you use.

Windows or Mac, Photoshop Elements' main reason for being is still to make your photos look better; and it's a powerhouse at that task. But all this power comes at a price. Elements is a great image editor, but it's also complex. Adobe Photoshop Elements is an easier-to-use, scaled-down version of Adobe Photoshop, a program legendary for its power and complexity. Photoshop Elements is missing some of Photoshop's high-end features, and it has some exclusive tools of its own. However, we said it in the last edition of this book, and we'll say it again:

Photoshop Elements Is Photoshop

What exactly do we mean by that? Well, we don't mean that Elements isn't *any* easier to use than Photoshop; Elements has an extensive, genuinely helpful Help system. And we also don't mean that Elements doesn't need its own *Dummies* book. (Perish the thought!) Here's what we mean: To get the most out of Photoshop Elements, you still have to come to grips with the same complex concepts and tools that Photoshop uses. And if you've ever experimented with Photoshop, you know that isn't easy.

You want examples? We've got examples. First, take a gander at this exceedingly cute cat photo in Figure 1.

Figure 1:
An
exceedingly
cute cat.

Exceedingly cute, huh? Maybe the photo's a little dark, but that can be corrected. Now, if you wanted to correct this somewhat dark photo with an image-editing application, and you saw a command called Brightness/Contrast, you'd be tempted to use it, wouldn't you? Heck, your TV has brightness and contrast controls! Brightness/Contrast it is!

Terrible move. Brightness/Contrast is among the worst commands that Photoshop and Elements offer. Sure, it's easy to use, but correcting photos on the computer is like many things in life: You get out of it what you put into it. Instead of Brightness/Contrast, what you should use to correct brightness — in Photoshop or Elements — is the Levels command. And Figure 2 shows you the Levels dialog box when applied to the exceedingly cute cat photo.

Yikes! What the heck is that jagged black blob? What do all those sliders and buttons do? And what does this monstrosity have to do with that exceedingly cute cat?

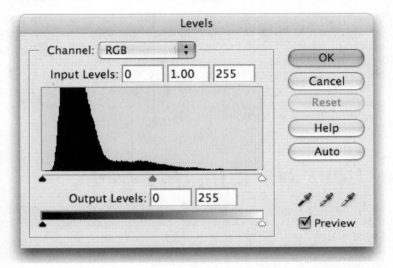

Figure 2:
The exceedingly cute cat photo, as represented in the Levels dialog box.

Well, in truth, Levels isn't really that difficult after you understand the concept it's based on, but we show it to you here to prove a point: Levels is a splendid tool for brightening images, but it's hardly intuitive. And Levels is the same in Elements as it is in Photoshop. If you think you would need help mastering Photoshop (and you would), you'll need help using Elements, too.

And that's where this book comes in.

About This Book

Because Elements' roots are in Photoshop, we hope you'll forgive us for feeling that we're particularly well suited to guide you through Elements. Deke has been using Photoshop since version 1.0 was introduced and has gone on to become the best-selling author of *Photoshop For Dummies, Photoshop Bible,* and a bevy of other books on digital imaging. Galen, slacker that he is, didn't get with Photoshop until version 2.0 came out in 1991, but since then he's used it almost daily. It's the benchmark against which he's judged many other image-editing applications as a reviewer for *Macworld* and *PC Magazine.*

For that matter, Deke — in cahoots with the fine folks at Total Training (www. totaltraining.com) — is officially responsible for introducing the Windows version of Elements 3.0 to the world! Windows users, just click the Product Overview icon on the main installer screen of your Elements installer CD, prop your feet up, and let Deke be your personal tour guide for a 30-minute introduction to Elements 3.0.

In this book, we set out to explain Photoshop Elements 3.0 from the ground up, assuming that you know nothing about the program or even about image editing in general. (That, incidentally, is what's meant by the word *Dummies* in the title. We know you're not a dummy about every topic, but the title *Photoshop Elements 3 For Dummies About Photoshop Elements 3* was deemed to be lacking in elegance.) Step by step, concept by concept, we gradually work through a thorough examination of Photoshop Elements 3.0 and the incredible things it can do for your images.

Conventions Used in This Book

Many times in this book, you'll be asked to press some keys on your computer keyboard to make Elements do its stuff. We tell you which keys to press like so:

> Ctrl+Shift+P (⌘+Shift+P on the Mac)

This means to press the Ctrl key, and then press the Shift key while still holding down Ctrl, and then press the P key while still holding down the other two keys. (Mac users, substitute the ⌘ key for Ctrl.) It doesn't matter whether you press Shift or Ctrl (⌘ on the Mac) first, but the letter key (P in this case) must always come last.

What You're Not to Read

Mac users, you can sit out Chapter 6; it deals exclusively with the Organizer component, available only in Windows. A few other short sections in the book are Mac-only or Windows-only, particularly in Chapter 18; look for the icons in the margins to alert you.

Foolish Assumptions

We assume only three things:

- You have a computer.
- It's turned on.
- It has Photoshop Elements 3 installed on it.

If you can meet these stringent requirements, we can take it from here.

How This Book Is Organized

To give you an overview of the kind of information you're likely to find in these pages, here's a quick rundown of the five parts.

Part I: Element-ary School

We begin at the beginning, by answering the question "What exactly *is* image editing, anyway?" From there we get face to interface with Elements, exploring the array of tools and palettes it places on your screen. We talk about opening images and then do a profile on the pixel, without which digital images wouldn't be. And although the last chapter is an examination of color, we hope it will be free of any purple prose.

Part II: Be Prepared

This is the part you'll skip because you're too eager to start cleaning up your photos, but you'll come back when you can't figure out what the heck is going on, or you can't find the photo you want to clean up. Chapter 6 introduces Windows users to the fabulous new Organizer component of Elements. Then Chapter 7 tells everyone about how to save their files in the proper format. Chapter 8 tells you how to correct your mistakes and also how to print your images when there are no more mistakes to correct. Chapter 9 focuses on isolating parts of your pictures with selections, and Chapter 10 introduces the multileveled concept of layers.

Part III: Realer Than Life

This part of the book details how to take a bad image and make it better, or how to take a good image and make it great. In Chapter 11, we get down and dirty with the topic of cleaning up your images. In Chapter 12, we check out the editing tools in Elements. Chapter 13 looks at the powerful tools for brightening up your images — including that eagerly anticipated Levels command.

Part IV: Unreality Programming

The preceding part was all about making images look better; this part begins with a chapter on how to make them look weirder, using the many distorting capabilities in Elements. From there we start with a clean canvas and explore the subject of painting and coloring. From painting pictures, we move on to how to create a thousand words (or fewer) with the type tools. And we wrap up this part with a bang as we reveal some extraordinary tricks that Elements can do all on its own.

Part V: The Part of Tens

The Part of Tens is a *For Dummies* tradition. You don't want to follow traditions? Don't read this part. But then you'll miss a couple of really neat Top Ten lists: ten important techniques to remember that utilize the keyboard, and ten reasons you might possibly want to upgrade from Elements to Photoshop someday.

Icons Used in This Book

After the release of the very first *For Dummies* books, a scientific study revealed that although most people were indeed learning great amounts from the books, a few were distracted by a compulsive need to doodle in the margins. The publishers decided there was only one solution: Do the margin doodling themselves. And so the *For Dummies* icon system was born. Over the years, the icons have taken on specific meanings, alerting you to the type of information the text may contain. In this section, we describe the meaning of the icons in this book.

This icon lets you know that we're talking about a new feature in Photoshop Elements 3.0 or a change that the program has undergone since the last version. This means that experienced Elements 2.0 users can just rifle through the book in search of this icon, culling all the juicy new bits and ignoring the rest of our deathless prose. (Sniff.)

This icon lets you know we're talking about a Windows-only feature.

When Windows readers see this icon, take a snooze; this info works on the Mac only.

You can pretty much bet there will be some eight- and nine-letter words in these sections. Technical Stuff is information that maybe isn't vital but can help enrich your understanding if you take a few minutes to wrap your brain around it.

This is the really good stuff. Generally, a Tip is a less-than-obvious technique for accomplishing the task at hand. Here's where you get to reap the benefits of our years of image-editing experience. Don't bother to thank us. It's our job. Oh, okay, you can go ahead and thank us.

Not that you should forget everything else, but these Remember sections contain particularly important points.

Okay, the worst thing that can happen when using Elements is that you'll lose a few hours of work. You're not going to find any warnings in this book that say "Clicking this command will make your laptop suddenly snap shut and break your fingers." But hey, lost work is no fun, either.

Well, this is the stuff that's not really technical, or a tip, or particularly worth remembering, or a warning about anything. And yet it seemed somehow icon-worthy. So . . . it's gossip. So there.

Where to Go from Here

Want to send us congratulations, compliments, or complaints? If so, you can visit Deke's Web site at www.dekemc.com and drop him a line, or stop by Galen's Web site at www.grundoon.com and e-mail him as well. We get a ton of e-mail, but we definitely read it all and respond to a fair amount of it as well. We'd especially appreciate suggestions for improving this book in its next edition.

You can also contact the publisher or authors of other *For Dummies* books by visiting the publisher's Web site at http://dummies.com or sending paper mail to Wiley Publishing, Inc., 10475 Crosspoint Boulevard, Indianapolis, IN 46256.

Part I

Element-ary School

In this part . . .

*I*f just thinking about the name *Photoshop Elements* makes you feel as though you're about to drown in a sea of confusing concepts and terminology, consider this part of the book a life preserver with your name on it. (Yeah, life preservers usually have the name of the ship on them, but whatever.) Taking in anything new can be intimidating, but we set out to make the process as painless as possible, starting with the very first chapter.

Speaking of that very first chapter, it seeks to answer the timeless question: "Just what exactly *is* Photoshop Elements, anyway?" We very slowly pick up steam in the next chapter; even if you're only vaguely acquainted with your own computer, you'll be fine. From there we look at the all-important topic of opening images and how to view them from different perspectives. Next, we take a penetrating look at that teeny tiny giant, the pixel. And finally, we teach you just enough about color theory to make you dangerous, yet keep your colors Web-safe.

By the end of Chapter 5, you won't know everything there is to know about Elements — otherwise, we could have dispensed with the chapters that follow it — but you'll know enough to phrase a few intelligent questions. And please remember that as you read these chapters, there's no shame in starting out uninformed. Millions of *For Dummies* readers would agree.

Chapter 1

Braving the Elements

As you know if you read the Introduction to this book, the image-editing powers of Photoshop Elements are inherited from another Adobe application called simply "Photoshop." But you still may not be aware that Photoshop is the most comprehensive and popular image editor around. In fact, there's probably not a single computer artist who doesn't use Photoshop almost daily. As an Elements user, you have most of that professional power coiled up inside your computer, waiting for you to discover how to harness it.

Even if you haven't yet used Elements or Photoshop, you probably have at least a vague idea of what they're all about. But just so we're all clear on the subject, the primary purpose of these applications is to make changes to photographic images that you've managed to get on disk, whether from a digital camera, a scanner, or other means. Windows users also have the Organizer component of Elements, which lets you organize and arrange your digital image collection. We examine the Organizer half of Elements in Windows in Chapter 6; for now, when we refer to "Elements," we're referring to the Editor component of the Windows version, which is basically equivalent to the entire Mac version.

If you've used Elements for only a week or so, you may have mistaken it for a fairly straightforward package. Certainly, on the surface, Elements comes off as quite friendly. But lurking a few fathoms deep is another, darker program, one that is distinctly unfriendly for the uninitiated but wildly capable for the stout of heart. Sigmund Freud would no doubt declare Elements a classic case of a split personality. It's half man, half monster; half mild-mannered shoeshine boy, half blonde-grabbing, airplane-swatting King Kong. In short, Elements has a Dr. Jekyll-and-Mr. Hyde thing going — only it's way scarier.

As you may recall from the last time you saw *Abbott and Costello Meet Dr. Jekyll and Mr. Hyde* — indisputably the foremost resource of information on this famous tale — this Jekyll character (not to be confused with the similarly named cartoon magpie) is normally your everyday, average, nice-guy scientist. Then one day, he drinks some potion or gets cut off in traffic or something and changes into his ornery alter ego, known at every dive bar in town by the surname Hyde. Elements behaves the same way, except no magical transformation is required to shift from the easy-to-use part of the program to the scary, technical side. Both personalities — both "elements," if you will — coexist simultaneously in symbiotic harmony.

This chapter explores both the cuddly and not-so-cuddly parts of Elements' brain. (We'll leave the exploration of Abbott's and Costello's brains for another book.) We'll also take a look at the built-in Help features, which are the chief means of distinguishing Elements from its not-so-friendly big brother, Photoshop.

The Bland but Benevolent Dr. Jekyll

To discover the benevolent Dr. Jekyll side of Photoshop Elements, you need look no further than the standard painting and editing tools. Shown in Figure 1-1, these tools are so simple they're practically pastoral, like the kind of household appliances your great-grandmother would have been comfortable with. The eraser tool erases, the pencil tool draws hard-edged lines, the brush tool paints, and so on. These incredibly straightforward tools attract new users just as surely as a light attracts miller moths.

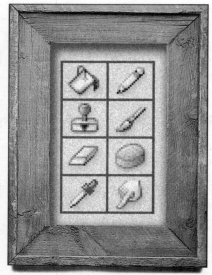

Figure 1-1: Many tools in Elements have an old-world, rustic charm that's sure to warm the cockles of the most timid technophobe.

But you quickly discover that these tools, just like the boring Dr. Jekyll, aren't super-duper exciting on their own. They don't work much like their traditional counterparts — a line drawn with the pencil tool, for example, doesn't look much like a line drawn with a real pencil — and they don't seem to be particularly applicable to the job of editing images. Generally speaking, you have to be blessed with pretty strong hand-eye coordination to achieve good results using these tools.

The Dynamic but Dastardly Mr. Hyde

When the standard paint and editing tools don't fit the bill, you might try to adjust the performance of the tools and experiment with the other image controls of Elements. Unfortunately, that's when you discover the Mr. Hyde side of the program. You encounter options that have meaningless names such as Dissolve, Multiply, and Difference. Commands such as Image Size and Brightness/Contrast — both of which sound harmless enough — can easily damage your image. It's enough to drive a reticent computer artist stark raving insane.

The net result is that many folks return broken and frustrated to the under-equipped and boring but nonthreatening painting and editing tools that they've come to know. It's sad, really. Especially when you consider all the wonderful things that the more complex Photoshop Elements controls can do. Oh sure, the controls have weird names, and they may not respond as you think they should at first. But after you come to terms with these slick puppies, they perform in ways you wouldn't believe.

In fact, the dreaded Mr. Hyde side of Elements represents the core of this powerful program. Without its sinister side, Elements is just another rinky-dink piece of painting software whose most remarkable capability is keeping the kids out of mischief on a rainy day.

It must be noted, however, that even the dastardly Mr. Hyde side of Elements can have a friendly face, namely in Elements' new Quick Fix mode. This mode lets you deal with the complex task of image editing using greatly simplified controls. Compared to a snarling, maniacal real-world encounter with the powerful Mr. Hyde, this is sort of the Hanna-Barbera cartoon version. We visit the Quick Fix mode in Chapter 12.

The Two Elements of Photoshop Elements

Generally speaking, the simple side and the complex side of Photoshop Elements serve different purposes. The straightforward Jekyll tools concentrate mostly on painting, and the more complex Hyde capabilities are devoted to image editing. Therefore, to tackle this great program, you may find it helpful to understand the difference between the two terms.

Painting without the mess

Painting is just what it sounds like: You take a brush loaded with color and smear it all over your on-screen image. You can paint from scratch on a blank canvas, or you can paint directly on top of a photograph. Notice in Figure 1-2 the charming young lady, possibly in costume to portray Glinda the Good Witch in her high school's production of the musical *Wicked*. We introduce this lovely person solely to demonstrate the amazing functions of Elements.

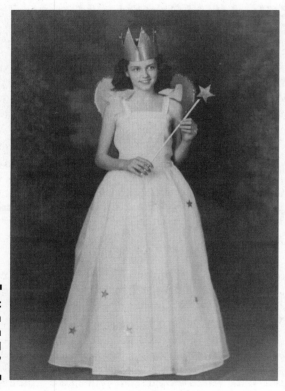

Figure 1-2:
Are you a good witch or a bad witch?

Were you to paint on our unsuspecting fairy queen, you might arrive at something on the order of the image shown on the left in Figure 1-3. All these changes were invoked using a single tool — the brush — and just two colors — black and white. Clearly, the artistic work here is a little, shall we say, unsophisticated. However, it's worth pointing out that the image isn't permanently damaged, as it would have been with a real-life paintbrush. Because the original image is saved to disk (as explained in Chapter 7), we can restore details from the original whenever we get the whim.

Editing existing image detail

The lady on the left in Figure 1-3 may be entertaining to look at, but she's nothing compared to what she could be with the aid of some image editing. When you *edit* an image, you distort and enhance its existing details. So rather than paint with color, you paint with the image itself.

The lady on the right in Figure 1-3 demonstrates what we mean. To arrive at this bizarre image, we started by doing a little plastic surgery on our subject, using the Liquify filter as a substitute for the traditional ugly stick. Liquify was also used to create her stylish hairdo. We selected her crown with the lasso tool and placed it back on her head at a mischievous tilt. Her skirt was turned into a sort of seahorse tail by the Twirl filter. We replaced her pitiful little fairy wings with a pair of eagle wings from another picture, and then cut the whole thing out and placed it on a new background. And finally, we used the custom shape tool to draw the yin-yang symbol at the end of her wand, and applied a couple of layer styles to give it dimensionality and a nice glow. We're not sure exactly what it all means, but she certainly has a little more credibility as an authentic magical fairy-type creature than she did in the left image, huh?

Mind you, you don't have to go quite so hog wild with image editing. If you're a photographer, for example, you may not care to mess with your work to the point that it becomes completely unrecognizable. Figure 1-4 shows a subtle adjustment that affects neither the form nor composition of the original image. These kinds of changes merely accentuate details or downplay defects in the image.

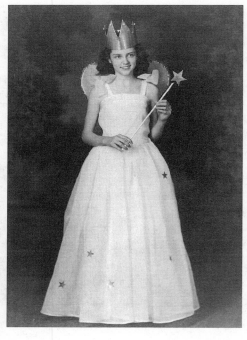

Figure 1-4:
You can apply more moderate edits to your image, such as sharpening and color correcting.

Just for the record, here are a few common ways to edit photographs in Elements:

- ✔ You can *sharpen* an image to make it appear in better focus, as in Figure 1-4. Generally, sharpening is used to account for focus problems in the scanning process, but you can sometimes sharpen a photograph that was shot out of focus.

- ✔ If you want to accentuate a foreground image, you can blur the focus of the background.

- ✔ If a photograph is too light or too dark, you can fix it in a flash through the miracle of color correction. You can change the contrast, brighten or dim colors, and replace one color with another. The image in Figure 1-4 has been color-corrected.

- ✔ Using the selection and move tools, you can grab a chunk of your image and physically move it around. You can also clone the selection, stretch it, rotate it, or copy it to a different image.

And that's only the tip of the iceberg. In the book's remaining chapters you'll see Photoshop Elements examined as both a painting program and an image editor. Some chapters contain a little bit of information on both topics, with Part III pertaining to image editing in particular. But you'll find all sides of Photoshop Elements' personality flourishing in this book.

Psychiatric Help: The Doctor Is Built In

Poor Dr. Jekyll. He spent all his time trying in vain to mix a drinkable antidote for that split personality problem of his, when all he needed was to seek help from another doctor — one of the *psychiatric* kind. Luckily, Photoshop Elements has seen the light, and the many built-in Help features that it puts at your disposal ensure that you'll never suffer by association with its split personality. Elements has woven the various aspects of its Help system together in such a way that help is always just a click away.

The Welcome screen

Let's start with first things first: The Welcome screen is the very first thing you'll see after you've fired up Photoshop Elements. (Don't worry if you don't know how to start Photoshop Elements yet — we'll cover that in the next chapter. If you feel lost, just smile and nod as you read and come back to this section later. We'll understand.)

The Mac Welcome screen

As Figure 1-5 makes clear, the Mac Welcome screen gives you these options:

- **Start from Scratch:** Click here to start out with a pristine new canvas, just waiting for you to express yourself all over it. You'll be asked to specify some properties of the new canvas; we'll get to those in the next few chapters.

- **Open File for Editing:** Click here to open the File Browser palette, which lets you search for images on your hard drive, giving you image thumbnails to help you find exactly the file you're looking for. We cover the File Browser palette thoroughly in Chapter 3.

- **Connect to Camera or Scanner:** Click here to start the process of bringing an image into Elements from a scanner, a digital camera, or an already captured video. You'll be taken to the Select Import Source window, where you can choose a source from the Import menu. Frankly, so many different scanners and cameras, each with its own quirks and oddities, are available that we can't possibly begin to thoroughly explain this process for each and every device. But if you have a scanner or a digital camera (and there's a chance that your copy of Photoshop Elements came bundled with just such a device), it's of primary importance that you've correctly installed the software that came with your digital device. For instance, if you've installed your scanner software properly, you should see that option listed in the Import menu. If your digital camera shows up as its own little hard drive when you connect it to your computer, you may have better luck using the File⇨Open command to import images from that camera instead of the Welcome screen. (See Chapter 3 for the skinny on opening files.)

You can also choose Frame from Video from the Import menu to be taken to the VCR-style controls, which let you import a frame from pre-captured video. Just click the Browse button to locate the video on your hard drive, use the controls to locate your frame, and click the Grab Frame button.

The Web site for the company that made your device can be a great place to turn for help as well as an easy source for downloading updated software for your device. And the Photoshop Elements manual that came with the program has a surprising amount of helpful information.

✓ **Recent Images:** If you've opened or created any images recently with Elements 3.0, you'll see them listed here. Just click a name to open the file.

✓ **Tutorials:** Click here and Photoshop Elements will fire up your Web browser to show you Elements tutorials on the Adobe Web site.

✓ **Close:** If every Elements option were this easy to understand, we'd never sell any books. But don't forget, you can always bring back the Welcome screen by choosing Window➪Welcome.

Okay, there's one more button in this window, though technically it's a check box. If you click the check box for Show at Startup to deactivate the Welcome screen feature, you'll receive a thoughtful reminder that this screen can be turned on again by choosing Welcome under the Window menu.

Figure 1-5:
The Mac Welcome screen helps get your Elements work session off to a quick start.

The Windows Welcome screen

Figure 1-6 shows the Windows Welcome screen, which gives you seven icons to click:

- ✔ **Product Overview:** Click here to find out a little general information about Photoshop Elements. You'll also find a link to special information for users of Elements 2.0.

- ✔ **View and Organize Photos:** Clicking this link takes you straight to the Organizer component of Elements, which we cover in Chapter 6.

- ✔ **Quickly Fix Photos:** This link takes you to the Quick Fix mode of the Editor component in Elements, giving you access to some simple image-editing controls.

- ✔ **Edit and Enhance Photos:** This link takes you to the Standard Edit mode of the Editor component.

- ✔ **Make Photo Creation:** Click here to open the Creation Setup window, part of the Organizer component. We cover Organizer's creations in Chapter 18.

- ✔ **Start from Scratch:** This link opens the Editor component and takes you straight to the New dialog box, where you can specify some properties for the new canvas you want to create. We explain those properties in the next few chapters.

- ✔ **Tutorials:** Click here and Photoshop Elements will fire up your Web browser to show you Elements tutorials on the Adobe Web site.

The Start Up In menu at the bottom-left corner of the screen lets you specify how you want your Elements sessions to begin. Welcome Screen is selected by default, which means when you start Elements, the first thing you see is this screen. You can also choose Editor or Organizer if you want to skip the Welcome screen and have Elements open in one of its two components. But you can always choose Welcome from the Window menu of either Editor or Organizer to access the Welcome menu again.

Adobe Help

Whether you're in Elements on the Mac or in either component of Elements in Windows, the first command available under the Help menu is Photoshop Elements Help. Here you have access to the built-in help information that Adobe provides. This help is divided into three sections: Contents, Index, and Glossary. You can access these sections by clicking the tabs at the top of the left panel in the Adobe Help window. Provided you have an Internet connection, clicking the Go to Adobe Help Online link in the lower-left corner of the window loads the Support page from Adobe's Web site. You can also open this page in your Web browser by choosing Help⇨Online Support. Adobe has many helpful features here, including the Forums link, which can take you to the online community of Photoshop Elements users.

Figure 1-6:
The
Windows
Welcome
screen
presents
several
options
which take
you to either
the Editor or
Organizer
component
of Elements.

The scores of warnings, messages, and dialog boxes that appear throughout the program often feature technical words that you may find confusing. These words are usually underlined and colored blue, like links on Web pages. Sure enough, clicking one of these words gives you a link straight to Adobe Help, where you'll find a definition of the word or term.

Yet another way to access Adobe Help is through the interface's Search field. On the Mac, this feature is located in the shortcuts bar; in Windows, it's in the main menu bar. By default, the field reads "Type a question for help"; if you follow its sage advice and then press Enter (Return on the Mac), you'll be taken to Adobe Help for the answer. You can also click the adjacent question mark icon to activate Adobe Help.

The How To palette

The How To palette, pictured in Figure 1-7, is the place to turn in Elements for the latest and greatest recipes. Now, if the thought of recipes makes you hungry, put down this book, make yourself a sandwich, eat it, and then come back to us when you're finished (but please wipe your hands first). These recipes can't help you remember how to make your great-aunt Naomi's meat-loaf, but they are a big help where Photoshop Elements is concerned.

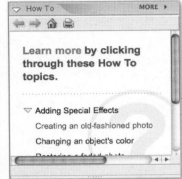

Figure 1-7:
The How To
palette
presents
you with
step-by-step
tutorials for
image
editing.

In the How To palette, you'll find an assortment of image-editing recipes for doing common tasks such as removing dust and scratches from scanned photos and restoring faded photos. You can click to be guided through the tutorial step-by-step. Browser-style forward and backward icons are at the top of the How To palette, as well as a printer icon you can click to print the current tutorial.

You know, there's another way you can apply the whole Jekyll/Hyde analogy to Photoshop Elements. Although Elements definitely has its wild and woolly Hyde side, full of intimidating tools and forbidding commands, the Dr. Jekyll side of Elements — represented by all the Help features — is dedicated to making sure you understand the darker side of the program. Doctors are generally helpful that way. So with this much help at your fingertips, why have we decided to write this book? Well, we thought you might want a second opinion.

Chapter 2

Dissecting Your Desktop

· ·

In This Chapter

▶ Launching Elements

▶ Taking some first, tentative looks at the Elements interface

▶ Working with the program window

▶ Choosing commands

▶ Using dialog boxes and palettes

▶ Picking up tools from the toolbox

▶ Using the photo bin

· ·

*I*f you're brand new to Photoshop Elements — or to computers in general — this is the chapter for you. You get the first of the basic stuff you need to know before you can begin using the program to distort the faces of all your family members.

Even if you're already familiar with the basic interface of Elements, you may want to give this chapter a once-over to make sure we're all speaking the same language. Here, we can calibrate brains, so to speak.

Giving Elements the Electronic Breath of Life

Before you can see the Elements interface, you have to start up, or launch, the program. Here's how to do this on the Mac:

1. **Locate the Adobe Photoshop Elements 3 folder.**

   Double-click your hard drive icon on the desktop (it's probably the one in the upper-right corner). Elements should be located in the Applications folder.

2. **Locate the Photoshop Elements 3 icon.**

   The Photoshop Elements 3 icon should be in the Adobe Photoshop Elements 3 folder.

3. **Double-click the icon.**

   While the program is loading, you should see the Elements splash screen. Finally, the Welcome screen should appear on your desktop.

4. **Close the Welcome screen.**

   You should see the Elements 3 interface on your desktop, as shown in Figure 2-1.

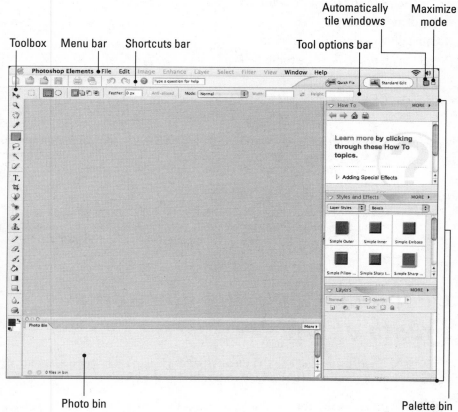

Figure 2-1:
The Elements interface, shown in Macintosh OS X, makes its first appearance.

To see the corresponding interface in Windows, you need to launch the Editor component of Elements. Here's how:

1. **Click the Start button in the taskbar.**

   A menu should appear, giving you access to programs and utilities installed on your hard drive.

2. **Click All Programs.**

   Another menu appears, listing the programs installed on your hard drive.

3. **Choose Adobe Photoshop Elements 3.0.**

   The Welcome screen appears on your desktop.

4. **Click the Edit and Enhance Photos icon.**

   The interface shown in Figure 2-2 should appear on your desktop.

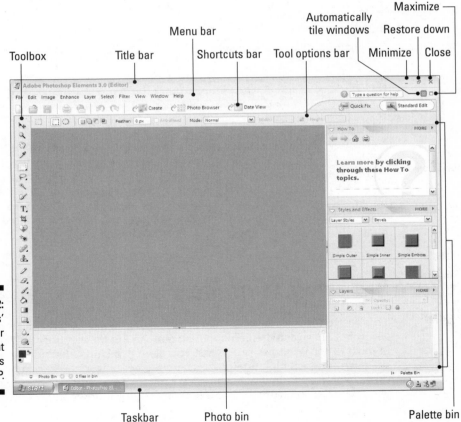

Figure 2-2:
Elements'
Editor
component
in Windows
XP.

Why does Elements give your computer amnesia?

If your computer says it's out of memory, it just means that a part of the machine is filled to capacity. Memory — known in computer dweeb circles as *RAM* (random-access memory, pronounced *ram*, like the sheep) — allows your computer to run programs. Elements needs lots of RAM, and the more the better. If you can't launch Elements because of a memory error, you have three options:

✔ Free up RAM by quitting all other programs that are currently running.

✔ PC users: Windows XP users, restart your computer by choosing Turn Off Computer from the Start menu and then click Restart.

Windows 2000 users, restart your computer by choosing the Shut Down command from the Windows Start menu and then choosing the Restart the Computer option. After your computer restarts, try to launch Elements again.

Mac users: Restart the computer by choosing Restart from the Apple menu.

✔ Buy and install more RAM.

If you've never tried to upgrade the RAM in your machine, seek out expert advice from your local computer guru.

Don't freak out and start running around the room in a frenzy if you're a little fuzzy on the meaning of *menu, taskbar,* and a few other terms. We cover all this stuff in fairly hefty detail in this very same chapter.

Note: As you read, you'll see that you can use the keyboard and mouse in tandem. For example, in Elements, you can draw a perfectly horizontal line by pressing the Shift key while dragging with the pencil tool. Or you can press Alt (Option on the Mac) and click the rectangular marquee tool in the upper-left corner of the toolbox to switch to the elliptical marquee tool. Such actions are so common that you often see key and mouse combinations joined into compound verbs, such as Shift+drag or Control-click.

Working with Windows

This section is relevant to PC users only. Mac people skip down to the "Switching between Elements and Macintosh Finder" section. In Elements, as in most other Windows programs, you have two kinds of windows: the program window, which contains the main Elements work area, and image windows, which contain any images that you create or edit. To see the program window, refer to Figure 2-2; for a look at image windows, see Chapter 3.

Elements windows — both program and image — contain the same basic items as those in other Windows programs, though they may look a little different in Elements. Just in case you need a refresher or you're new to this whole computing business, here's how the Elements program window works with Windows:

✔ Windows users can click the X in the upper-right corner of the program window to shut down Elements. If you have open images that haven't been saved, the program prompts you to save them. (For details on saving images, see Chapter 7.) The quickest way to close your program window (and Elements) is to press the keyboard shortcut for the Exit command, Ctrl+Q (as in Quit).

✔ Click the Minimize button (refer to Figure 2-2) to reduce the program window to a button on the Windows taskbar at the bottom of the screen. To redisplay the program window, just click the taskbar button.

✔ You can also use the taskbar buttons to switch between Elements' Editor and Organizer components, if they're both running. In the taskbar, just click the button of the component you want to use.

✔ The appearance of the Maximize/Restore Down (or just Restore) button changes, depending on the current status of the window. If you see two boxes on the button, the button is the Restore Down button. Click this button to shrink the window so that you can also see other open program windows. You can then resize the window by placing your mouse cursor in the lower-right corner of the window. Just drag the corner to resize the window. To move the window around, drag its title bar.

✔ After you click the Restore Down button, it changes to the Maximize button, which looks like a single box. Click the button to zoom the program window so that it consumes your entire screen. After the window zooms, the button changes back to the Restore Down button. Click the button to restore your screen to its former size.

Switching between Elements and Macintosh Finder

In back of the myriad components of the Elements interface, you Mac users can probably see the icons and open windows from Finder. (These are hidden in Figure 2-1 just to make the picture less confusing.) If you click a Finder window or the desktop, you're taken back to Finder, and the Elements toolbox and palettes disappear. If you have an image open, however, the image window remains visible.

Here are some tips to help you manage working between Finder and Elements:

- ✔ If you inadvertently click yourself out of Elements, go to the Dock (located at the bottom of the screen by default) and click the Elements icon. Or you can just click the Elements image window. The toolbox and palettes return to the screen to show you that Elements is back in the game.

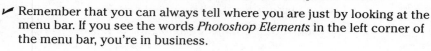

- ✔ You may be wondering why this program switching happens. Finder is a piece of software, just like Elements. The only difference is that Finder is running the entire time you use your Mac. This means that all the time you're using Elements, Finder is working away in the background. When you click the desktop or some other component of Finder, it comes to the foreground and Elements goes to the background. But both programs continue to operate until you quit Elements or shut down your computer.

- ✔ If the clutter from Finder gets too distracting when you're using Elements, choose the Hide Others command from the Photoshop Elements menu to hide every Finder element except the icons.

- ✔ Remember that you can always tell where you are just by looking at the menu bar. If you see the words *Photoshop Elements* in the left corner of the menu bar, you're in business.

Maneuvering through Menus

Elements, like all Windows and Macintosh programs, sports a menu bar at the top of its desktop (refer to Figures 2-1 and 2-2). Below that menu bar, though, are two things many other programs don't have: a shortcuts bar and a tool options bar. The shortcuts bar is a handy way to perform common functions with just a single click of the mouse.

On the Mac only, the shortcuts bar also contains four items, labeled in Figure 2-1: the help icon, the search field, the automatically tile windows icon, and the maximize mode icon. In Windows, these four items were moved up into the menu bar to make room for the Create, Photo Browser, and Date View buttons, all of which take you over to the Organizer component of Elements. Both the Mac and Windows shortcuts bars have icons to switch you to Quick Mix mode, and back again to the default Standard Edit mode.

The tool options bar gives you control over the tool you currently have selected. If you want to reset the options in the tool options bar, click the tool icon on the far left of the bar and choose Reset Tool to reset the options for that particular tool, or Reset All Tools to return them all to their default settings. We'll make frequent visits to both the tool options bar and the shortcuts bar when appropriate in the book; for now, let's belly up to that menu bar.

Each word in the menu bar — File, Edit, Image, and so on — represents a menu. A *menu* is simply a list of commands that you can use to open and close images, manipulate selected portions of a photograph, hide and display palettes, and initiate all kinds of procedures.

We explain the most essential Photoshop Elements commands throughout this book, but here's a bit of background information on how to work with menus:

✔ To choose a command from a menu, click the menu name and then move the mouse down to the command name and click again. Or you can press and hold the menu name, drag down to the command name, and release the mouse button at the desired command.

✔ Some commands display additional menus called *submenus*. For example, if you choose File⇨New, you display a submenu offering still more commands. If we ask you to choose File⇨New⇨Blank File, you choose New under the File menu to display the submenu and then choose the Blank File command from the submenu, all in one beautiful continuous movement. When you do it just right, it's like something out of Swan Lake.

You can access some commands by pressing keyboard shortcuts. For example, to initiate the File⇨Blank File command, you can press the keyboard shortcut Ctrl+N (⌘+N on the Mac) — that is, press and hold the Ctrl key (⌘ key on the Mac), press the N key, and then release both keys.

✔ Some keyboard equivalents select tools, and some perform other functions. Either way, we keep you apprised of them throughout this book. If you take the time to memorize a few keyboard shortcuts here and there, you can save yourself a heck of a lot of time and effort. (For some essential shortcuts, read Chapter 19. Also, tear out the Cheat Sheet at the front of this book and tape it up somewhere within easy ogling distance.)

✔ Elements offers you yet another way to access some commands. If you right-click (Control+click on the Mac) inside an image window, you display a context-sensitive menu. In nongeek-speak, a context-sensitive menu, also known as a *shortcut menu,* is a minimenu that contains commands related to the current tool, palette, or image, as shown in Figure 2-3.

Figure 2-3:
Right-click
(Control+
click on the
Mac) inside
the image
window
to access
context-
sensitive
menus.

Talking Back to Dialog Boxes

Elements reacts immediately to some menu commands. But for other commands, the program requires you to fill out a few forms before it processes your request. If you see an ellipsis (three dots, like so . . .) next to a command name, that's your clue that you're about to see such a form, known in computer clubs everywhere as a *dialog box.*

Figure 2-4 shows a sample dialog box. As the figure demonstrates, dialog boxes can contain several basic kinds of options. The options work as follows:

- A box in which you can enter numbers or text is called an *option box.* Double-click or click and drag in an option box to highlight its contents and then replace the contents by entering new stuff from the keyboard.

- Some option boxes come with *sliders.* Drag the triangular slider to the left or right to lower or raise, respectively, the associated numerical value.

- You can select only one *radio button* (not shown in Figure 2-4) from any gang of radio buttons. To select a radio button, click the circle or the option name that follows it. A black dot fills the selected radio circle; all deselected radio circles are hollow.

- Although you can select only one radio button at a time, you can usually select as many *check boxes* as you want. Really, go nuts. To select a check box, click the box or the option name that follows it. A check fills the box to show that it's selected. Clicking on a selected check box turns off the option.

- To conserve space, some multiple-choice options appear as *drop-down menus.* Click the menu to display the option choices. Then click the desired option in the menu to choose it, just as if you were choosing a command from a standard menu. As with radio buttons, you can choose only one option at a time from a drop-down menu.

- The normal, everyday variety of *button* enables you to close the current dialog box or display others. For example, click the Cancel button to close the dialog box and cancel the command. Click OK to close the dialog box and execute the command according to the current settings. Clicking a button with an ellipsis (such as Load. . . or Save. . .) displays yet another dialog box.

As you can with menus, you can select options and perform other feats of magic inside dialog boxes from the keyboard. The following shortcuts work in most dialog boxes:

- To advance from one option box to the next, press the Tab key. To back up, press Shift+Tab.

- In Windows, press Enter to select the button surrounded by a heavy outline (such as the OK button in Figure 2-4). On the Mac, you can always press Return to select the blue button. On either platform, press Esc to select the Cancel button.

- Press ↑ to raise a selected option box value by one; press ↓ to decrease the value by one. Pressing Shift+↑ and Shift+↓ raise and lower the value by ten, respectively.

- If you change your mind about choices you make in a dialog box, you can quickly return things to the settings that were in force when you opened the dialog box. In most dialog boxes, pressing the Alt key (Option key on the Mac) magically changes the Cancel button to a Reset button. Click the Reset button to bring back the original values.

A wonderful new feature of Elements 3.0 is *scrubbing* on words to change option values. For example, in the Hue/Saturation dialog box featured in Figure 2-4, if you place your cursor over the word Hue, the cursor turns into a pointing hand, with arrows coming out on either side of the finger. If you click and drag, the value for Hue will change as you drag. This works in most dialog boxes, as well as in the tool options bar. Of the many ways Elements gives you to change numeric options, we think you'll find scrubbing to be the easiest and fastest way of all.

If a dialog box gets in the way of your view of an image, you can reposition the box by dragging its title bar.

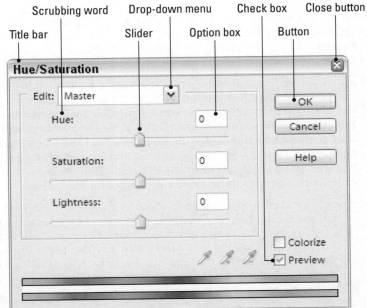

Figure 2-4: The anatomy of the dialog box.

Playing Around with Palettes

One of the chief features of the Elements interface is the palette. A *palette* is basically a dialog box that can remain on-screen while you work, providing access to options that change the appearance of images and otherwise assist you in your editing adventures.

Users of Elements 2.0 will notice the new version's palette bin, a wide vertical strip running down the right side of the desktop. If you think the palette bin is eating up too much of your desktop, you can make it thinner by clicking and dragging on its left edge. You can also choose Window⇨Palette Bin to make it disappear. Choose the command again to bring it back. Windows users can also click the *Palette Bin* text below the palette bin to hide and show the bin.

By default, the palette bin features the How To, Styles and Effects, and Layers palettes. You can collapse a palette in the palette bin by clicking the white triangle to the left of the palette's name. This is a great way to make room for viewing a different palette in the bin. You can also drag palettes out of the palette bin if you want, and place different ones inside.

When you drag a palette outside the palette bin, it becomes a floating palette that can be stationed wherever you want on the desktop. The palette's appearance changes as well; Figure 2-5 shows a floating palette.

We cover the specifics of using the palettes in chapters to come, but here's a brief introductory tour of how palettes work:

✔ What may look like just one floating palette can actually be a collection of palettes sharing the same palette window. For example, in Figure 2-5, the Color Swatches and Histogram palettes are housed in the same palette window. To switch to a different palette in a palette window, click its tab.

✔ When you've finished using a floating palette for the immediate future, you can click the Close button to make it vamoose. Exactly where it vamooses to depends on how you set the Place in Palette Bin option in the palette's More menu. When there's a check mark next to the option, clicking the Close button sends the palette into the palette bin. By default, the How To, Styles and Effects, and Layers palettes all have this feature turned on. If you drag one of them out of the palette bin and then click its Close button, the palette will appear in the palette bin again.

If no check mark appears next to Place in Palette Bin, clicking the Close button makes the palette disappear from your screen completely; the palette will reappear only when you choose its name from the Window menu. (Be aware that Place in Palette Bin is a toggling command, meaning that you turn it on and turn it off simply by choosing it.) In Windows, the Close button is on the far right of the palette's title bar; on the Mac, it's on the far left of the title bar. To hide and show palettes, you can also use the commands available in the Window menu.

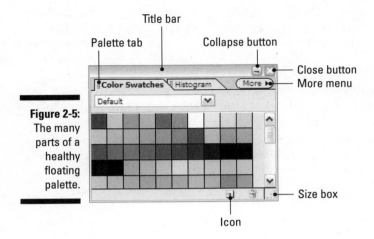

Title bar

Palette tab   Collapse button

Close button

More menu

Figure 2-5:
The many
parts of a
healthy
floating
palette.

Size box

Icon

✔ Pressing Tab can hide various parts of the interface to free up more screen space. On the Mac, pressing Tab hides pretty much everything, including the toolbox, free-floating palettes, the palette and photo bins, and the shortcuts and tool options bars. In Windows, pressing Tab hides just the toolbox (if it's in two-column mode, as explained later in this chapter) and any free-floating palettes; the bins and bars stay put. (Note that this trick doesn't work if there's an active option box in the tool options bar or in a palette.)

✔ Some palettes contain icons, just like the toolbox does. Click an icon to perform a function, such as adding or deleting a layer in the Layers palette (see Chapter 10).

✔ Drag the title bar at the top of a floating palette to move the palette around on-screen.

✔ Shift+click the title bar of a floating palette to snap the palette to the nearest corner of the screen. For example, if the palette is near the lower-left corner of the screen, Shift+clicking its title bar moves it all the way into the corner, giving you more space to view your image on-screen.

✔ Every palette except the Info and Histogram palettes has a size box, as labeled in Figure 2-5. Drag the size box to resize the palette. You can click the divider between palettes in the palette bin to resize palettes while they're in the bin.

✔ Click the Collapse button (the green Zoom button on a Mac) on a floating palette to hide all but the title bar and the palette tabs. You can also double-click a palette tab to accomplish the same thing.

✔ You can combine multiple floating palettes into a single palette window by dragging a tab from one palette into another, as shown in Figure 2-6. You can also break any floating palette into its own window by dragging the palette tab out of the current window.

✔ You can also dock floating palettes vertically. Move the tab of a palette to the bottom of a second palette and you should see a black outline at the bottom of the second palette, indicating that you can dock the first palette. You can also dock one palette to the top of another palette in the same manner.

✔ Press and hold the More button, located to the right of the palette's name, to display the palette menu. Here's yet another hiding place for commands.

✔ If you get your palettes in an unbearable muddle, you can always restore things to the way they were when you first launched Elements by choosing Window⊏>Reset Palette Locations.

Figure 2-6:
Drag a floating palette tab into another palette window to make the palettes share the same little apartment.

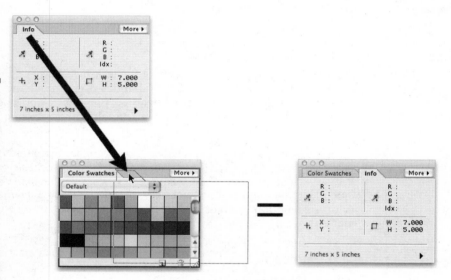

Opening Your Toolbox

As Figures 2-1 and 2-2 show, by default the toolbox is a long, thin one-column-wide strip, stretched along the left side of the screen. However, if you click the line of dots at the top of the toolbox and drag it to the right, the toolbox will resize itself and become transformed into the two-column beauty seen in Figure 2-7. To switch back to one-column mode, drag the toolbox by its top bar until it snaps to the left side of the screen, and then release.

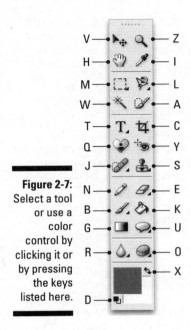

Figure 2-7:
Select a tool
or use a
color
control by
clicking it or
by pressing
the keys
listed here.

Whether in one- or two-column mode, the toolbox offers the same controls. As shown in Figure 2-7, the items in the toolbox fall into two basic categories: tools and color controls. Future chapters explain in detail how to use the various gizmos in the toolbox, but here's a basic overview of what's in store:

✔ The top five sections of the toolbox (refer to Figure 2-7) are devoted to an assortment of tools that you can use to edit images, just as you might use an assortment of pencils, markers, and scissors in a craft project. To select one of these tools, click its icon. Then use the tool by clicking or dragging it inside your image.

✔ A tiny, downward, right-pointing triangle in the bottom-right corner of a tool icon indicates that more tools are hidden behind that icon on a *flyout* menu. To display the flyout menu and reveal the hidden tools, press and hold the mouse button on the icon. Drag over and down the column of tools until your cursor is hovering over the tool you want to use and then release the mouse button.

✔ You can also Alt+click (Option+click on the Mac) on a tool icon to cycle through all the tools hidden beneath it.

✔ The bottom section of the toolbox contains color selection options. These icons respond immediately when you click them.

- If you've been clicking away on the toolbox icons and haven't seen any results, don't panic. Your copy of Elements isn't broken; the icons just don't do anything unless you have an image open. To find out how to open images, see Chapter 3.

- You can access all the tools and two of the color controls also from the keyboard. For example, to select the brush tool, you just press the letter B key. Figure 2-7 shows other keyboard equivalents.

- Elements includes a preference setting that determines how you use the keyboard to select tools that share flyout menus in the toolbox. Choose Edit➪Preferences➪General (Photoshop Elements➪Preferences➪General on the Mac). If the option Use Shift Key for Tool Switch is selected, adding the Shift key to the tool's keyboard shortcut lets you cycle through the tools on the flyout menu. For example, pressing Shift+B repeatedly will cycle between the brush, impressionist brush, and color replacement tools. However, if the preference option is deselected, you can cycle through the tools just by repeatedly pressing the single letter key.

- If you can't remember the keyboard shortcut of a particular tool, pause your cursor over its icon for a second or two. A little label known as a *tool tip* appears, telling you the name of the tool and its keyboard equivalent. You can even click these tool tips (it takes a slow and steady hand) to be whisked away to Adobe Help, where you can find more info about the tool in question. If the tool tips get annoying, you can turn off the feature by deselecting the Show Tool Tips option in the General panel of Preferences.

The Photo Bin

As your image-editing prowess progresses, there will be times when you'll have more than one image window open. Elements 3.0 offers a new tool for managing multiple image windows. The long, thin window stretching across the bottom of the desktop in Figures 2-1 and 2-2 is the new photo bin. When an image window is open, a thumbnail representing the image appears in the photo bin. When you have multiple images open, you can click a thumbnail in the photo bin to bring that image window to the front. You can also click the arrow icons in the lower-left corner of the photo bin to switch between images. To hide the photo bin, choose Window➪Photo Bin; to unhide the bin, choose the command again.

On the Mac, the photo bin is a floating palette that behaves basically like any other palette. In Windows, the photo bin is built into the interface; you can resize it by clicking and dragging its top edge, and show and hide it by clicking the photo bin icon in the lower-left corner of the program's interface.

Chapter 3

"Open!" Says Me

*P*hotoshop Elements presents you with a plethora of tools, menus, and palettes (just check out Chapter 2 if you don't believe us!). However, until you have an image open, those contraptions are intriguing but ultimately worthless — it's like having an easel, a full set of brushes, and a paint box full of paints, but no canvas. And with Elements, you can't even climb up on billboards and paint mustaches on the faces in the ads. (Not that we've ever done anything like that.) No, if you want to become a digital Picasso (or whatever artistic legend you choose), you need an open image.

This chapter explains how to open existing images and also how to create a new, blank canvas for an image you want to paint from scratch. Then we chart a course through the many ways you can navigate the vast sea of your image. So strap a parrot on your shoulder and hop aboard.

Don't Just Sit There — Open Something!

If you're a longtime computer buff, you may expect opening an image to be a straightforward process. You just choose File➪Open or press Ctrl+O (⌘+O on the Mac) and select the image file you want to display, right?

Well, in Elements *O* stands for *options* just as much as it stands for *open*. The main opening tool in Elements is the File Browser. As you can see in Figure 3-1, the File Browser is an excellent visual means of browsing through your computer and peeking at the graphics files contained therein.

Figure 3-1:
The File Browser not only lets you view thumbnails of your photos but also lets you rename and organize them. The Mac version, seen here, has a few options that the Windows version doesn't.

Opening with the File Browser

* Sometimes, have to press F5 twice!

Before we find out about opening files with the File Browser, you may well want to know how to open the File Browser itself. Take your pick: Choose Window➪File Browser, choose File➪Browse Folders, press Ctrl+Shift+O (⌘+Shift+O on the Mac), or press F5. Mac users can also click the Browse button in their shortcuts bar; it's the folder-with-magnifying-glass icon. Now that we have that out of the way, let's dissect the File Browser and see what makes it tick.

Anatomy of a browser

The File Browser has been greatly expanded for Elements 3.0, starting with the addition of its own little menu bar at the very top of the window. The menu bar contains a handful of commands, and some shortcuts-style icons as well. Because only the Windows version of Elements comes with the separate Organizer component, the Mac version of the File Browser has a few exclusive features to compensate. Among these are an Automate menu in the menu bar, giving Mac users easy access to many of the automated features that we cover in Chapter 18.

On the left side of the File Browser interface is a palette bin-like area composed of a series of tabbed panels. Although the default layout of these panels is a pretty good one, you can drag the panel tabs around to make different panels share the same space, similar to how you can arrange floating palettes, as described in Chapter 2.

By default, you'll find the Folders panel in the upper-left corner of the File Browser; this shows you a folder hierarchy of your hard drive with the desktop at the top. You can navigate and view the contents of folders by clicking the plus icons under Windows or by clicking the twirly arrows on the Mac. Note, however, that you can't see any image files in the Folder panel. Click a folder, however, and the contents of that folder take over the large thumbnail section on the right side of the File Browser, showing you a thumbnail image for every image file in the folder. If you make a few changes to the organization of your hard drive — such as adding, moving, and deleting folders — while the File Browser is open, those changes won't show up in the desktop view until you choose Refresh from the View menu.

The menu at the top left of the thumbnail panel shows you the folder path to the currently displayed folder. You can click the menu and choose another folder to navigate backward toward your desktop, or click the adjacent folder-with-an-arrow icon to move backward one folder. In the thumbnail panel, you can double-click an image to open it in Elements, and double-click a folder to see what's inside it. Clicking once on a thumbnail makes it appear in the resizable Preview panel on the left of the browser. Move your cursor to the top, bottom, or right edge of the preview area, and then click and drag to expand or shrink the preview.

If you want to hide the left side of the File Browser and devote the entire window to thumbnails, click the double-arrow (toggle expanded view) icon in the bottom-left corner of the Thumbnail panel.

The Metadata panel at the bottom left of the browser shows you a variety of information about the selected image. On the Mac, you can click to edit the description, author (photographer), and copyright info in the IPTC section of the Metadata panel. Click the Apply check mark button at the bottom of the Metadata panel to embed this information into the file's metadata, or click Cancel if you've changed your mind.

EXIF stands for Exchangeable Image File, which is a standard format for appending nonpixel information to an image. Many digital cameras use the EXIF format. This information is usually invisible, but the File Browser lets you see it, and it can be quite useful. It typically includes such information as the date and time the photo was taken, the type of camera, and the focal length.

If a thumbnail needs to be rotated, handy icons in the menu bar can accomplish just that. However, note that clicking these icons rotates only the thumbnail, not the actual image itself. If you rotate a thumbnail and then double-click it, Elements opens the full image on-screen with the same rotation applied. This is not a permanent change; if you close the image and don't save the changes to the file, the image on disk will not have the rotation applied. If you've rotated a thumbnail and you want to go ahead and rotate the image without opening it first, choose Edit⇨Apply Rotation from the File Browser's menu.

Organizing with the File Browser

As we mentioned earlier, Adobe partially makes up for the Mac's lack of the Organizer component by giving Mac users some exclusive organizing powers right here in the File Browser. In addition to the aforementioned Automate menu, you can also *flag* photos to make it easier to view them separately. Flagging the best photos in a batch allows you to view them apart from the other photos without moving them to a separate folder. To flag a photo, select it in the thumbnail view and then click the flag icon in the menu bar. A small flag icon appears below the thumbnail. You can then view only the flagged photos in a folder by choosing Flagged Files from the Show menu at the top of the Thumbnail panel. Other options in the Show menu let you view only unflagged photos, or both flagged and unflagged photos.

An even more powerful feature is the ability to apply *keywords* to images. Adobe has given Mac users a Keywords panel to accomplish this; by default, the Keywords panel shares a space with the Metadata panel in the lower-left corner of the File Browser. The Keywords panel contains descriptive keywords you can apply to photos, grouped into folders or *sets*. There are just a few keywords and sets by default, but you can create new ones by accessing the Keywords panel's More menu and choosing New Keyword or New Keyword Set. The More menu also holds commands for renaming and deleting keywords and keyword sets. To get things organized exactly the way you want, you can drag keywords from set to set within the Keywords panel.

To apply a keyword to a photo, select the photo and click to place a check mark in the Keywords panel in the box to the far left of the desired keyword. You can apply multiple keywords from multiple keyword sets to images. The more work and specificity you put into creating and applying keywords to your digital photo collection, the easier it will be to find the photo you're looking for using the Search function in the File Browser.

Searching for photos

To search for a photo in your digital photo collection using the File Browser, click the binoculars (search) icon in the menu bar. In the Search dialog box, the Source section lets you specify which folder you want to search inside. Click the Browse button to load the desired folder into the Look In menu, and click the Include All Subfolders check box if you want to search folders nested inside your selected folder.

The Criteria section of the Search dialog box lets you specify what aspects of the photo you want to search for. The first menu gives many types of search criteria, but the most powerful choice is Keywords. Let's say you've applied keywords to your digital photo collection. You want to find a picture of your good friend Julius taken in New York, but you're looking for a photo that doesn't also contain his good friend Michael. In this case, you would do the following:

- ✔ Choose Keywords from the first menu, Contains from the second menu, and type *Julius* in the option field. Then click the plus sign icon to add a new search criteria line.

- ✔ In the second line, choose Keywords from the first menu, Contains from the second menu, and type *New York* in the option field. Then click the plus sign icon again.

- ✔ In the third line, choose Keywords from the first menu, Does Not Contain from the second menu, and type *Michael* in the option field.

When you click the search icon, the File Browser searches the folder or folders you specified, and shows you the photos that contain the keywords *Julius* and *New York,* but not the keyword *Michael.*

On both Windows and the Mac, the File Browser's menu bar has a trash icon. If you select a thumbnail and click the trash icon, or just drag the thumbnail to the icon, Elements removes the image from its folder and places it in your computer's recycle bin or trash. This leads us to our next major point about the File Browser: It lets you not only view thumbnails of your files but also make changes to the names and organization of your images on your hard drive. For instance, in addition to relocating files to your recycle bin or trash, you can drag image thumbnails into the Folders panel of the File Browser to move them from the current folder to a new folder. If you want to rename an image, just click the name in the Thumbnail panel. Elements highlights the image name and lets you type in a new one.

how?

Opening the ordinary way

The File Browser aside, Elements has several other handy ways to open images. Chapter 1 looked at the Connect to Camera or Scanner options featured on the Welcome screen. The File⇨Import submenu is another place you can turn to for opening photos; this menu features the handy Frame from Video command, which lets you import a frame from a video clip on your hard drive.

Figure 3-2 shows a convenient one-click open icon found on the shortcuts bar; it's the second icon from the left, just past the new file icon. But if you'd rather maneuver through menus, you can choose File⇨Open. Or if clicking icons and choosing menu commands is too much work, just press Ctrl+O (⌘+O on the Mac). The Open dialog box rears its useful head, as shown in Figure 3-3.

Figure 3-2:
If you're the point-and-click type, the shortcuts bar was made for you. The Mac version, shown here, also has a Browse icon to summon the File Browser.

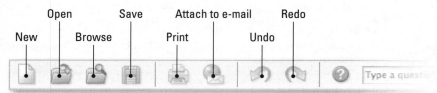

New · Open · Browse · Save · Print · Attach to e-mail · Undo · Redo

Figure 3-3:
This dialog box lets you locate and open images on your hard drive or some other disk.

Finding an item in the Open dialog box is similar to navigating in the File Browser's Folders panel. Just keep clicking and double-clicking to look inside hard drives and folders until you find the folder containing your desired image. If you're not sure whether it's the right one, selecting it with a single click will show you a small preview of the image. (Mac users need to have the Open window in multicolumn view mode to see the preview.) When you've found the right image, double-click it, press Enter (Windows) or Return (Mac), or click the Open button. You're good to go!

If you've had an image open recently, you may find it hiding in the File⇨Open Recently Edited File submenu. You can set the number of files that this submenu contains in the Saving Files panel of Elements' Preferences.

Creating an image

To create a new image instead of opening an existing one, Elements gives you a typically wide range of options. You can use the Welcome screen as mentioned in Chapter 1; use the new icon in the shortcuts bar (refer to Figure 3-2); choose File⇨New⇨Blank File; or press Ctrl+N (⌘+N on the Mac). Whichever method you use, Elements displays the New dialog box.

In the New dialog box, you can name your file; specify the width, height, and resolution (as discussed in Chapter 4); set the color mode (as discussed in Chapter 5); and determine whether you want the file to be filled with white, filled with the current background color, or transparent. Elements gives you a handy shortcut for setting the size and resolution of your file: the Preset menu. You can choose from a number of standard sizes for print, Web, and digital video work.

Behold the Image Window

After you open an image, Elements displays the image on-screen in a new image window. Several new items appear when you open an image, as labeled in Figure 3-4.

The following list explains all:

- ✔ The title bar lists the title of your image with the file extension (for more on file formats, see Chapter 7). The bonus is that you can drag the title bar to move the window to a different location on-screen. Easy stuff.

Is this a Mac screen?

Title bar   Image area   Scrollbar

Figure 3-4:
An open
image
causes
even more
Elements
features
to appear
on-screen.

Magnification   Information   Scroll arrows
box   box

Size box

✔ You can choose File⇨Close or press Ctrl+W (⌘+W on the Mac) to close an image window. (If you've made some changes to the image, Elements asks you whether you want to save the new and improved image, a process explained in great detail in Chapter 7.)

✔ For PC users: To change the size of the image window, place your cursor over a side or a corner of the window. When a double-headed arrow appears, just drag. For Mac users: Place your cursor over the size box in the lower-right corner of the window and drag. On both platforms, the image remains the same; you're just changing the size of the window that holds the image. Give it a try and see what we mean.

✔ Scrollbars let you navigate around and display hidden portions of the image in the window. Elements always initially opens an image so that the entire image fits on-screen; no scrollbars are necessary. However, if you shrink the window in both directions, you'll see two scrollbars, one vertical bar along the right side of the image and one horizontal bar along the bottom.

If you click a scroll arrow, you nudge your view of the image slightly in that direction. For example, if you click the right-pointing scroll arrow, an item that was hidden on the right side of the photograph slides into view. Click in the blank area on either side of the scrollbar to scroll the window more dramatically. Drag the scrollbar to manually specify the distance scrolled.

Using the scroll arrows isn't the only way to move around your image; in fact, it's probably the least efficient method. For some better options, check out the techniques presented in the section "The Screen Is Your Digital Oyster," coming up next.

✔ The area bounded by the title bar and scrollbars is the image area. The image area is where you paint, edit, select details, and otherwise have at your image. Obviously, you look at the image area a lot throughout the many pages of this book.

✔ You can open as many images on-screen as your computer's memory and screen size allow. But only one image is active at a time. To make a different image window active, just click its thumbnail in the photo bin or choose its name from the bottom of the Window menu.

✔ The commands in the Window⇨Images submenu give you tricks for managing multiple open image windows. One of the nicest of these is Tile, also accessible by clicking the Automatically tile windows icon (see Figures 2-1 and 2-2 in Chapter 2) in the menu bar in Windows or in the shortcuts bar on the Mac. Doing so makes multiple image windows automatically resize themselves in a neat, orderly, tiled fashion. Next to the tile icon in the interface is the maximize mode icon, which expands the active image window until it completely fills the available space on the desktop.

The Screen Is Your Digital Oyster

The Photoshop Elements toolbox includes two navigation tools: the hand tool, which lets you scroll the image in the window with much more ease than the silly scrollbars afford, and the zoom tool, which has the effect of moving you closer to or farther away from your image. The hand tool and the zoom tool are called *navigation tools* because they don't change the image; they merely alter your view of the image so that you can get a better look-see.

In addition to these tools, you have another navigational aid, appropriately called the Navigator palette. The palette gives you a super-convenient way to zoom and scroll your image. In fact, after you're familiar with the palette, you may not use the hand and zoom tools at all. But in the interest of fair play, we present all the various options for moving around within your image in the upcoming sections.

Using the hand tool

If you're familiar with other Windows and Macintosh programs, you need to know something about Elements: The scrollbars are relatively useless. Keep away from them. Promise that you'll always use the hand tool or the Navigator palette (explained shortly) instead. Promise? Good. As for you new users, don't worry — you have no old habits to break.

Consider the following example: The left image in Figure 3-5 shows a young woman displaying a fair amount of attitude. The problem is that the picture is wider than the image window, so you can't see what is motivating her defiant stance.

Hand cursor

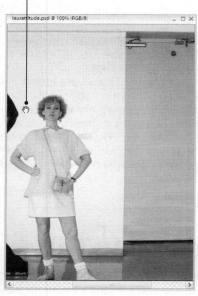 

Figure 3-5: Dragging with the hand tool reveals that imitation is the sincerest form of flattery.

To view the rest of the scene, select the hand tool by clicking its icon in the toolbox. Then position the hand tool in the image window, as shown in the first example in Figure 3-5, click, and drag to the right. The image moves with the hand cursor, as shown in the second example, and reveals the reason behind the young lady's posturing.

Dragging with the hand tool is like turning your head to view a new part of your surroundings, except you'll never get a crick in your neck. You can drag at any angle you please — up, down, sideways, or diagonally.

You can also select the hand tool by pressing the H key. To temporarily access the hand tool when another tool is selected, press the spacebar. As long as the spacebar is down, the hand tool is available. Releasing the space-bar returns you to the selected tool.

Using keyboard shortcuts

You can use keyboard shortcuts also to move about your image. Press Page Up or Page Down to scroll up or down an entire screen. Press Shift+Page Up or Shift+Page Down to scroll in smaller increments. Press Home to go to the upper-left corner of the image, and press End to move to the lower-right corner.

And as if that isn't enough, Elements offers keyboard shortcuts for moving right and left. Press Ctrl+Page Up or Ctrl+Page Down to scroll left or right an entire screen. Press Ctrl+Shift+Page Up or Ctrl+Shift+Page Down to scroll left and right in smaller increments. Mac users, substitute the ⌘ key for the Ctrl key here.

Zooming in and out on your work

When you first open an image, Photoshop Elements displays the entire image so that it fits on-screen. But you may not be seeing the details in the image as clearly as you want. If you want to inspect the image in more detail, you have to move closer. No, don't scoot your chair; read on.

Elements gives you several ways to zoom in and out on your work, as described in these next few sections.

Zooming doesn't change the size of your image in any way — not the size at which it would print, and not the size it would appear on-screen if you e-mailed it to somebody or posted it on the Web. It just temporarily adjusts the size at which you see the image on-screen. Zooming is like looking at some teensy-weensy life form under a microscope. The creature doesn't actually grow and shrink as you vary the degree of magnification, and neither does your image.

The zoom tool

Using the zoom tool is one avenue for changing your view of an image. Every time you click your image with the tool, you magnify the image to a larger size. Here's an example of how it works:

1. **Select the zoom tool.**

   Click the zoom tool in the toolbox. It's the one that looks like a magnifying glass. You can also press the Z key to grab the zoom tool.

2. **Click in the image area.**

   Elements magnifies the image to the next preset zoom size, as demonstrated in the second example of Figure 3-6. The program centers the magnified view about the point at which you click, as much as possible. In Figure 3-6, for example, the boy was zoom-clicked right on the nose.

3. **Repeat.**

   To zoom in farther still, click again with the zoom tool, as demonstrated in the bottom example of Figure 3-6.

Figure 3-6:
Clicking
with the
zoom tool
magnifies
your image
in preset
increments.

A setting in the tool options bar determines whether Elements resizes your image window to match the image when you zoom with the zoom tool. If you want your image windows to be resized when you zoom, select the Resize Windows to Fit option.

Here's some other zoom tool stuff to tuck away for future reference:

✔ To zoom out on your image, first switch to the zoom out icon in the tool options bar (the magnifying glass with the minus sign in it). Holding down the Alt or Option key when you click makes the zoom tool behave the opposite way from the mode selected in the tool options bar.

✔ As you zoom, Elements displays the *zoom factor* in the title bar and the tool options bar. A zoom factor of 100 percent shows you one screen pixel for every pixel in your image. (Pixels are explained thoroughly in Chapter 4.)

Keep in mind that a 100 percent zoom ratio more than likely doesn't correspond to the printed size of your image. If you want a rough idea of what the printed size will be, use the Print Size command, explained in the next section.

✔ To magnify just one section of an image, drag with the zoom tool to surround the area with a dotted outline. Elements fills the image window with the area that you surrounded.

✔ To temporarily access the zoom tool while another tool is selected, press Ctrl+spacebar (⌘+spacebar on the Mac). Press Ctrl+Alt+spacebar (⌘+Option+spacebar on the Mac) to get the zoom out cursor. In either case, releasing the keys returns you to the previously selected tool.

✔ You can also zoom in and out on your images from the keyboard. Ctrl++ (the plus sign) (⌘++ on the Mac) zooms in; Ctrl+– (the minus sign) (⌘+– on the Mac) zooms out. This keyboard shortcut always resizes the window, regardless of the settings in the zoom tool options bar. Note that, technically, the zoom-in shortcut is actually Ctrl+= (⌘+= on the Mac); in other words, it's not necessary to also press the Shift key to access the plus sign.

The View commands

The View menu offers some more ways to change the magnification of your image. The first two zoom commands on the menu, Zoom In and Zoom Out, aren't of much interest. They do the same thing as clicking and Alt+clicking (Option+clicking on the Mac) with the zoom tool, except that you can't specify the center of the new view as you can with the zoom tool. But you may find the other View commands helpful at times:

✔ Choose View⇨Fit on Screen or press Ctrl+0 (zero) (⌘+0 on the Mac) to display your image at the largest size that allows the entire image to fit on-screen.

✔ Choose View➪Actual Pixels or press Ctrl+Alt+0 (zero) (⌘+Option+0 on the Mac) to return to the 100 percent zoom ratio. This view size shows you one pixel on your monitor for every pixel in the image, which is the most accurate way to view your image.

✔ You can also choose the Fit on Screen view by double-clicking the hand tool in the toolbox. Double-click the zoom tool to change to the Actual Pixels view.

✔ Choose View➪Print Size to display your image on-screen in a rough approximation of the size at which it will print.

✔ When you have the hand or zoom tool selected, you can simply click the actual pixels, fit on screen, or print size button in the tool options bar.

✔ You can choose New Window from the very top of the View menu to create a second view of your image. Don't confuse this with duplicating an image, which creates a new file. New Window simply creates a second view of the same file. This can be useful when you are editing an image in a magnified view, but you want to see the overall results on your entire image without having to continuously zoom in and out.

Cool!

The magnification box

Clicking the zoom tool and choosing the View commands are great when you want to zoom in or out to one of the preset Elements zoom amounts. But what if you want more control over your zooming? For Mac users, the answer awaits in the magnification box, found in the lower-left corner of the image window.

To enter a zoom amount, just double-click or click and drag on the magnification box and type the zoom amount you want to use. If you know exactly what zoom amount you want, press Return to make Elements do your bidding. But if you want to play around with different zoom amounts, press Shift+Return instead. That way, Elements zooms your image but keeps the magnification box active so that you can quickly enter a new amount if the first one doesn't work out. When you're satisfied, press Return.

Regardless of your platform, another great way to change your image's magnification is with the Zoom option in the zoom tool options bar. Note that this setting is scrubbable; click the word *Zoom* and drag your cursor left and right to change the zoom amount.

Navigating by palette

The Navigator palette, shown in Figure 3-7, is the best navigational aid in Elements because it combines the functions of the zoom and hand tools in one location. Choose Window➪Navigator to make the Navigator palette appear on the desktop. To make the palette smaller or larger, drag the size box in the palette's lower-right corner.

Magnification box   Zoom slider

Zoom out   Zoom in

Figure 3-7:
The
Navigator
palette
provides a
nifty way to
zoom and
scroll your
image.

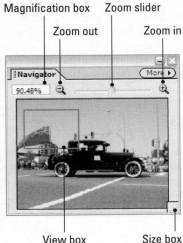

View box   Size box

The palette provides a handy, all-in-one tool for scrolling and zooming. It's especially useful when you're working on a large image that doesn't fit entirely on-screen when you're zoomed in for detail work. Here are the how-tos for using the palette:

✔ In the center of the palette, you see a thumbnail view of your image, as shown in Figure 3-7. The palette shows your entire image, even if it's not all visible in the main image window.

✔ See the red box that surrounds a portion of the thumbnail? That's called the view box. The area in the box corresponds to the portion of your image that's visible in the main image window. As you drag the box, Elements scrolls your image in the main image window to display the area that's surrounded by the box. You can also click an area in the thumbnail to move the view box over that portion of the image.

✔ Press and hold Ctrl (⌘ on the Mac), and the cursor in the palette changes to a zoom cursor. If you drag with the cursor while pressing Ctrl (⌘ on the Mac), you resize the view box, which, in turn, zooms the image in the image window.

✔ The palette also contains a magnification box, as labeled in Figure 3-7. Just enter a zoom factor and press Enter (Return on the Mac). The Shift+Enter (Shift+Return on the Mac) trick explained previously in "The magnification box" section works here, too.

✔ To zoom in or out in the preset Elements increments (as with the zoom tool), click the zoom in or zoom out icons, labeled in Figure 3-7.

✔ You can also zoom by dragging the zoom slider — drag left to zoom out, and drag right to zoom in.

If you're having trouble picking out the view box against the colors of your image, change the view box's color. Click the Navigator palette's More menu and choose the Palette Options command. Then choose a new color from the Color drop-down menu, or click the Swatch to open the Color Picker, where you can choose exactly the shade you want. For more on the Color Picker, see Chapter 5.

Tools for the Terribly Precise

As shown in Figure 3-8, a *grid* is an on-screen device that helps you align items in your image. For example, in the figure the grid was used to keep the words spaced both horizontally and vertically in the image.

Grid lines   Ruler

Figure 3-8: Our furry friend isn't really fenced in; he's just covered with grid lines.

In addition to grids, Elements offers rulers that run across the top and left sides of the image window. Grids and rulers come in handy when you're feeling the urge to be especially precise with your work. And the Info palette helps you get a bead on exactly what's going on in your image.

Switching on the rulers

To display rulers, choose View⇨Rulers or press Ctrl+R (⌘+R on the Mac). To hide the rulers, simply repeat.

By default, the rulers use inches as their unit of measurement. But if you want to use some other unit, say pixels instead of inches, go to the Units & Rulers panel of Elements' Preferences. (You can just double-click a ruler to do so.) In the Units section of the dialog box that appears, select a new unit of measurement from the Rulers drop-down menu. You can also right-click (Control-click on the Mac) on either ruler to access a shortcut menu where you can select your desired unit of measurement.

Preferences is in the Edit Sub Menu

Turning on the grid

The grid superimposes lines on your image at regular intervals. Although you can't move grid lines, you can turn them on and off, and change the spacing and color of the lines.

To turn on the grid, choose View⇨Grid. To change the spacing and appearance of the grid lines, go to the Grid panel of Elements' Preferences. Elements presents you with a dialog box in which you can choose a color and line style for the grid lines. Specify how far apart you want to space the grid lines, and choose whether you want to subdivide the grid with secondary grid lines. You can also choose a unit of measurement for the grid.

The lines of a grid have "snapping" capabilities — anything you drag near a grid line automatically snaps into alignment with that line. You turn snapping on and off by choosing View⇨Snap to Grid.

Information, please

The Info palette (Window⇨Info) can be a big help when you need to know precise values related to your image. By default, the Info palette is divided into four parts: The upper two sections give you the exact values for the color of the pixel your cursor happens to be over, the bottom-left section tells you exactly where in the image your cursor is located, and the bottom-right section tells you the dimensions of an active selection.

The units of measurement are changeable in two ways. You can click the tiny little arrows next to the eyedroppers and the crosshair, or you can use the Info palette's More menu.

The bottom-left section works on an x and y coordinate system. Assuming you've set the units of measurement for this section to pixels (usually the most helpful setting, by the way), if you move your cursor into the upper-left corner of the image, you'll notice that the x and y coordinates are both at 0. Move your cursor to the right across the upper edge of the image — along the x-axis — and you'll see the x coordinate grow. Move your cursor down — along the y-axis — and you'll see the y coordinate grow.

At the bottom of Elements 3.0's Info palette is a new informational area. The information that appears here depends on how you set the menu, which is accessible by clicking the black triangle button in the lower-right corner of the palette. The available options can tell you a wide variety of not particularly helpful information, from the document's pixel dimensions to the current tool that's being used. On the Mac, this information is also available in the Information box at the bottom of an image window when you click the adjacent black triangle.

Chapter 4

Pixels: It's Hip to Be Square

● ●

In This Chapter

▶ Taking a close look at the pixels in an image

▶ Choosing ideal and acceptable resolutions

▶ Cropping images

▶ Rotating and flipping your image

● ●

*I*mages that you create and edit in Photoshop Elements — or in any other image-editing application for that matter — are made up of tiny squares called *pixels*. Understanding how pixels work in an image can be enormously confusing to beginners. Unfortunately, managing your pixel population correctly is essential to turning out professional-looking images, so you really do need to come to grips with how pixels work before you can thoroughly master Elements.

This chapter explains everything you need to know to put pixels in perspective, including how the number of pixels in an image affects its quality, printed size, size on-screen, and size on disk. You'll also see how to reduce or enlarge the size of the on-screen canvas on which all your pretty pixels perch. In other words, this chapter proffers pages of particularly provocative pixel paragraphs, partner.

Welcome to Pixeltown

Imagine that you're the victim of a scientific experiment that has left you 1 millimeter tall. After recovering from the initial shock, you discover that you're sitting on a square tile that's colored with a uniform shade of blue. Your tile is surrounded by other blue tiles, aligned in a perfect grid, just like standard floor tiles but without the grout. You notice upon further inspection that each blue tile differs slightly in shade and tone. As you slowly turn, it becomes evident that you're surrounded by these colored tiles as far as your infinitesimally tiny, pinprick eyes can see.

You cry out in anguish and fling your dust-speck body about in the way that folks always do when plagued by these terrifying scientific experiments. As though in answer to your pitiful squeals, you start to grow. In a matter of moments, you increase in size to almost 5 centimeters tall. A bug that was considering devouring you has a change of mind and runs away. You can now see that you sit in the midst of a huge auditorium and that all the tiles on its vast and unending floor are colored differently, gradually changing from shades of blue to shades of green, red, and yellow. You continue to grow: 10 centimeters, 20, 50, a full meter tall. The tiles start to blend to form some kind of pattern. You grow 2 meters, 5, 10. Your massive head bursts through the flimsy ceiling of the room. This must be how Alice felt in Wonderland. You've now grown several times beyond your normal height, reaching 20 meters tall.

When you reach the height of a 50-story building, your growth spurt comes to an end. You look down at the ruined auditorium, whose walls have been reduced to rubble by the edges of your tremendous feet, and you notice a peculiar thing. You stand not on a floor, but on a picture, as rich in color and detail as any you've seen. Although you would expect the result to have the rough appearance of a mosaic, the tiny tiles have blended into what looks like a continuous-tone photograph.

The vision inspires you to claw at your temples, fling your arms about in circles, and shriek, "What's happening to me?!" The answer, of course, is nothing (other than a little overacting, that is). You see, when you get far enough away from a perfect grid of colored tiles, the tiles disappear, and an overall image takes shape.

What does this little trip down sci-fi lane have to do with Elements? A lot, actually. Like the image on the auditorium floor, your Elements image is made up of a grid of colored squares. In this case, the squares are called *pixels*. These tiniest of image particles are at the heart of what makes Elements and your electronic images tick.

Every single painting and image-editing function in Elements is devoted to changing the quantity, arrangement, or color of pixels. It sounds so simple that you figure it must be a joke, an exaggeration, or just a plain lie. But it's the absolute truth. Image editing is just a sophisticated way to count, color, and arrange pixels, and nothing more.

Screen Pixels versus Image Pixels

Like the tiles in the preceding story, each pixel in a computer image is perfectly square, arranged on a perfect grid, and colored uniformly — that is, each pixel is one color and one color only. Put these pixels together, and your brain perceives them to be an everyday, average photograph.

The display on your computer's monitor is also made up of pixels. As with image pixels, screen pixels are square and arranged on a grid. For instance, a typical monitor display measures 1024 screen pixels wide by 768 screen pixels tall. These screen pixels are kind of tiny, so you may not be able to make them out. Each one generally measures around ½ inch across.

To understand the relationship between screen and image pixels, open an image. After the image appears on the screen, double-click the zoom tool in the toolbox. The Zoom option in the tool options bar lists the zoom amount as 100%, which means that you can see one pixel in your image for every pixel displayed by your monitor.

To view the image pixels more closely, click the zoom tool once in the middle of the image to increase the zoom amount to 200 percent. A 200% zoom amount magnifies the image pixels to twice their previous size so that one image pixel measures two screen pixels tall and two screen pixels wide. If you change the zoom amount to 400% by clicking the zoom tool twice more in the image, Elements gives you a total of 16 screen pixels for every image pixel (four screen pixels tall by four screen pixels wide). Figure 4-1 illustrates how different zoom amounts affect the appearance of your image pixels on-screen.

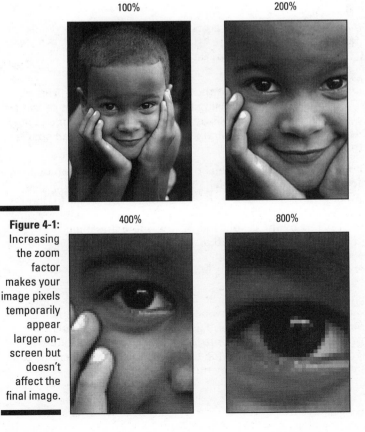

Figure 4-1: Increasing the zoom factor makes your image pixels temporarily appear larger on-screen but doesn't affect the final image.

Remember that the zoom factor has nothing to do with the size at which your image prints or appears if e-mailed to a friend or posted on the Web — it affects only how your image looks on-screen at that moment in Elements. If you want to see on-screen an approximation of your image's print size, choose View➪Print Size. Bear in mind, though, that this is only a rough approximation.

Image Size, Resolution, and Other Tricky Pixel Stuff

An image has three primary attributes related to pixels: *file size, resolution,* and *physical dimensions,* as explained in the following list. You control these attributes through the Image Size dialog box, shown in Figure 4-2.

To display the dialog box, choose Image➪Resize➪Image Size. Here's some stuff to consider about an image's size:

- The *pixel dimensions* of the image are a measure of how many pixels the image contains. The image in Figure 4-1 is 256 pixels wide and 384 pixels tall, for a total of 98,304 pixels. Most images contain hundreds of thousands or even millions of pixels.

- The *resolution* of an image refers to the number of pixels that print per inch (or per centimeter, if you're using the metric system). For example, the resolution of the first image in Figure 4-1 is 180 pixels per inch *(ppi).* That may sound like an awful lot of pixels squished into a small space, but it's actually on the low side.

- Not to be confused with pixel dimensions, the *document size* of an image is its physical width and height when printed, as measured in inches, centimeters, or your unit of choice. Resolution is a key factor in determining document size. You can calculate the document size by dividing the number of pixels by the resolution. For example, the image of the little boy in Figure 4-1 measures 256 pixels ÷ 180 pixels per inch = 1⅜ inches wide and 384 pixels ÷ 180 ppi = 2⅛ inches tall. Measure the image with a ruler, and you see that this is indeed the case.

No problem, right? Sure, this stuff is a little technical, but it's not as though it requires an advanced degree in cold fusion to figure out what's going on. And yet, the Image Size dialog box may well be the most confusing Elements dialog box. You can even damage your image, so be extremely careful before you make changes in the Image Size dialog box. (The upcoming sections tell you everything you need to know to stay out of trouble.)

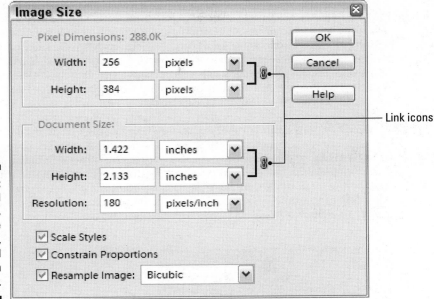

Figure 4-2:
You control
file size,
image
dimensions,
and
resolution
here.

You can change the print size of your image with other dialog boxes, chiefly Print Preview (File➪Print). On the Mac, you can also change the print size with the Page Setup command (File➪Page Setup). On either platform, it's also possible that your printer software may give you yet another option for changing the print size. When using any of these methods, your image is scaled to the new size only during the print cycle. However, the interaction of possibly four different commands telling your printer how large to print an image can be, to put it mildly, confusing. Your best bet is to stick with the Image Size command; it's entirely possible to change the print size with Image Size and yet not affect the quality of your image in any way.

Resolving resolution

Although the Resolution option box seems like just another option in the Image Size dialog box, it's one of the most critical values to consider if you want your images to look good.

The Resolution value determines how tightly the pixels are packed when printed. It's kind of like the population density of one of those ridiculously large urban areas cropping up all over the modern world. Take Lagos, Nigeria, for example, which is a city of approximately 15 million people. The population density of Lagos is such that there are roughly 267,000 people packed into each square mile.

To increase the population density, you have to either increase the number of people in a city or decrease the physical boundaries of the city and scrunch everyone closer together. The same goes for resolution. If you want a higher resolution (more pixels per inch), you can either decrease the document size of the image or increase the pixel dimensions by adding pixels to the image. For example, the two images in Figure 4-3 have the same pixel dimensions, but the top image has a smaller document size, giving it twice the resolution of the larger image — 180 ppi versus 90 ppi.

Conversely, population density goes down as people die, as people move out, or as the boundaries of the city grow. For example, if we were to mandate that Lagos spread out evenly over the entire 357,000 square miles of Nigeria, the population density would temporarily drop to 42 people per square mile (assuming, of course, that the other residents of Nigeria happened to be on vacation at the time). Likewise, when you increase the document size of an image or delete some of its pixels, the resolution goes down.

Figure 4-3:
Two images with the same number of pixels but subject to two different resolutions.

Before you get the mistaken idea that this analogy is completely airtight, we should in all fairness mention a few key differences between a typical image and Lagos:

- Lagos, like any city, has its crowded spots and its relatively sparse areas. An image, by contrast, is equally dense at all points. Therefore, unlike population density, resolution is constant across the board.

- An image is always rectangular. Lagos can best be described as free-form.

- Population density is measured in terms of area — you know, so many folks per square mile. Resolution, on the other hand, is measured in a line — pixels per linear inch (or centimeter). So an image with a resolution of 180 pixels per inch contains 32,400 pixels per square inch. (That's 180 squared, in case you're wondering.)

- The pixels in an image are absolutely square. The people in Lagos are shaped rather arbitrarily, with arms and legs jutting out at irregular and unpredictable angles.

- You have total control over the size and resolution of an image. You can move to Lagos and thereby increase the population by one, but otherwise the population of Lagos is entirely out of your hands.

Changing pixel dimensions

The top two option boxes in the Image Size dialog box enable you to change an image's *pixel dimensions* — the number of pixels wide by the number of pixels tall. Unless you really know what you're doing when it comes to pixels, it might be best to avoid these options.

Lowering the Pixel Dimensions values can be dangerous because what you're really doing is throwing away pixels. And when you delete pixels, you delete detail. Figure 4-4 shows what we mean. The document size of all three images is the same, but the detail drops off from one image to the next. The first image contains 64,000 pixels and is printed at a resolution of 140 ppi; the second contains ¼ as many pixels and is printed at 70 ppi; the third contains only 4,000 pixels and has a resolution of 35 ppi. Notice how details such as the shadows from the girl's eyelashes and the distinction between individual hairs in her eyebrows become less pronounced and more generalized as the pixel population decreases.

Increasing the Pixel Dimensions values isn't such a hot idea either because Elements can't generate image detail out of thin air. When you raise the Pixel Dimensions values, Elements adds pixels by averaging the existing pixels (a process computer nerds call *interpolation*) in a way that may result in image softening and never results in the miraculous reconstruction of detail.

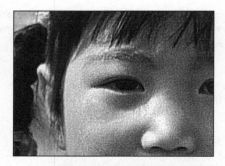

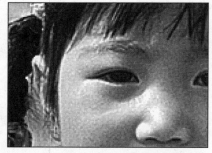

Figure 4-4:
Three
images,
each
containing
fewer pixels
and printed
at a lower
resolution
than the
image
above it.

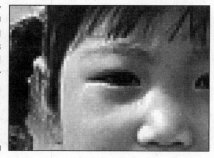

If changing the pixel dimensions is dangerous, you may wonder why Elements gives you the option to do so. Well, although we don't recommend ever adding pixels to an image, you may need to lower the pixel dimensions. If your file size is really large — that is, your image contains a ton of pixels — you may want to toss some of the pixels overboard.

In an ideal world, you'd want as many pixels as possible because more pixels mean greater image detail. But if you're posting your image on the Internet, you may need to reduce your pixel dimensions so that the image will download more quickly and so that it can fit on your users' screens. Also, the more pixels you have, the more of your disk space the image consumes, which can be a problem if you're working with limited computing resources.

Even when you want to dump pixels from an image, it's best not to attack the job from the Pixel Dimensions option boxes. You discover a better way in the "Using the Image Size dialog box safely" section, later in this chapter.

Changing the physical dimensions of the image

The Width and Height boxes in the Document Size portion of the Image Size dialog box reflect the actual printed size of your image. The drop-down menus next to the Width and Height options let you change the unit of measure displayed in the option boxes. The percent option in the drop-down menu enables you to enter new width and height values as a percentage of the original values. Enter a value higher than 100% to increase the print size; enter a value lower than 100% to reduce the print size.

Yeah, okay, but what resolution should I use?

All kinds of formulas are available for calculating the optimal resolution for various types of output. But rather than try to explain any of these — what with your head already spinning with Lagos population data — we'll just go ahead and simply list some ideal and acceptable values for certain kinds of print jobs. See whether these work for you.

Type of Job	Ideal Resolution	Acceptable Setting
Full-color image for magazine or professional publication	300 ppi	225 ppi
Full-color slides	300 ppi	200 ppi
Color inkjet printers	300 ppi	200 ppi
Color image for laser printing or overhead projections	180 ppi	120 ppi
Color images for multimedia productions and Web pages	72 ppi	72 ppi
Black-and-white images for imageset newsletters, flyers, and so on	180 ppi	120 ppi
Black-and-white images for laser printing	120 ppi	90 ppi

Keep in mind that there are no hard-and-fast rules for resolution settings. You can specify virtually any resolution setting between the ideal and acceptable settings and achieve good results. Even if you go with a resolution value that's lower than the suggested acceptable setting, the worst that can happen is that you'll get fuzzy or slightly jagged results. But there's no wrong setting; if it looks good, it *is* good.

Keeping things proportionate

Both pairs of Width and Height option boxes in the Image Size dialog box list the dimensions of your image. If you enter a different value in an option box and click the OK button, Elements resizes your image to the dimensions you specified. Pretty obvious, eh?

But strangely, when you change the width or height value, by default the other value changes, too. This is nothing more than a function of the Constrain Proportions check box, which is turned on by default. Elements is simply maintaining the original proportions of the image.

If you click the Constrain Proportions check box to turn it off, Elements permits you to adjust the width and height values independently. Notice that the little link icons (labeled back in Figure 4-2) disappear, showing that the two options are now maverick independents with reckless disregard for one another. You can now create stretchy effects like the ones shown in Figure 4-5. The first example has the width value reduced, with the height value unchanged. In the second example, the height value was reduced, leaving the width value unaltered.

However, to deselect the Constrain Proportions check box, you have to select the Resample Image check box. As we explained in the highly anticipated section "Using the Image Size dialog box safely," when you change the width or height of your image with the Resample Image check box selected, Elements either adds or deletes pixels from your image. Obviously, to stretch an image as shown in Figure 4-5, pixels have to be added or deleted. Therefore, if you want to turn off Constrain Proportions, you have to turn on Resample Image.

Using the Image Size dialog box safely

As mentioned earlier in the section "Image Size, Resolution, and Other Tricky Pixel Stuff," three image attributes — size, resolution, and dimension — are vying for your attention and affecting each other. Change any one of these attributes, and at least one of the others has to change proportionately. If you decrease the pixel dimensions, for example, either the document size or resolution (number of pixels per inch) must also decrease. If you want to increase the document size, you have to increase the pixel dimensions — add pixels, in other words — or decrease the resolution.

Thinking about all the possible permutations can drive you crazy, and besides, they aren't the least bit important. What is important is that you understand what you can accomplish with the Image Size dialog box and that you know how to avoid mistakes. So, now that you have all the background you need, it's finally time for a modicum of fatherly advice:

✔ The first question to ask yourself when using the Image Size command is: "Do I want to change the number of pixels in my image?" If the image is intended for print, the answer is almost certainly "No." In this case, the first thing you should do is deselect the Resample Image check box. Deselecting this box enables you to change only the document size, affecting the size of the image when it is ultimately printed. However, as you adjust the width or height values, you must keep an eye on the resolution to make sure that it doesn't fall below an acceptable value. (See the chart in the "Yeah, okay, but what resolution should I use?" sidebar for ballpark figures.)

✔ If your document is intended for the Web, however, you may well want to change the number of pixels in your image. Even a one-megapixel digital camera produces images with too many pixels to be seen on most computer screens. In this case, make sure that Resample Image is selected. You can ignore the Document Size portion of the Image Size dialog box; when preparing images to be seen on a computer screen, the only thing that matters is the Pixel Dimensions portion.

Some other things to keep in mind:

✔ When you deselect the Resample Image check box, the Image Size dialog box changes, and the Pixel Dimensions portion of the dialog box become unavailable to you. A link icon also connects the Document Size's Width, Height, and Resolution option boxes, showing that changes to one value affect the other two values as well.

✔ If you manage to mess up everything in the Image Size dialog box, you can return to the original settings by Alt+clicking (Option+clicking on the Mac) the Cancel button. Pressing Alt (Option on the Mac) changes the word *Cancel* to *Reset;* clicking resets the options.

✔ In the Resample Image drop-down menu, you'll want to avoid using the Nearest Neighbor and Bilinear choices, which give ugly results on regular images. But Elements 3.0 now offers three flavors of Bicubic resampling, all of which have merit. The default Bicubic setting gives all-around excellent results, but when you're lowering the number of pixels in an image, Bicubic can at times soften the image undesirably. In that case, Bicubic Sharper can help keep details sharp. Conversely, increasing the number of pixels in an image (while not generally recommended) can result in jagged edges. In such a case, Bicubic Smoother can help smooth things out.

✔ If you want to change the unit of measure that appears by default in the Image Size dialog box drop-down menus, choose Edit➪Preferences➪Units & Rulers (in Windows) or Photoshop Elements➪Preferences➪Units & Rulers (on the Mac) and choose a different option from the Rulers drop-down menu.

Figure 4-5: This little girl was allowed to use the Image Size dialog box without parental supervision, providing clear examples of what can happen when the Constrain Proportions check box falls into the wrong hands.

What Does the Canvas Size Command Do?

Another important command related to the topic of image sizing is Image⇨ Resize⇨Canvas Size. Unlike the Image Size command, which in some manner changes the size of the existing image, the Canvas Size command changes the size of the "canvas" on which the image sits. If you increase the size of the canvas, Elements fills the new area outside the image with a solid color of your choosing, assuming that the image has a background layer (see Chapter 10 for more on layers). If you make the canvas smaller, Elements crops the image. Have you ever written a sign on a piece of poster board and found as you got to the end of a line that you'd been writing too large, giving you no other choice but to scrunch up your letters in an unreadable clump? That's the sort of thing that Canvas Size can correct for you (but only on the computer, needless to say); it can tack on that little bit of extra space to your digital poster board.

When you choose Image⇨Resize⇨Canvas Size, the dialog box shown in Figure 4-6 pops up from its virtual hole. You can play with the options found in the dialog box as follows:

✔ Enter new values into the Width and Height option boxes as desired. You can also change the unit of measurement by using the drop-down menus, just as in the Image Size dialog box.

✔ When the Relative check box is active, Canvas Size automatically *adds* the amounts you enter in the Width and Height boxes *to* the current dimensions. This is great for adding, say, a 20-pixel border around an image; just type 40 into both the Width and Height fields, and you're finished. Relative works when you're cropping images with Canvas Size too; just select Relative and type negative numbers, such as –40.

✔ The Anchor section shows a graphic representation of how the current image will sit in the new canvas. By default, the image is centered in the canvas. But you can click inside any of the other eight squares to move the image. If you move the image to, for example, the upper-right corner, the canvas would be added to or subtracted from the left and bottom of your original image.

✔ The new Canvas Extension Color option lets you specify a color for the additional canvas you're adding to your image. You can choose from the foreground and background colors, white, black, or medium gray. Choosing Other at the bottom of the menu takes you to the Color Picker, where you can specify your own color. You can access the Color Picker also by clicking the small square color chip to the right of the menu.

✔ If you reduce either the width or height value and press Enter (Return on the Mac), Elements asks whether you really want to clip (or crop) the image. If you click the Proceed button and decide you don't like the results, you can always click the step backward icon or press Ctrl+Z (⌘+Z on the Mac) to restore the original canvas size.

✔ As with Image Size, if you want to change the unit of measure that appears by default in the Canvas Size dialog box, choose Edit⇨Preferences⇨Units & Rulers (in Windows) or Photoshop Elements⇨Preferences⇨Units & Rulers (on the Mac) and choose a different option from the Rulers drop-down menu.

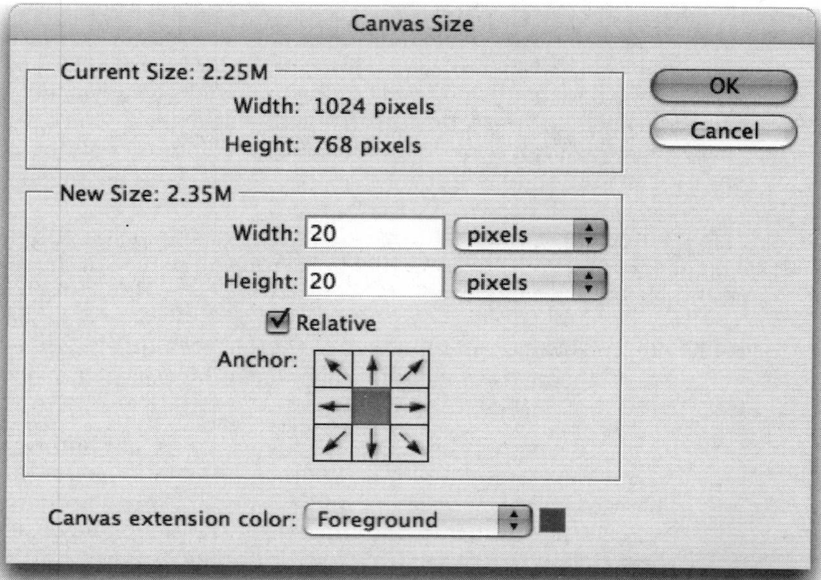

Figure 4-6:
Use the
Canvas Size
dialog box
to change
the size of
the virtual
page on
which the
image sits.

Trimming Excess Gunk Off the Edges

Although you can use the Canvas Size command to crop images, it's hardly the best tool at your disposal. Elements, the handy-dandy application that it is, has specialized tools for the job. The Image Size command can definitely turn an 8-x-10 wedding photograph into a nifty wallet-size snapshot without trimming anyone's vital body parts. But suppose that your spouse up and runs off to Lagos with your next-door neighbor? What do you do then? Why, you crop the cretin out of the picture.

The sharp edges of the crop tool

In your effort to cut out background flack as you're framing a picture in your camera, you could overcompensate and cut off Grandma's head or the right half of little Joey. The fact is, it's better to have too much stuff in your photos than too little, for the simple reason that excess stuff can be cut away but missing stuff is gone forever. Since photography was invented, production artists have been taking knives and scissors to just about every image that passes over their light tables in an effort to clip away the extraneous gook around the edges and hone in on the real goods. Called *cropping,* this technique is so pervasive that professional photographers purposely shoot subjects from too far away knowing that someone, somewhere, will slice the image and make it right. As with the Canvas Size command, cropping changes the pixel dimensions and the document size of your image without changing the resolution. (Of course, the content of your image changes, too.)

In Elements, you can cut away the unpalatable parts of an image by using the crop tool. To select the crop tool without messing with the toolbox, press C.

Here's how to use the crop tool:

1. **Drag with the tool around the portion of the image you want to retain.**

   In Figure 4-7, that's the floating spaceman. A dotted rectangle called a *marquee* follows your drag to clearly show the crop boundaries. After you've drawn your marquee, Elements covers the area outside the marquee with a translucent *shield* to better frame the image. You can use the shield controls in the tool options bar to specify the color and opacity of the shield or to turn it off entirely. Don't worry if you don't draw the perfect marquee; you get the chance to edit the boundary in the next step.

2. **Drag the crop boundaries as desired.**

   After you release your mouse button, Elements displays square handles around the edges of the marquee (refer to Figure 4-7). If the marquee isn't the right size, drag a handle to change the crop boundary. Your cursor changes to a double-headed arrow when you place it over a handle, indicating that you have the go-ahead to drag the handle. You can drag as many handles as you please before cropping the image. Holding down the Shift key while dragging from one of the corner handles constrains the proportions of the crop. Holding down the Alt key (the Option key on the Mac) makes the resizing of the crop boundary occur around the visible center point of the crop.

   If you've created a crop boundary and can't get it to resize as you want, click the cancel icon in the tool options bar. Then click the Clear button, and drag your crop boundary again. See the upcoming section "More good news about cropping" to find out about the Front Image and Clear buttons.

   If you move the cursor outside the crop boundary, the cursor changes to a curved, double-headed arrow. Dragging then rotates the crop boundary.

   After the crop boundary is rotated, dragging from one of the square handles with the Alt key pressed (the Option key on the Mac) enables you to create a nonrectangular crop, without right angles at the corners. When you accept the crop (see Step 3), Elements does the necessary distortions to convert the nonrectangular crop back into a rectangular image. You probably won't ever want to do this, but then again, who knows?

3. **After you get the crop boundary the way you want it, double-click inside the boundary to crop the image or click the commit (check mark) icon on the tool options bar.**

   You can also just press Enter (Return on the Mac). Elements throws away all pixels outside the crop boundary. If you rotated the crop boundary in Step 2, Elements rights the rectangular area and thus rotates the image, as shown in Figure 4-8.

Handle   Resize cursor   ┌ Crop boundary

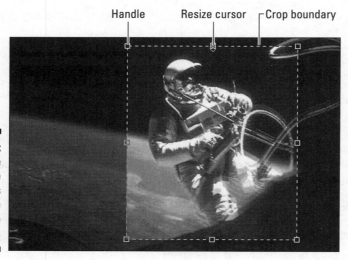

Figure 4-7:
Drag the
square
handles
to change
the crop
boundary.

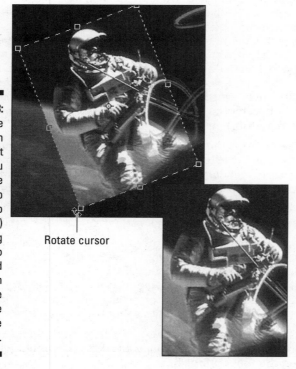

Figure 4-8:
If the
photograph
isn't
straight, you
can rotate
the crop
boundary to
match (top)
while telling
Elements to
crop and
straighten
the image
at the
same time
(bottom).

Rotate cursor

When you rotate an image in this way, Elements *resamples* your image — that is, it rearranges the pixels to come up with the rotated image. As discussed earlier, resampling can slightly damage your image by making the details softer. For best results, don't rotate your image more than once. However, if you rotate your image only in 90-degree increments (which the Shift key makes easy), Elements doesn't resample your image.

More good news about cropping

Do you think that's all a generous application such as Elements has to offer in terms of cropping images? Ha! Elements has so many terrific cropping techniques that one would be tempted to refer to them as a "bumper crop," if one liked painfully bad puns. Here's some more cropping info:

- ✔ After you selected the crop tool, but before you started dragging with it, you may have noticed some other choices in the options bar. The Width, Height, and Resolution settings are useful for cropping an image to exact dimensions.

- ✔ The new Preset Options menu gives you several standard cropping sizes for photos. Just choose an option such as 6 in x 4 in from the menu, and those measurements are automatically entered into the Width and Height fields. When you drag to create your cropping marquee, you'll automatically be constrained to the correct aspect ratio for a 6 x 4 print. If you actually wanted a 4 x 6 print instead, just click the new double arrow button between the Width and Height fields to swap the amounts. When you want to return to free-form cropping, click the Clear button to void the Width and Height fields.

- ✔ Another option that can be useful is the Front Image option. It enables you to crop one image so that it's the same size as another image. Suppose that you want to make image B the same size as image A. First, open both images. Make sure that image A is the foremost image by clicking its title bar. Select the crop tool and click the Front Image button in the options bar. Elements loads the size and resolution settings from image A to the tool options bar. Select image B. Drag the crop tool on the canvas and frame your image; you'll notice that the marquee always stays in the same proportions as image A. When you press Enter (Return on the Mac) to execute the crop, Elements automatically resizes image B to match image A. Note that Elements resamples image B if necessary to match the size of image A. Click the Clear button to escape this cropping mode.

- ✔ If you've created an active crop boundary and you then change your mind about cropping the image, press Esc or Ctrl+period (⌘+period on the Mac) to get rid of the cropping boundary. Or you can also click the cancel (slashed circle) icon in the tool options bar.

✔ To move the cropping boundary in its entirety after you've drawn the marquee, just drag inside the boundary.

✔ In addition to using the crop tool, you can crop a *selected area* (see Chapter 9) by choosing Image⇨Crop. The selection doesn't even have to be vaguely rectangular; it can be elliptical, polygonal, even feathered. Elements can't really crop to an irregular shape, but it gets as close to the boundary as it can.

✔ As mentioned, you can also crop an image by using the Canvas Size command. You may want to consider this method if you need to trim your image on one or more sides by a precise number of pixels to get the image to a certain size; the Relative option can really come in handy here.

The new cookie cutter tool can cut a shape out of an image and throw away the unused pixels like so much excess cookie dough. The tool even has a cropping mode to reduce the pixel dimensions of your image, which is why we mention it here. We cover the cookie cutter tool in depth in Chapter 15.

The Divide Scanned Photos command

From the very first version of Elements, the Image⇨Rotate submenu has had two commands called Straighten Image and Straighten and Crop Image. If you place a picture crookedly in your scanner, Straighten Image is designed to automatically correct the rotation of the scan. Straighten and Crop Image goes one step further by automatically cropping the edges of the straightened scan.

These commands have never worked very well, and the bad news is that they're apparently no better in version 3.0 of Elements. The good news, however, is that Elements 3.0 has a new command on loan from Photoshop CS. The new Divide Scanned Photos command out-straightens and out-crops the Straighten and Crop Image command, plus performs a nifty trick all its own.

Scan an image — don't even worry about placing it correctly on the scanning bed — and choose Image⇨Divide Scanned Photos. The command automatically analyzes the scan, corrects the rotation, and crops out the scanned underside of your scanner lid so that you're left with nothing but the image. It's great to finally have a command in Elements that can perform this task reliably.

But wait — it gets better. As Figure 4-9 shows, you can place several images on your scanning bed at once — known in scanning circles as a "gang scan" — and Divide Scanned Photos can work its magic on each and every member of the gang. A formerly difficult, time-consuming, and tedious task has been automated in Elements 3.0. Now if the command could only clean the glass on your scanning bed, we'd really have progress.

Figure 4-9:
The Divide Scanned Photos command can chop a "gang scan" (left) into individual images (right).

Image Gymnastics

If you visit the Image⇨Rotate menu to pay your last respects to the Straighten and Crop Image command, you'll notice a submenu of rotation commands lurking there. Here's the lowdown on them:

- ✔ **90° Left, 90° Right,** and **180°:** These commands rotate the entire canvas. Left is counterclockwise; Right is clockwise. These commands can be useful if your image was scanned on its side or upside down, but it doesn't need cropping or straightening. 90° left and right rotation is also available in Quick Fix mode.

- ✔ **Custom:** Rotates your canvas a specific amount. If you rotate anything other than 90° or 180°, the canvas size will grow to accommodate the rotated image.

- ✔ **Flip Horizontal:** Creates a mirror image of your canvas.

- ✔ **Flip Vertical:** Creates a mirror image of your canvas and turns it upside down.

For the most part, the other commands in the Rotate submenu perform identically to the commands listed here, but they apply only if your image has an active selection (see Chapter 9) or layers (see Chapter 10). The one exception is the Free Rotate Layer command (which becomes Free Rotate Selection when there's an active selection). This command puts you in Free Transform mode, which is discussed freely in Chapter 10.

Chapter 5

Over (and Under) the Rainbow

As you may have guessed from the title, this chapter is all about color — the same kind of color that Dorothy encountered when she passed over the weather-beaten threshold of her old Kansas home onto a path of lemon-yellow bricks in that beloved classic, *Fight Club*. Or was it *The Wizard of Oz*? Maybe so. Anyway, when Dorothy was in Kansas — "under" the rainbow — everything was black and white. But as soon as she went "over" the rainbow and stepped out of her ramshackle house into the Land of Oz, things were in color. (Yeah, we know that the movie's "black and white" scenes are actually in sepia tone. What are you trying to do — screw up our otherwise-relevant analogy with trivial facts?)

So what's the lesson here? Kansas seemed pretty dreary and depressing next to Oz, with its helium-voiced midgets, combative trees, and bipedal jungle cats. Color must have it all over black and white, huh?

Well, little Dorothy Gale didn't ultimately think so. And, in truth, the absence of color can offer its own special attractions. It's the refreshingly personal vision of a 16mm short-subject film you stumble across one evening on Bravo. It's the powerful chiaroscuro of an Ansel Adams photograph. In an age when every screen, page, and billboard screams with color that's more vivid than real life, black and white can beckon the eye like an old friend.

Kansas is starting to sound better and better, huh? No surprise, really. The Sunflower State is truly as lovely as its nickname, whereas the Munchkins — to hear Judy Garland tell it — were a bunch of randy booze hounds.

Whether you choose black and white or color, this chapter tells you how it all works. You find out how to use and create colors that you can apply with the painting tools. Not bad for a chapter based on an old MGM musical, eh?

Looking at Color in a Whole New Light

To understand color, you have to understand a little color theory. If you've had a color image open in Elements, you may have noticed the telltale initials *RGB* in parentheses on the image title bar. These initials mean that all colors in the image are created by blending red, green, and blue light.

Red, green, and blue? Weren't we taught in kindergarten that the primary colors were red, *yellow,* and blue? Well, red, green, and blue are the primary colors of *light*. And it just so happens that these colors correspond to the three kinds of cones inside your eyeball. So, in theory, your monitor projects color in the same way your eyes see color.

Go ahead and turn to Color Plate 1 (but keep a finger here, of course). The colorful photo at the bottom of the plate looks very much like it would on your monitor. But lurking under the surface, as illustrated at the top of the plate, are three different color channels: red, green, and blue. When you see a color image like this on your monitor, you're actually seeing the combination of these three channels. The red image on the left is the one being sent to the red cones in your eyes; the green image in the middle is hitting your green cones, and the blue image goes right to your blue cones.

Pretty nifty, huh? Here's another way to think about it: If you were to take the images you see in the red, green, and blue channels, print them to slides, put each of the slides in a different projector, and shine all three projectors at the same spot on a screen so that the images precisely overlapped, you would see the full-color image in all its splendor.

Yet another way to think about the color channels is as black-and-white images, as shown in Figure 5-1. Areas in the red channel that are very light will have a lot of red in the corresponding full-color image. And where things are dark in the red channel, there won't be much red at all. The same holds true for the green and blue channels. Compare the boy's blue shirt, red shorts, and the green grass behind.

Every color channel contains light areas and dark areas, just like a black-and-white image. The light and dark pixels from each channel mix to form other colors. In Elements, this is basically an invisible process. But it's important to know that the three color channels are always there, lurking beneath the surface of your color images.

The following list explains how corresponding pixels from the different channels mix to form a single, full-color pixel:

 ✔ A white pixel from one channel mixed with black pixels from the other two channels produces the color from the first channel. For example, if the red is white, and green and blue are black, you get a red pixel.

Figure 5-1:
Shown here in black and white are the red (left), green (center), and blue (right) channels that combine to make the full-color image in Color Plate 1.

✔ White pixels from the red and green channels plus a black pixel from the blue channel form yellow. This description may sound weird — two colors, red and green, mixing to form a lighter color — but that's exactly how things work in the world of RGB. Because you're mixing colors projected from a monitor, two colors projected together produce a still lighter color.

Do you follow? No? Well, suppose you had a flashlight with a red bulb and your friend had one with a green bulb. Maybe it's Christmas or something. At any rate, if you were to point your flashlight at a spot on the ground, the spot would turn red. No surprise there. But if your friend pointed her green flashlight at the same spot, the spot wouldn't get darker, it would get lighter. In fact, it would turn bright yellow.

✔ White pixels from the green and blue channels plus a black pixel from the red channel make a bright turquoise color called cyan. White pixels from the red and blue channels plus a black pixel from the green channel make magenta.

✔ By a strange coincidence, cyan, magenta, and yellow just happen to be the main ink colors used in the color printing process. Well, actually, it's not a coincidence. Color printing is the opposite of color screen display, so the two use complementary collections of primary hues to produce full-color images. The difference is that because cyan, magenta, and yellow are pigments, they become darker as you mix them. Yellow plus cyan, for example, make green.

Your monitor creates white by mixing the lightest amounts of red, green, and blue — the opposite of how things work on the printed page. Color printing exploits the fact that sunlight and man-made light (both referred to as "white light") contain the entire spectrum of visible light, including all shades of red, green, and blue. The primary printing inks — cyan, magenta, and yellow — are actually *color filters*. When white light hits cyan ink printed on a page, the cyan ink filters out all traces of red and reflects only green and blue, which mix to form cyan. Similarly, magenta is a green light filter, and yellow is a blue light filter, as illustrated in detail in Color Plate 2. This and other factors (such as purity of inks, variation of ink tints, whiteness of paper, and lighting conditions) result in the CMYK world. (The *K*, incidentally, stands for *blacK*.)

✔ White pixels from all three channels mix to form white. Black pixels form black. Equally medium pixels make gray.

Although this discussion is highly stimulating, it would probably make more sense if you could see it. If you're the visual type, take a look at Color Plate 3. The left side of the figure shows the RGB combinations just discussed. The right side shows RGB mixes that result in other colors, including orange, purple, and so on. Give it the once-over and see if you can't feel your brain grow by leaps and bounds.

In Elements 3.0, an "8" shares the parentheses with the "RGB" in an image's title bar, as in "(RGB/8)". This 8 signifies that the image is using 8-bit color, which (due to a technical process) means that potentially 16.8 million colors are available for your use in the image. However, Elements 3.0 offers limited support for 16-bit color images. You can now open a 16-bit image, but you can't do very much with it unless you choose Image➪Mode➪Convert to 8 Bits/ Channel to convert it to 8-bit color. You'll know you have a 16-bit image if you see "(RGB/16)" in the title bar.

Did you know that 16-bit color offers a mind-blowing theoretical 281.5 *trillion* colors? But because your monitor can display only 16.8 million colors, and because 16-bit color images have much bigger file sizes than 8-bit images, and because Elements' support for 16-bit is extremely limited, you have little reason to worry about 16-bit color.

Managing Photoshop Elements Color

Now that you have some basic color theory, it's time for basic color management. Ideally, you want to have a true WYSIWYG (What You See Is What You Get) world. In other words, you want to be able to look at your monitor and see the exact colors you'll get coming out the other end. This "other end" can be in the form of printouts or just an image on the Web viewed from another monitor.

Gimme good gamma

Getting exact color is next to impossible. Devices can help — expensive hardware and software calibrators that come with high-end monitors deliver very good results — but most of us average Joes and Jos have to manage this dilemma on our own. For Windows users at least, Elements comes with a little help in the form of the Adobe Gamma Control Panel:

1. **In Windows XP, choose Start⇨Control Panel, click Appearance and Themes, and then click Adobe Gamma. For Windows 2000, choose Start⇨Settings⇨Control Panel and double-click Adobe Gamma.**

2. **Take the deluxe guided tour of the Adobe Gamma Control Panel by choosing Step by Step and letting the wizard show you the way. Click the Next button.**

   If you're supremely confident, choose the Control Panel option. The Control Panel appears, as shown in Figure 5-2, giving you all the necessary setup options in one dialog box. Otherwise, choose Step by Step along with the rest of us dummies.

3. **Give your monitor profile a distinctive name, and then click Next.**

   What you're doing here is creating a *monitor profile,* a settings file that describes how your monitor displays color.

4. **Adjust the brightness and contrast controls on your monitor, and then click Next.**

   Your monitor most likely has these controls somewhere, probably on the front. Follow the on-screen instructions.

5. **Choose a setting for your monitor's phosphors, and then click Next.**

   We're guessing you don't know this information right off the top of your head. We'll also surmise that this information may not be contained anywhere in your head whatsoever. If you can't find anything about phosphors in the documentation that came with your monitor, don't sweat it; just accept the default setting and click Next. The really important stuff is coming up next anyway.

6. **Deselect the View Single Gamma Only check box, adjust the three sliders, and then click Next.**

   The idea here is to make the middle rectangles blend in as closely as possible with the outer rectangles. It may help you to move as far away from your monitor as possible, to squint, or to actually look above the rectangles and use your peripheral vision. Sounds weird, we know, but give it a try. Keep the Gamma setting at Windows Default and click Next.

7. **Measure your hardware white point, and then click Next.**

   This defines the general color cast of your screen. Again, you probably don't know this setting by rote. Luckily there's a way to measure this one. Click the Measure button and follow the on-screen instructions.

8. **Use the default setting as your Adjusted White Point, and then click Next.**

   Just leave this set at Same as Hardware.

9. **Compare the before and after as desired, and then click Finish.**

   Here you can compare how things looked before you went through Adobe Gamma with how they look now.

10. **Save your profile to disk.**

    The default location is perfect; Elements will know just where to find your profile. Click OK, and Elements has the scoop on your monitor.

Mac users don't need to feel left out in the cold because they don't have Adobe Gamma; an excellent monitor-profiling tool is built right into the Mac. Go to your Displays System Preferences and click the Color tab. Then click the Calibrate button, turn on Expert Mode (who's a dummy here?), and click Continue to be guided step-by-step through the calibrating process.

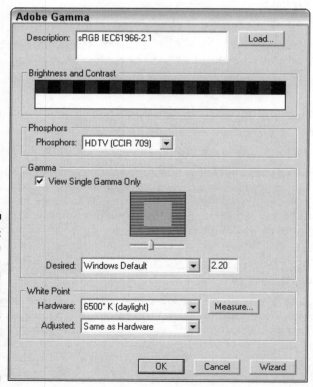

Figure 5-2:
The Adobe
Gamma
Control
Panel is the
no-frills
method for
calibrating
your
monitor.

Choosing your color settings

Trying to get consistent color is without question the most complex and confusing aspect of working with digital images on the computer. In Elements' granddaddy application, Photoshop, the Color Settings dialog box is an intimidating myriad of options and technical terms designed to make even seasoned pros curl into a ball on the floor and whimper. Thank your lucky stars, then, that this has all been simplified quite eloquently for Elements. Follow along; we promise this won't hurt a bit:

1. **Choose Edit⇨Color Settings. (On the Mac, choose Photoshop Elements⇨ Color Settings.)**

   You should see a dialog box that bears an uncanny resemblance to the one in Figure 5-3. Only three options to choose from — this doesn't look so bad, does it?

2. **Decide how you want to manage color:**

   • **If you're happy with the status quo, leave things at the default setting of No Color Management.**

   After all, things have worked pretty well so far, right? If you're happy with the colors you see on-screen and in print, there's no reason to change a thing.

   • **If you're going to be working with images for the World Wide Web, you can choose Limited Color Management.**

   This setting lets you work in a color space called sRGB, which takes into consideration what images look like when displayed on the average PC monitor (which, after all, is what most Web surfers are using). sRGB is a generally agreed-upon standard, endorsed by many hardware and software companies.

   • **If you're working on images for print, you can choose Full Color Management.**

   This setting lets you work in a color space called Adobe RGB, a good choice for print work. When we say "print," we're talking about the world of *professional* printing — and if you're doing a lot of professional print work, it may behoove you to move up from Elements to the full version of Photoshop anyway. But this setting will help you get by in a pinch. It embeds a hidden *profile* into the code of your images when you save them. This profile gives the next person to come along an idea of what the image looked like the last time you worked on it. Full Color Management also preserves existing profiles in images you might open, and lets you choose between sRGB (for the Web) and Adobe RGB (for print) if you open an image that doesn't have a profile.

TIP

The downside to both Limited and Full Color Management is that not all applications and devices understand color spaces or embedded profiles, meaning that things could potentially look worse for your efforts. The safest bet, all things considered, is to use No Color Management. But know that the other options are available to you, if you find yourself in a situation where you know they'll come in handy.

3. Click OK.

There now, that wasn't so bad, was it?

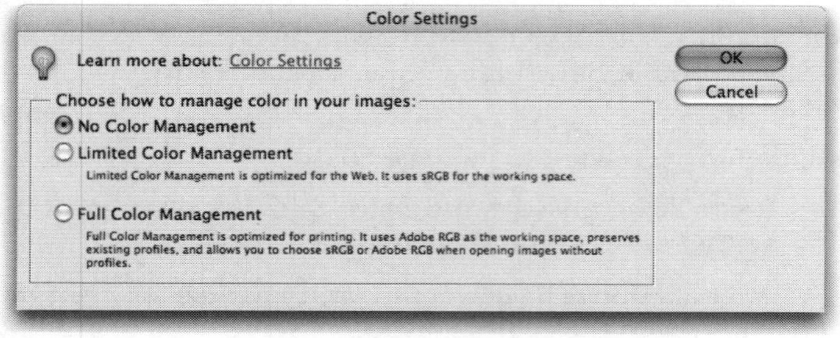

Figure 5-3:
The Color Settings dialog box makes color management a simple affair.

> Color Settings
>
> 💡 Learn more about: <u>Color Settings</u>   OK
>   Cancel
>
> ─ Choose how to manage color in your images: ─
> ⦿ No Color Management
> ◯ Limited Color Management
>   Limited Color Management is optimized for the Web. It uses sRGB for the working space.
>
> ◯ Full Color Management
>   Full Color Management is optimized for printing. It uses Adobe RGB as the working space, preserves existing profiles, and allows you to choose sRGB or Adobe RGB when opening images without profiles.

Choosing Color the Mix-and-Match Way

So after luring you into this chapter by comparing the subject matter to a beloved classic family movie, we've done nothing but bore you to tears with talk of color theory and color settings. But all that sleep-inducing talk about color is important to understand if you're going to get the most out of Elements. However, now it's time to turn to more practical color matters. Things such as "How do I choose colors?" and "Where can I keep them after I've chosen them?" Read on, Mac- (or PC-) duff.

Juggling foreground and background colors

In Elements' toolbox, you can work with two colors at a time: a *foreground color* and a *background color.* Most tools and commands paint your image with the foreground color, but a few splash it with the background color.

The toolbox displays two colors at its bottom. As shown in Figure 5-4, the foreground color is on top and the background color is on the bottom. To get some idea of how these colors work, read the following list:

✔ The foreground color is applied by the painting tools, such as the brush and pencil.

✔ When you use the eraser tool, you're actually painting with the background color. (Unless you're on a layer, in which case you erase to transparency. For more on layers, see Chapter 10.)

✔ The gradient tool, by default, creates a gradual shift between the foreground and background colors.

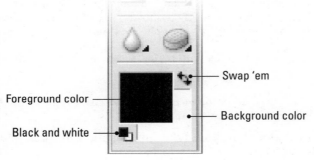

Figure 5-4:
The collection of color icons at the bottom of the toolbox.

Foreground color
Black and white
Swap 'em
Background color

The toolbox includes icons that enable you to change the foreground and background colors, swap them, and so on. Here are some guidelines to get you started:

✔ Click the foreground color or background color icon to display the all-important Color Picker dialog box. Press Esc or click Cancel to leave that dialog box.

✔ Click the black and white icon (refer to Figure 5-4) to make the foreground color black and the background color white.

✔ Click that little two-way arrow icon — childishly labeled swap 'em in the figure — to swap the foreground and background colors.

✔ You can access the black and white and swap 'em icons also from the keyboard. Press D to make the foreground black and the background white. Press X to swap the foreground and background colors.

Defining colors

You can define the foreground and background colors in Elements in three ways:

✔ Click the foreground color or background color icon in the toolbox to summon the Color Picker.

✔ Use the eyedropper tool to lift colors from your image.

✔ Use the Color Swatches palette.

Using the Color Picker

To access the Color Picker, shown in Figure 5-5, click the foreground color or background color icon. The first thing you should notice is the enormous square of color on the left of the dialog box; this is known to Elements cognoscenti as the *color field.* To its immediate right, you'll see a rainbow-colored bar commonly referred to as the *color slider.* The color rectangle in the upper-right corner of the controls is known, strangely enough, as the *color rectangle.* And below that you'll see a handful of option boxes and radio buttons. Introduce yourself to all the controls, and get to know their names, because you'll be spending a lot of time in the Color Picker.

Do you want to know the quick and dirty way to select a color using the Color Picker? Okay, here goes:

1. **Click the foreground color or background color icon in the toolbox, depending on which you want to set.**

2. **Drag in the color slider to set the specific hue you want. (Make sure the radio button next to H is selected first.)**

3. **Drag around in the color field to set the brightness and saturation for the hue.**

4. **Click OK.**

And that's it. Following these simple steps can reliably get you the color you want. Sometimes, however, you'll need to specify certain aspects of colors, and the preceding method won't suffice. It's for times such as these that we now present: The Rest of the Story.

The Color Picker also lets you choose colors numerically by entering values in the option boxes. You can work numerically with three color modes. The option box at the bottom is for specifying hexadecimal colors, which is useful for Web design professionals but generally classified as *too technical* for our purposes here. The top three option boxes (H, S, and B) let you specify colors according to their Hue, Saturation, and Brightness. We'll skip these for now, and instead turn our attention to the bottom three option boxes. Those three letters might look vaguely familiar to you by now: R, G, and B stand, of course, for Reginald, Gertie, and Bert.

Okay, just seeing if you were paying attention. Here, actually, is more proof that those red, green, and blue color channels we were yammering on about earlier really exist. When using the Color Picker, you can think of red, green, and blue as ingredients in baking the perfect color. With regular 8-bit color, you can add 256 levels of each of the primary hues, 0 being the darkest amount of the hue, 255 being the lightest, and 128 being smack dab in the middle. For example, if you set the R value to 255, the G value to 128, and the B value to 0, you get a vibrant orange, just like the one shown in the upper-right corner of Color Plate 3.

Color rectangle

Color field   Color slider   Web safe color alert

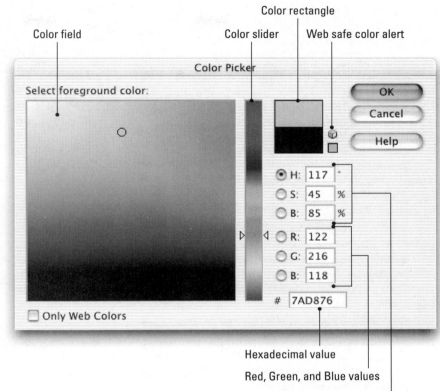

Figure 5-5:
The Color
Picker
cordially
invites you
to pick a
color . . . any
color.

Hexadecimal value

Red, Green, and Blue values

Hue, Saturation, and Brightness values

If you've never mixed colors using red, green, and blue, the process can be a little perplexing at first. For example, folks often have a hard time initially accepting that all yellows and oranges are produced by mixing red and green. We encourage you to experiment. Better yet, we order you to experiment.

If you followed our little orange recipe, you've probably noticed that the mysterious color rectangle now has a two-toned effect going on. The top half is sporting that spiffy orange color, but the bottom half is modeling the old foreground or background color you started with. That's what the color rectangle is all about: letting you compare your new color against the old one.

The HSB color mode is simply another way of describing color. Rather than break color down into three color channels such as red, green, and blue, the HSB color mode breaks color down according to its *hue* (which you can think of as the "color" of the color), *saturation* (how rich the color is), and *brightness* (how bright or dark the color is).

In truth, using the numeric values in the Color Picker is a complicated, confusing affair. It works on the principle that the property with the selected radio button gets mapped to the color slider. The color slider then gives you the full range of options for that one property. The other properties are then mapped to the color field, and you can drag around inside the field to hone in on the color you want. Just experiment with this concept for a second, clicking the various radio buttons and dragging around in the color slider and color field. How do you feel? Wait — don't smash your monitor with this book. Just click the H radio button again. There now, isn't that better?

It can't be just sheer luck that the Color Picker defaults to having the hues mapped to the color slider. The whole dang dialog box just seems to make sense that way. So keep it that way, we say.

If you're wondering about that almost-omnipresent little 3-D cube that pops up next to the color rectangle, it's there to warn you that the color you've chosen isn't Web-safe and might not display correctly on an old monitor. As more and more people upgrade from their old 256-color monitors, this becomes less and less of an issue. But if it concerns you, click the colored square beneath the cube to change to the nearest Web-safe color, or just click the Only Web Colors check box beneath the color field.

Lifting colors with the eyedropper tool

You can change the foreground and background colors also by lifting them from the image. Just select the eyedropper tool — the one near the top of the toolbox that looks like an eyedropper — and click inside the image on the color you want to use.

Here's some stuff to know about this incredibly easy-to-use tool:

- ✔ You can press I (for I-dropper) to select the eyedropper tool instead of clicking its toolbox icon.

- ✔ The eyedropper by default determines the foreground color. To set the background color, Alt+click (Option+click on the Mac) with the eyedropper.

- ✔ You can temporarily access the eyedropper tool when using many of the other tools by pressing the Alt key (Option key on the Mac). As long as the key is down, the eyedropper is available. You can change only the foreground color this way.

- ✔ Elements lets you sample color not just from the image but from anywhere on-screen. The trick is that you still have to first click the eyedropper inside the image. But then, while still holding down the mouse button, drag outside the image and onto your desktop, sampling colors from other open images, the desktop, the menu bar, or whatever you desire.

- ✔ As you use the eyedropper, you can keep tabs on the exact R, G, and B values for the colors you're sampling by looking in the upper-left section of the Info palette.

✔ The Sample Size option in the tool options bar determines precisely how the eyedropper tool chooses a color. When set to Point Sample, it chooses the color of the precise pixel it's clicked on. When set to 3 by 3 Average, the eyedropper looks at not only the clicked pixel but every adjacent pixel. It averages the colors of those nine pixels, and that average color becomes the chosen color. Likewise for 5 by 5 Average; the eyedropper looks in a 5-pixel-by-5-pixel square and averages the color of those 25 pixels. This can be useful if, for example, you want to sample the color of the sky and you're not as concerned with getting the color of any one pixel as you are with getting the general color of the sky.

Using the Color Swatches palette

At this point you may be thinking that being able to keep only two colors around — the foreground and the background color — is a trifle, shall we say, limiting. Enter the Color Swatches palette, as accurately depicted in Figure 5-6. No, it has nothing to do with stylish timepieces; the Color Swatches palette is nothing less than a repository for color.

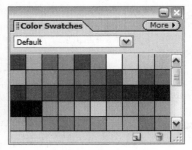

Figure 5-6: The Color Swatches palette. Okay, it loses a little something in black and white.

To activate the Color Swatches palette, choose Window⇨Color Swatches. As you can see, the Color Swatches palette already contains a pleasing assortment of colors. If you want a little more information about those colors, click the More button and choose Small List from the menu. You'll see the color swatches along with their descriptive names.

To set one of those colors as the foreground color, move your cursor onto a swatch — like magic, the cursor turns into the eyedropper tool. Just click, and there you go! If you want to set the background color instead, Ctrl+click (⌘+click on the Mac) on a swatch. Simple, huh?

Elements comes with several preset swatch libraries available from the menu at the top of the palette, but the real power of the Color Swatches palette lies in its ability to let you create and save your own customized swatch libraries. To add the current foreground color to the Color Swatches palette, just move the cursor into the blank area at the bottom of the swatches. (You may need to scroll down or expand the palette to get to the blank area.) The cursor automatically turns into the paint bucket tool. Just click, and Elements will ask you to enter a name for your swatch. If you want to dispense with the naming ceremony and just accept the default name, add the Alt key (the Option key on the Mac) as you click. You can also go to the More menu and choose New Swatch, bypassing the paint-bucket-clicking method altogether.

When you add a swatch to the default swatch set, an asterisk appears before the word Default in the menu at the top of the Color Swatches palette. This notifies you that the default set has been changed. Should you want to use the menu to switch to another swatch set, you'll first get a message asking whether you want to save your changes to the default swatch set. It's important to know that unless you reply in the affirmative, the swatches you added to the default set will be lost forever.

So if you want to keep those added colors around, click Yes (Save on the Mac). Accept the Untitled Color Swatches name, or give the swatch set a new name if you want. But definitely save the set inside the suggested Color Swatches folder; that way Elements will know where to find the swatches again.

Now, to access the swatch set you just saved, choose the Load Color Swatches command from the Color Swatches palette's More menu. Choose the name of the set you saved, click Load, and the set appears again in the Color Swatches palette, complete with the colors you added.

If you want to check out all the preset swatches, brushes, gradients, and patterns that Elements has to offer, you can always go to Edit⇨Preset Manager. All the various categories of presets are accessible via the Preset Type drop-down menu. To the right of each scrolling list of preset icons is a More menu that gives you reset, replace, and viewing options, as well as accessibility to the various libraries under each preset category. And, finally, you can also load, save, rename, and delete libraries using the buttons on the right side of the dialog box.

Going Grayscale

Now that we've wasted most of the chapter in the colorful Land of Oz, you may be wondering when we're ever going to decide there's no place like home, click our heels, and head back to good old monochromatic Kansas. Take heart: The heralded hour of black-and-white images has arrived.

The first thing to understand about black-and-white images is that the black-and-white world offers more colors than just black and white. It includes a total of 256 unique shades of gray and is therefore more properly termed *grayscale*. Each one of these shades is a color in its own right, which is why the term "black and white" can inspire fisticuffs among some grayscale devotees.

Second, all the stuff about creating colors in the previous sections of this chapter holds true for grayscale image editing as well. You have a foreground and background color. You can define colors in the Color Picker. (No matter what color you choose in the Color Picker, the color will appear as some shade of gray in the foreground color or background color icons.) And you can lift colors from a grayscale image using the eyedropper tool.

But some aspects of grayscale editing are different than full-color editing, which leads us to the next two sections.

The road to grayscale

Most images that you'll come across will be in color. This means that working in grayscale generally requires a conversion in Elements.

Unlike a three-channel RGB image, a grayscale image includes only one channel. If you plan to print in black and white, you should jettison all the extraneous color information, for two reasons. First, it's easier for Elements to keep track of one channel than three. In fact, given the same image size and resolution, Elements performs faster when editing a grayscale image than when editing in color. Second, you can better see what your printed image will look like. When you're designing an image to be printed in black and white, color just gets in the way.

To convert a color image to grayscale, just choose Image⇨Mode⇨Grayscale. Elements asks whether you want it to discard color information. (The "Don't show again" check box is just Elements' way of asking you whether you want it to ask you about this in the future.) You can click OK to convert to grayscale (or chicken out and cancel). That's all there is to it. You now have a single-channel grayscale image.

to go to
b&w

Before you change a color image to grayscale, you may want to make a backup copy of the original image, just in case you ever want to have the image available in color in the future. For details on saving images, see Chapter 7.

If you have a layered file and want to remove color from only one layer, choose Enhance⇨Adjust Color⇨Remove Color or press Ctrl+Shift+U (⌘+Shift+U on the Mac). Elements drains the selected layer of all its color. (You can also apply Remove Color to just a selected portion of a layer.) Note that Remove Color doesn't convert the image to grayscale; even if the image consists of only one layer and you apply Remove Color, the image will still be RGB.

A few more tips in black and white

Here are some final grayscale tidbits:

✔ To add color to a grayscale image, first convert the image back to RGB by choosing Image⇨Mode⇨RGB Color. Elements won't automatically add a bunch of colors to the image, but it will now let you add colors of your own.

✔ If you use the Image⇨Mode⇨Grayscale conversion method and your color image contains more than one layer (as explained in Chapter 10), Elements asks whether you want to flatten your image. If you want to keep your layers, click the Don't Flatten button.

Part II
Be Prepared

The 5th Wave   By Rich Tennant

"Why don't you try blurring the brimstone and then putting a nice glow effect around the hellfire."

In this part . . .

Yeah, we know. You want to start doing some image editing. You were very patient through the first part of this book: Jekyll and Hyde, dialog boxes, File Browser, zoom tool, floor tiles, Image Size, Wizard of Oz, grayscale. All very nice, very interesting, and exceedingly well written (?), but now — if we don't mind too terribly much — you'd really like to get down to doing some image editing, because you have this picture of yourself from your recent vacation to Maui that you want to e-mail to all your friends, but in the picture you have this unsettling disturbance on your chin that you'd really like to do something about . . .

Yeah, we know. But here's the cold, hard truth: You need to know a few more things before you start image editing. For instance, if you're a Windows user, you'll definitely want to know about the new digital image organizing component in Elements. And no matter what kind of computer you have, Photoshop Elements offers a truly bewildering array of options for saving files; you can choose from over a dozen file formats. And what if you make a mistake as you're editing that vacation photo and manage to give yourself a chin of Jay-Leno-sized proportions? How can you go back and undo your work? Maybe you know about pressing Ctrl+Z on the PC or ⌘+Z on the Mac, but do you know about Elements' phenomenal time-traveling tool, the Undo History palette? And how much do you really know about printing? For that matter, only when you come to grips with the power of making selections and using layers will you begin to realize the possibilities that Elements contains.

So patience, Gentle Reader. We get to the really exciting stuff, we promise. Just make it through this part of the book with us, and it will be nothing but actual image editing from there to the end. Come on, that vacation photo can wait. Chin up.

Chapter 6

Get Organized (Before It Gets *You*)

***W**elcome*, Windows users . . . especially the sloppy ones. After talking about the Editor component for the last five chapters, we now turn to the other half of Photoshop Elements, namely its amazing Organizer application. Is your digital photo collection in a state of disarray? Does it take you an hour of searching your hard drive to find the photo you're looking for? If so, Organizer is just the thing to help you organize and arrange your vast collection of digital images.

Actually, if you've used Photoshop Album 2.0, Organizer's interface (seen in Figure 6-1) will look familiar. Organizer is, essentially, Photoshop Album 3.0, an updated version of Adobe's image organizing and archiving software. But Organizer is a fully integrated part of Elements, and it's easy to switch back and forth between programs as the need arises.

In this chapter, we take a look at Organizer from the ground up, starting with how to import your existing photo collection into the program. Then we move on to examining tags and collections, two key tools that Organizer uses to help you group and arrange your images. After your images are tagged, searching for specific photos is a much simpler task. Organizer also makes it easy to create backup CDs and DVDs to archive your photo collection.

What we *won't* look at in this chapter is the ways Organizer enables you to use and share your images with others. We put that information in Chapter 18.

Find bar
Timeline   Shortcuts bar

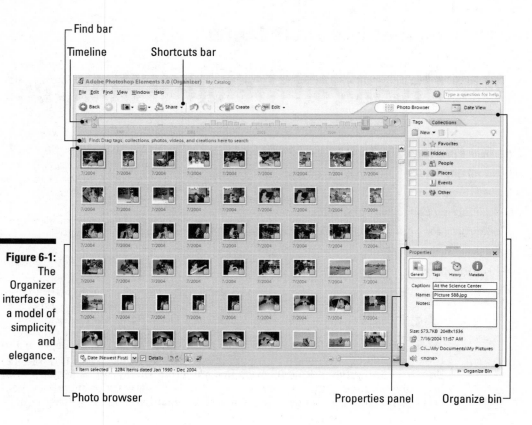

Figure 6-1:
The
Organizer
interface is
a model of
simplicity
and
elegance.

Photo browser   Properties panel   Organize bin

Before we begin, we should mention that Organizer keeps track of not only image files, but other media files such as audio and video clips. Indeed, when you first start the program, you'll see some excellent-quality audio clips Adobe has included for free.

We went over this in the first chapter, but it's worth pointing out again precisely how to start Elements' Organizer component. From the Welcome screen, click the View and Organize Photos icon. (If you want to enter the Editor component from the Welcome screen, click the Edit and Enhance Photos icon.) If you're already using Editor and you want to launch Organizer, you can click the Photo Browser button or the Date View button in Editor's shortcuts bar.

Your installer CD has a half-hour movie showing the highlights of Elements, hosted by none other than Deke, one of this book's co-authors! Deke spends the first half of the movie giving an introduction to Organizer. To see the movie, just click the Product Overview link from the installer CD's main screen.

Getting Photos into Organizer

If you've tried to organize your digital images without the aid of special software, you've no doubt realized it's an uphill battle. Maybe you create a folder for a given year — 2004, let's say. After you accumulate a couple thousand photos in your 2004 folder, you realize it would be a good idea to organize even further, so you create subfolders for each month and divide the photos accordingly. Even so, in some months you probably took hundreds of photos, and it's a pain to sort through them to find just the one you want. This leads to a sense of futility, in turn spawning an entirely different form of organization: just dumping all your photos in one common folder and letting them fight it out themselves. Whatever your previous technique, Organizer can enormously simplify the task of managing your photos and of helping you find the photo you're looking for out of possibly tens of thousands of others.

Organizer's main power stems from the fact that it isn't based on Windows' file-organizing system. Even if related photos are scattered hither and yon on your hard drive, Organizer can deal with them as if they were in a single location and display them all in the same window. But Organizer doesn't move your photos to accomplish this; instead it stores information in a *catalog file*. A catalog file is really just a database that contains information about your photos, including where they're actually located on your hard drive.

After Organizer catalogs a photo, that doesn't mean that you can now delete it from your hard drive! Remember that Organizer just creates a link from the catalog to wherever your photo is located on your hard drive. Delete the file, and you won't be able to access it again through Organizer either.

By default, Organizer creates a catalog for you, naming it, appropriately, "My Catalog." Although you can create as many different catalogs as you want by choosing File⇨Catalog, it's probably best to stick with just your single, default catalog. You can't view photos from more than one catalog at the same time, which can be a big limitation. Organizer gives you so many ways to view and sort your images that unless you have a very special reason to isolate a group of photos from the rest, you should stick with your default catalog and manage all your photos inside it.

So how do you get your photos to show up inside your catalog along with Adobe's free included audio files? That all depends on where the images are to begin with.

Importing existing photos

The first step in allowing Organizer to manage your photo collection is to have it take command of the photos already on your hard drive. To do this, choose File⇨Get Photos⇨By Searching to summon the Get Photos By Searching for Folders dialog box, pictured in Figure 6-2. If you have multiple hard drives connected to your system, you can narrow Organizer's search if you want by choosing a single drive from the Look In menu. However, you'll probably just want to keep the default setting of All Hard Disks to make sure Organizer looks at every disk drive you have.

Many application folders contain various graphics files for use with the particular application. You probably don't want these graphics imported into your personal photo collection, so keeping the Exclude System and Program Folders check box selected is a good choice. Likewise, Exclude Files Smaller Than 100 KB can keep tiny images such as thumbnails from appearing in your collection. You can deselect this check box if you don't want to limit the search by file size, or enter a different file size in the numeric field.

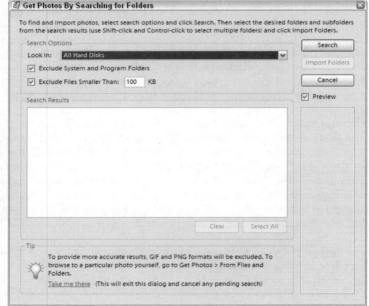

Figure 6-2:
Step one in
Organizer's
bid for Total
Photo
Domination.
Resistance
is futile . . .
and foolish,
frankly.

After you've set your options, click the Search button, and Organizer starts rummaging through your computer, scavenging for photos. When it finishes, a list of folders appears in the Search Results window. You can select one or more folders in the window, or just click the Select All button if you want to import everything that Organizer found. Then click the Import Folders button.

A succession of dialog boxes will follow:

✔ The Getting Photos window gives you a progress report, showing you thumbnails of the images being imported into the catalog.

✔ Next, you'll probably see an Items Not Imported window, telling you which images failed to import, and why. If you left the Exclude Files Smaller Than 100 KB check box checked, you'll probably see a lot of files in the list that didn't import for that reason. Scan the list if you want, and then click OK.

✔ Finally, you'll get a message telling you that the only items currently displayed in Organizer are the ones you just imported. If you're just getting started with Organizer, that should be everything except the default audio files. Click OK, and your initial import will be complete.

The By Searching method is definitely the way to begin using Organizer, but there's not much reason to ever use it again. Sure, you'll eventually want to import more images from your hard drive, such as photos you receive by e-mail and save to your desktop. To do this, choose File➪Get Photos➪From Files and Folders (Ctrl+Shift+G), or click the camera icon in the shortcuts bar and choose From Files and Folders. In the dialog box that follows, navigate to the folder containing the image or images you want to import and select it in the large window. The Get Photos from Subfolders check box means that Organizer will also look in any folders that your selected folder might contain. You can also select single images if you want. Then click Get Photos, and let the importing begin.

Importing from CDs

If you want to import photos from an inserted CD into your catalog, use the From Files and Folders command, navigate to the CD, and select it. By default, Organizer will want to copy the files from the CD onto your hard drive, as opposed to having the photos be *offline* where Organizer can't continually access them. Obviously, this is going to take up hard disk space, and you might have burned these files to CD to free up disk space in the first place.

If you don't want Organizer to copy the files to your hard drive, click the Keep Original Photo(s) Offline check box. Organizer will generate a small proxy version of the file and create a link from the proxy to the full-resolution version on the CD. If you want to edit the image later, Organizer will prompt you to enter the original CD; enter the name of the CD in the Optional Reference Note for Disc field so that you'll know which CD to insert.

TIP

If you're using offline images, a little CD icon appears in the upper-left corner of the image in the photo browser as a reminder that the image is only a proxy for the high-resolution version on CD.

Importing photos from a camera or a card reader

After your camera is hooked up to your computer and turned on — or your camera's memory card is inserted into the connected card reader — Organizer jumps into action, ready and eager to help you download photos to your hard drive. This is true even when Organizer isn't running.

When Organizer is open, the Get Photos from Camera or Card Reader dialog box (seen in Figure 6-3) appears to guide you through the process. If Organizer isn't open, you'll get basically the same dialog box, but it is renamed Adobe Photo Downloader and has an Advanced Options button, which allows you to specify the catalog you want to import the images into.

Figure 6-3:
When Organizer is on duty, it sends this dialog box to escort your camera's photos to safety.

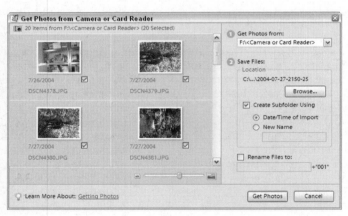

The dialog box features a large window on the left with previews of the images on the card. You can deselect an image's check box if you don't want to download it. On the right are a few options for downloading. By default, Organizer wants to create a subfolder in the My Pictures⇨Adobe⇨Digital Camera Photos folder, named with the date and time of import. We strongly suggest that you follow these defaults, though you can save the images to another place or rename the folder if you have a special reason.

You can also click the Rename Files To check box if you want all the images to be named similarly, such as "vacation001," "vacation002," and so on. When you click the Get Photos button, the photos will download, and if necessary Organizer will open to import the photos into your catalog.

As a final step, the Delete Files on Device? dialog box can clear your camera's memory card of the files you just downloaded. This is generally a good idea, simply because it frees up space on the card for more photos. (However, it's important that you back up your photo collection; see the "Backing It All Up" section, later in this chapter.) Even if you don't delete the photos from your card, Organizer is clever enough to not download the same photos again.

Scanning photos

Although your own scanning software will play the major role in scanning photos to import into your catalog, Organizer does ask a few questions before you proceed. Choose File➪Get Photos➪From Scanner or click the camera icon in the shortcuts bar and choose From Scanner. In the Get Photos from Scanner dialog box, you can click Browse to specify another place to store the scanned image if you don't like the default My Pictures➪Adobe➪Scanned Photos path. Our advice is to keep the default, and let Organizer be in charge.

The Save As menu lets you choose a file format for your scan. JPEG files are compressed, resulting in some degradation of the image. However, if you keep the JPEG setting and slide the Quality slider all the way to the right, you'll end up with a relatively small file size and excellent image quality. If you want a totally uncompressed image, choose TIFF from the Save As menu. After you've adjusted these few settings as desired, click OK and your scanner's software should kick into action, completing the scanning process.

Organizing your cell phone photos

In truth, Organizer really isn't any help in getting photos from your camera phone to your computer. Whether you connect your phone to your computer using a cable or you just e-mail the pictures to yourself from your phone, Organizer stays out of it. If you choose File➪Get Photos➪From Mobile Phone (Ctrl+Shift+M), you can then click the Browse button to specify a folder into which you want to download cell phone photos. You can then use the File➪ Watch Folders command and designate the chosen folder as a folder to "watch." When Organizer is watching a folder, it notices when photos are added to that folder, and can either notify you of the fact or automatically add the photos to the Organizer.

Getting photos from an online sharing service

Photoshop Elements 3 is now a proud part of Adobe Photoshop Services, an online photo sharing and printing service. Adobe Photoshop Services is a collaboration between the good people at Adobe and the equally good people at Ofoto, which is a division of Kodak.

With Ofoto, you can set up digital photo albums containing groups of photos, and then the service can automatically e-mail your friends with an invitation to come see your latest photos. You and your friends can order prints of these images, and the prints will be delivered in the mail. Just to be clear, we're talking about real prints that you can hold in your hand and stick to your refrigerator door with a magnet. And they're delivered to you in the real mail, not by e-mail. It's a great way to get high-quality prints of your images, even if you don't own a printer. In addition, Ofoto lets you order enlargements of your photos, plus it provides you with easy ways to turn photos into cards, calendars, and photo albums.

Choosing File⇨Get Photos⇨From Online Sharing Services enables you to download photos from your friends' Ofoto accounts. Of course, you and your friends need to set up Ofoto accounts if you don't have them already, but doing so is easy, painless, and absolutely free. See the section "Printing and Sharing Your Photos Online" at the end of this chapter for more information.

Organizing Photos

After you have your photos in Organizer, it follows that the next step is to organize them. Organizer gives you plenty of ways to accomplish this, and although the process is hardly automatic, it's sort of fun. But first, it's important to know that Organizer is making certain assumptions about your images — assumptions that might not be correct and might cause trouble down the road.

Correcting the date

There's more to a digital photo than meets the eye. A photo file contains not only the millions of pixels that make up the actual photo, but also *metadata* information about the camera that was used to take the photo, about the exposure settings, and so on. This metadata comes in the EXIF (Exchangeable Image File) format. You don't normally see EXIF data when you look at an image on-screen, but certain applications — such as Elements, for instance — can show it to you.

Included in EXIF data are the date and time that the photo was taken. This information is drawn from the date and time setting on your camera. But if your camera's date is set incorrectly — maybe the battery ran down, or maybe you never set it to begin with (shame on you!) — the wrong date and time get embedded into the photos' EXIF metadata.

Scanning photos will also leave them with incorrect dates. Organizer looks at the date and time the scanning took place, and uses that info for the photo's date and time. Of course, compared to when the photo was actually snapped, this may be wrong by decades.

For a program that likes to sort photos chronologically, these wrong dates can really mess things up. Luckily, Organizer makes it easy for you to assign new dates to photos, even going so far as to rewrite the EXIF metadata to set things right.

To change the date and time for a photo or a range of photos, first select the photo or photos in the main photo browser window. Turn on the Details check box below the photo browser window if necessary, and click the date and time below a selected photo. You can also choose Edit⇨Adjust Date and Time (of Selected Items) or press Ctrl+J. If you have more than one photo selected, you'll be presented with a dialog box containing four options:

- ✔ Choosing the first option, Change to a Specified Date and Time, takes you to the Set Date and Time dialog box. Here, you can set the year, month, day, and time for the photo. For each of these options, you have a chance to choose ??? (for unknown) if you don't know the exact details of when the photo was taken. Setting an option to ??? means that you can't specify any subsequent options; for instance, if you know a photo was taken some time in 2000, setting the Month to ??? means that you can't specify a day or time for the photo.

- ✔ The second option, Change to Match File's Date and Time, sets the EXIF metadata date to the file's creation date. Choosing this option for a scanned image adds EXIF metadata to the scan and embeds the date and time of the scanning into the metadata.

- ✔ The third option, Shift to New Starting Date and Time, is a great setting to use if your camera's clock was wrong when a series of photos were taken. Even though all the selected photos in the series will have wrong dates and times, the dates and times will be correct *relative to each other*. When you choose this option (multiple photos have to be selected to access it), you then set the date and time for the *earliest* of the photos in the series. All the subsequent selected photos will have their dates and times adjusted, relative to the earliest file.

✔ The final option, Shift by Set Number of Hours (Time Zone Adjust) can adjust photos over a set number of hours to account for time zone differences. If your camera's clock is set to Seattle time but you flew to Orlando for a vacation at Disney World, the 7 p.m. fireworks display you photographed will be time stamped at 4 p.m. No problem; just choose this option, and in the Time Zone Adjust dialog box, move the time Ahead 3 Hours. Click OK, and you're finished.

Tags — you're it

If we had to sum up Organizer's awesome power in one word, that word would be *tags*. In Organizer, tags are sort of like visual keywords you can apply to your images and use to search your photo collection. Suppose you have a picture of little Billy playing with your cat, Mr. Toodlepaws, on Halloween. You apply three tags to the image, one each for Billy, Mr. Toodlepaws, and Halloween. After you tag your thousands of images, you can sort them by tag; double-click the Billy tag in the organize bin, and Organizer shows you just the hundreds of photos you've applied the Billy tag to. Add the Mr. Toodlepaws tag to the mix, and the browser window displays only the dozens of photos that have both the Billy and Mr. Toodlepaws tags. Then throw in the Halloween tag, and Organizer shows your one photo of Billy and Mr. Toodlepaws on Halloween.

Although Organizer has many ways to group, arrange, and view your photos, tags are really the backbone. Take the time to understand them.

Creating tags

In the organize bin — that's the long, vertical panel down the right side of your screen — is a Tags tab that shares space with the Collections tab. This Tags tab leads to the Tags panel, which is Grand Central Station for tags in Organizer, letting you create, delete, and organize your tags. By default a few tags are already created: Favorites tags are used to rank images by quality, the Hidden tag is for images you don't want to see in your collection on a day-to-day basis (yet you don't want to delete either), and you also have a few categories and subcategories, such as People, Family, Places, and Events.

To create a tag, click the New button at the top of the Tags panel and choose New Tag (Ctrl+N). In the Create Tag dialog box, choose the Category you want the tag to appear under, type a name in the Name option, and append a note if you want. You can set a photo icon for your tag by clicking the Edit Icon button, though it's easier and more flexible to set the icon for a tag after the tag has been applied to images (we explain how to do this in a minute). Click OK to create the tag.

Unless you specified an icon for the tag when you first created it, the first image you apply the tag to becomes that tag's icon. You can edit a tag (including its icon) at any time by selecting it and clicking the pencil icon at the top of the Tags panel. This displays the Edit Tag dialog box.

In the dialog box, click the Edit Icon button and you'll be taken to the Edit Tag Icon dialog box. Here you can choose a different icon from among the images the tag has been applied to by clicking the left and right arrow buttons. You can also click the Find button to see all the tag's images in a window. Otherwise, clicking the Import button allows you to set the icon by choosing an image to which the tag hasn't been applied.

After you select your icon image, resize the square cropping boundary to zoom in to a detail of your image; tag icons are quite small, so it's often best to crop closely into a face or other detail. When you're finished, click OK, then click OK again to close the Edit Tag dialog box, and your new tag icon takes effect.

Creating categories and subcategories

You can create new categories and subcategories by choosing New Category or New Sub-Category from the New button at the top of the Tags panel. Categories and subcategories are not only helpful for organizing your tags hierarchically but are also tags themselves.

When you create a category, you can choose an icon from the clip-art-style icons available on the Create Category dialog box's Category Icon menu. You also get the chance to choose a representative color for this category; the color shows up not in the category tag itself but in any subcategories and tags that you place within that category.

To delete a tag, category, or subcategory, click to select it in the Tags panel and then click the trash can icon at the top of the panel.

You can drag and drop tags, subcategories, and categories in the Tags panel to rearrange and reorder things, easily creating sorting hierarchies and nested subcategories at will.

Tagging photos

Applying tags to photos is a simple matter; just drag the tag from the Tags panel onto the pertinent photo. If you want to apply a tag to multiple photos, Shift+ or Ctrl+click the photos to select them first, and then drag the tag onto any selected photo.

You can tell by looking at a photo in the photo browser whether or not it's been tagged , though the appearance of the tag depends on the current size of the thumbnails in the browser. When thumbnails are small, you'll just see a generic tag icon in the thumbnail, but as thumbnails get larger, as in Figure 6-4, you see the category icon and tag name below the image in the Details section. You can also click the Show properties button at the bottom of the browser window to reveal the Properties panel in the organize bin. Click the Tags section of the Properties panel, and you can view the tags applied to the selected image.

If you have a group of photos on your hard drive assembled in an appropriately named folder — perhaps as a relic of the days before you got Elements 3.0, when you were trying to keep your photos organized with a folder system in Windows — you can quickly create a tag from the name of the folder, and tag all the contained photos with the tag.

To do this, first switch to the Folder Location view using the Photo Browser Arrangement menu in the lower-left corner of the browser window. You'll see that the browser is now divided up into sections, with horizontal dividers marking each image folder, and with a folder's images appearing below its divider. Click the divider's Instant Tag button, and the Create and Apply New Tag dialog box appears. By default, the folder name will be used as the tag name. Make any changes if you want and then click OK. All images in the folder will be tagged. This is a quick way to capitalize on any pre-Elements organizational work you may have tried to perform on your photos.

Figure 6-4:
The tags applied to an image appear in the Details section below the image thumbnail in the photo browser.

Collections

Another way Organizer lets you arrange your photos is by putting them in collections. *Collections* are very much like tags; you create and apply them in the same way, you assign icons to them, and you can create hierarchies with them by also creating collection groups. The chief difference is that collections are designed to be used as the first step toward making a creation (see Chapter 18 for info about creations). Also, when you view a collection of photos, each photo is numbered with a small numeral in the upper-left corner; you can drag photos around within a collection to reorder them to your liking.

To work with collections, click the Collections tab at the top of the organize bin. The same rules for creating tags apply here for collections. Click the New button to make new collections or collection groups, click the pencil icon to edit the collection or group, and click the trash can icon to delete a collection or group. To bring a photo into a collection, drag the collection icon from the organize bin onto the photo, just as with tags. One difference here is that unlike tag categories and subcategories, collection groups can't be applied to photos.

Stacks and version sets

At the beginning of our discussion of tags, we mentioned the pre-made Hidden tag, which causes a photo to not display in the photo browser window. Organizer provides a couple of other ways to keep photos from appearing in the browser. If you have a series of images that are all basically the same — maybe you took several shots of the same subject, with very slight variations — you might want only the best shot of the series to appear in the photo browser. Organizer's Stacks feature lets you "stack" the series of photos so that they take up only one thumbnail space in the browser window.

Stacks

To stack photos, Ctrl+ and Shift+click to select the similar photos. Then choose Edit⇨Stack⇨Stack Selected Photos or press Ctrl+Alt+S. A stack icon appears in the upper-right corner of the thumbnail to show that other photos are stacked behind the visible one. To view the photos in a stack, choose Edit⇨Stack⇨Reveal Photos in Stack or press Ctrl+Alt+R. You can then select one of the revealed photos in the stack and choose Edit⇨Stack⇨Remove Photo from Stack to unstack that single photo or choose Edit⇨Stack⇨Set as Top Photo to designate the selected photo as the one to appear in the browser window when the photos are stacked.

You can permanently unstack a stack in two ways. Choosing Edit⇨Stack⇨ Unstack Photos places all stacked photos back in the browser window. Choosing Edit⇨Stack⇨Flatten Stack deletes all the photos from your catalog except for the designated top photo. This command also has an option to delete the photos from your hard drive as well.

Version sets

Version sets are similar to stacks but are based not on slightly different photos but on different versions of the same photo. To create a version set, do the following:

1. **Select a photo in the photo browser.**

   Choose a JPEG that needs a good bit of editing work.

2. **Click the Edit button in the Organizer's shortcuts bar and choose Auto Fix Window from the drop-down menu.**

   The selected photo opens in Organizer's Auto Fix window.

3. **Edit the image.**

   Do your worst. Or do your best; it's entirely up to you. We look a little more closely at the Auto Fix window in the upcoming section "Editing Your Photos," but for now, just do what you can with the four Auto commands available in the window. But don't click the More Editing button, which would open the image in Elements' Editor component.

4. **Click OK.**

   You'll get a message telling you that your image is being saved with "_edited-1" appended to its name.

5. **Click OK again.**

When you go back to Organizer, notice that the thumbnail now reflects the edited version of the photo, and a version set icon appears in the upper-right corner of the thumbnail. The Edit⇨Version Set submenu has commands similar to the Edit⇨Stack submenu for revealing, flattening, and setting top photos.

You can also create a version set by choosing Go to Standard Edit from the Edit button's drop-down menu in the shortcuts bar. After you've completed your edit, choose File⇨Save As, and check the Save in Version Set with Original check box. When you click Save, a version set will be created in Organizer.

Captions and notes

Organizer gives you the opportunity to enter a caption for each photo in your catalog, as well as any notes about the image you might want to record. These captions can be used later when making creations (see Chapter 18). To enter captions and notes, select a photo and click the Show Properties button at the bottom of the browser window, or just press Alt+Enter. View the General section of the Properties panel in the organize bin, and you'll see fields where you can enter the caption and notes.

You can also enter a caption for a photo by choosing Edit⇨Add Caption (Ctrl+Shift+T). If multiple photos are selected, this command adds the same caption to all the photos. If you're viewing a photo in Single Photo view (maximum thumbnail size), you can also follow the advice of the Click Here to Add Caption text that appears below the photo.

Organizer also lets you record audio captions for photos; these can then be used in the soundtrack for slide shows you create in Organizer. To do this, select a photo and click the Audio caption button at the bottom of the General panel of the Properties palette. (You can display the Properties palette by clicking the Show Properties button at the bottom of the browser window.) In the Select Audio File dialog box, you can either choose File⇨Browse to find a prerecorded audio file, or click the red Record button to record the caption live. (Of course, your computer will need a properly set up microphone for this feature to work.) Click the Stop button to stop recording. If you want to re-record your caption, choose Edit⇨Clear and try again. When you're satisfied, close the window and Organizer will prompt you to save your audio caption.

for adding audio clips

Viewing and Finding Photos

You've already been introduced to the chief viewing location for photos, Organizer's photo browser. Here are a few more fast facts about it:

- ✔ You can switch between Photo Browser view and Date view by clicking the buttons on the right end of the shortcuts bar or by pressing Ctrl+Alt+O for the browser and Ctrl+Alt+C for date view.

- ✔ The Photo Browser Arrangement menu in the bottom-left corner of the browser lets you view your photos in chronological order, reverse chronological order (by date but not by time), by folder location, or by the batch in which they were imported.

- ✔ The thumbnail size slider in the bottom-right corner of the browser window determines how large the thumbnails are, and therefore how many thumbnails you can view at one time. You can drag the slider to change the size, click the icons at either end of the slider to go instantly to the smallest or largest thumbnail size, or use the Ctrl++ (plus) and Ctrl+− (minus) keyboard shortcuts to change the size by a smaller increment.

- ✔ When you're viewing an image at maximum thumbnail size, you're in Organizer's Single Photo view. The image's caption appears below the image, along with the date and time. You can browse through the photos in your catalog while in Single Photo view using the arrow keys; the down and right arrow keys move forward through the catalog, and the up and left arrow keys move backwards.

✔ At the top of the photo browser is a find bar you can use to perform searches and view your search criteria. To search for tagged photos or photos in a collection, drag the tag or collection from the organize bin into the find bar.

✔ The Matching check boxes in the find bar let you broaden or narrow your search results. For instance, if only the Best check box is selected when you drag two tags into the find bar, you'll see only those photos that have both tags attached. If only the Close check box is selected, you'll see photos that have either tag applied, but not both. The Not check box displays photos that don't match any of your search criteria.

You've also taken a quick look at the Properties panel, but here are some other facts about it you may want to know:

✔ Click the Show or Hide properties button at the bottom of the browser window to make the Properties panel appear in the organize bin. Click the X in the upper-right corner of the panel to close it. You can also press Alt+Enter to toggle opening and closing the panel.

✔ The Properties panel has four sections. The General section lets you view or enter the selected photo's caption, name, and a note about the photo. You can also view the file size, pixel dimensions, date and time, and file path, and hear or record an audio caption.

✔ The Tags section of the Properties panel shows you the tags that have been applied to the selected image.

✔ The History section of the Properties panel gives you a rundown of the selected image's past life, including when it was imported, edited, printed, used in a creation, and to whom it was e-mailed.

✔ The Metadata section of the Properties panel displays the embedded EXIF metadata for the selected image, and is available in either Brief or Complete form by clicking the appropriate radio button at the bottom of the panel.

Reviewing and comparing photos

Even when you're viewing an image at the largest thumbnail size in the photo browser, it can be difficult to see details. When you're using Organizer to examine your photos, determining which ones you want to print or e-mail, sometimes you'll need to be able to zoom in or compare two images closely side-by-side. For moments such as these, Organizer has the Photo Review and Photo Compare viewing modes.

Photo Review

Organizer's Photo Review mode is a sort of slide show, letting you view a group of selected images one after the other. If no images are selected, Photo Review will feature all images currently visible in the photo browser. To start Photo Review, click the photo review button at the bottom of the browser window, press F11, or choose View⇨Photo Review.

In the Photo Review dialog box, you can customize your slide show by adjusting the presentation options as follows:

- ✔ If you want to hear music while you're viewing your photos, choose an imported audio file from the Background Music menu or click the Browse button and navigate to an appropriate audio file.

- ✔ If you've recorded audio captions and want them to play during Photo Review, click the Play Audio Captions check box.

- ✔ The Page Duration option lets you specify how long you want each image to display. You can choose an option from the menu or type a number directly into the field to set the display duration.

- ✔ To include text captions in Photo Review, click the Include Captions check box.

- ✔ The Allow Photos to Resize check box allows low-resolution images to expand to fill the screen when you view your Photo Review. The results of enlarging a low-resolution photo may not be very attractive, so deselecting the check box makes the images display at Actual Pixel size during Photo Review. The Allow Videos to Resize check box does the same for videos.

- ✔ If you want your Photo Review to start over again from the beginning when it reaches the end, select the Repeat Slide Show check box.

After you've set your presentation options, click OK. If any of your selected photos are offline, a dialog box will appear prompting you to insert the proper CD. If you don't want to do this, you can choose options to use the proxy images or to skip the offline photos altogether.

The Photo Review screen consists of three main elements: a large area for viewing the current photo, a vertical thumbnail bin running down the right side of the screen, and a control strip. When you start Photo Review, the first image is selected in the thumbnail bin and displayed in the viewing area. Your background music will begin automatically, but the Photo Review won't begin until you click the green Play button in the control strip. Click the button, and the slide show begins; each image in turn becomes selected in the thumbnail bin and displays in the viewing area. Clicking a thumbnail in the thumbnail bin displays that image and halts the slide show. Click Play Again to resume.

The control strip features several controls for manipulating images or Photo Review itself:

✔ On the left are controls for playing and pausing the slide show, navigating manually from image to image, and stopping Photo Review.

✔ To the right of the navigation controls are controls for rotating the current photo and deleting it.

✔ The Action menu lets you perform a variety of tasks to the current image, such as tagging, adding to collections, and performing an Auto Fix. (Most of these are available by right-clicking a photo as well.) If you mark a photo for printing, Elements will remind you of the fact after you exit Photo Review.

✔ You can switch from Photo Review to Organizer's Photo Compare mode by clicking the photo compare button.

✔ The zoom controls let you fit the photo in the window, view the image pixel-for-pixel on your monitor, or zoom in and out.

Photo Compare

As seen in Figure 6-5, Photo Compare is a variation of the Photo Review mode, letting you judge two images side-by-side. To access Photo Compare, choose View⇨Photo Compare, press F12, or click the photo compare button in the control strip while in Photo Review mode.

The Photo Compare viewing area is partitioned in two sections either horizontally or vertically, depending on whether you choose Side by Side or Above and Below from the Photo Compare menu in the control strip. To load an image into one half of the viewing area, click in the viewing area to select the partition you want to load the image into, and then click the thumbnail in the thumbnail bin.

Photo Compare gives you access to the same controls in the control strip as in the Photo Review mode, with additional access to the sync pan and zoom button. When this button is active, the zooming and panning changes you make to an image in one partition of the viewing area occur also in the other partition.

Navigation controls   Action menu

Delete   Photo Review

Rotate   Photo Compare   Sync pan and zoom

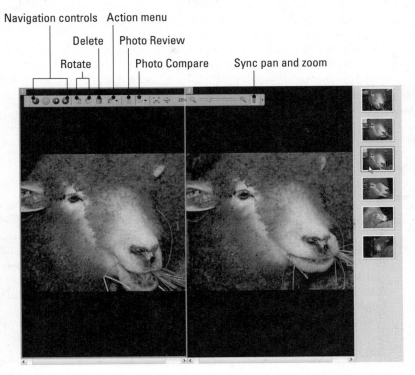

Figure 6-5:
Photo
Compare
lets you
perform a
side-by-side
analysis of
two similar
photos.

Searching by date

If you're looking for a photo and you know the date it was taken, you could of
course just scroll through the photo browser (set to one of the Date options
in the Photo Browser Arrangement menu) until you find the photo. But just
below the shortcuts bar is Organizer's timeline, an excellent visual aid for
finding photos according to when they were snapped.

The timeline

As seen in Figure 6-6, time is represented in the timeline in horizontal fashion
from left to right, and there's a vertical bar in the timeline for each month in
which you've snapped photos. The height of this bar reflects how many photos
you snapped for the month. To move from month to month, you can drag the
blue sliding viewfinder or just click a bar to advance the viewfinder to the
month you want to view.

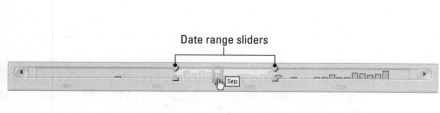

Figure 6-6:
Organizer's
timeline
shows you
a graph
depicting
how many
photos
you've taken
for any
given
month.

Date range sliders

To help you focus your search efforts, the timeline also lets you restrict the range of images displayed in the photo browser. Drag the date range sliders on either end of the timeline to narrow the time span. You can also narrow the date range by choosing Find⇨Set Date Range or by pressing Ctrl+Alt+F to display the Set Date Range dialog box. To clear the date range and go back to viewing all your photos, choose Find⇨Clear Date Range (Ctrl+Shift+F) or just drag the timeline's date range sliders back to either end of the timeline.

Date view

Photo browser aside, Organizer has an entire mode dedicated to letting you find your photos according to when they were taken. Clicking the Date View button in the shortcuts bar switches the Organizer interface to a big, friendly calendar. The buttons at the bottom of the screen let you view a year at a time, a whole month (pictured in Figure 6-7), or just a single day.

Here's the rundown on each view:

✔ In Year view, you can navigate from year to year with the buttons that appear on either side of the year at the top of the calendar. Within a year's calendar, each day for which you have photos in your catalog is assigned a color. The color is usually blue, but it turns to magenta if that day is also some sort of holiday or special occasion. (If there are no photos for a special day, the day's numeral appears in magenta.)

You can tell Organizer which holidays you want to mark as special in Date view by choosing Edit⇨Preferences⇨Calendar. You can also use the Preferences to add your own special events to Date view.

To view the photos taken on any given day, click the calendar to select the day. The first photo taken on that day appears in the thumbnail preview on the right side of the screen. You can then view the other pictures taken on that day by clicking the navigational arrows under the thumbnail or navigate to a different day with the arrows above the thumbnail.

✔ Month view operates almost identically to Year view, with a couple of exceptions. For each day of the month, a thumbnail appears in the calendar showing the first picture taken that day. The actual names of holidays and special events also appear below the thumbnails.

✔ Day view resembles the Photo Review mode, with its large viewing area for images and the thumbnail bin to the right. The bin contains all the photos that were taken on that day.

If you want, a photo other than the first one shot on a given day can be the photo that represents that day in Month view. To designate a different photo, just select the day in question while in Month view, and then switch to Day view. Next, right-click the photo in the thumbnail bin that you want to be the representative photo, and choose Set as Top of Day.

Figure 6-7:
The Date view can help you chart your photo-taking activity over the course of a month.

Searching by tags and collections

As mentioned, searching for photos by tag assignment is a simple affair. In the Photo Browser mode, just double-click a tag in the Tags panel and any photos given that tag will appear in the browser. The find icon (a pair of binoculars) appears next to the tag in the Tags panel. To filter these search results with another tag, click in the empty box to the left of the second tag's icon to set the find icon for that tag as well. Assuming that the Best check box is active in the Find bar, the browser now displays only photos that match both tags.

You can also use tags to *exclude* photos from the browser. Suppose you want to find all photos containing little Billy that *don't* also contain the cat Mr. Toodlepaws. Double-click the Billy tag, and then right-click the Mr. Toodlepaws tag and choose the Exclude Photos with Mr. Toodlepaws tag from Search Results. The photos are filtered away, leaving you with Toodlepaws-free search results.

Searching by collections works exactly the same as for tags: Just double-click the collection in the organize bin, and the browser displays all the photos in the collection. The only difference is that you can't add to or refine a collection search like you can a tag search.

Searching by caption or note

Another potential clue to use when trying to locate a photo is to search for words in a caption or note you may have assigned to the photo. Choose Find⇨By Caption or Note or press Ctrl+Shift+J to display the Find by Caption or Note dialog box. Here you can enter text to search for in your photos' captions and notes. The dialog box includes two radio buttons that allow you to specify how Organizer should match the term you specified. The first radio button (which is the default) instructs Organizer to match your text only to the beginning of words; if you enter *photo,* for example, the search results might include *photograph, photocopy,* and *Photoshop.* If you select the second radio button, your search results might also include words in which *photo* doesn't occur at the beginning, such as *telephoto.*

Searching by filename

Choose Find⇨By Filename or press Ctrl+Shift+K to reach the Find by Filename dialog box. Here, as with searching for captions and notes, you can enter text that Organizer will search for in your photos' filenames.

Searching by history

Because Organizer keeps track of each photo's history — when you imported the photo, when you printed it, who you e-mailed it to — searching this history can be a powerful way to find an image. Choosing Find⇨By History displays a submenu full of options, each one specifying a particular aspect of history you want to search by.

For example, choosing Find⇨By History⇨Imported On takes you to a dialog box that lists each session during which you imported photos into your catalog. Click to select a session, click OK, and the photo browser displays the photos that were imported from that session.

You can view a photo's history in the History section of the Properties panel.

Searching by media type

Don't forget that Organizer keeps track of more than just photos. Using one of the choices in the Find⇨By Media Type submenu searches for that particular type of media, be it photo, video, or audio. There are also searching options for creations and for files with audio captions.

Searching by the rest

A few more commands are available in the Find menu. Three of these — Items with Unknown Date or Time, Untagged Items, and Items Not in Any Collection — are easy enough to figure out. The fourth item, By Color Similarity with Selected Photo(s), needs a bit of an explanation.

Select one or more photos in photo browser, and choose Find⇨By Color Similarity with Selected Photo(s). Unlike other searches, Organizer doesn't just display photos that match the search criteria. Instead, it rearranges all photos in order of how well they match the colors of the selected photo or photos. This is as close as Organizer can come to analyzing the contents of your photos without your having applied tags to them.

Editing Your Photos

Yes, we know, there's another half of Elements devoted to editing your photos. But Adobe still gave Organizer some editing power. Here's the lowdown on the four choices available to you when you click the Edit button in the shortcuts bar to access the menu of Edit options:

- ✔ **Auto Fix Window:** This choice takes you straight to Organizer's own Auto Fix window, seen in Figure 6-8. In the General section of the window, you can apply Auto Smart Fix, Auto Levels, and Auto Contrast, just as you can in the Editor component of Elements. There's also an Auto Sharpen feature, roughly analogous to Editor's Sharpen filter. To use these tools, just click the button on the right side of the screen.

Auto Fix - reflection.psd (Edits will be saved to reflection_edited-1.psd)

General | Crop

General Fixes

Auto Smart Fix
Auto Levels
Auto Contrast
Auto Sharpen

Reset Image
More Editing...

35%

OK | Cancel

Figure 6-8:
The Auto Fix window is Organizer's exclusive image fixer-upper.

The Crop section lets you, no surprise, crop your photo. We are actually quite fond of Auto Fix's cropping function, because it's more intuitive and simpler than the one found in Editor's toolbox. Not that it does anything that you *can't* do in Editor; it's just easier to understand here. Choose an aspect ratio from the menu, or set the menu to No Restriction if you want to free-form crop your image. When you're finished, click the Apply button.

Note that there's also a More Editing button; clicking this button opens the image up in Editor, the same as if you had chosen Go to Standard Edit from the Edit button's menu in the shortcuts bar.

To leave the dialog box, click OK. The edited image will be saved in a version set with the original image.

✔ **Go to Quick Fix:** This choice automatically opens the Editor component of Elements and opens the image in Editor's Quick Fix dialog box, where you can perform simple editing tasks. Note that if you save any changes you make in the Quick Fix dialog box without renaming the file, you'll overwrite the original version of the file. To save the edited version of the image in a version set with the original, click the Save in Version Set with Original check box when you save the file. When you switch back to Organizer, the edited image and the original will be stacked in a version set.

✔ **Go to Standard Edit:** This opens the image in Editor. As with the Go to Quick Fix option, you can turn on the Save in Version Set with Original option when you save the image to save your edited image in a version set with the original.

✔ **Edit with Photoshop:** This option opens your image in Adobe Photoshop. There's a slight catch, however: You have to actually have Photoshop installed on your computer. The folks at Adobe aren't *that* generous.

When an image that's included in your Organizer catalog is open for editing in the Editor component of Elements, a red band and a lock icon appear across the image's thumbnail in Organizer. This lets you know that an edit is in progress on this particular image.

Backing It All Up

You've no doubt heard the expression "An ounce of prevention is worth a pound of cure." But if you lose the only copies of your digital photos due to hardware failure, theft, or for any reason, there sadly is no cure. In that case, an ounce of prevention is worth more like several days of crying, lamentation, self-reproach, and mourning. So be smart, and prevent such sadness by using Organizer to back up your photos.

Organizer clearly thinks this is a good idea. First, it presents you with periodic messages reminding you to back up your photos. Second, it gives you two different backup-related commands under the File menu — Burn and Backup — even though they lead you to the same dialog box. The Burn/Backup dialog box, shown in Figure 6-9, lets you decide whether you want to copy or move selected files to a CD or DVD to save disk space or to give the disc to others, or whether you want to perform an "ounce of prevention" and preserve both your catalog file and the photos it's tracking. We'll explore this last option first.

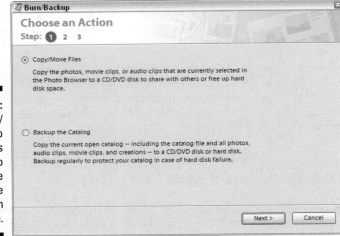

Figure 6-9:
The Burn/ Backup dialog box is the first step you'll make along the Prevention Path.

Backing up your catalog

After you've selected the Backup the Catalog option in the Burn/Backup dialog box, click the Next button. The ensuing Missing Files Check Before Backup dialog box appears, suggesting you click its Reconnect button to make sure Organizer knows the locations of all the images you want to back up. We suggest you follow its sage advice; that way, if you've moved any photos to a different location on your hard drive, Organizer can find them and back them up.

If Organizer finds any files missing, it tries its best to locate them for itself, though it may present you with the Reconnect Missing Files dialog box to enlist your aid. If this happens, select a photo in the Files Missing from Catalog list on the left. If you know where to find the missing photo, navigate to its location in the Locate the Missing Files section on the right. Click to select the photo, and then click the Reconnect button. If you can't find the missing photo, click the Delete from Catalog button. Click the Close button when you're finished.

The second step in the Burn/Backup dialog box is to choose between a full backup and an incremental backup. As the dialog box itself explains, you should do a full backup the first time you back up your catalog, because the backup will include your catalog file and all the photos in it. Subsequently, an incremental backup will back up your catalog file and only the new photos added since the last time you backed up. Make your choice — if you're reading this section of the book to learn how to back up photos, you're probably backing up for the first time and should choose Full Backup — and then click the Next button to proceed to Step 3.

In the Destination Settings portion of the Burn/Backup dialog box, click to select your CD or DVD burner in the Select Destination Drive window. Based on your selected Write Speed, Organizer will present you with the file size of your backup in megabytes, and the estimated length of time the backup will take. Click Done, and you'll get a dialog box telling you how many discs you'll need for the backup. Click No if you need to run out to buy more discs, or click Yes and let the burning begin.

To verify or not to verify? Organizer presents you with this choice after it's burned a disc. We join with Organizer in recommending that you verify. Sure, it takes a lot longer, but these are your precious photos we're talking about. It would be a shame if one of your backup discs turned out to be faulty, so spend the extra time and let Organizer verify the discs.

Making copies or moving files

If you just want to copy images to a CD or DVD to share with a friend, or you want to move some photos offline to free up disk space, Organizer can do that, too. First, select the photos you want to copy or move, and then choose

File⇨Burn. With the Copy/Move Files option selected in the Burn/Backup dialog box, click the Next button.

If you're trying to free up disk space, select the Move Files check box. After the images are copied to CD or DVD, they are deleted from your hard drive and replaced with low-resolution proxy versions. To access your original high-resolution versions, you'll have to insert the CD. However, if you just want to copy some images to a disc to share with a friend, definitely uncheck the Move Files check box. You can also include all the files in a stack or a version set by checking the appropriate check boxes.

Then click Next one final time, and you're taken to the Destination Settings portion of the Burn/Backup dialog box. Make sure your CD or DVD burner is selected in the Select Destination Drive menu, click Done, and burn, baby, burn.

Printing Your Photos

A large chunk of Chapter 8 is devoted to the subject of printing from the Editor half of Elements. But Organizer has its own printing command, with its own special options. Select the photo or photos you want to print, and then click the printer icon in the shortcuts bar, choosing Print from the menu that appears. You can also press Ctrl+P. Either way, the Print Selected Photos dialog box appears. Organizer gives you three steps to successful printing, but the choice you make in the second step determines exactly what the third step will be.

Step 1 is to choose your printer from the list. Epson's PIM and EXIF Print technologies are designed to help your print look more like the original image. If your digital camera supports these technologies, you can enable them by clicking the appropriate check boxes.

We deal with two of the options under Step 2 — Contact Sheet and Picture Package — in Chapter 18. Here's the lowdown on the other two options:

- ✔ The Individual Prints option is set up almost identically to Editor's Print Preview dialog box, which we cover thoroughly in Chapter 8. You can access additional Individual Prints options by clicking the More Options button at the bottom of the dialog box.

- ✔ The Labels option features presets for common label sheet layouts from makers such as Avery. Choose your label package in the Select a Layout menu, and then choose an optional frame from the Select a Frame menu. If you find your print job doesn't exactly line up with the labels on the sheet, you can adjust things in the Offset Print Area to a fineness of one tenth of a millimeter.

Printing and Sharing Your Photos Online

Don't forget that Elements lets you print your photos even if you don't own a printer! You can accomplish this nifty magic trick by taking advantage of Adobe's partnership with Ofoto, the online photo sharing and printing service.

To get started sharing photos online, select the desired photo or photos, click the Share button in the shortcuts bar, and choose Share Online. Provided that you have an Internet connection, Elements will go online and connect to Ofoto. If you currently have an Ofoto account, fill in your e-mail address and password and then click the Next button at the bottom of the screen. If you don't have an Ofoto account, we strongly recommend that you get one. It's perfectly free, and it will open up a whole new world of photo sharing opportunities. To set up an account, click the Join Now link and fill in the necessary information. Then click the Next button at the bottom of the screen, and you're on your way!

After you've created or accessed your account, you'll see a Share Online screen that enables you to enter the names of people you want to notify that you're sharing your photos online. These recipients will receive an e-mail inviting them to visit Ofoto and view your photos in an online album. Click the Add New Address link to be taken to a new screen where you can enter information about your recipient, and then click Next to be returned to the Share Online screen. Then, place a check mark in the box next to your desired recipient or recipients, and click Next. From here, you can follow the easy directions to upload your photos, and your recipients will be automatically notified through e-mail.

Ordering prints is a similar process. Select the photo or photos you want to print, and choose File⇨Order Prints. You'll then be taken step-by-step through the ordering process, specifying the size and number of prints you want for each image, designating recipients, paying for the order, and finally uploading the images.

Online sharing is a great way to let others enjoy your photos, but the Organizer component of Elements 3 is packed with other ways to spread the love. We examine some of these sharing and creating options in Chapter 18.

Chapter 7

Saving with Grace

....

....

1 f you've used a computer before, you may be wondering why we would devote an entire chapter to saving files. After all, you just press Ctrl+S (⌘+S on the Mac) and you're finished, right? For that matter, Photoshop Elements (Windows users, we're talking here about the Editor component of Elements) lets you click a handy save icon in the shortcuts bar — the one that looks like the floppy disk. "What's to know about saving?" you ask. Well, if we were talking about any other program, you'd be right. If this book was about Microsoft Word, for example, we'd say, "Not to worry, Gentle Reader, saving a file is so simple, a newborn lemur could pull it off with only the most cursory supervision from a parent or older sibling."

But this book is about Photoshop Elements. And Elements, as you may or may not be aware, enables you to save images in more flavors than Willy Wonka manages to squeeze into an Everlasting Gobstopper. In the computer world, these flavors are called *file formats,* and each one has a different purpose.

This chapter offers a thorough explanation of the saving process, including an exhaustive — well, okay, pretty decent — review of the various file formats you can use. We'll also be taking a look at Elements' powerful Save for Web command. With this chapter by your side, saving can be a pretty easy thing to do, after all.

Save an Image, Save a Life

Although we don't know you from Adam — or Eve for that matter — you're probably the kind of person who doesn't like to spend hours editing an image only to see your work vanish in a puff of on-screen smoke as the result of some inexplicable and unforeseen computer malfunction. If you are indeed that kind of person, finding out how to save your image is essential. By saving your image early and often, you improve your chances of weathering any digital storm that may come your way.

Saving for the very first time

If you're working on an image that you created from scratch in Elements by using the File⇨New⇨Blank File command, choosing the Save As command displays the Save As dialog box. If you're working on an image that's already been saved to disk, such as a photograph from a digital camera or scanner, you'll probably want to save another copy of the image containing your changes while leaving the original unaltered. So, before you begin making changes to your image, use the Save As command to save it under a new name and specify where you want to store it on disk. If you do this, the original image remains untouched so that you can return to it at a later date for inclusion in a different project. Here's how to save your image:

1. **Choose File⇨Save As.**

    The dialog box shown in Figure 7-1 appears.

    You can also open the dialog box by pressing Ctrl+Shift+S (⌘+Shift+S on the Mac).

Figure 7-1:
Use the Save As dialog box to name your image and decide where you want the image to hang out on disk. The Windows version is on the left; the Mac version is on the right.

2. **Enter a name.**

   PC users: Enter a descriptive filename in the File Name box. If you're saving another copy of an existing file, the filename may be followed by a period and a three-character file extension that indicates the file format (explained shortly). To ensure maximum compatibility with other operating systems, don't use any spaces or special characters, such as ampersands or brackets, in your filenames; stick with regular letters and numbers. You don't have to enter the extension because Elements does that for you. Also, make sure there's a check mark in the Use Lower Case Extension box at the bottom of the Save As dialog box, because this aids compatibility as well.

   Mac users: Enter a descriptive filename in the Save As box. In addition to entering a filename, you also have the option of adding a three-character extension (such as tif) that indicates the file format (explained shortly in "The Elemental Guide to File Formats" section). The Append File Extension option is located in the Preferences command under the Saving Files panel. You can choose Never, Always, or Ask When Saving. You can also choose to save a file with a lowercase extension (a good idea). If you select the Ask When Saving option, check boxes for Append and Use Lower Case appear in the Save As dialog box.

3. **In the Format drop-down menu, choose a format.**

   This is the point at which you have to deal with the image flavors touched on in the introduction to this chapter. The drop-down menu provides all kinds of options, such as TIFF, JPEG, and PICT. We discuss the ramifications of the important formats later in this chapter.

   Some formats are restricted to certain kinds of images. For example, images that contain layers can be saved only in the Photoshop (PSD), TIFF, or PDF format. If you try to save a layered image in a format that doesn't accept layers, such as JPEG, the Save As a Copy option is applied automatically.

4. **Navigate to the folder you want to save the image into, and select it.**

5. **Select one or more of the next options. Note that option availability is based on the type of image and whether the image has layers (more about layers in Chapter 10).**

   - **As a Copy:** Instead of giving your image a different name, you can check the As a Copy option. This option automatically adds the word "copy" after your filename, thereby ensuring your original remains intact.

   - **Layers:** With this option checked, your image preserves all its layers. If unchecked, your image is flattened into a background.

   - **Color:** Checking this option embeds a color profile into the code of your image (see details in the Color Settings discussion in Chapter 5).

- **Include in Organizer:** For Windows users, this option automatically makes the image show up in your catalog in the Organizer component of Elements.

- **Save in Version Set with Original:** If you've just performed an edit on an image already in your Organizer catalog in Windows, this option creates a version set containing the original image and this edited version. For info on version sets, see Chapter 6.

6. **Click the Save button or press Enter (Return on a Mac).**

7. **If another dialog box appears, fill out the options and press Enter (Return on the Mac).**

    Some formats present additional dialog boxes that enable you to modify the way the image is saved. We explain these later where appropriate.

Your image is now saved! Come heck or high water, you're protected.

The Thumbnail check box(es) at the bottom of the dialog box are visible (Mac) and accessible (PC) only if you've selected Ask When Saving in your Preferences under Saving. If you don't check the Thumbnail options when you save an image, you may not get a preview when you later try to open that image, depending on your operating system.

To make sure that Elements always saves previews, go to the Saving Files panel of Elements' Preferences. When the Preferences dialog box appears, choose the Always Save option from the Image Previews drop-down menu. Click OK to exit the dialog box. Now a thumbnail will be saved by default, and you don't have to worry about it anymore.

The only time not to save a preview is when you're saving images for posting on the Web. Previews make the file size a little bigger, leading to longer download times. If you're saving images for the Web, however, you'll want to use the Save for Web command discussed later in this chapter.

Joining the frequent-saver program

After you name your new or altered image and save it to disk for the first time, from this point onward press Ctrl+S (⌘+S on a Mac) or choose File⇨ Save every time it occurs to you. Think of it as a nervous twitch you actually want to develop. Elements updates your image on disk, without any dialog boxes or options popping up and demanding your attention. Then when your computer crashes — notice that we said *when,* not *if* — you won't lose hours of work. A few minutes, maybe, but that comes with the territory.

The Elemental Guide to File Formats

Selecting a format in which to save your image is a critical decision. So, you need to pay attention to the upcoming sections, even if the subject is a dry one — which it is. Get a double espresso if you need one, but don't skip this information.

What is a file format, anyway?

Glad you asked. (But do you have to use that bold, italic tone of voice?) A *file format* is a way of saving the electronic bits and pieces that make up a computer file. Different formats structure those bits and pieces differently. In Elements, you can choose from about a zillion file formats when you save your image to disk, which makes things a tad bit confusing.

Luckily, you can ignore most of the file format options. The Photoshop Raw format, for example, sacrifices colors and other image information, so avoid it. (Don't confuse this with the Camera Raw format, which we discuss in Chapter 13; it's a different thing.) Scitex CT is a sophisticated format used by sophisticated (and well-funded) creative types, so you can forget about it, too. JPEG 2000 is a relatively new format that offers lossless compression, but support for it among other applications is still sparse. Use the Pixar format if you want your toys to come to life and behave in vastly amusing ways, but only when you're not in the room. (Just kidding.)

Actually, you'll probably use only a handful of formats: TIFF, PDF, JPEG (as opposed to JPEG 2000), GIF, and perhaps most importantly, the native format, PSD, which Elements inherited from the application that gave it life — Photoshop. The following sections explain the most important file formats and when to use them. (We deal with JPEG, GIF, and also the PNG format in the "Saving for the Web" section coming up in this chapter.)

TIFF: The great communicator

One of the best and most useful formats for saving Elements images is TIFF (pronounced "tiff"), which stands for Tagged Image File Format. TIFF was developed to serve as a platform-independent standard so that both Macintosh and Windows programs could take advantage of it. TIFF is an excellent file format to use for images that are destined to be printed. It can be imported into virtually every page layout and most drawing programs.

When you select the TIFF option from the Save As drop-down menu and click the Save button, Elements displays another dialog box, shown in Figure 7-2. In the area labeled Byte Order, you can tell Elements whether to save the TIFF image for use on a Macintosh or Windows program. Neither option is likely to give you a problem regardless of the platform you're working on, so just choose your favorite and don't sweat it.

The TIFF Options dialog box offers several compression methods. If you select one of the methods, Elements compresses your image file so that it takes up less room on disk. LZW compression doesn't sacrifice any data to make your file smaller and is great for compressing images with large sections of a single color. It's known as a *lossless* compression scheme. ZIP compression is also a lossless scheme and works well with images containing large areas of a single color. ZIP compression is common in the Windows world. The last compression method is JPEG, a *lossy* compression scheme, meaning that some of the data that makes up your image will be lost. The term is used with special frequency by Scottish nerds trying to impress women: "Och, ye've got a be-oo-tifully compr-r-ressed image ther-r-r-re, Lossy!" (Sorry, that's a terrible joke. We should be kilt.) There's more on JPEG in the "Saving for the Web" section of this chapter.

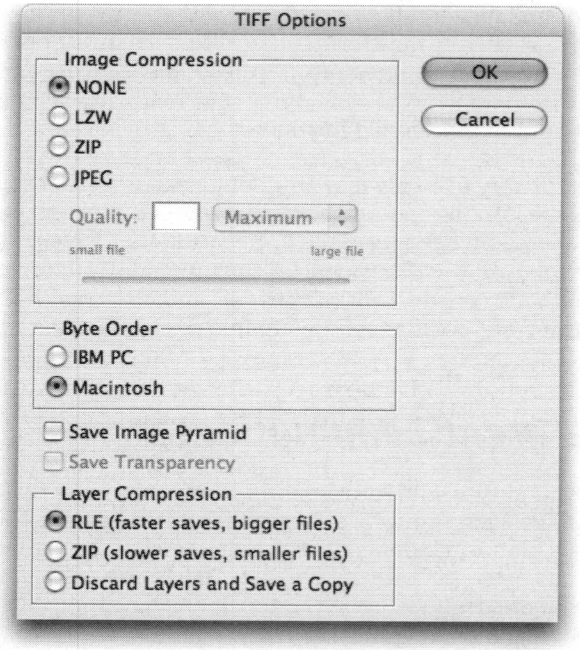

Figure 7-2: The options that appear when you save a TIFF file.

Your best bet is to use LZW. Most programs that support TIFF also support LZW. For example, you can import an LZW compressed TIFF image into InDesign, PageMaker, or QuarkXPress. Only obscure programs don't support LZW, so there's really no reason not to select this option. LZW compression does make your files open and save a bit more slowly, but the savings in disk space are worth it.

TIFF also supports saving with layers. If the term *layers* is fuzzy to you, check out our upcoming book, *Layers For Dummies*. What the heck — on second thought, we'll just roll that stuff into Chapter 10 of this book. Lucky you.

Not many programs support pyramid files right now, so it's best to leave the Save Image Pyramid option unchecked. The Save Transparency option has no effect if you're opening your image back up in Elements; transparency will always be preserved. The option applies only if you're opening the file in another program that supports PDF transparency (read on for more about PDF). And if you're saving layers in your TIFF file, the self-explanatory Layer Compression options give you a choice in the "disk space versus speed" equation.

Photoshop PDF: The can-do kid

PDF is a versatile, powerful format and another excellent choice for cross-platform work. Short for Portable Document Format, PDF was created by Adobe, so it's little surprise that you'll find it heavily supported by Adobe applications such as Illustrator, InDesign, and PageMaker. In fact, PDF has become an almost universally accepted format; all a person needs to view a PDF document is free Adobe Reader software (which is available for download from www.acrobat.com). And if you want to save your Elements image with layers, PDF is one of only three options.

When you choose Save As, select Photoshop PDF from the Format drop-down menu, click Save, and another dialog box appears. Choose ZIP encoding if you want lossless compression; otherwise select JPEG and choose a Quality setting. As noted in the TIFF section, JPEG is a lossy compression format, but the upside is that the PDF file will be smaller. If your image contains Transparency, you'll have the option of keeping it within your PDF document. The Image Interpolation option means that low-resolution images in your PDF file will be smoothed out rather than appear pixelated. It's probably best to turn off the option because the interpolation process can't improve low-resolution images and usually just makes them appear fuzzy.

BMP: The wallpaper glue for PC users

BMP is a popular PC format for saving graphics that you want to make part of your computer's systems resources, such as the wallpaper that you see behind your desktop. Programmers also use BMP to create images that appear in Help files.

When you save a file in the BMP format, don't worry about changing any of the options in the dialog box; use the defaults that Elements chooses for you.

What about Elements' native Photoshop format?

One strong bit of proof that Photoshop Elements is the offspring of Photoshop (a sterling lineage indeed) is that Elements' native file format is the Photoshop format. The three-letter extension for the Photoshop format is PSD.

PSD, TIFF, and PDF are the only formats that can save the layers in your image; all the other formats "flatten" (merge) the layers together.

As do TIFF and PDF, the Photoshop format offers a lossless compression scheme. And Elements can open and save images faster in its native format than in any other format. But some other programs don't support the Photoshop format. So, use the PSD format when you're sure the program you plan to import the image into supports it and you don't need compression.

What format to use when

Ooh, you cheated, didn't you? You skipped right over the sections on how formats work and why they were invented. Instead of reading all that juicy background information — information that would help you make your own decision about which format to use — you want easy answers.

Okay, fine. Because you plunked down good money so that understanding Elements would be easy for you, we'll give you a break just this once. Think of the following list as your study guide to file formats. But when you're standing around at a cocktail party and the discussion turns to JPEG compression versus LZW and you don't have an intelligent word to offer, we don't want to hear about it.

- ✔ If you're just going to use the image in Elements, save the image in Elements' native Photoshop (PSD) format. 'Nuff said.

- ✔ If your image contains layers ("Layers?" you ask. "Chapter 10!" we answer.) and you want to preserve those layers, you can choose the PSD (Photoshop), TIFF, or PDF format.

- ✔ If you want to import your image into another program, TIFF is probably the most compatible choice.

✔ If you want to import your image into another program, and if saving disk space is a priority, and if TIFF's LZW compression making the file small enough, use JPEG compression.

✔ If you're a Windows user and want to create wallpaper to amuse your co-workers or just yourself, use BMP.

✔ If you're working on a photograph to be sent by e-mail or posted on the Web, use the JPEG file format. For graphics or partially transparent images, use CompuServe GIF. For more on these formats, read the following section.

Saving for the Web

Yes, JPEG and GIF are the two standard file formats to use when saving images for posting on the Web. Yes, you can choose File➪Save As and save your image as a JPEG or GIF. But don't.

Why not? Because (fanfare, please) there is a better way! Using Elements' terrific Save for Web command is, for the most part, vastly superior to using the Save As command to create JPEGs and GIFs. Not only do you get a side-by-side preview of your original uncompressed image versus the compressed version, but also it's easy to switch back and forth between JPEG and GIF to determine which is the better format to use in terms of image quality and download time. The Save for Web command gives you almost every option you have when you choose JPEG or GIF from the Save As command; we'll cover the few additional options that Save As provides in the sections that follow.

Hey — what about PNG?

In addition to saving JPEGs and GIFs, the Save for Web command also lets you save images in the PNG file format. PNG stands for *Portable Network Graphics* and was originally designed to replace the popular GIF format. PNG is better than GIF in just about every way, except one: Even the major browsers, Internet Explorer on Windows and Safari on the Mac, don't offer full support for all of PNG's features. JPEG and GIF are still better choices.

If you want to go ahead and give PNG a chance, you have two flavors to choose from: PNG-8 and PNG-24. The options for saving a PNG-8 file are virtually identical to saving a GIF file, so refer to the GIF section in this chapter for details. Saving a PNG-24 file gives you precious few options, but again, you can refer to the GIF section for more information.

The Save for Web command

To open the Save for Web dialog box, choose File⇨Save for Web, or press Ctrl+Shift+Alt+S (⌘+Shift+Option+S on a Mac). You'll see the large window in Figure 7-3. Elements shows the original image on the left along with a copy on the right with compression applied, as it would appear when opened in a Web browser. You can modify the settings along the right side of the window.

To get a closer view, you can zoom and scroll the previews using the zoom and hand tools in the small toolbar in the upper-left corner of the window. You can also change the zoom ratio by changing the Zoom value in the lower-left corner of the window. To preview settings in your favorite Web browser, choose it from a list of available browsers in the Preview In menu, which is at the bottom of the window below the compressed view of your image. From then on out, you can just click the Preview In button; your image appears in your selected browser window.

If you meant to make your image smaller for posting on the Web using Image⇨Resize⇨Image Size, but you forgot to, Elements gives you a convenient way to scale down your image in the Save for Web dialog box. The New Size settings let you do the job by entering pixel dimensions or a new percentage. You'll probably want to keep Constrain Proportions checked, unless you want to squash or stretch your image. After you've made your adjustment, click the Apply button and watch your image shrink!

Aside from that, using Save for Web is just a matter of adjusting the various other options along the right side of the window. The predefined settings appear in the drop-down menu at the head of the Preset area. Some of these may work perfectly for you, or perhaps you'll want to select one as a jumping-off point for creating your own settings with the options below the menu. These options change according to the file format you choose. In the next sections, we examine the options in the Save for Web dialog box when you choose JPEG and GIF.

Clicking the arrow button located to the right of the menu at the top of the Preset area gives you access to the new Optimize to File Size dialog box, an excellent addition to Save for Web. If the ultimate file size of the compressed image is your major concern, Optimize to File Size lets you specify the file size first, and then compresses the image to match. Type a number in the Desired File Size box to specify your desired file size.

In the Start With section of the Optimize to File Size dialog box, the Current Settings option will cause the command to create the file in the format already specified in the Preset section, be it JPEG, GIF, or PNG. Clicking the Auto Select GIF/JPEG option causes Elements to examine the image and determine whether you're better off saving the file as a JPEG or a GIF.

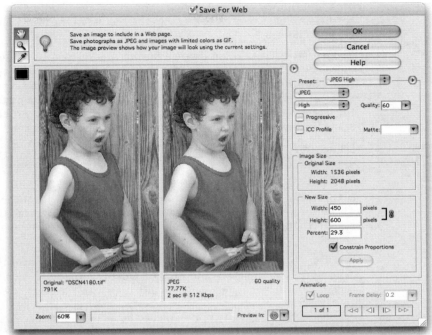

Figure 7-3:
The Save for
Web
command
lets you
compare
your original
image to
a Web-
compressed
version.

JPEG: The best choice for photos

JPEG stands for Joint Photographic Experts Group, but who cares? What's important to remember is that although JPEG can provide very good results with photographs, it does use lossy compression, meaning that some of your image data will be missing.

The good news, however, is that you'll probably never miss what's not around anymore — sort of like when you were a kid and you "lost" your little brother at the park. Depending on the level of compression used, you may notice a slight difference in your on-screen image after you save the file using JPEG. But if the image is saved at High or Maximum quality and then printed, the compression is usually undetectable. As with TIFF's LZW compression, JPEG compression saves you lots of disk space. In fact, a JPEG image takes up less space on disk than an LZW-compressed TIFF file — half as much space, maybe a tenth as much, depending on your settings.

Here are the JPEG settings available in Save for Web:

✓ **Compression Quality (Low, Medium, High, Very High, Maximum):** Choose an option from the drop-down menu immediately below the word JPEG to set the image quality to one of Elements' predefined settings. The Maximum option is best because it preserves the most image data, but the Very High and High options usually produce very good results as well. Color Plate 4 shows the results of the four Compression Quality choices.

✔ **Progressive:** This option makes your image download from the Web in incremental stages. A rough draft version of the image will appear relatively quickly in your browser, and the image will become clearer in subsequent passes. Although it's nice to quickly give users a hint of what the image will ultimately look like, this option can cause problems in some browsers. For fullest compatibility, leave it unchecked.

Using the Save As JPEG Options dialog box instead of the Save for Web command gives you the opportunity to specify the number of passes, or scans, it takes for your image to load fully.

✔ **ICC Profile:** This check box embeds a color profile with the JPEG image. The color profile adds about 3K to the file size. Even though that's a negligible amount, support for reading ICC Profiles in browsers is pretty sparse, so the extra 3K is wasted. Leave it unchecked.

✔ **Quality:** This option gives you more incremental control over the quality of compression than the Compression Quality drop-down menu does. Higher values give better image quality but larger file sizes; lower settings give lesser quality but smaller file sizes. You can specify a setting by entering a value in the Quality option box or by using the slider. Whereas the JPEG Options dialog box (available when choosing File➪Save As) divides the range of compression into 13 increments, from 0 to 12, the Save for Web value gives you a lot more incremental control, ranging from 0 to 100.

✔ **Matte:** This option applies only when you have transparency in your image. If your image has transparent or translucent pixels — maybe it has an oval, feathered outline that gradually fades to transparency — you must choose a background color to be matted into the image, because JPEG doesn't support transparency. For instance, if blue is selected, and the same shade of blue is used as the background for a Web page, the edges of the image would appear to gradually fade into the Web page. Totally transparent pixels would be filled with the specified blue, and translucent pixels would be mixed with blue.

The Matte menu gives you several options for selecting a color. You can use the eyedropper tool located in the upper-left corner of the dialog box. You can also choose Other or click the Matte color box to display the Color Picker with three Web-specific options, spotlighted in Figure 7-4. Click the Only Web Colors check box to select exclusively from the 216-color Web-safe palette. Click the cube icon to the left of the Help button to replace a color with its nearest Web-safe equivalent. And if you're a hexadecimal geek (and proud of it!), you can enter the desired hexadecimal color value into the # option at the bottom of the dialog box.

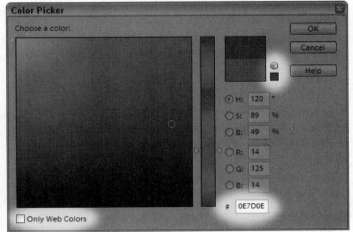

Figure 7-4:
Color Picker
has three
options
specifically
for Web
designers.

GIF: The choice of choosy Web designers

Computer hacks are divided on how you pronounce GIF. Some folks swear that the proper pronunciation is with a hard *G* — as in one *t* short of a *gift*. Other experts insist that you say it with a soft *g*, so that the word sounds just like that famous brand of peanut butter. (No, we don't mean Skippy.) Regardless of which camp you decide to join (we're in the peanut butter camp ourselves), GIF is best used for high-contrast images, illustrations created in Elements or imported from a drawing program, screen shots, and text. The biggest drawback to GIF is that it can save images with only 256 colors or less. However, it's the format you want to use for simple — no computer programming skills required — animations, called *animated GIFs*. We look at animated GIFs in Chapter 18.

Here are the GIF options available in the Save for Web command:

- **Color Reduction Algorithm (Perceptual, Selective, Adaptive, Restrictive):** This drop-down menu controls how the colors are reduced from 16 million to 256 or fewer. The color reduction algorithm creates a palette containing the colors used in the image.

  - **Adaptive** selects the most frequently used colors in your image. If an image contains relatively few colors and you want to keep the colors as exact as possible, apply this palette.

  - **Perceptual** is a variation on the Adaptive palette, which varies the reduced color palette to suit the image. But where Adaptive maintains the most frequently used colors, Perceptual is more intelligent, sampling colors that produce the best transitions. Use this palette with photographic images (if for some reason you don't want to use JPEG), where smooth transitions are more important than actual color values.

- **Selective** is also a variation on the Adaptive palette but it better preserves Web colors. Use this palette when an image contains bright colors or sharp, graphic transitions.

- **Restrictive (Web)** is a palette of 216 colors and is usually used for graphics that display on ancient 8-bit monitors. There are better palettes to use than Restrictive.

✔ **Transparency:** If a layered image contains transparent areas, you can keep them transparent by turning on this check box. Bear in mind, however, that transparency in a GIF file is on or off; there are no soft transitions as in an Elements layer.

✔ **Animation:** Applies only when you're creating animated GIFs, covered in Chapter 18.

✔ **Interlaced:** This option results in an interlaced GIF file, in which the image fades into view incrementally as it is downloaded by the Web browser. Although this is a nice option when it works correctly, there can be problems with browser compatibility. Use with caution.

✔ **Colors:** Here's where you specify the number of colors in an image. You can also choose predefined settings using the drop-down menu. Start with a low setting (such as 64), and see what happens to your image. Use the lowest number of colors that keeps your image reasonably intact. You may find that photographic images, especially those with a wide range of colors, require a higher setting than nonphotographic images or photos with a limited color range. And JPEG may be a better option for photos anyway.

✔ **Dither:** This wonderful option controls the amount of dithering applied. Lower values produce harsher color transitions but lower the file size. It's a trade-off. Keep an eye on the preview to see how low you can go.

✔ **Matte:** This is similar to the JPEG Matte setting. When Transparency is turned off, the Matte color is blended in with translucent pixels, and transparent pixels are completely filled with the Matte color. When Transparency is turned on, the Matte color still blends with translucent pixels, but transparent pixels remain transparent. This setting is useful for making an image blend in with the background color of a Web page.

Choosing CompuServe GIF in the Save As dialog box displays the Indexed Color dialog box (pictured in Figure 7-5), which gives you a few additional options:

✔ **Palette:** This is the same as the Color Reduction Algorithm option in the Save for Web dialog box. There are a few other choices here:

- **Exact:** If an image already contains less than 256 colors, the Exact palette appears by default. If this happens, leave it as is.

- **System (Mac OS)** and **System (Windows):** Use this palette only if you want to add a graphic to your system (like a desktop pattern or a file icon that will appear on your desktop).

- **Web:** This option converts the colors in your image to the 216 Web-safe colors.

- **Uniform:** The worst palette of the lot. Consists of a uniform sample of colors of the spectrum. Don't use it.

- **Previous:** When available, this palette uses the last look-up table created by the Indexed Color command. Usually used when creating a series of high-contrast graphics that need to maintain a consistent look.

Notice that the Palette menu also provides Master versions of the Perceptual, Selective, and Adaptive palettes. Local palettes are based on the colors in the open image, whereas master palettes take into account all currently open images.

✔ **Forced:** Sometimes an adaptive palette can change extremely important colors. For example, the white background of an image may turn a pale red or blue, even if white was a predominant color. With this option you can lock in important colors so that they don't change. Black and White locks in black and white. Primaries protects eight colors — white, red, green, blue, cyan, magenta, yellow, and black. And Web protects the 216 colors in the Web-safe palette. Very helpful indeed.

✔ **Preserve Exact Colors:** This option preserves areas of flat color when you select Diffusion in the Dither menu. It's best to leave this check box turned on. By doing so, colors in your image that are also in the palette aren't dithered; therefore, lines, text, and other small details in your Web images have better on-screen quality.

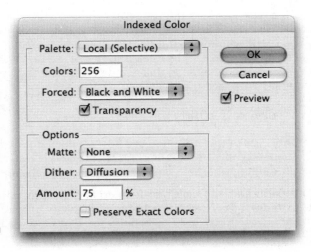

Figure 7-5:
The Indexed Color dialog box controls the appearance of GIF images.

Any GIF file can store transparency information. After saving a GIF file with indexed color, you can make all occurrences of one of those colors transparent using the Color Table command. Choose Image➪Mode➪Color Table to display the dialog box shown in Figure 7-6, and then select the eyedropper icon below the Preview check box. Now click a color in the palette or in the image itself. Either way, that one color becomes transparent.

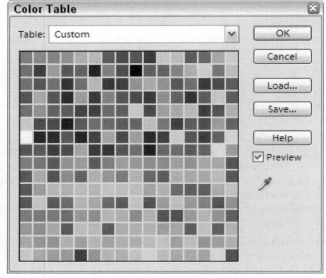

Figure 7-6:
Use the eyedropper tool to select a color that you want to make transparent.

The Preview menu

Before you exit the Save for Web window, we have one last set of options to explain. At the top of the window, to the right of the compressed image preview, you see an arrowhead in a circle. Click it to reveal the Preview menu, shown in Figure 7-7. The commands in this menu control the appearance and feedback provided by the image previews.

The commands are divided into three sections:

 - **Browser Dither:** Select this option to see how a selected preview will look when displayed on an 8-bit monitor. This method is exceedingly useful for determining whether you need to go with a Web-safe palette.

 - **Color Compensation:** Colors shift from one screen to the next and from the Mac to Windows. There's no way to predict exactly how an image will look on another screen, but you can use the four color commands to get an idea of how it will appear. By default, Uncompensated Color is active, so Elements makes no attempt at a prediction. Select Standard Windows Color or Standard Macintosh Color to see how the colors might look on another platform. The final color command, Use Document Color Profile, uses the profile embedded in the document, if one exists (see Chapter 5 for more on color profiles).

✔ **Size/Download Time:** The final twelve commands let you specify an Internet connection speed to see how long your image will take to download at the selected speed. The info appears underneath the compressed image preview.

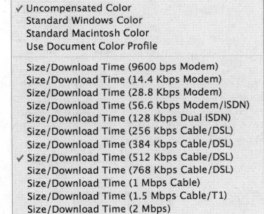

Figure 7-7: Choose a command from the Preview menu to affect the compressed preview.

File Association Manager

If you're a Windows user and you have more than one image-editing program on your hard drive — particularly if you use both Elements and Photoshop — it can be a real crap shoot knowing which application is going to open an image when it's double-clicked. The File Association Manager is just the tool to settle the matter once and for all. Choose Edit↔File Association, and the dialog box shown in Figure 7-8 appears. Using the File Association Manager is a simple affair; just place a check mark in the box corresponding to the type of file you want to assign to Elements. If you want Elements to open every possible image format, click the Select All button; if you want it to keep its mitts off every format, click Deselect All; and if you want to restore things as they were, click Default.

Figure 7-8:
The File
Association
Manager
lets you
grant
Elements
the authority
to open
various
image
format
types.

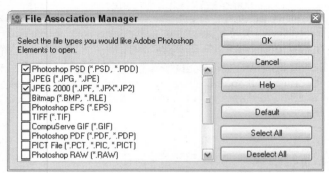

Although this is a Windows-only feature, Mac users have the same sort of control built into the operating system. While in the Finder, single-click an image file to select it and then choose File⇨Get Info or press ⌘+I. In the Open With section of the window, choose an application from the menu. After you've chosen the desired application, click the Change All button and then click the Continue button to make the change final. All image files with the same extension will be opened by the application you chose.

Good Night, Image — and Don't Let the Programming Bugs Bite

To put Elements to bed for the night, choose File⇨Exit (Photoshop Elements⇨Quit Photoshop Elements on the Mac) or press Ctrl+Q (⌘+Q on the Mac). Elements may display a message asking whether you want to save the changes you made to your image. Unless you have some reason for doing otherwise, press Enter (Return on the Mac) to select the Yes or the Save button. The program then shuts down. If you don't want to save your changes, press the N key for "No" (press D for "Don't Save" on the Mac). If you decide that you aren't ready to say good-bye to Elements after all, click the Cancel button or press the Esc key. Sweet dreams.

Note that if Windows users also have the Organizer component of Elements open, quitting the Editor component won't quit Organizer as well. Organizer has its own File⇨Quit command for that purpose.

Chapter 8

It's Perfect. No, Wait! Okay, Print.

*H*ere's how you know that you're a consummate computer nerd: When you snag your favorite sweater, say something highly objectionable to your spouse, or spill a well-known staining agent on your newly installed carpet, your first reaction is not one of panic or regret. You merely think, "Undo."

Unfortunately, the real world provides no Undo command. After a horrible deed is done, it takes an obscenely disproportionate amount of fussing, explaining, or scrubbing to correct the transgression.

Not so in the magical world of personal computing. Photoshop Elements, in fact, gives you access to *multiple undos*. You not only can undo as many as 1,000 actions but also *skip* backwards over previous steps. In other words, if you've performed five actions and want to return to the way your image looked after your second action, you aren't required to first undo steps five, four, and three. You merely select step two in the digital undo command headquarters — the Undo History palette. As this chapter explains, you can not only turn back the digital clock but also travel back in time.

And after you're done undoing, what do you do? Chapter 7 looks at the Save for Web command, a great choice if your final destination is an image you can e-mail to friends or post on the Web. But if you want your image to have a life on the other side of the monitor, the on-screen image is really just a figment of your computer's imagination. You won't be able to actually *feel* your work until the ink hits the paper. (Even so, try to wait until the ink dries.)

In this chapter you find out how to go from an on-screen, imaginary image to hard copy. But it's hard to explain this process when it has so many unknown variables: what kind of printer you're using, what kind of cabling is installed, and even whether the printer is located in your home or your office. In other words, we're suffering from a terrific deficit of knowledge. So when we start talking about printing, your sympathy and understanding will be appreciated as we explain — very briefly — how to print from Elements using an everyday, generic printer. But first things first: Here's how Elements lets you do the Big Undo.

Time Traveling

The more you work with Elements, the more reflexive your actions become. Certainly, this means that you can work more quickly, but it also means that you're likely to make more mistakes. Reflexive, after all, is a close cousin to thoughtless. And when you don't think, you can wander into some pretty nasty situations.

Exploring the Undo History palette in nine easy steps

Elements ensures that you aren't punished for working reflexively. To get a sense of just how wonderful this flexibility can be, try out these steps:

1. **Open the Undo History palette.**

2. **Create a new image.**

   The size is unimportant; just make it big enough so that you have room to paint a few brush strokes. Use White for the Background Contents. After you create the image, notice that the Undo History palette now has its first state, labeled New. A *state* is a record of exactly what an image looked like at a certain point in time — in this case, the New state shows you what the canvas looked like before you painted anything on it. You can't do anything with this first state; just affirm its existence. That'll make it feel good.

3. **Select the brush tool and drag across the image.**

   Press the B key to get the brush tool, but make sure you get the brush and not its suitemates, the impressionist brush or the color replacement tool. Also, press the D key to set the foreground color to black. Draw a single brush stroke, and no more. Now take a gander at the Undo History palette. You have a new highlighted state labeled Brush Tool under the New state. Again, for now, just notice this.

4. **Take a break.**

   You've worked hard; you deserve it. Watch TV for your daily allowance of 16 hours. Take up macramé. Paint a wall and watch it dry. The point is, no matter how long you're away, Elements remembers the last operation you performed (as long as you leave the image open in Elements and don't have a power outage or some similar computing disaster).

5. **Click the undo icon (the curvy downward-left-pointing arrow) in the shortcuts bar.**

   You should notice two things: Your brush stroke disappears from the image window, and the Brush Tool state becomes dimmed in the Undo History palette.

6. **Click the redo icon (the curvy downward-right-pointing arrow) in the shortcuts bar.**

   Your brush stroke reappears, and the Brush Tool state in the Undo History palette becomes active again. Are you beginning to see how the undo and redo icons and the Undo History palette are interrelated?

7. **Paint three more strokes.**

   Make sure each stroke is separate from the others. You should now have three more Brush Tool states in the Undo History palette, for a total of four.

8. **This time, rather than clicking the undo icon, use the default keyboard shortcut of Ctrl+Z (⌘+Z on the Mac). Repeat twice.**

   After you've traveled back to your very first brush stroke, try Ctrl+Y (⌘+Y on the Mac) to step forward in time, bypassing the Redo icon in the shortcuts bar. Go ahead and step forward to the last Brush Tool state.

9. **Click the first Brush Tool state in the Undo History palette.**

   This is yet another way to time travel in Elements: By clicking directly on states in the Undo History palette, you can travel backward or forward in leaps without revisiting every state.

Undo (Ctrl+Z on the PC, ⌘+Z on the Mac) lets you keep undoing until you run out of history states. Redo (Ctrl+Y on the PC, ⌘+Y on the Mac) lets you do just the opposite, allowing you to keep redoing until you reach the last action you performed.

Undoing and redoing work whether you have the Undo History palette open or not.

Travel restrictions

WARNING!

Undoing and redoing give you a great deal of flexibility as you work. However, here are some important things to keep in mind about these tools:

✔ The only actions you can undo or step through are ones that could actually change the image. For instance, using the zoom or hand tool isn't reversible because they affect only temporarily what part of the image you're seeing on-screen.

✔ You also can't reverse changing a foreground or background color, adjusting a Preference setting, hiding or displaying palettes, changing a setting in the options bar, or selecting a tool.

✔ After you close an image, you wipe the entire slate clean for that image. Elements has no memory of the steps you took to arrive at your current masterpiece.

The Undo History palette

Let's take a closer look at the powerful Undo History palette, which is depicted in Figure 8-1. This palette records all your operations and creates a running list of the steps — in other words, the states of your image at those points in history. As you perform each operation, Elements names each state and displays a corresponding icon according to the tool or command used. It records only operations that make a change to the pixels in your image.

Here's a list of the Undo History palette's features and functions and how to take advantage of them:

✔ To return to a previous state, click the desired state. Notice that Elements temporarily undoes all steps after that state, and those steps appear dimmed.

✔ The dimmed states are referred to as *undone states*. You can redo an undone state by clicking it. If you perform a new operation when you have undone states in the Undo History palette, the undone states disappear.

✔ To step backward through the palette one state at a time, press Ctrl+Z (⌘ +Z on the Mac). To move forward, press Ctrl+Y (⌘+Y on the Mac). These commands are accessible also through the Undo History palette's More menu.

✔ The keyboard equivalents for undoing and redoing can be customized with the Preferences⇨General command.

✔ Drag the history state slider (refer to Figure 8-1) up and down to scroll through and see each state rapidly disappear and reappear in order.

✔ Elements lets you save up to 1,000 history states. You can establish the maximum number of history states you want to retain in the Preferences⇨ General command. If your computer is low on RAM, you may not want to set this value too high. After you exceed your maximum, the oldest step disappears, then the next oldest, and so on.

✔ If you're absolutely sure you're happy with your image, and your computer is slowing down or running out of memory, you can delete the history states by choosing Clear Undo History from the More menu. If you have multiple files open, you can clear all their histories simultaneously by choosing Edit⇨Clear⇨Undo History.

✔ If you're working in Elements and you need to manage the number of states in your Undo History palette, you may find it handy to delete the last few states you performed. To do this, select the oldest state you want to delete and choose Delete from the More menu. Elements will delete the selected state and all subsequent states.

✔ Every image has its own history; therefore, you can work on multiple images simultaneously and independently of each other.

✔ After you close your image, its history disappears forever. The states in the Undo History palette aren't saved with the file.

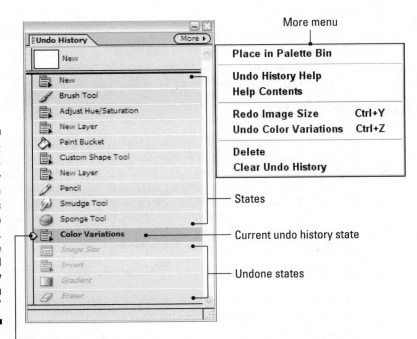

Figure 8-1:
The Undo History palette records every step you take. The Police recorded "Every Breath You Take."

Undo history state slider

Abandoning Edits en Masse

Sometimes you make small mistakes, and sometimes you make big ones. If, after several minutes of messing about, you decide that you hate all your edits and want to return the entire image to its last saved appearance so that you can just start over again, you can possibly do one of two things. First, you may be able to select the top state in the Undo History palette. Selecting the top state theoretically restores the image back to the way it appeared when you first started working on it. However, if you've already exceeded your maximum number of history states as set in the General panel of Preferences, the New or Open state has been bumped off the top of the Undo History palette. If this happens, you can choose Edit➪Revert to Saved. The program reloads the image from disk and throws away all your changes.

Provided that you have a large enough number of undo history states available, there's an advantage in using the Undo History palette rather than the Revert to Saved command. The Undo History palette can restore the *original* image regardless of whether you saved along the way, whereas Revert to Saved reloads the last saved version, which may include some undesirable changes.

Just in case you change your mind or your fingers slip, you can reverse Revert to Saved, so breathe easier. The Undo History palette records the Revert to Saved command.

The Command Formerly (and Currently) Known as Print

If you've ever wasted a sheet of expensive photo paper on a terrible print, you'll agree that someone really needs to work on being able to undo the act of printing. Imagine if Print appeared as a state in your Undo History palette; clicking the undo icon would feed the paper back into your printer, the ink would be sucked off the page and back into the cartridges, and then the printer would spit out a pristine white sheet of paper into the feeder tray. Alas, this is not to be. So let's take a close look at printing, and see whether we can figure out how to get it right the first time.

For starters, we're going to be totally rash and assume the following:

- You have a printer.
- Your printer is plugged in, it's turned on, and it doesn't have a 16-ton weight sitting on top of it. In other words, your printer works.
- The printer is properly connected to your computer. A cable running out of your computer and into your printer is probably a good sign.

✔ The proper printer software is installed on your computer.

✔ Your printer is stocked with ink, paper, ribbon, toner, film, pacifiers, little bits of felt, spring-like gizmos that go "ba-zoing," or whatever else is required in the way of raw materials.

If you've used your printer before, everything is probably ready to go. But if something goes wrong, call your local printer wizard and ask for assistance.

This May Be All You Need to Know about Printing

When things are in working order, printing isn't a difficult process. Although it involves slightly more than picking up your mouse and saying "print" into it, printing doesn't require a lot of preparation. In fact, a quick perusal of the following steps may be all you need to get up to speed:

1. **Turn on your printer.**

   And don't forget to remove that printer cozy your uncle knitted for you.

2. **Choose File➪Save or press Ctrl+S (⌘+S on the Mac).**

   Although this step is only a precaution, it's always a good idea to save your image immediately before you print it because the print process is one of those ideal opportunities for your computer to crash. Your computer derives a unique kind of satisfaction by delivering works of art from the printer and then locking up at the last minute, all the while knowing that the image saved on disk is several hours behind the times. If you weren't the brunt of the joke, you'd probably think that it was amusing, too.

3. **Check that the image fits on the page.**

   Click the print icon (the one that looks like a printer) in the shortcuts bar. (Windows users, we're talking about printing in Elements' Editor component here; see Chapter 6 for the lowdown on printing from the Organizer component.) You can also choose File➪Print, or press Ctrl+P (⌘+P on the Mac). Elements displays a preview of how your image fits on your chosen paper size. The white area in the Print Preview represents the size of the page. If your image fits entirely inside the white area, it will fit on the printed page. If it exceeds the boundaries of the white area, the image is too big for the page; you need to reduce the image or change the page orientation. To change the page orientation, read on.

4. **Select a printer, paper size, and page orientation.**

   You accomplish all this in the Page Setup dialog box, which you can display by clicking the Page Setup button in the Print Preview dialog box.

You can also visit Page Setup ahead of time by choosing File⇨Page Setup or pressing Ctrl+Shift+P (⌘+Shift+P on the Mac). When you've verified your settings, click OK to leave the Page Setup dialog box.

You can also click the rotate icons below the preview to change the orientation of the image on the page.

5. **Click the Print button in the Print Preview dialog box.**

   Elements displays the Print dialog box. Here you can specify how many copies of the image you want to print.

6. **Press Enter (Return on a Mac).**

   Experts say that this is the easiest step. Well, one guy got a blister on the end of his finger, but otherwise the vote was unanimous.

Congratulations! You have hard copy. But on the off-chance that you're unclear on how a couple of the preceding steps work or you're simply interested in excavating every possible nugget of information from this book, go forward to probe the depths of the rest of this chapter.

Choosing a Printer in Windows

If you have only one printer hooked up to your computer, you can skip this section. But if you're part of a network or you have more than one printer available to you, you need to tell Elements which printer you want to use.

To select a printer, open the Page Setup dialog box. You can do this by choosing File⇨Page Setup or pressing Ctrl+Shift+P. In Windows XP, you then click the Printer button at the bottom of the Page Setup dialog box to open yet another Page Setup dialog box, similar to the one shown in Figure 8-2. (Yours may look slightly different depending on your printer and which version of the operating system you're using.)

Figure 8-2:
In Windows, you select a printer in this dialog box.

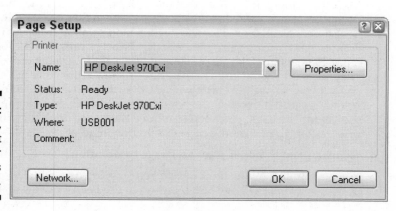

To select a printer, just choose the printer name from the Name drop-down menu. Click OK or press Enter to exit the dialog box.

Choosing a Printer on a Mac

The hub of "All Things Printing in Mac OS X" is the Printer Setup Utility, located in the Utilities folder, which is in your Applications folder. Opening the Printer Setup Utility displays the Printer List, as shown in Figure 8-3; just click the printer you want to use and you're finished.

Figure 8-3:
You can choose your printer here in the Printer List on the Mac.

Getting Image and Paper in Sync

The Print Preview dialog box, immortalized in Figure 8-4, offers much more than a preview of your printed image. Here are some of its other wonders:

- **Print Size:** This new menu lets you choose from among some popular preset print sizes. If you don't see any you like, you can create your own in the next area on the screen.

- **Scaled Print Size:** These settings enable you to reduce or enlarge the image for printing only. Enter any percentage less than 100 percent to reduce the dimensions of the printed image. The printer still prints all the pixels in the image, but the pixels are printed smaller. You can also enter a value in the Height or Width boxes, or turn on Show Bounding Box and resize the image in the preview by dragging from the sides or corners. You'll notice that the Scale, Width, and Height options are linked, meaning that changing any one affects the other two.

  If you select a portion of your image before you display the Print Preview box (using one of the tools we discuss in Chapter 9), you can print only the selected area with the option that says, surprise, Print Selected Area. If you just want to take a quick look at an isolated area, you can use this option to save time and ink.

✔ **Position:** Check the Center Image check box to center your image on the page. To enter other position values, deselect Center Image and type values in the Top and Left fields or turn on Show Bounding Box and simply drag your image preview to the desired location on the page.

✔ **Show Bounding Box:** This option places a box with handles around your image, showing the precise image boundaries and enabling you to reposition and resize the thumbnail image on the page.

✔ **Rotate:** Click the icons below the preview to rotate the image 90 degrees one way or the other.

✔ **Crop to Fit Print Proportions:** If you've specified a preset option in the Print Size menu, this option crops your image if necessary so that it will fit within the proper aspect ratio you've chosen.

✔ **Border:** If you want to print a border around your image, specify the size in inches, millimeters, or points, and click the swatch to choose a border color from the Color Picker.

✔ **Print Crop Marks:** As the name says, this option prints crop marks to aid you in cutting your image out of the paper.

✔ **Show More Options:** This displays the Label and Color Management options. More on these in a moment.

✔ **Label:** The File Name option prints the filename above the image. The Caption option allows you to print a caption below your image. If Windows users have already entered a caption for the image in Organizer, that caption will print below the image. Otherwise, you first have to cancel out of the Print Preview box and choose File⇨File Info. Type your desired caption in the Description field, and click OK. When you return to the Print Preview dialog box, you'll be able to see where your caption will print under the image preview.

✔ **Color Management:** These options are based on the idea of *color spaces.* Monitors, desktop color printers, and high-end offset printers all have their own color space. The Color Management options enable you to convert the color space of your image while printing. For example, if you created an RGB Elements document with Full color management turned on in the Color Settings, your Document Source Profile is Adobe RGB (1998), and you can use the Print Space menu to choose to have your image's color converted to another color space upon printing. (For more on color management, see Chapter 5.)

✔ **Transfer Printing:** If you're printing out an iron-on transfer, the Invert Image option will give you a mirror image of your print, so that when the image is ironed on, it will appear unflipped.

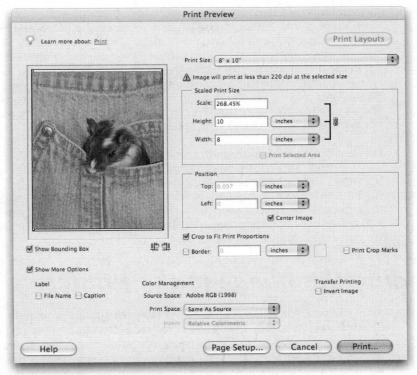

Figure 8-4:
You can
preview
how the
image fits
on the page
by using
the Print
Preview
dialog box.

The Page Setup dialog box lets you make additional choices that will affect your final printed output. To open Page Setup, choose File➪Page Setup, press Ctrl+Shift+P (⌘+Shift+P on the Mac), or simply click the Page Setup button in the Print Preview dialog box.

You can rotate your image in the Page Setup dialog box as well as in Print Preview. For example, if the image is wider than it is tall, you can print it horizontally by rotating the page 90 degrees. Somewhere in your Page Setup dialog box you should find two choices for Orientation: Portrait and Landscape. (It may be necessary to click the Properties button to access the Orientation options.) If you choose Portrait, your image prints upright on the page; if you choose Landscape, Elements rotates the image so that it prints sideways on the paper.

The specific options in the Page Setup dialog box vary depending on the kind of printer you're using. Note that the Page Setup dialog box also offers a scaling option.

As mentioned in Chapter 4, many factors can determine the size at which your image prints. Although the Image Size command (covered in Chapter 4) is the only one that can potentially damage your image, keeping this from happening is relatively easy (turn off the Resample Image check box). To avoid confusion and unpredictable results caused by the interaction of so many different influences on the final print size (and to avoid wasting expensive printer paper), we recommend using only Image Size to determine the size at which your image prints. Find out how to use Image Size correctly and you'll never be surprised by the results.

One last note: In the upper-right corner of the Print Preview dialog box, you'll find a button that enables you to print multiple files on the same page. On the Mac, the Print Layouts button cancels the Print Preview dialog box and opens the Picture Package command. In Windows, the Print Multiple Images button fires up Organizer (if necessary) and opens that component's Print dialog box. We cover both of these multiple-image printing techniques in Chapter 18.

Sending the Image to the Printer

After you've made it past the obstacle course of options provided by the Print Preview and Page Setup dialog boxes, you're almost home free. All you need to do is make a few last-minute calls, such as how many copies you want to print. Click the Print button in the Print Preview dialog box to display the Print dialog box, shown in Figure 8-5. As with the Page Setup dialog box, the options available in the Print dialog box may vary depending on your printer.

If the image is still too large for the page, Elements displays an error message when you click Print in the Print Preview dialog box. The message warns you that a portion of your image will be cut off the page and asks whether you want to proceed. If you cancel, the error message disappears, and you can then resize the image to fit the page, as discussed earlier in this chapter. If you say that you want to go ahead and print anyway, the Print dialog box appears.

If you're absolutely confident that your image should fit on your selected paper size, but Elements still barks at you that it won't fit, check the page orientation (portrait or landscape) in your Page Setup dialog box. Even if your image fits on the paper, Elements sometimes thinks the image is too large if it isn't oriented correctly.

That's it. Just click the OK button (Print on the Mac) or press Enter (Return on a Mac), and you're off. Depending on the size of the image and the speed of your printer, you should have hard copy in a matter of a few minutes.

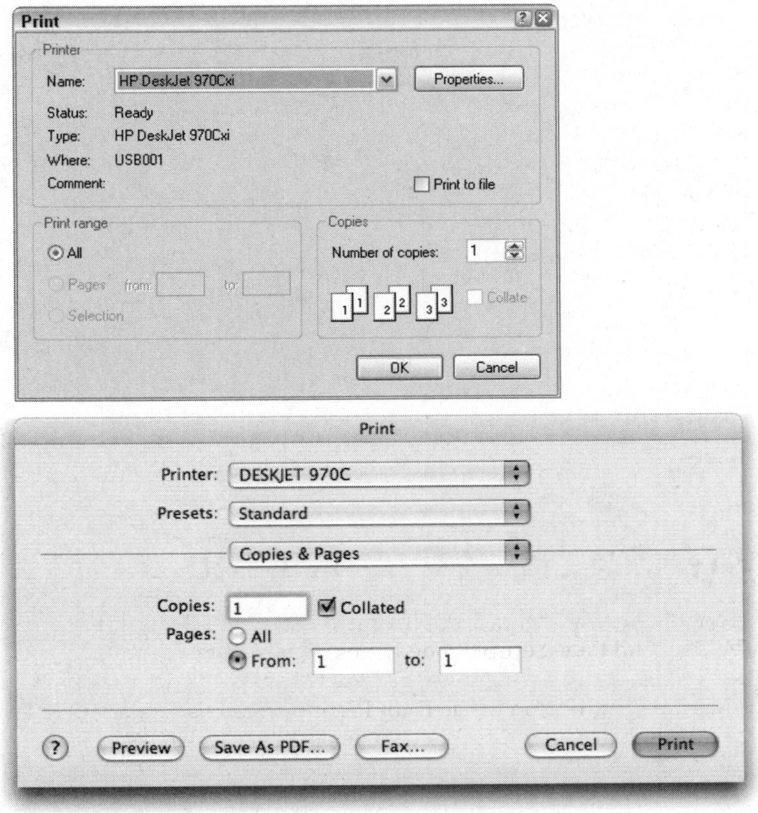

Figure 8-5:
The Print
dialog box in
Windows
(top) and on
the Mac
(bottom).

Chapter 9

Making Selections on the Pixel Prairie

*I*f you're an old ranch hand, you may find it helpful to think of the pixels in your image as a bunch of cows. A pixel may not have any horns, and you don't have to watch where you step when you're around it, but it's like a cow all the same. Consider these amazing similarities: Both pixels and cows travel in herds. (Come on, when's the last time you saw one pixel out on its own?) They're both dumb as dirt. And — here's the clincher — you can round them both up by using a lasso.

The only difference between pixels and cows is in the vernacular. When you lasso a cow or two on the lone prairie, it's called ropin'. When you lasso a mess of pixels, it's called selectin'. And after you select the desired pixels, you can do things to them. Selecting lets you grab hold of some detail or other and edit it independently of other portions of your image. It's a way of isolating pixels to manipulate them.

Granted, you can select pixels in a few other ways: with a magic wand, with a couple of marquee tools, and perhaps best of all with a tool called the selection brush. But whichever means you choose, this chapter is all about selecting portions of an image. With a little practice, you can rustle pixels better than most ranch hands rope dogies, and that's no bull.

Learning the Ropes of Selecting

Photoshop Elements provides several selection tools, all labeled in Figure 9-1. These tools include two marquee tools, the lasso, the polygonal lasso, the magnetic lasso, an automatic color selector known as the magic wand (phoenix feather not included), and the selection brush. Here's how they work:

✔ The rectangular marquee tool lets you select a rectangular area. Just drag from one corner of the area you want to select to the other. The outline drawn with the tool looks like chaser lights — which is how "marquee" managed its way into the tool's name.

✔ The elliptical marquee, which shares a flyout menu with the rectangular marquee, draws oval selections. The word *ellipse,* incidentally, is what mathematicians say when they're talking about ovals. In fact, we could just call it the ovoid marquee tool, but you might forget and think we were talking about some home pregnancy test.

✔ Drag inside the image with the lasso tool to select free-form areas. The shape of the selection conforms to the shape of your drag.

✔ Use the polygonal lasso tool, which shares a flyout menu with the regular lasso tool, to select pixels that are married to more than one other pixel. Oops, sorry — that's the *polygamal* lasso. The polygonal lasso draws selections made up of straight sides.

✔ Sharing the flyout with the other two lasso tools is the magnetic lasso tool (which sounds like the perfect tool for ropin' a mechanical bull). Click the magnetic lasso on the edge of your object and then move the lasso around that edge.

✔ The magic wand selects areas of continuous color. For example, if you want to select the sky without selecting the clouds, just click in the sky. At least, that's the way it's supposed to work, but the magic wand isn't always as magical as you might think.

✔ The selection brush lets you paint over the area you want to select. While in Selection mode, working with the selection brush is similar to working with the other selection tools, but in Mask mode the real power of the tool becomes visibly apparent.

An active selection in Elements is represented by a line of ever-moving dots, referred to in the digital imaging community as *marching ants.* (Just stare at a selection outline for a while and you'll see the resemblance.) Anything enclosed in the outline is selected; anything outside the outline is not selected. Although this is a fairly effective means of indicating an active selection, you may eventually feel that working with these ants is, well, no picnic. The upcoming section, "Hiding the Ants," tells how to make the distracting ants turn temporarily invisible, and the selection brush tool offers an effective ant alternative. Read on for details.

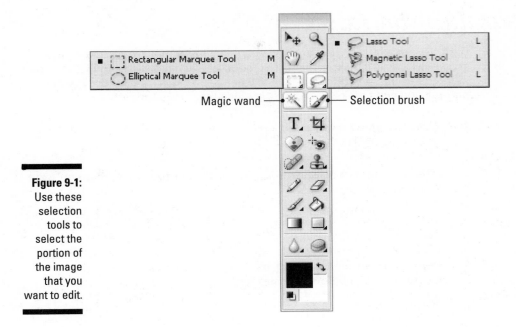

Figure 9-1:
Use these selection tools to select the portion of the image that you want to edit.

Now that you know how the tools work, let's see how to get to the tools. The arrow in the lower-right corner of the marquee and lasso tools in the toolbox indicates that a flyout menu of hidden tools lurks beneath each icon (see Chapter 2 for more information).

To switch between the tools on the flyout menus, you can Alt+click (Option+click on the Mac) whichever tool happens to be visible in the toolbox at the time. You can also use the buttons available on the far left of the tool options bar. Or, you can select tools using these keyboard shortcuts:

- ✔ Press the M key to access the active marquee tool. Whichever marquee tool is active, press Shift+M to get the other one.

- ✔ Press L to get the lasso tools. As with the marquee tools, a common shortcut switches you between the three lasso tools: If the regular lasso tool is active, pressing Shift+L toggles between the regular, polygonal, and magnetic lassos.

- ✔ Press W to get the magic wand. If W stands for *wand,* it also stands for the *wrong* results you frequently get with the magic wand.

- ✔ Press A to get the selection brush. You can remember that *A* is for *artistic,* and painting on the image is unquestionably the most artistic means of making a selection.

Throwing lassos

Both the regular lasso tool and the polygonal lasso tool are so easy to use your newborn can master them. If you don't have a newborn, you'll have to muddle through on your own. The magnetic lasso is trickier, however, but nothing you can't pick up with a little guidance from a toddler.

Using the regular lasso tool

Here's a complete set of instructions for using the regular lasso tool:

1. **Click and drag to trace around the portion of the image that you want to select with the tool.**

   That's it. In Figure 9-2, for example, we dragged around the frog to select it independently of its surroundings. As the figure shows, Elements displays a dotted outline — those wacky marching ants — around the selected area after the mouse button was released. This outline represents the exact path of the drag. (If you release before completing the shape — that is, before meeting up with the point at which you began dragging — Elements simply connects the beginning and ending points with a straight line.)

Selection outline   Lasso cursor

Figure 9-2:
We selected the frog by dragging around it with the lasso.

Granted, it's not easy to draw the outline just right, as in Figure 9-2. There's no trick to it; just get plenty of practice. If you have a graphics tablet, such as those made by Wacom, you may find it easier to select with a stylus rather than with the mouse. However, if your outlines aren't perfectly accurate, don't sweat it. You can modify the outline in plenty of ways after you draw it.

Drawing straight-sided selections

Suppose that you want to select a cube sitting in the center of an image. You can try to drag around those straight edges by hand with the lasso tool, but a better option is to use the polygonal lasso, which makes it easy to create selections with straight sides.

To select an object in this manner, click with the polygonal lasso to set the beginning of the first line in the selection. Then move the mouse cursor to the point where you want the first line to end and click again. Keep clicking to create new line segments. To complete the selection, you have two options. If you double-click, Elements draws a segment between the spot you double-clicked and the first point in your selection. You can also move the cursor over the first point in your selection until you see a little circle next to the polygonal lasso cursor. Then click to close the selection.

You can use the polygonal lasso also for images with both curved and straight segments. You can switch to the regular lasso in midselection to create a curved segment. Just press and hold down Alt (Option on the Mac) and drag to draw your curved line. When you release Alt (or Option), the tool reverts to the polygonal lasso.

You can also press Alt (Option on the Mac) while drawing a selection with the regular lasso to access the polygonal lasso. Press Alt (or Option) and click to set the endpoints of your straight-sided segments, as you normally do with the polygonal lasso. To start another curved segment, just drag. You can keep the Alt (or Option) key down or not — it doesn't matter. But be sure that the mouse button is down any time you press or release Alt (or Option), or Elements completes the selection outline.

Selecting with the magnetic lasso

The magnetic lasso tool takes a little getting used to and may not produce a great selection in all cases. But the concept behind it is simple, and if you take some time to understand the method behind its madness, it can be a quick remedy for your selection needs.

The magnetic lasso works best with high-contrast images — that is, when the object you want to select is a different color than the background. Taking the tool options bar settings into account, the magnetic lasso analyzes the difference in the color of the pixels between the object you want to select and the background, and snaps to your object's edge. Here's how to use this quirky tool:

1. **Select the magnetic lasso tool.**

2. **Click the edge of the object you want to select.**

3. **Move the cursor around the edge of the object.**

   Don't press the mouse and drag — just move the mouse. The magnetic lasso creates an outline with square anchor points around the edge of the object. If the line is off the mark, back up your mouse and try again. If you need to delete an anchor point as you are moving around the edge, press Backspace (Delete on the Mac). To create your own anchor points, click with the mouse. Adding your own anchor points can be helpful if the magnetic lasso seems reluctant to stick to the edge you want to select.

4. **Continue around the object, until you are back to the starting point.**

   A small circle next to your cursor indicates that the outline is about to be closed.

5. **To close the outline, click your starting anchor point.**

   As soon as you release the mouse, a selection marquee appears.

6. **Press Esc or Ctrl+period (⌘+period on the Mac) to cancel the magnetic lasso in midselection.**

To create a straight segment while using the magnetic lasso, press Alt (Option on the Mac) and click with the mouse. You can see that your cursor temporarily changes to the polygonal lasso. Release Alt (or Option) and drag for a second to reset the tool back to the magnetic lasso.

Exploring your lasso options

Whether you use the regular lasso, the polygonal lasso, or the magnetic lasso, you can modify the performance of the tool using the options common to all three tools in the tool options bar (see the next section for options specific to the magnetic lasso). Although small in number, the options for the lasso tools are some tough little hombres:

- ✔ Normally, you'll want selections drawn with the lasso tools to have soft, natural looking edges. This softening is called *anti-aliasing*. If you want to turn off the softening, deselect the Anti-aliased check box in the tool options bar. From now on, outlines drawn with the tool will have sharply defined and sometimes jagged edges.

- ✔ Both Feather and Anti-aliased affect future selection outlines drawn with the lasso tools, not currently active selections. In short, Feather makes the outline fuzzy, and Anti-aliased slightly softens the edge of the outline. If you want to modify an outline that you've already drawn, you have to choose a command under the Select menu (more on this in the section "Automatic selection shifters").

✔ Figure 9-3 shows two lassoed selections moved to reveal the white background in the image. In the left example, the Anti-aliased check box was turned off; in the right example, the option was turned on. The edges of the left example are jagged; the edges of the right example are soft. (Chapter 10 explains all the ways to move selections. But if you want to try moving a selection now, just drag it with the move tool.)

✔ Most of the time, you want to leave the Anti-aliased check box turned on. Just turn it off when you want to select precise, hard-edged areas. (Which may be never. Who knows?)

✔ Enter a value into the Feather option box to make the next outline you draw fuzzy. The value determines the radius of the fuzziness in pixels. If you enter a value of 3, for example, Elements extends the fuzzy region 3 pixels up, 3 pixels down, 3 pixels to the left, and 3 pixels to the right. As shown in the first example of Figure 9-4, that's a lot of fuzz. A higher value results in a more fuzzy selection outline, as witnessed in the right example, which sports a Feather value of 10.

Anti-aliasing off; jagged edges   Anti-aliasing on; soft edges

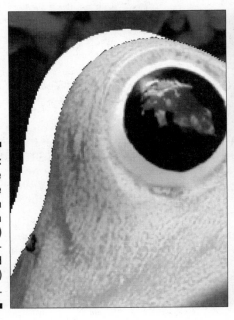 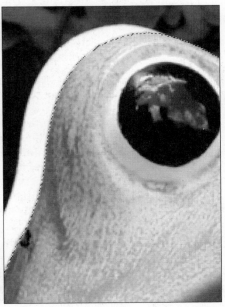

Figure 9-3: The difference between dragging a jagged (left) and anti-aliased (right) selection.

Feather 3 pixels   Feather 10 pixels

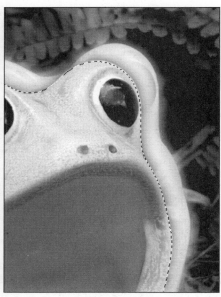

Figure 9-4:
A bigger
Feather
value
means a
fuzzier
froggy.

Looking at the unique magnetic lasso options

The magnetic lasso has unique options in the tool options bar that are related to the sensitivity of the tool's operation. They are as follows:

- **Width:** This option determines how close to an edge you have to move the mouse for Elements to "see" the object. You can set it to a higher number for smooth, high-contrast objects, and it will still hug the edge of the object. Set it to a lower value if the image has a lot of nooks and crannies or the contrast isn't that high. The range of the Width option is 1 to 256 pixels. To change it while you're using the tool, press the [key to lower the number and the] key to raise the number.

- **Edge Contrast:** This option tells the magnetic lasso how much contrast is required between the object and the background before the lasso can "be attracted to," or "hug," that edge. The range for the Edge Contrast option is 1% to 100%. If you find a good deal of contrast between the object and the background, use a higher value to get a cleaner selection. If the image is low contrast, lower the value for this option.

- **Frequency:** The number in the Frequency option tells the magnetic lasso when to automatically insert anchor points. The range for Frequency is from 0 to 100. If you want more points, insert a higher number; for fewer points, use a lower value. Don't forget that you can add your own anchor points at any time by clicking.

Start with the default settings for the previous magnetic lasso options, carefully make your selection, and see how it works. If your image is low contrast, you may want to lower the Edge Contrast to 5% or so. If edges are jagged or rough, try raising the Frequency to around 70 and lowering the Width to 5 pixels. If all else fails, and the magnetic lasso just isn't behaving, you can always go back to the regular lasso and the polygonal lasso. They may not be as high tech, but they're reliable.

Using the marquee tools

If you want to create a selection that's rectangular or elliptical, you use — guess what — the rectangular or elliptical marquee tool, respectively. These tools are so easy to use that they make the lasso look complicated. You just drag from one corner to the opposite corner and release the mouse button. (Okay, ovals don't have corners, so you have to use your imagination a little bit.) The dotted marquee follows the movements of your cursor on-screen, keeping you apprised of the selection outline in progress.

If you're in the midst of using a marquee tool and you decide that you don't like where you began drawing the marquee, press the spacebar while the mouse button is held down. Doing so lets you drag the entire marquee-in-progress to a new location. When you're happy with the new spot, release the spacebar, and finish drawing the marquee.

Elements has never been one to provide you with only one way to use a tool — or, in this case, two tools. For example, you can also use these tools to select perfect squares or circles. The program's cup of flexibility forever runneth over, and the marquee tools are no exception.

Grabbing a square or circle

Every so often, you may feel the urge to apply some puritanical constraints to your selection outlines. Enough of this random width and height business — you want perfect squares and circles. Lucky for you, Elements obliges your fussbudget impulses by letting you constrain shapes drawn with the marquee tools:

✔ To draw a perfect square, press the Shift key as you drag with the rectangular marquee tool. To draw a perfect circle, press Shift as you drag with the elliptical marquee tool.

✔ Drawing squares and circles is a little trickier than you might expect. For the best results, you should get in the following habit: begin dragging, press and hold the Shift key, drag to the desired location, release the mouse button, and finally release Shift. In other words, press Shift after you start the drag and hold it until after you complete the drag.

✔ If you press Shift before dragging, you run the risk of adding to the previously selected area, which you may not want to do. Here's the deal: If a portion of your image is already selected, holding down the Shift key first and then dragging will add the new selection to the previous one, rather than constrain the new selection to a square or circle. Befuddling, huh? If this happens to you, deselect everything and start over again. However, if you actually want to add a square or circular selection to a previously made selection, here's what you do: Hold down Shift, begin to drag, and then keep the mouse button pressed down as you release and press the Shift key again. Weird, but it works.

Getting even more control over selections

Are you crazed for control? Do your tyrannical desires know no bounds? If so, you probably aren't appeased by drawing a square or a circle. What you want is to apply even more stringent constraints.

For example, suppose that you're the sort of pixel-oppressor who wants to select a rectangular or an oval area that's exactly twice as wide as it is tall. With your marquee tool selected, choose Fixed Aspect Ratio from the Mode drop-down menu in the tool options bar. The Width and Height option boxes come to life, letting you specify an *aspect ratio,* which is a precise proportion between the width and height of a marquee. To make the marquee twice as wide as it is tall, enter 2 as the Width value. Then press Tab to highlight the Height value and enter 1. When you drag, the deed is done.

To constrain the marquee to an exact size, choose Fixed Size from the Mode drop-down menu, and then enter the exact pixel dimensions of your desired marquee in the Width and Height option boxes. Then click to create the marquee.

The new, dual-arrow icon between the Width and Height option boxes in the tool options bar lets you instantly swap the amounts entered in those option boxes. Always innovating, those good folks at Adobe.

One last item submitted for your approval: As with the lasso options discussed earlier in this chapter, the marquee options sport Anti-aliased and Feather options, which, respectively, soften the selection outline and make it blurry. However, the Anti-aliased check box is dimmed when you use the rectangular marquee tool. Perpendicular edges never need softening because they can't be jagged. Anti-aliasing, therefore, would be a waste of time.

Drawing from the center out

As mentioned earlier, you draw a rectangle or oval from corner to opposite corner. But you can also draw a marquee from the center outward. To do this, press Alt (Option on the Mac) as you drag with a marquee tool.

To draw a square or circle from the center outward, press both Shift and Alt (Option on the Mac) as you drag with the appropriate marquee tool. If you already have an active selection and you press Shift and Alt (Option on the Mac) before you begin dragging, you end up selecting the intersection of the two selections, as explained later.

Wielding the wand

The magic wand is even easier to use than the marquee tools. (Pretty soon, things will get so easy you won't need us at all.) But it's also the most difficult selection tool to understand and predict. To use the tool, you just click inside an image. Elements then selects the color that you clicked in the image.

'Scuze me while 1 click the sky

Figure 9-5 shows how the magic wand works. In the first image, the magic wand tool was clicked in the sky above the dinosaur. Elements automatically selected the entire continuous area of sky. In the second example, the selection was made more apparent by pressing Ctrl+Backspace (⌘+Delete on the Mac), which filled the selection with the white background color. The selection outline is gone because the selection was hidden. (Don't worry, hiding selections is explained in full, rich detail in the section "Hiding the Ants.")

Notice that the wand by default selects only uninterrupted areas of color. The patch of sky below the creature's tail, for example, remains intact. Also, the selection seeped slightly into the edges of the dinosaur. Pressing Ctrl+ Backspace (⌘+Delete on the Mac) removed very small pieces along the top of the plastic behemoth.

Teaching the wand tolerance

You can modify the performance of the magic wand by accessing the ever-popular tool options bar, which offers four basic options: Tolerance, Anti-aliased, Contiguous, and Use All Layers.

We cover Anti-aliased earlier in this chapter, in the section "Exploring your lasso options," so we're not going to beat that poor horse anymore. The Use All Layers option comes into play only when your image contains more than one layer (see Chapter 10). When Use All Layers is turned off, the magic wand selects colors on only the active layer. If you want the magic wand to select colors from all visible layers, turn the option on.

When Contiguous is active, the magic wand selects only adjacent pixels. If the option is not active, the magic wand looks throughout the entire image for any pixels in the Tolerance range.

This brings us to Tolerance, which has the most sway over the performance of the magic wand. Tolerance tells Elements which colors to select and which not to select. A lower Tolerance value instructs the wand to select fewer colors; a higher value instructs it to select more colors.

Figure 9-5:
Here's what happens when you click in the sky above the T-Rex with the magic wand (top) and fill the selection with white (bottom).

Figure 9-6 shows what we mean. Each row of images demonstrates the effect of a different Tolerance value, starting with the default value of 32 at the top and working up to 180 at the bottom. In each case, the magic wand was clicked at the same location, just to the right of the big giraffe's schnoz. The left image in each row shows the selection outline created when we clicked the magic wand; the right image shows the selection filled with white and then hidden.

Tolerance: 32

Tolerance: 90

Figure 9-6:
A Tolerance
value of 32
selected too
little sky. A
value of 180
selected all
the sky but
also got
some huge
chunks of
the giraffe's
face and
the rolling
foothill. A
value of 90
appears to
be just right.

Tolerance: 180

The problem is that finding the best Tolerance setting is a random exercise
in the frustrating art of trial and error. As with changes to any tool setting,
changes to the Tolerance value have no effect on the current selection. You

have to click with the magic wand to try out each and every new value. There's no magic here; just a whole lotta clickin' and tweakin' goin' on.

One more option affects the performance of the magic wand, but it isn't located in the magic wand's tool options bar. Guess what it is. Give up? Click the eyedropper tool to find out. The Sample Size setting determines how many pixels the eyedropper looks at when it samples a color. The default setting, Point Sample, means that the eyedropper will sample only the precise pixel on which it's clicked. However, choose 3 by 3 Average, and the eyedropper also looks 1 pixel in every direction — making for a 3-by-3 square. The eyedropper averages the colors of those 9 pixels, and that average color becomes the foreground color. Likewise, 5 by 5 Average makes the eyedropper look in a 5-by-5 square, and it averages the colors of those 25 pixels.

And here comes The Weirdest Thing About Photoshop Elements: That Sample Size option in the eyedropper's tool options bar *affects the behavior of the magic wand.* If you set the option to 3 by 3 Average and then switch to the magic wand and click, the wand's selection will be based not just on the pixel it's clicked on, but also on the 3-by-3 square of surrounding pixels. And likewise for 5 by 5 Average. Why? We don't know. It's spooky. It's weird. But it's true. And we thought you should know.

Greatness with a brush

The premise of the selection brush is simple: You paint in the image to create a selection. With the Mode menu in the tool options bar set to Selection, the selection brush uses the now-familiar marching ants to show where the selection occurs. However, switch to Mask mode and things are different. Now the selection brush paints on the image in a strange red overlay. Areas covered with the red overlay are unselected; clear areas are selected. Therefore, when in Mask mode, the selection brush becomes in effect a *de*-selection brush, masking areas of the image that you want to protect from change.

Follow along, and we'll show you what's so darned great about Mask mode:

1. **Select the elliptical marquee tool.**

2. **Set a high Feather value in the tool options bar.**

   Maybe something like 30 or so.

3. **Draw a selection.**

   Doesn't look very feathered, does it? The problem is that those marching ants have no way of demonstrating to you that a selection is feathered. They're brilliant at marching around in a 1-pixel-wide circle but lousy at conveying the soft gradual transition of a feathered edge.

4. **Select the selection brush.**

   Don't deselect your marquee selection; keep it active.

5. **In the tool options bar, switch to Mask mode and view the selection.**

   Aha! Now *there's* a feathered selection! The overlay is red where the image is totally unselected, clear where the image is totally selected, and gradual fades between red and clear in the area in-between. So when soft edges are important, the selection brush is clearly the way to go. Color Plate 5 gives full-color proof of this fact.

Let's take a look at the settings in the selection brush's tool options bar:

- ✔ **Brush menu:** You can select the type of brush you want to use for your selection from this menu. For much more about brushes, see Chapter 15.

- ✔ **Size:** You can select the size of your brush here. Scrub the word Size, type a pixel value, or click the arrow and drag the slider. However, it will probably be most convenient for you to use the [and] keys to lower and raise, respectively, the size of the brush.

- ✔ **Mode:** Switch between Selection (marching ant) mode and Mask (red overlay) mode.

- ✔ **Hardness:** This setting determines how feathered the brush selection will be. Low settings create a very soft edge; high settings create a hard edge. Experiment in Mask mode and you'll get the idea.

- ✔ **Overlay Opacity (Mask mode only):** This setting determines the transparency of the overlay. A setting of 100 percent obscures the underlying image and is probably best avoided; likewise, a setting of 0 percent makes the overlay disappear completely and is useless.

- ✔ **Overlay Color (Mask mode only):** If your underlying image has a great deal of red, it's quite possible that a red overlay isn't the wisest choice. Click the color square to access the Color Picker and choose a more contrasting color, or click the arrow adjacent to the color square to choose a color from the swatches.

One other thing you should know about the selection brush: Holding down the Alt (or Option) key makes the tool behave in the opposite manner. So, holding down Alt (or Option) in Selection mode makes the tool deselect selected areas. Holding down Alt (or Option) in Mask mode makes the selection brush paint in "clear," erasing the overlay and thereby selecting areas of the image.

Selecting everything

When no part of an image is selected, the entire image is up for grabs. You can edit any part of it by using the paint or edit tools or any of about a billion commands. But you can also make the entire image available for edits by choosing Select⇨All or pressing Ctrl+A (⌘+A on the Mac) to select everything.

Beginning to see the mystery here? If you can edit any part of the image by deselecting it, why choose Select⇨All, which also lets you edit everything? Because some operations require a selection, that's why. For instance, if you want to copy an entire photo and paste it into another image (more on copying and pasting in Chapter 10), you need to select the entire photo first.

Deselecting everything

Before we plow into all that whiz-bang, awesome stuff that Elements lets you do to a selection outline, let's touch on selection's opposite, deselection. Although this may seem at face value to be a ridiculously boneheaded topic — one that hardly merits space in a scholarly tome such as this one — deselecting is actually an integral step in the selection process.

Suppose, for example, that you select one part of your image. Then you change your mind and decide to select a different portion instead. Before you can select that new area, you have to deselect the old one. You can deselect an existing selection outline in several ways:

- ✔ Click anywhere in the image with the marquee tools or with the lasso.
- ✔ To get rid of an existing selection and create a new one at the same time, just drag or click to create the new selection as you normally would. Elements automatically deselects the old selection when you create a new one. Note that the selection brush is an exception to this rule; using the selection brush always preserves an already active selection.
- ✔ Click inside the selection with the magic wand. (If you click outside the selection, you not only deselect the selection, but also create a new selection.)
- ✔ Choose Select⇨Deselect or press Ctrl+D (⌘+D on the Mac). Choosing Select⇨Reselect or Ctrl+Shift+D (⌘+Shift+D on the Mac) regains your most recent selection. You can do this even after you've performed numerous actions.
- ✔ Click the state preceding the final state in the Undo History palette.

Saving and Loading Selections

A selection can take quite a while to perfect, and you never know when — in the minutes, hours, days, or months to come — you might just need that complicated selection again. Elements solves this dilemma by letting you save selections. The information for the selection is embedded into the code of the image, so if you close and reopen the image, you can still load the selection.

To give this a try, make a selection and choose Select⇨Save Selection. The only option available is to give your selection a name; after you do this, click OK. Go ahead and deselect your selection — heck, go ahead and close the image entirely, saving changes. Reopen the image, and now choose Select⇨ Load Selection. The name of your saved selection is visible in the Selection menu; go ahead and click OK, and voila! There's your old selection. Pretty neat, huh?

The other Save Selection options come into play when you're dealing with multiple selections. If you choose Save Selection when you already have a selection saved, choosing the name of a selection in the Selection menu (rather than choosing New) means that you want to overwrite that selection. The Operation options give you four choices for combining your new selection with the old one. You can replace the old selection, add the new and old selections together, subtract the new selection from the old one, or keep only the intersection of the two selections.

When you loaded your selection a couple of paragraphs ago, you probably noticed the Invert check box. Selecting this check box inverts the selection before it loads, so what was selected becomes deselected, and vice versa. Load Selection also lets you use the Selection menu to choose the saved selection you want to load. The Operation options function just like the ones in the Save Selection dialog box, letting you determine how the loaded selection should interact with any other currently active selections in the document.

And finally, choosing Select⇨Delete Selection lets you select a selection to delete from the Selection menu. Whew.

Hiding the Ants

In the View menu, you'll find the Selection command. The Selection command hides the "marching ants" of the active selection outline. This makes it much easier to see what you're doing as you work, particularly around the edges of the selection; those distracting ants turn invisible. Note, however, that this is not the same thing as deselecting the selection. When you choose View⇨ Selection, the selection is still active; the visible evidence of the active selection (the marching ants) has just become invisible. Choose the command again to make the selection visible.

As with all subsequent editions, the final chapter of the first edition of *Photoshop Elements For Dummies* was entitled "Ten Reasons You Might Possibly Want to Upgrade to Photoshop One Day." The number one reason we gave was the keyboard shortcut Ctrl+H (⌘+H on the Mac), which hides selections in Photoshop. Lo and behold, version 2 of Elements came along, and Adobe had given Elements users this shortcut. So in *Photoshop Elements 2 For Dummies,* we chose Photoshop's healing brush as our top most-desired

Photoshop tool. We asked for it — you got it! This new version of Elements has not one but *two* healing brushes at your disposal. Clearly, Adobe is hanging on our every word, and we are awestruck by our power. So Adobe, for Elements' next version, here's what we want: cash in the box! An instant $50 rebate! Don't let us down.

Although hiding selection outlines is a crucial tool, it also leads to the number one most common mistake while working with Elements. You'll make a selection, press Ctrl+H (or ⌘+H on the Mac) to hide the selection, work inside your selection without distraction, and then move to working outside the selection — and nothing will happen. You won't be able to edit your image where you want. You'll get annoyed, start to fume, decide that the problem is that you're just not pressing on your mouse HARD ENOUGH — and then become convinced that Elements and your computer are plotting against you. Just take a deep breath, calmly ask yourself, "Did I hide my selection outline?"; answer yourself, "Yes, as a matter of fact, I did"; and then press Ctrl+D (⌘+D on the Mac). All is well.

Editing Selections

The first selection outline you create is almost never perfect. Whether you use a lasso, a marquee tool, the magic wand, or the selection brush, there's almost always some problem with the selection. Maybe you didn't get the hair selected right, or a finger is clipped off. Whatever the problem, you can remedy it by adding to the selection outline or by subtracting from it.

Adding to and subtracting from a selection

When you've made a selection with a lasso, a marquee tool, or the magic wand and you then want to add onto it or take away from it with the selection brush, it's a no-brainer. The selection brush always respects previous selections and doesn't automatically wipe them out when you use it. And regardless of your Mode setting, you can always switch the behavior of the selection brush by holding down the Alt key (Option key on the Mac).

However, if you want to use a lasso, a marquee tool, or the magic wand to add to or take away from a previous selection, it's a different matter. The four selection modifier icons in the tool options bar, as pictured in Figure 9-7, enable you to make a new selection, add to a selection, subtract from a selection, or intersect a selection. Simply click your desired selection modifier icon and then drag. For instance, if you've made a rectangular selection with the rectangular marquee tool and you also need to make a circular selection, first switch to the elliptical marquee. Click the second selection modifier icon, add to selection. Now when you drag out your circular selection, the rectangular selection won't disappear; instead, the circular selection will be added to it.

Figure 9-7:
The four
selection
modifier
icons in the
tool options
bar let you
modify your
existing
selection.

New selection   Subtract from selection

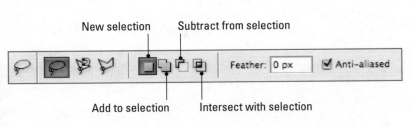

Add to selection   Intersect with selection

It's also possible — and probably more convenient after you get up to speed with Elements — to modify selections using the keyboard. If you do use the keyboard, the selection modifier icons automatically become active when you press the appropriate keys anyway.

To add an area to the current selection, Shift+drag with a lasso or marquee tool, or Shift+click with the magic wand. It doesn't matter which tool you used to select with previously, nor does it matter whether you Shift+click inside or outside the selection.

For example, if you want to select the sky in a photo similar to the one in Figure 9-8, first select the top part of the sky by clicking it with the magic wand, as shown in the top example. To add the other areas to the selection, press the Shift key and click those areas with the magic wand as well, creating the selection outlines shown in the bottom example. To remove an area from a selection, Alt+drag (Option+drag on the Mac) with a lasso or marquee tool or Alt+click (Option+click on the Mac) with the magic wand.

When you're adding to a selection, a little plus sign appears next to your cursor. When you're subtracting from the selection, a little minus sign appears. And when you're selecting the intersection of two selections (as explained next), a little multiplication sign appears. See, your math teacher was right — knowing arithmetic comes in handy in all kinds of situations.

Intersecting a selection with a selection

If you press the Shift and Alt (Option on the Mac) keys together while clicking with the magic wand or dragging with a lasso or marquee tool, you select the intersection of the previous selection and the new one. Confused? Let's see whether a picture can be worth at least those 39 words. Take a look at Figure 9-9. If you first drag around the black rectangle, then Shift+Alt+drag

(Shift+Option+drag on the Mac) around the gray rectangle, you get the inter-section of the two rectangles. Elements selects all portions of the second marquee that fall inside the first marquee and deselects everything else, leaving the selection shown in the right half of the figure. That's an *intersection*.

Figure 9-8:
To select all areas of the sky, you can first select just the top (first image), and then press the Shift key and click the other areas with the magic wand to select them, too (second image).

Figure 9-9:
Holding
down
Shift+Alt
(Shift+
Option on
the Mac)
when you
drag around
the gray
rectangle
(left) results
in the
intersection
of two
selections
(right).

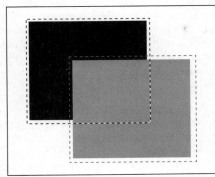 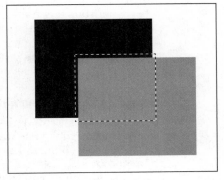

Avoiding keyboard collisions

You can use the lasso and marquee tools in a variety of ways while pressing keys. Pressing Alt (Option on the Mac) while using one of the lasso tools, you may recall, temporarily accesses one of the other lasso tools. Pressing Shift while using a marquee tool results in perfect squares and circles.

But what happens when you start combining those shortcut keys with all the add, subtract, and intersect shortcut keys we've just talked about? We touched on this topic briefly earlier, but the following list should answer your most burning questions:

✔ As previously noted, to add a square or circular area to an existing selection, start by Shift+dragging with the appropriate marquee tool. You get an unconstrained rectangle or oval, just as though the Shift key weren't down. Then midway into the drag — here's the catch — release the Shift key and then press it again, all the while keeping the mouse button down. The shape snaps to a square or circle with the second press of Shift. Keep the Shift key down until after you release the mouse button.

✔ Pressing Alt (Option on the Mac) to temporarily access the polygonal lasso when the regular lasso is active causes trouble when you have an existing selection. This is because pressing Alt (or Option) in that scenario sets you up to subtract from the selection. So, if you want to add or subtract a straight-sided selection, use the polygonal lasso — don't try to Alt+click (Option+click on the Mac) with the regular lasso.

Automatic selection shifters

Shift+dragging, Alt+dragging (Option+dragging on the Mac), and all those other wondrous techniques are wildly helpful when it comes to selecting complex details. But they aren't the only selection modifications you can make. Elements offers a handful of automatic functions that reshape selection outlines, blur them, and otherwise mess them up. All the commands discussed in the next few sections reside on the Select menu.

Extending the magic wand

Two commands, Grow and Similar, are extensions of the magic wand tool. (For details on the magic wand, see "Wielding the wand," earlier in this chapter.) The Grow command expands the size of the selection to include still more continuous colors. For example, if clicking with the magic wand doesn't select all the colors you want it to, you can either increase the Tolerance value in the tool options bar and reclick with the tool, or just choose Select⇨Grow to incorporate even more colors. It's kind of a clunky method, especially because the Grow command doesn't have a keyboard shortcut. You'll usually get better results if you Shift+click with the wand tool, but every once in a while, the Grow command works as you want. (You can use the Grow command also with selections made with tools other than the magic wand, by the way.)

The Similar command selects all colors that are similar to the selected colors, regardless of whether they're interrupted by other colors. In other words, Similar selects all the contiguous colors that Grow selects, as well as all similarly colored pixels throughout the image.

Both Grow and Similar judge color similarity exactly as the magic wand tool does — that is, according to the Tolerance value in the tool options bar. So, if you increase the Tolerance value, the commands select more colors; if you decrease the value, the commands select fewer colors. For example, if you want to select all colors throughout the image that are exactly identical to the ones you've selected so far, enter 0 in the Tolerance option box, and choose Select⇨Similar.

Swapping what's selected for what's not

Sometimes it's easier to select the stuff you don't want to select and then tell Elements to select the deselected stuff and to deselect what's selected. (It's certainly easier to *do* this than to *write* it.) This technique is called *inversing a selection,* and you do it by choosing Select⇨Inverse or pressing Ctrl+Shift+I (⌘+Shift+I on the Mac).

For example, suppose that you want to select the clock tower shown on the left side of Figure 9-10. A typical work of baroque madness, this building has more spikes and little twisty bits than a porcupine. Therefore, selecting it would prove a nightmare.

Figure 9-10:
This building (left) is too darned ornate to select easily, but it's a snap to select the sky and then inverse the selection. Filling the selection with white (right) shows how accurate the selection is.

Selecting the sky, on the other hand, is quite easy. By clicking and Shift+ clicking a couple of times with the magic wand tool (set here to the default Tolerance of 32), you can select the entire sky in a matter of two or three seconds. Then choose Select⇨Inverse to invert the selection so that the building is selected and the sky is deselected. To better show off the selection, it's filled with white in the example on the right, and the selection is hidden. The second example of Figure 9-8 is primed for this technique as well; if we inversed that selection, the arch would be selected and the sky deselected.

Making the selection fuzzy around the edges

You can blur the edges of a selection you're going to create with the lasso or marquee tools by increasing the Feather value in the corresponding tool options bar. But more often than not, you want to leave the Feather value set to 0 and apply your feathering after you finish drawing the outline.

To feather an existing selection, choose Select⇨Feather or press Ctrl+Alt+D (⌘+Option+D on the Mac). In the dialog box that appears, enter the amount of fuzziness, in pixels, that you want to apply to the selection and press Enter (Return on the Mac). The selection outline probably won't change very much — as we noted before, marching ants are useless for demonstrating a feathered selection — but you can always pop over to the selection brush and take a gander at the selection in Mask mode to see the results.

You can use feathering to make an image appear to fade into view. For example, take a look at the winsome example on the right side of Figure 9-11. If you want to pull off the same effect, first encircle the little charmer with the elliptical marquee tool. Then choose Select⇨Inverse to select the background instead and choose Select⇨Feather; we used a value of 15 pixels here. Finally, use Ctrl+Backspace (⌘+Delete on the Mac) to fill the selection with white. The result should look something like a locket photo with fuzzy edges, as shown on the right side of Figure 9-11. This effect is also possible using the Vignette choice from the Frames category of Effects in the Styles and Effects palette (see Chapter 18 for more information on Effects).

Figure 9-11: A well-dressed lad (left) receives a classic vignette treatment (right).

Using Border, Smooth, and the rest

The remaining selection outline modifiers, found in the Select⇨Modify submenu, aren't quite as useful, but they do come in handy every now and then:

- ✔ The Border command selects an area around the edge of the selection. You tell Elements the width, in pixels, of the border you want to select. This command is probably the least useful command of the bunch. If you want to color the outline of a selection, it's easier to use stroking. (See Chapter 16 for more on stroking.)

✔ Smooth rounds off the corners of a selection outline. If the selection is very irregular and you want to straighten the twists and turns, use the Smooth command. You can enter a value from 1 to 100 to tell Elements how far it can move any point in the outline. Start with 2 or 3 to be safe.

✔ If you want to increase the size of a selection a few pixels outward, choose Expand and enter the number of pixels. The maximum value is 100 pixels; if you want to expand the outline farther, you have to choose Expand a second time.

✔ Contract is the opposite of the Expand command. This command shrinks the selected area by 1 to 100 pixels all the way around.

Moving selection outlines

To move a selection outline without moving the image inside it, select a tool other than the Move or Crop tool and nudge the selection outline with the arrow keys. You can also drag the selection outline if you choose one of the selection tools and position it within the outline. This is a great way to reposition a selection outline without disturbing so much as a single pixel in the image.

o collapsing layers, changing PSD's to JPG's sharpening, resizing

figure out ↗

Chapter 10

Fifty Ways to Love Your Layer

In This Chapter

▶ Combining images

▶ Working with layers

▶ Locking layers for safety

▶ Moving and cloning selections

▶ Applying transformations to layers and selections

Insofar as "high art" is concerned, the heyday for surrealism was 70 to 80 years ago. But the problem with guys such as Max Ernst, René Magritte, and even Salvador Dalí was that they never got around to learning how to use Photoshop Elements. Oh, sure, they were long dead by the time Elements debuted. But still, think of what they could have done with Elements' layers. A paintbrush is great, but it pales when compared to Elements as a means for merging photo-realistic images to create flat-out impossible visual scenarios.

Color Plate 6 provides ample evidence. No matter how hard you worked at it, you could never assemble these subjects in a photo shoot. If you had talent streaming like fire-hydrant jets out your ears, you might be able to paint the image, but most of us would have thrown in the towel before we even began.

Because it may be difficult to distinguish every one of the eight images in Color Plate 6, we show each layer individually in Color Plate 7. The arrows indicate the order in which the layers are stacked on top of each other. For example, the grinning gremlin in the lower-right corner of Color Plate 7 lies at the bottom of the composition in Color Plate 6; the butterfly in the upper-left corner of Color Plate 7 rests at the top of Color Plate 6. The image in Color Plate 6 appears as if you cut out and pasted a picture of the gremlin onto a page, pasted the boat on the gremlin, pasted the tops of the two guys' heads in front of the boat, and so on.

This is the point at which you ask, "Yeah, yeah, yeah, but how in the world do I begin to pull off something like that?" Well, wouldn't you know it — that's what this chapter is all about. And, remarkably, it's all a lot easier than you may think.

Pasting Images Together

Let's use another couple of fishy images as an example. Suppose that you want to paste the fish image on the left of Figure 10-1 into the neighboring kelp image. How do you go about it? Here's one approach:

1. **Open the fish image and select the fish.**

   To find out about selections, refer to Chapter 9.

2. **Choose Edit⇨Copy or press Ctrl+C (⌘+C on the Mac).**

   Copying places a copy of your selection onto the clipboard. The *clipboard* is a temporary storage area for image data. The fish displaces any previous occupant of the clipboard (sent there by Edit⇨Copy or its close cousin, Edit⇨Cut).

3. **Open the kelp image.**

4. **Choose Edit⇨Paste or press Ctrl+V (⌘+V on the Mac).**

   Pasting dumps the current contents of the clipboard into your image. The original fish image remains intact because the fish you pasted into the kelp was merely a copy.

But these steps aren't the only way to combine images. You also have these options at your disposal:

- ✔ To cut a selection from one image and paste it into another, choose Edit⇨Cut or press Ctrl+X (⌘+X on the Mac). Then switch to the other image and choose Edit⇨Paste. The selection is removed entirely from the first image and planted in the second.

- ✔ Simplest of all, you can clone a selection between images by dragging it with the move tool or Ctrl+dragging (⌘+dragging on the Mac) it with most other tools.

  This method of cloning between images is known in the computer world as *dragging and dropping,* by the way.

- ✔ The Copy command copies the contents of the selection from only the currently selected layer. To copy from all layers in the image, choose Edit⇨Copy Merged.

- ✔ For a weird but occasionally useful trick, choose Edit⇨Paste Into Selection to paste an image in an existing selection, as described in the upcoming section "Filling a selection with a selection."

Whether you use the Paste command or drag and drop a selection from one image to another, Elements places the pasted image on a new layer. For details, turn to the section "Excuse Me, but What's a Layer?"

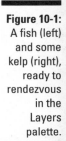

Figure 10-1:
A fish (left)
and some
kelp (right),
ready to
rendezvous
in the
Layers
palette.

Filling a selection with a selection

The Edit➪Paste Into Selection command lets you insert an image into an existing selection outline. For example, suppose you want to paste the fish behind some of the vegetation in the neighboring kelp image so that the fish would appear to be intertwined with its environment. As shown in the first example of Figure 10-2, select an area inside the kelp stalks and feather the selection by choosing Select➪Feather. Then choose Paste Into Selection or Ctrl+Shift+V (⌘+Shift+V on the Mac) to create the fish-inside-the-kelp shown in the second example. (Note that the selection has been deselected in the second example so that you can better see the transitions between fish and stalks.) Elements pastes the selection into the currently selected layer.

Resizing an image to match its new home

When you bring two images together, you always have to deal with the issue of relative size. Suppose that the fish image is much larger than the kelp image. Here's how to ensure that the two images you want to combine are sized correctly:

1. **Magnify the two images to the same zoom factor.**

   To see them side by side, a zoom ratio of 50% or smaller may be necessary.

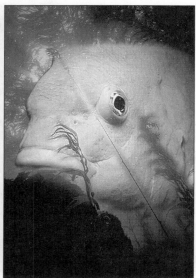

Figure 10-2:
After selecting an area of kelp (left), use the Paste Into Selection command to introduce the fish to his new kelpy home (right).

2. **If either of the two images appears disproportionately large, scale it down by choosing Image⇨Resize⇨Image Size.**

In this case, you don't care at about the document size or resolution of the image; all you care about is the pixel dimensions — that is, the number of pixels that make up the image. If the image you want to copy or drag (the fish) is too large, scale it down just enough to fit inside the destination image. If the destination image (the kelp) is too large, reduce it as desired. Don't forget about Ctrl+Z (⌘+Z on the Mac) in case you accidentally go too far. (See Chapter 4 for more information about the Image Size command.)

Be careful not to overreduce! Remember that you're throwing away pixels and, therefore, sacrificing detail. Err on the side of keeping the image a little bit too big. If you go too far, you can always restore the original by choosing Edit⇨Revert to Saved, or by undoing your steps using the Undo History palette, as discussed in Chapter 8.

3. **Combine the two images.**

Copy and paste or drag and drop — it's your call.

4. **Position the image more or less where you want it.**

5. **Choose Image⇨Resize⇨Scale.**

A marquee with four corner handles surrounds the image; this is known as the *transform box*. This command lets you fine-tune the relative size of the imported image with respect to its new home. (More on this command at the end of the chapter, in the section "Using the transform tool.")

6. **Drag a corner handle to scale the image.**

   Shift+drag a handle to scale the image proportionally, as the first example in Figure 10-3 illustrates. After you release the handle, Elements previews how the resized image will look. Don't worry if the preview is a little choppy; the scaled image will be smooth.

   For the best results, don't scale the image up; only scale it down. Otherwise, Elements has to make up pixels, and it's best to avoid that if possible.

7. **Move your cursor inside the transform box and double-click.**

   After you resize the image as desired — you can drag the corner handles all you want — move your cursor inside the box. Double-click or press Enter (Return on the Mac) to accept the image's new size and tell Elements to work its magic. You can also click the commit icon (the check mark icon) at the end of the tool options bar. The resized image will appear perfectly smooth.

Figure 10-3: Use the Scale command to refine the image size.

Excuse Me, but What's a Layer?

Here's a little analogy to get things rolling. Imagine that you have three sheets of acetate — you know, that stuff folks used to slide into overhead projectors to bore audiences before they started using multimedia presentations to bore them. Anyway, you draw a fish on one sheet, a fishbowl on the second, and a table on the third. When you stack all the sheets on top of each other, the images blend to create a seamless view of a fish in a bowl on a table. (This is the way cel animation works, if that means anything to you.)

Layers in Elements work just like that. You can keep different parts of your image on separate layers and then combine the layers to create a composite image. You can rearrange layers, add and delete layers, blend them using different opacity values and blend modes, and do all sorts of other impressive things. And as we mentioned earlier, when you drag and drop between images or use the Paste command, you're creating a new layer. You aren't restricted to the layers that Elements creates automatically, however. You can create as many new layers as your computer's memory allows.

Another advantage of using layers is that you can edit or paint on one layer without affecting the other layers. That means you can safely apply commands or painting tools to one portion of your image without worrying about messing up the rest of the image — or without bothering to first select the part you want to edit.

Finding your way around the Layers palette

The Layers palette, shown in Figure 10-4, is Grand Central Station for managing layers. Here's what you need to know to navigate the Layers palette:

- ✔ The background is the bottom layer in the image. Every image has a background (unless the background has been deleted or turned into a regular layer — read on to see how).

- ✔ The order of the layers in the Layers palette represents their order in the image. The top layer in the palette is the front layer in your image, and so on.

- ✔ You can make edits to only one layer at a time — the active layer. The *active layer* is highlighted in the Layers palette and has a little brush icon to the left of its layer name. To make another layer active, just click its name.

- ✔ Press Alt+] (right bracket) — Option+] on the Mac — to move up one layer; press Alt+[(left bracket) — Option+[on the Mac — to activate the next layer down. Press Shift+Alt+] (Shift+Option+] on the Mac) to move to the top layer; press Shift+Alt+[(Shift+Option+[on the Mac) to move to the background or bottom layer.

- ✔ An eyeball icon next to a layer name means that the layer is visible. To hide the layer, click the eyeball. To display the layer, click where the eyeball was to bring it back.

Create adjustment layer

Lock transparent pixels

Create a new layer | Delete layer | Lock all | Active layer

More menu

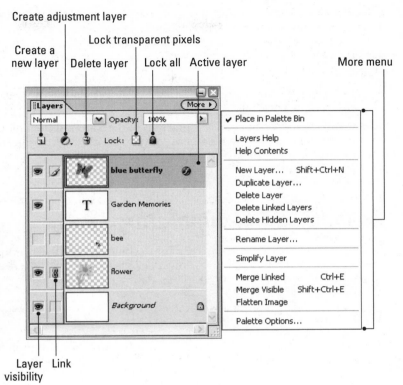

Figure 10-4:
The Layers palette is key to managing your layers.

Layer visibility | Link

✔ To hide all layers but one, Alt+click (Option+click on the Mac) on the eyeball in front of the name of the layer you want to see. Alt+click (Option+click on the Mac) again to redisplay all the layers.

✔ If you hide the background layer, you see a checkerboard pattern wherever the background would have shown through the layers. The checkerboard represents the transparent areas of the visible layers.

✔ This gray and white checkerboard can be customized in the Transparency section of Preferences. You can specify the size and color of the squares that Elements uses to represent transparency.

✔ To find out how to use the blending mode pop-up menu and the Opacity setting at the top of the palette, refer to Chapter 14.

✔ To create a new, blank layer, click the create new layer icon (refer to Figure 10-4). If you hold down Alt (Option on the Mac) when you click, you'll get a dialog box where you can name your layer. To create a duplicate of an existing layer, drag the layer to the create new layer icon.

When you simply click the create new layer icon, Elements gives the layer a generic name such as Layer 1. If you want to name the layer later, double-click the layer name in the Layers palette and type a new name in the highlighted field.

✔ To delete a layer, select it and click the trash icon, or just drag the layer to the trash icon. Be aware that you're throwing away the layer along with the image on it.

✔ If you ever want to create a selection outline around the objects on a layer, Elements gives you an easy way to do it. Just Ctrl+click (⌘+click on the Mac) on the layer in the Layers palette. For more on selections, see Chapter 9.

Moving and manipulating layers

Layers are flexible things — you can move them, shuffle their order, and rearrange them as though they were a deck of playing cards. Here's a look at some of the more common layer manipulation moves you may need to make:

✔ To move a layer, drag it with the move tool. To move the layer in 1-pixel increments, select the move tool and tap an arrow key. To move the layer in 10-pixel increments, press Shift as you tap the arrow key.

✔ Check the Auto select layer check box in the tool options bar to switch to a layer when you click with the move tool on any nontransparent part of that layer.

The Auto select layer option has a drawback, in that it makes it very easy to switch layers when you don't want to.

✔ The Show bounding box option, which also appears in the tool options bar when the move tool is active and is switched on by default, surrounds the contents of the layer (or the selection) with a box with handles. This box lets you transform a layer without choosing a command. (For more on transformations, see "Transforming Layers and Selections," later in this chapter.)

✔ To link an active layer to another layer, click the second column of the Layers palette — just to the right of the eyeball icon — next to the layer that's not active. A link icon appears in the column. Now you can move, scale, and rotate both layers simultaneously. To unlink the layers, click the link icon.

✔ To delete linked layers in one fell swoop, select one of the layers in the group, and Ctrl+click (⌘+click on the Mac) the trash icon in the Layers palette.

✔ If you right-click (Control+click on the Mac) an object in the image with the move tool selected, Elements presents you with a little pop-up menu, which lists every layer that contains pixels at the precise point where you clicked. From the menu, you can select the layer you want to make active. You can also activate the Auto select layer option on the fly if you want. With the move tool selected, Alt+right-click (Control+Option+click on the Mac); Elements automatically activates the appropriate layer. Again, throw the Ctrl key (the ⌘ key on the Mac) into the mix when you have a tool other than the move tool selected. (This works for most but not all tools.)

✔ After you have a few layers in your image, you can move one in front of or behind another by dragging it up or down in the list of layers in the Layers palette. As you are dragging, a black line shows where the layer will be inserted. You can't reorder the background or move any layer below the background until you convert it to a layer. To convert, choose Layer➪New➪Layer from Background. Or just double-click the background in the Layers palette, type a name for the layer, and press Enter (Return on the Mac).

✔ When there's no background layer and you want to convert an active layer to the background layer, choose Layer➪New➪Background from Layer. Elements will make the conversion, moving the selected layer to the bottom of the stack if it wasn't already there.

✔ Another way to rearrange layers is to use the commands in the Layer➪ Arrange submenu. Click the layer that you want to move in the Layers palette. Then do one of the following:

- Choose Bring to Front (Shift+Ctrl+]/Shift+⌘+]) to make the layer the topmost layer.

- Choose Bring Forward (Ctrl+]/⌘+]) to move the layer up one level.

- Choose Send Backward (Ctrl+[/⌘+[) to move the layer down one level.

- Choose Send to Back (Shift+Ctrl+[/Shift+⌘+[) to move the layer to just above the background layer.

✔ You can copy an entire layer to a new image by selecting the layer in the Layers palette and dragging and dropping the layer into the new image. The layer drops at the spot where you release the mouse button and resides one layer above the formerly active layer in the new image.

Flattening and merging layers

Layers are fun, but they do come at a price. If an image contains layers, saving it in any format other than PSD (Elements' native format), PDF, or TIFF merges all the layers into one. Every layer you add also makes your file size grow, which can slow down Elements. If your computer is getting a little long in the tooth, it's best to juggle as few layers at a time as possible. When things get out of control, operations can slow to a snail's pace, and that's an insult to the snail. Here are your merging options:

- ✔ To merge several layers into one, hide all layers except the ones you want to merge. In other words, in the Layers palette, an eyeball icon should appear next to the names of each layer you want to merge. Hide the eyeball if you don't want to merge the layer. Then choose Merge Visible from the More menu or from the Layer menu at the top of the screen. Or, even simpler, press Shift+Ctrl+E (Shift+⌘+E on the Mac).

- ✔ You can merge one layer with other layers to which it has been linked. Choose Merge Linked from the More menu or from the Layer menu. Easier yet, press Ctrl+E (⌘+E on the Mac). Note that the Merge Linked command changes to the Merge Down command if you have no linked layers selected. Merge Down merges your selected layer with the layer residing below it.

- ✔ If you want to flatten the entire image and get rid of all the layers, choose the Flatten Image command from the More menu or from the Layer menu.

Locking Layers

In the last chapter, we talked about creating selections to limit the active working area. For instance, you can paint inside a selection outline to make sure you leave the surrounding areas untouched. But when you send a selection to a layer, the selection outline disappears. So how do you paint only inside the image on a layer? For example, maybe you want to paint stripes on an object on a layer without going outside the edges.

One solution is to click the lock transparent pixels icon near the top of the Layers palette, as shown in Figure 10-4. The transparent areas around the object stay transparent, letting you paint only inside the opaque and translucent pixels. For a quick way to turn the lock transparent pixels icon on and off, press the forward slash key (/).

Clicking the adjacent lock all icon prevents you from painting, editing, moving, or transforming your layer. (But you can still make selections.)

Moving and Cloning Selections

Chapter 9 looks at moving a selection outline without moving the contents of the selection. Now that you have a working knowledge of layers, let's look at the related topic of moving selections *along with* the pixels they contain:

✔ To move a selection, grab the move tool (press V to select the tool from the keyboard) and drag. A bounding box appears around the selection to show that you're about to move it from its current home, and the move tool sprouts a little pair of scissors. When you move a selection on the background layer, the area where the selection used to be is filled with the background color, as shown in Figure 10-5.

Figure 10-5:
After selecting the Washington Monument (top), it's dragged to a more convenient location (bottom).

- You can temporarily access the move tool by pressing Ctrl (⌘ on the Mac) when most other tools are selected.

- Moving a selection with the keyboard is just like moving the entire contents of a layer, as described earlier. To nudge a selection 1 pixel, press one of the arrow keys while the move tool is selected. Or press Ctrl (⌘ on the Mac) and an arrow key when any tool other than the hand or shape tool is selected. The up arrow nudges the selection 1 pixel up; the right arrow nudges it to the right, and so on, just as you'd think. To nudge a selection 10 pixels, press Shift along with an arrow key while the move tool is selected.

- To clone and move a selection, Alt+drag (Option+drag on the Mac) with the move tool or Ctrl+Alt+drag (⌘+Option+drag on the Mac) with any tool other than the hand or shape tool.

- To clone and nudge, select the move tool and then press Alt (Option on the Mac) and one of the arrow keys. Or, when most other tools are selected, press Ctrl+Alt (⌘+Option on the Mac) as you press the arrow keys. Add Shift to clone the selection and move it 10 pixels.

- You can move and clone selections between two different images as well. Just drag the selection from its current window into the other image window.

Transforming Layers and Selections

The end of Chapter 4 looks at commands that can flip and rotate the entire canvas. Now let's take a look at the related subject of transforming. In Elements parlance, *transforming* means spinning, stretching, and generally distorting. Technically, even moving is transforming. You can transform a layer or selection when it's surrounded by a bounding box, such as the bounding box that appears by default when you select the move tool. You can drag from the square handles of the bounding box to transform the layer or selection.

Using the Image menu's commands

The Image menu has three submenus that contain transforming commands: Rotate, Transform, and Resize. The Rotate submenu has the Free Rotate Layer/ Free Rotate Selection command (along with other commands that mirror the ones covered in Chapter 4). The Transform submenu has four transforming commands, and the bottom of the Resize submenu has the Scale command.

These commands work with or without selections. If there's no selection, the commands work on the entire layer. If there's an active selection, the commands affect only the selected area. The only exception to this is the background layer, which must have an active selection to be transformed. If you try to transform the entire background layer, you'll get a message asking you whether you first want to change the background into a full-fledged, first-class layer.

Using the transform tool

There's a secret tool hiding inside Elements that's nowhere to be found in the toolbox: the transform tool. Just choose one of the transforming commands or drag a handle of the move tool's bounding box, and the transform tool's mysterious icon appears on the far left of the tool options bar (see Figure 10-6), exactly where you'd see, say, the zoom tool icon if you had that tool selected. This implementation in Elements is somewhat confusing; you can manipulate your transformation using the tool options bar, or you can freely choose from among the transforming commands under the Image menu. The latter option is by far the easiest, so let's take a closer look at the relevant commands:

- ✔ **Free Rotate Layer/Free Rotate Selection:** This command changes depending on whether there's an active selection. The command is a scaled-back version of the free transform tool, which allows you to only rotate and move the selection. Move the cursor toward the edge of or outside the selection to rotate; move the cursor toward the center to move the selection.

- ✔ **Free Transform:** This option allows you to scale, move, and rotate the selection. You can invoke Free Transform from the keyboard by pressing Ctrl+T (⌘+T on the Mac).

- ✔ **Skew:** Skew permits distortion on a given axis.

- ✔ **Distort:** Distort enables handles to move independently with no axis restrictions.

- ✔ **Perspective:** When you choose this command, dragging a corner handle makes the opposite corner handle on the same side move as well.

- ✔ **Scale:** Drag any handle to scale your selection. Press Shift+drag to maintain proportions. Press Alt+drag (Option+drag on the Mac) to scale from the center point outward. (This behavior is similar to that of the crop tool, as covered in Chapter 4.)

The most useful control found in the tool options bar is the reference point location option (the first option on the left). This sets the point around which the transformation happens and is especially useful when rotating the selection. Click in one of the white squares to move the transformation point.

Figure 10-6:
The tool
options bar
for the
stealthy
transform
tool.

Ending your transformation

After you finish transforming, press Enter (Return on the Mac), double-click inside the transform box, or click the commit (check mark) icon in the tool options bar. To cancel, press Esc or Ctrl+period (⌘+period on the Mac), or click the cancel icon (the "no" icon).

You have many more options available in the Layers palette — blend modes, text layers, adjustment layers, shape layers, fill layers — but we thought it was important to give you a basic introduction to the Layers palette relatively early in the book. Don't worry: We peel away the many layers of the Layers palette as we proceed.

Part III
Realer Than Life

In this part . . .

Photographs are supposed to be little records of a moment in time, right? Sure, it can be a drag to stop whatever fun you're having and smile for the camera. But in the back of your mind you know it's going to be worth it down the road. You can just imagine yourself in the twilight of your years, reflecting on those halcyon days of yore (whatever that means). Was the sky really that blue? Was your face really that wrinkle-free? Was life ever really that brilliantly in focus?

If now, in the prime of your youth (did we lose anyone there?), you give your photos a working over with Photoshop Elements, the answers to those questions will be no, no, and no. You see, Elements has a phalanx of tools designed to make your images look better than they ever did in real life. And we're not just talking about eliminating a case of flash-induced red eye — although Elements can certainly do that. Elements can dig deep within the shadows and find hidden details, take a gray sky and make it blue, and soften those wrinkles with no surgery required.

The three chapters in this part tell you how to use Elements to make your images look better — "realer" than life, if you will. Although doing this to your photos now might give you a glorified sense of the past in your later years, there will be an easy remedy. Just take your 54-megapixel digital camera, snap a photo, import it into your 5 googolhertz computer, give it a workout using Photoshop Elements Version 36.0, and compare with your old photos. With all the advancements in technology, you'll be able to make the new reality look much better than the old reality ever could.

Chapter 11

The Midas Retouch

*I*f you've ever scanned an image, you know the story. You start with a lovely photograph that you've cherished all your life, gingerly place it in your scanner, and the scan ends up looking like someone stuck it inside a dryer's lint trap. Big, gnarly hairs wiggle across the image. Little dust flecks seem to have reproduced like rabbits. And if you really hit the jackpot, you may even spy a few fingerprints on your image. It's enough to make you clean the house, shave the cats, and have your fingerprints sanded off.

Ultimately, that won't get you anywhere. But the retouching tools discussed in this chapter are just the thing to scrub away imperfections from the image or its subject, and make the final result appear absolutely spotless. Elements offers several retouching tools, shown in Figure 11-1:

✔ The clone stamp tool lets you copy portions of an image to cover up other portions. Using this tool is labor intensive, but the results can be downright miraculous.

✔ Um . . . what's better than miraculous? The healing brush, that's what. The clone stamp is still the champ for some forms of retouching, but when it comes to removing imperfections such as blemishes, the new healing brush and its companion, the spot healing brush, can out-clone stamp the clone stamp.

✔ The new red eye removal tool makes it easier than ever to remove that demonic flash-induced glow from your subjects' eyes.

We start this chapter with a look at filters, a collection of commands that can do amazing things for cleaning up your images (and that's just for starters).

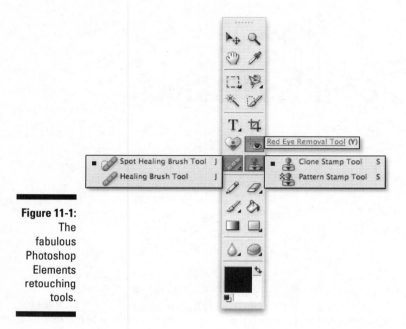

Red Eye Removal Tool (Y)

Spot Healing Brush Tool   J   Clone Stamp Tool   S

Healing Brush Tool   J   Pattern Stamp Tool   S

Figure 11-1:
The
fabulous
Photoshop
Elements
retouching
tools.

Introducing Filters

If you are a photographer or have at least taken a photography course or two, you know how photographic filters work. They refine or refract light to modify the image as it comes into the camera. But real-life filters present some problems, chiefly that you have to decide which filter you want to use before shooting the photo. It's difficult to experiment through a viewfinder, and whatever decision you make is permanent. If you go with a fish-eye lens, for example, you can't go back and "undistort" the image later.

The filters in Elements are another story:

- All filters reside in a single palette (called the Styles and Effects palette).
- You can undo a filter if you don't like the results.
- You can preview the outcome of almost every filter.
- You can apply several filters in a row and even go back and revisit a single filter multiple times.
- Most Elements filters have no real-world counterparts, which means that you can modify images in ways that aren't possible inside a camera.

If you're a professional photographer, you may want to forgo a few of your camera's filters and take up Elements' filters instead. Granted, you may still want to use corrective lenses to adjust color and keep out reflected light, but avoid a special-effects filter that makes the image look like more than what your eyes can see. Such filters merely limit the range of effects you can apply later in Elements.

And if you aren't a photographer, filters open up a range of opportunities that no other Elements function quite matches. Filters can make changes automatically, so there's no need to be an artist (although an artistic vision certainly comes in handy). Filters can make poor images look better and good images look fantastic. And you can use them to introduce special effects, such as camera movement and relief textures. Frankly, filters turn Elements into a lean, mean, photo-munching machine.

Applying filters

You have three basic ways to apply Elements' filters: the Filter menu, the Filters category of the Styles and Effects palette, and the new Filter Gallery. In the Filter menu, all filters are grouped into submenus; in the Styles and Effects palette and Filter Gallery, filters are grouped into categories. Most filters present a dialog box that lets you tweak various aspects of the filter.

A few filters in the Filter menu aren't available in the Styles and Effects palette. None of the filters from the Filter menu's Adjustments submenu (Equalize, Gradient Map, Invert, Posterize, Threshold, and Photo Filter) are accessible in the palette. Also missing are Average (from the Blur submenu), Displace (from Distort), Fibers and Texture Fill (from Render), and Read Watermark (from Digimarc).

In the Styles and Effects palette, choose Filters from the left-hand menu at the top of the palette. You can then switch between categories by using the right-hand menu at the top of the palette, or just set the menu to All if you like having your filters organized strictly by alphabetization. Each filter has a thumbnail of a green apple showing the effects of the filter applied to a sample image. To apply a filter from the Styles and Effects palette, double-click the filter in the palette or just drag the filter from the palette to the image window. Heck, you can even choose the Apply command from the Styles and Effects palette's More menu if you want. The filter will be applied to the active layer or selection.

What happens next depends on precisely which filter you applied. Some filters, such as Blur, just apply themselves to the image, no muss, no fuss. Other filters, such as Gaussian Blur, display a dialog box, where you can tinker with settings for the filter before you click OK to apply it. Still other filters, such as Colored Pencil, bring up the massive and new Filter Gallery. We'll examine a typical dialog box filter and the Filter Gallery in a bit.

A few fast filter facts

Here are some important things to know about using filters in general:

- The Styles and Effects palette has two viewing modes: list view and thumbnail view. You'll probably find list view to be more helpful in the long run, with its side-by-side before-and-after views of the green apple thumbnail.

- If you select some portion of your image, the filter affects the selection and leaves the rest of the image unmodified. If you don't select a portion of the image, the filter affects the entire layer.

- To create smooth transitions between filtered and unfiltered areas in an image, blur the selection outline by choosing Select⇨Feather (see Chapter 9).

- After you apply a filter, you can reapply it with the same settings by choosing the first command in the Filter menu or by pressing Ctrl+F (⌘+F on the Mac).

- If the last filter you applied invoked either a dialog box or the Filter Gallery, press Ctrl+Alt+F (⌘+Option+F on the Mac) to redisplay the dialog box or Filter Gallery and apply the filter again using different settings.

Dialog box filters

A large number of filters perform their task with the aid of a dialog box, which provides some controls you can manipulate and a preview window so you can get an idea of the effect the filter will have on your image. In the case of the Liquify filter (see Chapter 14), the dialog box is so enormous and gives you so many tools that it's like a mini-application running inside Elements. Most dialog boxes, however, are much simpler affairs.

We'll take a look at dialog box filters by examining the Dust & Scratches filter. This filter is designed to eradicate problems such as the ones described back at the very beginning of this chapter. We're not big fans of Dust & Scratches (the healing brush is a more labor-intensive but much better alternative), but it will serve well as an example.

To apply the filter, choose Filters from the Styles and Effects palette's main menu and set the second menu to Noise. Then double-click Dust & Scratches. You can also go to the Filter menu and choose Noise⇨Dust & Scratches. Elements displays the strange and mysterious Dust & Scratches dialog box, shown in all its glory in Figure 11-2.

If you select a portion of your image before you choose Dust & Scratches or any filter, the command affects just the selected area.

Preview box

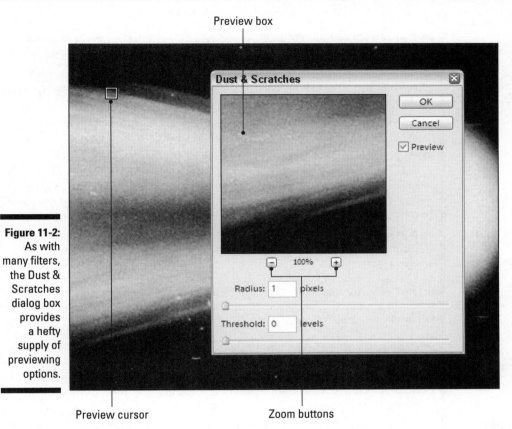

Figure 11-2:
As with
many filters,
the Dust &
Scratches
dialog box
provides
a hefty
supply of
previewing
options.

Preview cursor   Zoom buttons

Previewing the filter effects

The makers of the Dust & Scratches dialog box knew that at first glance it
wouldn't make a lick of sense, so they thoughtfully provided some preview
options (shown in Figure 11-2) to enable you to see what happens when you
make some otherwise-meaningless adjustment. Here's how these preview
options work:

- ✔ The preview box shows how your modifications look when applied to a
  portion of the image.

- ✔ If you move the cursor outside the dialog box, the cursor changes to a
  hollow square. Click an area in the image to capture it inside the preview box.

- ✔ You can also scroll the contents of the preview box by dragging inside
  the box. Your cursor changes to a little hand.

- ✔ To magnify or reduce the contents of the preview box, click the plus
  zoom icon or the minus zoom icon, respectively.

- You can access the standard magnifying glass cursor inside the preview box by pressing Ctrl (⌘ on the Mac) to zoom in or Alt (Option on the Mac) to zoom out.

- Adding the Shift key to the preceding keyboard shortcut makes the image window's zoom amount change along with the preview.

- As long as the Preview check box is selected, Elements previews your settings in the image window as well as in the preview box.

- You can even use the standard Hand and Zoom cursors *inside the image window* while the Dust & Scratches dialog box is open. Just press the spacebar to get the hand cursor, or press Ctrl or Alt (⌘ or Option on the Mac) to get the zoom cursors. This technique is a great way to preview a filter at two zoom ratios; one inside the dialog box and one outside.

- If Elements seems to be slowing down too much as it tries to preview a filter in the image window, just click the Preview check box to turn off the function.

The Dust & Scratches dialog box offers just two options: the Radius and Threshold sliders. (These options are found in several other filters, as well.) The sliders work as follows:

- Change the Radius value to indicate the size of the dust specks and the thickness of the hairs that you want to eliminate. In geometry, radius means half the width of a circle, so the Radius value is half the width of a dust speck. The minimum value is 1, meaning that the filter wipes out all specks and hairs up to 2 pixels thick.

"Ah, ha," you may think, "If I just crank up the Radius value as far as it goes (100 pixels), that should be enough to eliminate entire warrens of dust bunnies." Well, no. The Dust & Scratches filter doesn't really know a speck from a tiny bit of detail. So, if you have it rub out 100-pixel dust globs, it also rubs out 100-pixel details, such as Uncle Ralph's head.

- The Threshold value tells Elements how different the color of a dust speck has to be from the color of the surrounding image to be considered a bad seed.

The default Threshold value of 0 tells Elements that dust and image need to be only 0 color levels different from each other. Because all colors are at least 0 levels different, Elements ignores the Threshold value and considers only the Radius value.

By raising the Threshold value, you tell Elements to be more selective. If you set the value to 10, speck and image colors must vary by at least 10 levels before Elements covers up the speck. If you raise the Threshold to 20, Elements disregards still more potential impurities.

The Filter Gallery

If you're wondering why only some filters get to take up residence in the lovely new Filter Gallery, the answer goes way back to the early days of Photoshop. In the 1990s, Adobe acquired a suite of imaging filters called Aldus Gallery Effects, and rolled them into Photoshop. With the release of Photoshop CS, Adobe put the Gallery Effects filters in a Filter Gallery, and now Elements 3.0 has inherited this Filter Gallery from Photoshop CS. Not that it matters much, but now you know.

Choosing any filter in the Artistic, Brush Strokes, Sketch, or Texture categories (from the Filter menu or the Styles and Effects palette) will display the Filter Gallery, pictured in Figure 11-3. In addition, three of the Distort filters (Diffuse Glow, Glass, and Ocean Ripple) and one Stylize filter (Glowing Edges) will invoke the Filter Gallery. You can also simply choose Filter Gallery from the Filter menu.

Figure 11-3: Behold the Filter Gallery, the only place to be when you want to apply an artistic filter to your image.

Here's a brief rundown of the Filter Gallery's special features:

✔ The large preview area on the left shows you how your image will look with the filter or filters applied. The regular Ctrl and Alt shortcuts (⌘ and Option on the Mac) give you the zoom in and zoom out tools, respectively.

✔ Click the triangle next to a folder in the middle section of the Filter Gallery to view thumbnail images of the available filters in that given category. Click the thumbnail for the filter you want to apply to your image.

✔ After you click a thumbnail, that filter's controls become available in the rightmost area of the dialog box. Note that the filter name appears in the Filter Gallery's mini layers palette in the lower-right corner of the dialog box. This mini layers palette is the Filter Gallery's best and most innovative feature, and one that makes us wish that all the filters were available in the Filters Gallery.

You can click the arrow icon in the upper-left corner of the rightmost panel to collapse the middle panel and provide a bigger preview area.

✔ The mini layers palette enables you to apply multiple filters in the Filter Gallery, and then change the order in which the filters are applied. To utilize this feature, apply a filter — let's say you choose Glowing Edges in the Stylize category. After you have the settings tweaked to your satisfaction, click the little New effect layer button at the bottom of the mini layers palette. A copy of Glowing Edges appears above the filter you applied in the mini layers palette. You can tell it's selected from its gray appearance. Now choose another filter — let's say it's Stained Glass from the Texture category. The stained glass effect is applied to the glowing-edged-version of your image.

But suppose that's not the effect you were looking for when combining those two filters. No problem; just click the top Stained Glass filter layer and drag it down below the Glowing Edges filter layer. Now the Stained Glass filter is applied first, and the Glowing Edges filter is applying itself to the edges of the stained glass panes, not to the edges in your image. You can add as many filter layers as you want, and drag them up and down in the stack to rearrange them. If you want to get rid of a layer, select it and click the trash can icon at the bottom of the mini layers palette. When you're finished, just click OK.

If only all the filters in Elements were available in the Filter Gallery! The ability to experiment after the fact with the order in which filters are applied is a powerful thing.

Experimenting with the Highly Ethical Clone Stamp Tool

If you're willing to expend a little energy and you can stand up to your friends when they call you compulsive, the clone stamp tool is your friend. This tool lets you take a good portion of an image and paint it onto a bad portion. This process is called, quite naturally, *cloning*.

Stamping out splatters

Want to see how the clone stamp tool works? Try out these steps:

1. **Select the clone stamp tool from the toolbox.**

   To select the clone stamp tool from the keyboard, press the S key.

2. **Make sure that the Aligned box is checked in the clone stamp's tool options bar (seen in Figure 11-4).**

   This option lets you clone from relative points in your image. You'll see how it works in a second.

Figure 11-4:
Options for the clone stamp tool.

3. **Start dragging randomly inside your image.**

   Whoops, you got an error message, didn't you? As the friendly error message tells you, to use the clone stamp tool, you have to tell Elements which portion of your image you want to clone before you begin cloning it. Elements isn't a mind reader, you know.

   Now that you've grasped this valuable lesson, grab a pen and put a big X through Step 3 so that you never make the same mistake again.

4. **Alt+click (Option+click on the Mac) the portion of the image that you want to clone.**

   As Figure 11-5 shows, to fix that big goober near the beginning of the lower tail in this ancient picture of Halley's comet, Alt+click (Option+click on the Mac) at a location that appears to contain similar gray values to the comet stuff that surrounds the goober. The point is to choose a portion of your image that blends in with areas around the blemish you want to eliminate.

5. Now click or drag on the offending blemish.

To apply the digital zit cream, just click directly on said goober. No muss, no fuss; the glitch is gone.

When you click or drag with the clone stamp tool, Elements displays a cross cursor along with the stamp cursor, as shown in Figure 11-6. (For clarity's sake in this figure, the painting cursors are set to Standard in the Display & Cursors section of Preferences.) This cross represents the clone source, or the area that you're cloning from. As you move the mouse, the cross cursor also moves, providing a continual reference to the portion of your image that you're cloning. The distance between the clone source (cross) and destination (stamp cursor) is set by the first two clicks you make: the Alt+click (Option+click on the Mac) to set the source and the click when you begin cloning. (Things work differently when you have the Aligned option unchecked in the tool options bar, however, as explained in the next section.)

If the cloned area doesn't blend in well, just click the undo button in the shortcuts bar or press Ctrl+Z (⌘+Z on Mac) and then Alt+click (Option+click on the Mac) in the image with the clone stamp tool to specify a better source for your cloning. Click or drag with the tool to test out a different clone. You may have to do this several times to get it just right.

Just for the sheer heck of it, Figure 11-7 shows the comet after a 15-minute workout with the clone stamp tool.

The dreaded cosmic goober

Alt+click with clone stamp

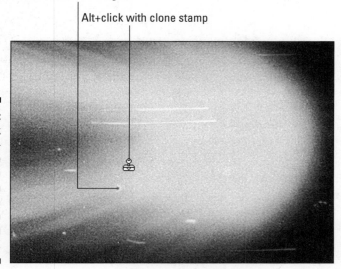

Figure 11-5:
Alt+click (Option+ click on the Mac) on a good portion of an image to establish the cloning source.

Clone source   Clone stamp cursor

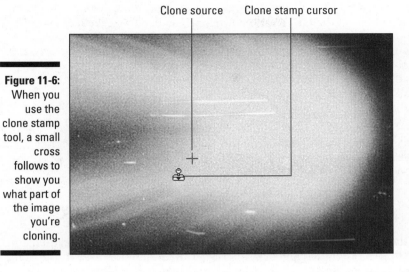

Figure 11-6:
When you use the clone stamp tool, a small cross follows to show you what part of the image you're cloning.

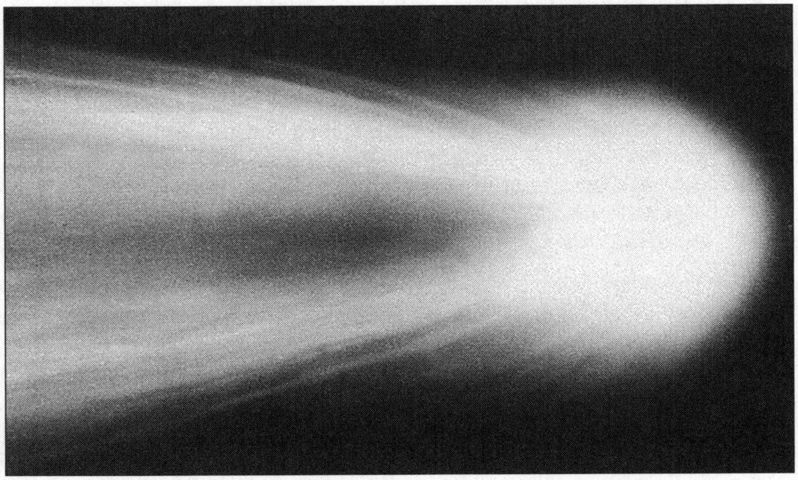

Figure 11-7:
Halley's comet, all dressed up and nowhere to go for another 74 years.

Performing more magic with the clone stamp tool

If you never find out another thing about the clone stamp tool, you'll be able to clean images quite easily after reading the preceding section. But the clone stamp is an amazing tool with more facets and capabilities than most tools in Elements:

✔ To change the size or shape of the cloning area, change the brush with the palette on the far left of the tool options bar. Click the downward-pointing arrow and choose a brush. You'll probably want to stay away from the more exotic brushes when using the clone stamp tool. You can also use the Size control in the tool options bar, or better yet change the size of the brush on the fly by tapping the [and] keys. For much more on brushes, see Chapter 15.

✔ To adjust the translucency of the cloning, use the Opacity option in the tool options bar. A setting of 100 makes your clone opaque. You can change the opacity by tapping the number keys; tap 5, for instance, to get 50 percent opacity, or 5 twice in quick succession to get 55 percent opacity.

✔ To clean up a straight hair or scratch, Alt+click (Option+click on the Mac) with the tool to specify the source for the cloning as you normally would. Then click at one end of the scratch and Shift+click at the other.

✔ If the first clone doesn't look exactly right but is pretty close, you may want to modify the clone slightly rather than redo it. Lower the Opacity setting in the tool options bar and then clone from a different position by again Alt+clicking (Option+clicking on the Mac) and dragging. This enables you to mix multiple portions of an image together to get a more seamless blend.

✔ Normally, the clone stamp tool clones from a relative location. If you move your cursor to a different location, the clone source moves with you. But what if you want to clone multiple times from a single location? In this case, deselect the Aligned box in the tool options bar. Now, you can Alt+click (Option+click on the Mac) once to set the source and click multiple times to duplicate that source.

✔ The pattern stamp tool, which shares a flyout menu with the clone stamp tool in the toolbox, clones an area with a repeating pattern. The Pattern pop-up palette in the tool options bar gives you access to Elements' large library of preset patterns. You can also define your own pattern by choosing Edit⇨Define Pattern or by first selecting a rectangular area and then choosing Edit⇨Define Pattern from Selection. Give the pattern a name, and then select your custom pattern from the bottom of the Pattern pop-up palette in the tool options bar. Drag with the pattern stamp tool, and you'll see the pattern appear. It's cool but generally not useful.

✔ Speaking of cool but not generally useful, there's an Impressionist option in the pattern stamp tool's tool options bar, which makes the pattern stamp tool do . . . well . . . an *impression* of the impressionist brush. If you want to obliterate your image with whirling, swirling pattern effects, this tool was made to order. And it's fun to experiment with, anyway. You can switch to the pattern stamp when the clone stamp is active by clicking the pattern stamp icon on the left side of the tool options bar.

✔ You can clone between images with the clone stamp tool. If you have two images open, you can Alt+click (Option+click on the Mac) in one image to specify the source and drag in the other image to clone. It's like painting one image onto another.

✔ Figure 11-8 shows an example Deke created of cloning between images. Starting with the two images on the left side of the figure (which he scaled to the same file size by using Image⇨Resize⇨Image Size, as discussed in Chapter 4), he Alt+clicked (Option+clicked on the Mac) inside the top image and then dragged with the clone stamp tool in the bottom image. He cloned the woman's face and blouse using a large fuzzy brush and then switched to a smaller brush for the touch ups. To match the skin tones in the forehead and the base of the nose, he cloned from the woman's cheeks at an Opacity setting of 50%. Pretty amazing, huh?

✔ If your image contains layers (as discussed in Chapter 10), remember that the clone stamp tool normally clones only from the active layer. If you select the Use All Layers check box in the tool options bar, the clone stamp tool reads the pixels in all visible layers as the clone source. When you then click or drag with the clone stamp tool, Elements paints the clone onto the active layer.

✔ The clone stamp tool also lets you clone using effect modes, which can create special effects by blending the colors of pixels. *Effect modes* are basically the same thing as blending modes, which are discussed at length in Chapter 14. In the meanwhile, if you have half an hour to waste, play with the different modes and see what you can do. Or spend the time with a loved one instead. Nah, check out those effect modes.

Figure 11-8:
By cloning from the top-left image onto the bottom-left image with the clone stamp tool, the two images were merged to create the strange but nonetheless believable specimen on the right.

The clone stamp tool is unquestionably one of Elements' two or three most useful tools. Take the time to get to know it well.

Performing Miracles with the Healing Brushes

If the clone stamp tool is one of Elements' two or three most useful tools, the new healing brush must be one of Elements' one or two most useful tools. Introduced in Photoshop 7, we frankly figured Adobe would forever keep the healing brush as a Photoshop-exclusive tool, one for which Elements users would have to upgrade to Photoshop to use. Happily, we were way, way wrong. Just wait until you get your mitts on the healing brush and its new friend, the spot healing brush.

The healing brush

Although the internal workings of the healing brush are very different from those of the clone stamp tool, the operating instructions are identical. Alt- or Option-click to set a source point, and then click and paint with the tool over the blemish you want to conceal. But where the clone stamp tool just basically pastes another chunk of image over the blemish, the healing brush blends the pixels of the source point with the pixels *outside* where you paint. You don't have to be anywhere near as careful as you do with the clone stamp to match the color of the source point to the color of the area you want to conceal. The healing brush takes care of that for you.

Take a gander, for example, at Figure 11-9, which shows a scar recently engraved on the forehead of Galen Fott, one of the co-authors of this book. (He walked into a partially rolled-up garage door that he himself partially rolled up, if you must know. Yes, this is the caliber of brain that is bringing this book to you.) In the left example, we clicked to set the source point in the relatively smooth part of the skin above the scar, and then painted a single brush stroke over the scar. The healing brush blended the smoothness and texture of the source point with the smoothness and texture of the pixels that lie directly outside the brush stroke, but not *within* the brush stroke. The result is on the right in Figure 11-9. More evidence of the healing brush's wonderful work can be found in Color Plate 8.

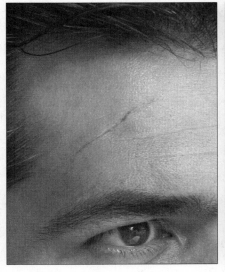 

Figure 11-9:
The healing
brush can
remove a
scar (left)
without
resorting to
expensive
cosmetic
surgery
(right).

Here's a rundown of the tool options controls available with the healing brush:

- **Size:** This controls the size of the brush. The larger the brush, the farther away from the blemish will the healing brush look for pixels to blend with the source point, so don't use too large a brush.

- **Mode:** As with the clone stamp, different effect modes are available, but you'll most likely want to keep this set to Normal.

- **Source:** You can click the Pattern radio option to deactivate the healing brush's Alt- or Option-clicking to set the source point. Instead, the tool will paint in the pattern specified in the adjacent Pattern pop-up palette. Although fun to experiment with, this falls outside the main purpose of the tool. For your basic healing needs, keep this set to Sampled.

- **Aligned:** Select this option if you don't want the healing brush to refer back to the source point for each brush stroke you paint. This is generally a more helpful option with the clone stamp tool than with the healing brush, and you'll probably want to keep this turned off.

- **Use All Layers:** As with the clone stamp, this option makes the healing brush draw from all layers in an image, and not just the active layer.

The spot healing brush

If the healing brush is a successful attempt to improve on the clone stamp (in terms of blemish removal, at least), the spot healing brush is a somewhat successful attempt to make the healing brush simpler than it already is. You don't Alt- or Option-click with this tool. Just drag to paint a selection-brush-style outline around the offending blemish in the image, and the spot healing brush attempts to do the rest itself. True to its name, the spot healing brush tends to work better on offending spots (such as pimples) than on larger areas such as scars.

Aside from the brush controls, only one tool option is available: the Type menu. Setting it to Proximity Match makes the spot healing brush look for its own source point outside the selected area. This is usually the best choice, though sometimes the tool makes wildly inappropriate choices for the source point, resulting in eyes floating in the middle of foreheads and things like that. The other setting, Create Texture, causes the spot healing brush to analyze the surrounding area and fill the selection with synthesized data.

By all means, give the spot healing brush a shot. It may work just fine on your image. If not, you'll have to fall back on the utterly miraculous healing brush. We should always have such appealing second choices.

Getting the Red Out

If you've been on the business end of a modern camera recently, you've probably witnessed a startling display of light just before the picture snapped, something akin to a laser light show at your local planetarium. The multiple strobes that many camera flashes emit nowadays are all about shrinking your pupils to keep out red eye, the longtime scourge of photographers everywhere. If the flash on a camera is too close to the lens, the light from the flash enters the eye, hits the retina, and bounces back into the lens, creating the glowing effect. The modern strobe flashes are indeed quite effective at stopping red eye before it happens.

And that's a good thing, because red eye is difficult to correct digitally. The reflected light often blasts away detail, and if it spreads into the iris there's no way to know what color the person's irises are supposed to be. Elements 3.0's new solution for this problem is the red eye removal tool. If the red eye problem in an image isn't too severe — and especially if the glow is confined to the pupil, and doesn't bleed out into the iris — the tool does a smashing job. The proof — as the popular saying goes — is in Color Plate 9.

Press Y to access the red eye removal tool. Then zoom into a single pupil afflicted with red eye, and click in the red. Repeat for the other pupil. You can also use the tool to drag a rectangle around an afflicted pupil, which works better in some cases. But really, as far as using the tool is concerned — that's pretty much it. The new red eye removal tool's strongest point is its simplicity.

Although the default settings tend to work very well, here's the rundown on the two options available to you in the red eye removal tool's tool options bar:

✔ **Pupil Size:** In severe cases of red eye, where the red bleeds out into the iris as well as the pupil, this control can help approximate the size of the pupil within the red glow. Just remember, however, that the tool has no way of knowing what color the iris was. If your subject had pale blue irises that were obliterated with red eye, you're probably not going to achieve satisfactory results no matter what you do.

✔ **Darken Amount:** If you feel the red eye removal tool is turning the pupils too black, lower this amount from the default value of 50 percent. Likewise, if you think the pupils are too light, raise the amount.

We think the red eye removal tool is a big improvement over Elements 2.0's red eye brush. It's certainly simpler to use and is generally more effective. Note, however, that true to its name, the red eye removal tool works on *red* eye problems, but not the green and amber flash problems that typically appear in animal eyes. If Scruffy or Fydo's eyes need a good working over — or if you have a stubborn case of human red eye — give the color replacement tool or the Replace Color command a try. We deal with these tools in Chapter 13.

Chapter 12

Darkroom Déjà Vu

*B*ack in the old days, retouching a photograph was a formidable task. Many an hour was spent in dank and dingy darkrooms, using primitive techniques to try to improve an image. If the darkroom was no use, the only other resource available was airbrushing. Anyone short of a trained professional would more often than not make a complete mess of the project and wish to heck it had never been started. Even the pros found it difficult to match flat colors on a palette to the ever-changing landscape of a photograph.

The beauty of Photoshop Elements is that you can paint not only with specific colors (as explained in Chapter 15) but also with colors and details already found in the image. Using the editing tools — smudge, blur, sharpen, dodge, burn, and sponge — you can subtly adjust the appearance of pixels by shifting them around, boosting contrast between them, or lightening and darkening them. And where the blur and sharpen tools leave off, the Blur and Sharpen filters pick up and go the extra mile.

We start this chapter with a look at Elements' easy-to-use Quick Fix mode, where sharpening is one of the many image-editing tasks available. Although the best techniques that Elements provides for correcting images are generally found in the Standard Edit mode, you can't beat Quick Fix mode's simplicity and convenience. As we noted in Chapter 1, Quick Fix is sort of the friendly, Dr. Jekyll-like face that Adobe has put on the Mr. Hyde-like world of image editing. So let's pay a visit to the good doctor, shall we?

Getting a Quick Fix for Your Image

The entire Mac version of Elements is basically analogous to just the Editor component in the Windows version. The Windows version also has an Organizer component, which operates in two modes, Photo Browser or Date View. The Editor component of Elements (which is all Mac users have) also has two modes, called Standard Edit and Quick Fix. In most of this book we assume you're working in the Standard Edit mode. That's because Quick Fix mode is pretty easy to figure out; if all of Elements was this user-friendly, there wouldn't be much need for this book. (Shudder!)

Windows users can access Quick Fix mode by clicking the Quickly Fix Photos icon on the Welcome screen. If you're already in the Organizer component, click the Edit button in the shortcuts bar and choose Go to Quick Fix from the menu. If you're already in the Editor component, just click the Quick Fix button in the shortcuts bar. Mac users also have a Quick Fix button in the shortcuts bar to access Quick Fix mode.

As seen in Figure 12-1, the Quick Fix mode replaces the flexible palette bin on the right side of the screen with four permanently fixed palettes, one each for General Fixes, Lighting, Color, and Sharpening. The toolbox is gone; only four tools — zoom, hand, crop, and red eye removal — stick around in Quick Fix mode. No toolbox and no Layers palette mean there's no selecting, painting, or working with layers. Therefore, the Edit, Layer, and Select menus are by and large full of nothing but dimmed commands.

Figure 12-1:
The Quick Fix mode is your one-stop shopping center for many of Elements' one-click commands.

Now that you know what you *don't* get in Quick Fix mode, you may well be wondering what you *do* get. Well, the chief attraction here is the large preview window, and its ability to split into several different before-and-after comparison modes. From the View menu underneath the preview, you can choose between:

- ✔ **After Only:** This choice shows you the image after the editing you've done in Quick Fix mode.

- ✔ **Before Only:** This shows you the image as it looked before you entered Quick Fix mode.

- ✔ **Before and After (Portrait):** This gives you a side-by-side view of the image before and after the Quick Fix changes you've made.

- ✔ **Before and After (Landscape):** This choice shows a top-and-bottom view of the image before and after your Quick Fix changes.

Another thing to be said for Quick Fix mode is that the four palettes on the right give you fast access to some critical image-editing tools. It must be noted, however, that these palettes don't offer anything you can't find in Standard Edit mode. The General Fixes palette gives you options that can be found in the Image and Enhance menus. The Lighting palette gives you access to the Enhance menu's Auto Levels, Auto Contrast, and Shadows/Highlights commands. The Color palette gives you the Enhance menu's Adjust Hue/Saturation command and the Photo Filter filter. And the Sharpen palette does the work of the Sharpen submenu of the filters.

If you spend a lot of time hunting around in Standard Edit mode's menus looking for the right command, give Quick Fix mode a try. You may find that you like it. It's certainly a fast and convenient way to approach image editing, and we have nothing against that. But bear in mind that Standard Edit, in general, offers more powerful ways to make the same changes to your images. We explore these alternatives in this and the next few chapters. This chapter, for instance, teaches you how to use the oh-so-powerful Unsharp Mask filter, which is much more customizable than the controls in Quick Fix's Sharpen palette. But before we look at giving images an overall sharpening, let's look at ways to retouch specific problem areas in your photos with the editing tools.

Touching Base with Retouching Tools

Unlike the pencil and brush tools, the editing tools don't have any common real-world counterparts. But editing tools would be extremely useful in real life if only someone would get around to inventing them. Take the task of touching up the walls in your rec room. (Come on, everyone has a rec room!

Where else would you do your reccing?) Using paintbrushes and rollers alone, this job can be a nightmare. The paint on the walls and the paint in the can may no longer exactly match. If you have to scrape away any dry paint, you'll have a heck of a time matching the texture.

But scan the walls of the rec room into Elements and your problems are solved. Even if you have to retouch both paint and wallpaper, the editing tools, shown in Figure 12-2, can handle the job without incident:

✔ Use the smudge tool to smear colors from a pristine area of the wall to the bare spots and the stains. You can smear the paint as far as you want, just as though it were still wet and in infinite supply. (The section "Smudging Away Imperfections," later in this chapter, discusses the smudge tool further.)

✔ If the transitions between objects in the wallpaper are a little ragged — for example, if the pixels in the little polka-dot mushrooms don't seem to blend naturally with those in the cute little frogs sitting beneath them — you can smooth the pixels out with the blur tool, which looks like a water drop. This tool blurs the edges between colors so that the colors blend together.

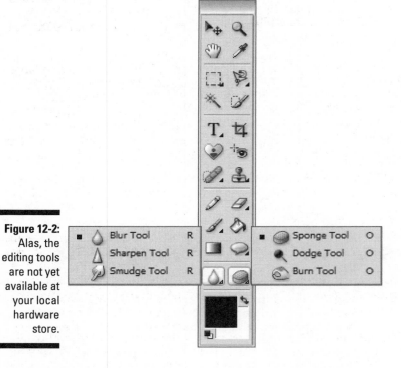

Figure 12-2:
Alas, the editing tools are not yet available at your local hardware store.

- To rebuild textures, drag with the sharpen tool — which looks as though someone took the water-drop-shaped blur tool and, well, sharpened it. (Must be very hard water.) The sharpen tool increases the amount of contrast between colors and builds up edges.

- To lighten a dark area in the wallpaper, drag with the dodge tool, which looks like a lollipop. This tool lightens up the area evenly.

- If an area on the wall has become faded over the years, you can darken it by using the burn tool, which looks like a hand making the shape of an O.

- Are the colors just too darn garish? Or has the color been drained right out? Okay, so these aren't common rec room problems, but if they do occur, you can take up the sponge tool to remedy them.

See, don't you wish you had a crack at using these tools in real life? Seems to me that Bob Vila or Tim Allen should get to work on them. There are millions to be made.

Smudging Away Imperfections

As you may recall from the earlier rec-room analogy, the smudge tool pushes color from one portion of your image into another. When you drag with this tool, Elements "grabs" the color that's underneath your cursor at the start of your drag and smears it in the direction of your drag.

The smudge tool can be used for smearing away scars, wrinkles, overly large noses, droopy ears, and all the other things that plastic surgeons keep their eyes out for. Figure 12-3 shows a before-and-after view of a scarred shark receiving a thorough makeover with the smudge tool. (For the sake of clarity, the cursor has been set to the Standard mode in the Display & Cursors panel of Preferences.) The various sharkish defects are smoothed away to the point that the guy looks like he's made out of porcelain.

Light on the smudge, please

Notice that in Figure 12-3, the smudge tool is being rubbed *with* the grain of the detail. It's tracing along the shark's gills, rubbing along the length of the shark's fins, and dragging up the shark's snout, all in short, discreet strokes. (It's very bad to rub a shark the wrong way.) You get more natural-looking results if you carefully trace along the details of your subject and don't simply drag haphazardly all over the place.

Retouching with the smudge tool requires a certain amount of discretion. If you really go nuts and drag over every single surface, you get an oil-painting effect. You can create some cool stuff this way, but excessive smudging is not the same as retouching.

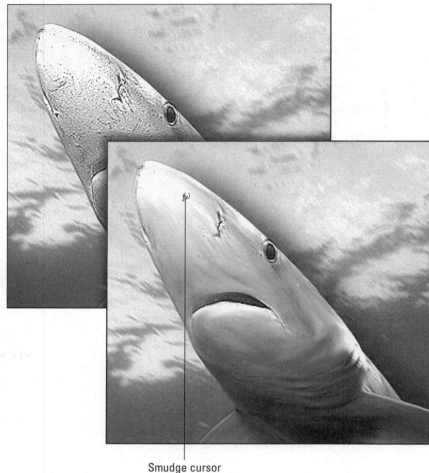

Smudge cursor

Figure 12-3:
As these before (top) and after (bottom) photos prove, the smudge tool can take years off a shark's face.

Smudge-specific controls

You can modify the performance of the smudge tool by using the Smudge tool options bar (see Figure 12-4):

✔ Click and Shift+click to smudge in a straight line. You can also Shift+drag to smudge horizontally or vertically. These Shift+click and Shift+drag techniques work for all the edit tools, by the way.

✔ Select another brush in the Brushes palette and change the Size option to enlarge or reduce the size of the smudge brush. You can likewise change the brush size for all the edit tools. To display the Brushes palette, click the downward-pointing arrow next to the brushstroke icon in the tool options bar. (For much more on changing brushes, see Chapter 15.)

✔ The tool options bar has various smudge options. For example, you can lower the Strength setting to create more subtle retouching effects. Increase the Strength setting to make the effect more pronounced.

✔ Remember that you can change the brush size from the keyboard by pressing the bracket keys and change the Strength setting by pressing the number keys.

✔ The Mode drop-down menu's Darken and Lighten options let you smear only those colors that are darker or lighter than the original colors in the image. You also have the Color effect mode, which lets you smear the colors in an RGB image without harming the detail. Pretty nifty. The other effect modes — Hue, Saturation, and Luminosity — range from nearly useless to completely useless. Don't worry about them.

✔ Select the Finger Painting check box to dip your brush into the foreground color before smudging. Elements applies a little dab of foreground color at the beginning of your drag and then begins to smear into the existing colors in the image as usual.

✔ The Use All Layers check box doesn't make any difference unless you're editing an image with layers. It enables you to pierce through and pick up the colors from all your layers.

✔ Although the smudge tool can be fun, there are better options at your disposal. If you want to push around pixels to create distortions in your image, the Liquify filter is sort of like the smudge tool on steroids. To check out the Liquify filter, head on over to Chapter 14. And if your wish is to repair your image, getting rid of imperfections and such, the healing brush and clone stamp tools will give you better results. Chapter 11 has the skinny on these tools.

Figure 12-4:
The options that affect the smudge tool.

Dodge? Burn? Those Are Opposites?

Wondering why the dodge and burn tools look the way they do? It's because they have their roots in traditional stat camera techniques in which you shoot a photograph of another photograph to correct exposure problems. The dodge tool is supposed to look like a little paddle that you wave around to block off light, and the burn tool is a hand focusing the light.

(handwritten margin note:) ① CLICK ON SPONGE TOOL. THAT BRINGS UP A TOOL BAR THAT HAS THE DODGE AND BURN PLUS OTHER SETTINGS. CLK ON EITHER DODGE OR BURN TOOL FOR THEIR RESPECTIVE TOOL BARS

Here's a handy key for remembering which tool does what:

- ✔ The dodge tool lightens images, just as a dodge ball lightens your body by about ten pounds when it knocks off your head.

- ✔ The burn tool darkens images, just as a sunburn darkens your body and eventually turns it a kind of charbroiled color.

Generally, you adjust the performance of the dodge and burn tools just like the other edit tools and the paint tools. You can find all the tool options, including brush sizes, in the tool options bar:

- ✔ The Exposure option indicates how much an area will be lightened or darkened. Lower the value to lessen the effect of the tool and raise the value to increase the effect.

- ✔ The Range menu contains just three options: Highlights, Midtones, and Shadows. The default setting is Midtones, which lightens or darkens medium colors in an image and leaves the very light and dark colors alone. Figure 12-5 shows the result of dragging all over the shark with the dodge tool while Midtones was the active range.

- ✔ The Shadows range ensures that the darkest colors are affected, whereas Highlights affects the lightest colors. In Figure 12-6, the dodge tool was scribbled with while the Range was set to Shadows. The payoff is a shark that looks like it ate a tanker full of glowworms. Even the darkest shadows radiate, making the image uniformly light.

- ✔ To darken an image with similar uniformity, select the burn tool and set the Brush mode to Highlights.

Figure 12-5: By setting the Range to Midtones and dragging indiscriminately with the dodge tool on the left image, the shark was lightened without eliminating contrast (right).

Figure 12-6: Using the dodge tool on the left image with the Range set to Shadows makes the shark's darkest shadows tingle with light (right).

Playing with the Color Knob

The sponge tool is designed for use on full-color images. Don't try using it on grayscale images because it doesn't do any good. It's not that it doesn't work — it does — it just doesn't work correctly. On a grayscale image, the sponge tool either lightens or darkens pixels like a shoddy version of the dodge or burn tool.

When you work on a color image, the sponge tool increases or decreases saturation. Ever used the color knob on an old television? Turn the knob up, and the color leaps off the screen; turn it down, and the colors look gray. What you're doing is adjusting the TV's saturation. Increasing saturation makes the colors more vibrant; decreasing saturation makes the colors more drab. The sponge tool works in much the same way.

Here's how you use the sponge tool:

1. **Select the sponge tool.**

   Press the O key, or press Shift-O if the dodge or burn tool is active. Elements displays the appropriate tool options bar.

2. **Select the desired Mode option from the menu in the tool options bar.**

   Select Saturate to make the colors vibrant; select Desaturate to make the colors drab.

3. **Press a number key to change the Flow value.**

   You can also scrub the word *Flow* to change the value. Either way, the setting affects the intensity of the sponge tool.

4. **Drag with the tool inside a color image.**

   Watch those colors change.

One good use for the sponge tool is to provide a focal point for your image. Suppose that you have a color photo of a group of people and want to have one person stand out among the others. Select your person (see Chapter 9 for selection methods) and then choose Select➪Inverse. Now, carefully take the sponge tool, set the Mode to Desaturate in the tool options bar, and drag over the image. You see the colors in the group wash out while your deselected person remains bright and stands out among the crowd.

Focusing from the Hip

From what we've discovered about the smudge tool, it's clear that it can be a handy device. But it's not always the right tool for the job. For example, suppose you have a harsh transition between two colors. Maybe one of our shark's teeth looks a little sharp, or you want to soften the edge of a fin. The problem with the smudge tool is that you can't get a nice, smooth transition no matter how hard you try.

Meanwhile, an edge softener is sitting nearby waiting for you to snatch it up. If you drag over a sharp edge with the blur tool — whether you drag perfectly straight or wobble the cursor back and forth a bit — you get a softened edge, no smudging required.

Here are a few other items about the focus tools in general:

- ✔ Just as the blur tool softens transitions, the sharpen tool firms the transitions back up.

- ✔ At least, that's what the sharpen tool is supposed to do. In practice, it tends to make an image overly grainy. Use this tool sparingly.

- ✔ You can adjust the impact of the blur and sharpen tools by changing the Strength settings in the tool options bar. As a jumping-off point, try working with the strength set to about 60% for the blur tool and 30% for the sharpen tool.

- ✔ When you work with the focus tools, you have access to the same blending modes as you do when using the smudge tool. Again, the important ones are Darken, Lighten, and Color. Any of the three can help downplay the effects of the sharpen tool and make it more usable. For more on blending modes, see Chapter 14.

If you want to adjust the focus of large areas of an image — or an entire image — your best bet by far is to go with the Blur and Sharpen filters. These commands work much more uniformly than the focus tools, and with better results.

Sharpening Those Wishy-Washy Details

No matter how good an image looked before you scanned it, chances are that it appears a little out of focus on-screen. The image in Figure 12-7 is an exaggerated example. Snapped around the time Stonehenge was built, this photo looks so soft you'd swear that it was sculpted out of gelatin.

The solutions to softness are the four filters found in the Sharpen category of the Filter menu and in the Styles and Effects palette. The following sections explain how these filters work and when — if ever — to apply them.

Figure 12-7: Antique images such as this one are notoriously soft on focus.

The single-shot sharpeners

The first three sharpening filters — Sharpen, Sharpen Edges, and Sharpen More — are *single-shot filters.* You choose them, and they do their work without complex dialog boxes or other means of digital interrogation. These filters, with their straightforward names, are a breeze to use.

Unfortunately, when it comes to Elements, you get back what you put in. In other words, if you don't have to work at something, it's liable to deliver rather mediocre results. As demonstrated in Figure 12-8, all three Sharpen filters sharpen, but none satisfactorily remedies the image's focus problems.

Figure 12-8 shows the results of applying each of the three single-shot sharpeners to a detail from the original image (shown in the top row). In each case, the filter was applied once (as shown in the middle row) and then a second time (as shown in the last row). For the record, here's what each of the filters does:

- ✔ Sharpen, as shown in the first column, enhances the focus of the image very slightly. If the photo is already well focused but needs a little extra fortification to make it perfect, the Sharpen filter can do the trick. Otherwise, forget it.

- ✔ The Sharpen More filter, shown in the second column, enhances focus more dramatically. Although it's easily the most useful of the three single-shooters, it's still fairly crude. For example, the center image in Figure 12-8 isn't sharp enough, whereas the bottom image is so sharp that little flecks — called *artifacts* — are starting to form in the woman's dress. Boo, hiss.

- ✔ The Sharpen Edges filter, as seen in the third column, is a complete waste of time. It sharpens the so-called edges of an image without sharpening any of the neutral areas in between. In the figure, for example, the filter sharpens the outline of the guy's face but ignores the interior of his jacket. The result is an inconsistent effect that eventually frays the edges and leaves non-edges looking goopy by comparison.

As you may have gathered by now, we don't wholeheartedly recommend the single-shot sharpening filters. We do endorse Unsharp Mask, which we talk about next.

Color Plate 1: The red, green, and blue color channels lurking behind the scenes in Photoshop Elements act like slides in separate projectors pointed at the same spot on a screen. You may find it hard to believe that three primary hues could mix together to produce a full range of colors, but it's true.

Background texture: Sandpaper effect

Color Plate 2: Pure white light from the sun (or a man-made light source) is made up of red, green, and blue light. When light passes through the cyan, magenta, or yellow printing ink, the ink filters out the red, green, or blue light and lets the other two pass through.

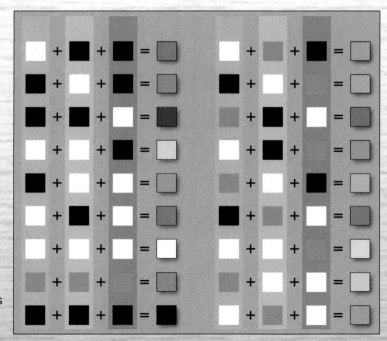

Color Plate 3: This figure shows the way light, dark, and medium pixels in the red, green, and blue channels mix to form various sample colors. Altogether, you can create more than 16 million color variations.

Background texture: Brushed Metal layer style

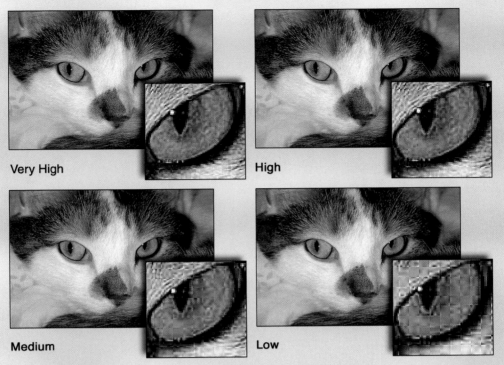

Very High

High

Medium

Low

Color Plate 4: The Save for Web dialog box gives you five default compression quality settings for JPEG files; four are pictured above. Even the Low setting can provide excellent results with a high-resolution photo like this one, but the magnified and sharpened inset eyes show that the image data has definitely been compromised.

Color Plate 5: Cute subject; terrible background. The selection brush gives you two modes for making selections: Selection mode (left) surrounds the selected area with a moving dotted line, whereas Mask mode (right) uses a translucent red overlay, letting you actually see the feathered edge of the selection.

Background texture: Tie-Dyed Silk layer style

Color Plate 6: This homage to an anchovy pizza bedtime snack was constructed from a multitude of different layers, organized and manipulated using the Layers palette. The Soft Light blending mode gives the heads peering over the edge of the boat their ghostly appearance.

Background texture: Angled Spectrum layer style

Color Plate 7: The eight images that comprise "Dyspepsia." The grinning gremlin at the lower right had Filter ⇨ Adjustments ⇨ Invert applied. The "DYSPEPSIA" text layer at the top right was first simplified before the metallic border was added to it.

Background texture: Wood — Pine effect

Color Plate 8: The ancient photo at left not only has nicks and tears, but the corners have been cut to fit a round frame. Although the clone stamp tool was useful for filling out the cut corners (right), the new healing brush was able to seamlessly remove the gash across the faces (see insets), yielding a better result than was possible in Photoshop Elements 2.0.

Color Plate 9: The red eye removal tool was able to quickly remove that familiar eerie red glow (left) from the eyes of an innocent youth (right).

Background texture: Sunset effect

Original

Auto Levels

Auto Smart Fix

Auto Color Correction

Auto Contrast

Levels

Color Plate 10: The original scanned slide seen at upper left is very dark and suffers from a severe violet color cast. Auto Levels and Auto Color Correction corrected the image fairly well, but seemed to introduce a bluish cast of their own. Auto Contrast simply brightened the discolored image, and Auto Smart Fix is barely distinguishable from the original. Although the Levels command is definitely a lot more work, by applying it to each color channel individually we were able to both correct the brightness and eliminate any hint of a color cast.

Background texture: Rusted Metal effect

Color Plate 11: The Shadows/Highlights command can take a dark image (left) and bring out details hiding in the shadowy foreground while balancing the contrast with the bright background (right).

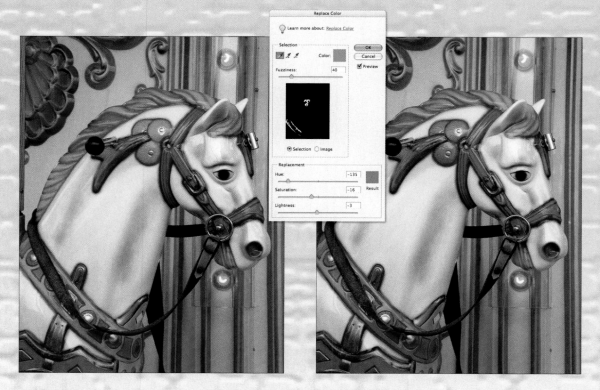

Color Plate 12: The Replace Color command was used to select the pink decorations on the carousel horse (left) and convert them to a brilliant blue (right).

Background texture: Ancient Stone layer style

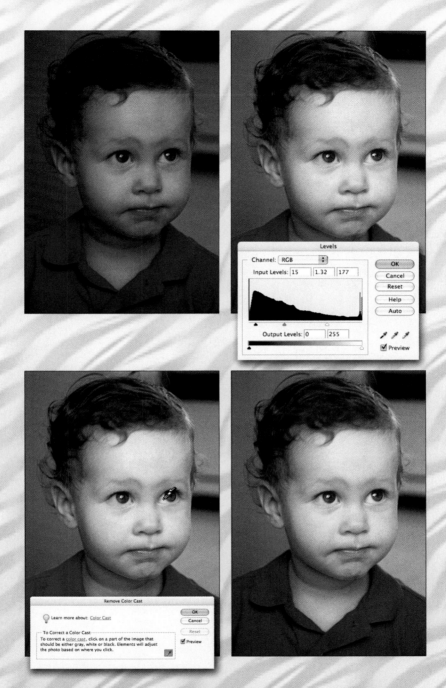

Color Plate 13: Starting with a dark, violet-tinged scan of a slide (upper left), we used the Levels command on the RGB composite to lighten the image (upper right). And although the Remove Color Cast command is far from a sure thing, clicking it here on the white of the young tike's eye (lower left) did a highly respectable job of correcting the colors in the image (lower right).

Background texture: Waves layer style

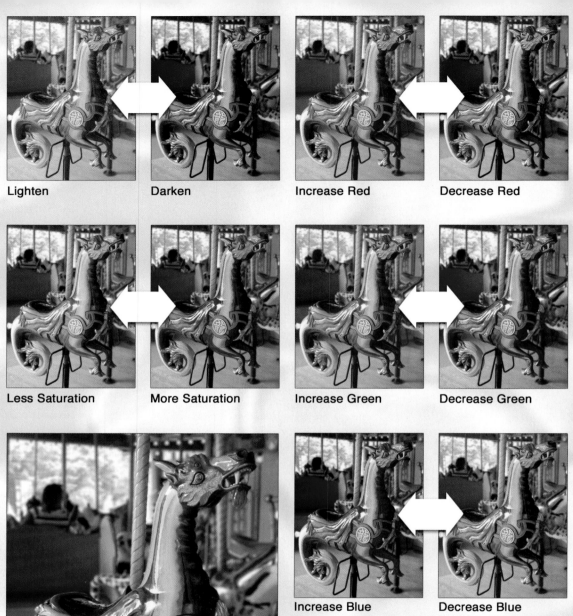

Lighten

Darken

Increase Red

Decrease Red

Less Saturation

More Saturation

Increase Green

Decrease Green

Increase Blue

Decrease Blue

Original

Background texture: Satin Sheets layer style

Color Plate 14: The Color Variations command is another effective way to correct an image. Shown here are the results of various changes to the original image's midtones, using the default intensity.

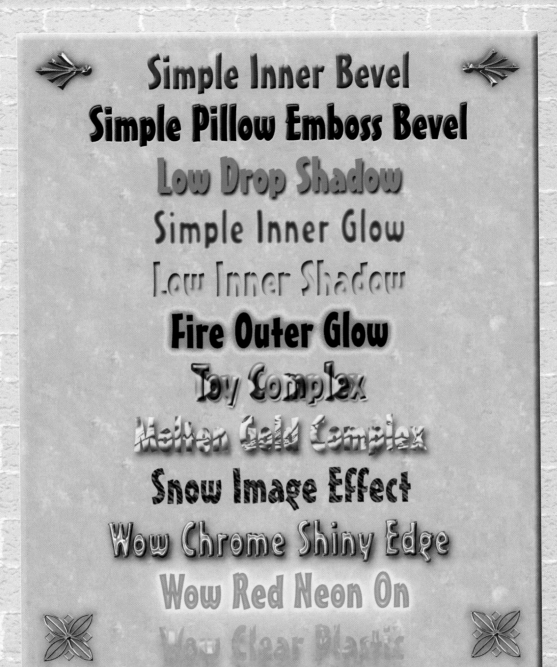

Simple Inner Bevel

Simple Pillow Emboss Bevel

Low Drop Shadow

Simple Inner Glow

Low Inner Shadow

Fire Outer Glow

Toy Complex

Molten Gold Complex

Snow Image Effect

Wow Chrome Shiny Edge

Wow Red Neon On

Wow Clear Plastic

Color Plate 15: Layer styles can work wonders on ordinary text with a single click. The texture behind the text is the Yellow and Orange Complex layer style; the ornaments in the corners were drawn with the custom shape tool and given the Wow Chrome Textured layer style.

Background texture: Bricks effect

Original

Artistic — Cutout

Artistic — Poster Edges

Artistic — Sponge

Artistic — Watercolor

Brush Strokes — Accented Edges

Brush Strokes — Crosshatch

Brush Strokes — Spatter

Sketch — Bas Relief

Sketch — Chalk & Charcoal

Texture — Craquelure

Texture — Patchwork

Color Plate 16: The filters found in the Filter Gallery can add interesting, "handmade" touches to your photos.

Background texture: Denim layer style

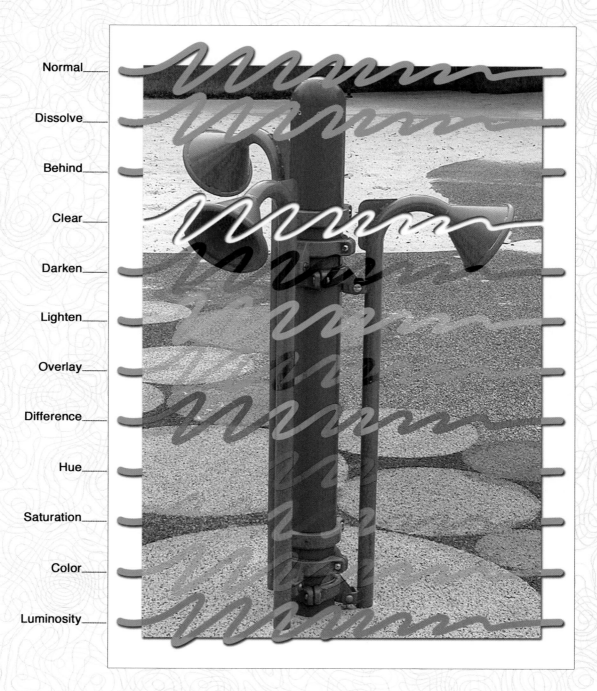

Normal

Dissolve

Behind

Clear

Darken

Lighten

Overlay

Difference

Hue

Saturation

Color

Luminosity

Color Plate 17: The brush tool's different painting modes can mix the foreground color with the image's colors in interesting and dynamic ways. This plate shows a dozen representative painting modes applied to an image. A Drop Shadow layer style has been added to the image to give a dimensional effect; note that the Clear painting mode basically acts as an eraser, completely wiping out the image and revealing the white layer underneath.

Background texture: Psychedelic Strings effect

Color Plate 18: In this plate, various style settings for the impressionist brush were used to give a hand-painted effect to the original image (inset).

Color Plate 19: The area behind the jar was filled with custom gradients created by using the Gradient Editor.

Background texture: Wood — Rosewood effect

Color Plate 20: The Create Web Photo Gallery command available in the Macintosh version of Photoshop Elements can instantly assemble a Web page out of a folder of your images. Shown here is the Spot Light style, one of many presets available.

Background texture: Batik layer style

July　　　　　2004

Sun	Mon	Tue	Wed	Thu	Fri	Sat
				1	2	3
4	5	6	7	8	9	10
11	12	13	14	15	16	17
18	19	20	21	22	23	24
25	26	27	28	29	30	31

Color Plate 21: The Windows version of Photoshop Elements provides easy-to-use layouts for making personalized creations such as the fun wall calendar pictured here.

Background texture: Green Slime effect

Figure 12-8: The effects of applying each of the single-shot sharpeners are shockingly shabby.

Unsharp Mask: The filter with the weird name

If the Adobe programmers had been in charge of naming Superman, they would have called him "Average Guy from Krypton." Rather than describing what the guy does, the programmers would describe his origins. That's exactly what they did with the Unsharp Mask filter. Rather than calling the filter "Supersharpen," which would have made a modicum of sense and may have even encouraged a few novices to give it a try, they named it after an ancient stat camera technique that a few professionals in lab coats pretend to understand to impress each other.

So forget Unsharp Mask and just think "Supersharpen." To use the "Supersharpen" command, choose Unsharp Mask. The "Supersharpen" dialog box appears, as shown in Figure 12-9.

Like the Dust & Scratches dialog box (see Chapter 11), the Unsharp Mask dialog box, shown in Figure 12-9, enables you to preview what happens when you change the values in the three option boxes. You can preview the filter in the dialog box and in the main image window. If you can't quite remember how these previewing functions work, check out Chapter 11.

Figure 12-9:
Experts
agree that
the Unsharp
Mask dialog
box really
should be
called the
*Super-
sharpen*
dialog box.

To sharpen an image, use the three slider bars like so:

✔ Change the Amount value from 1% to 500% to change the amount of sharpening. Higher Amount values produce more sharpening — but you were probably sharp enough yourself to figure that out.

✔ Adjust the Radius value to specify the width of the edges you want to sharpen. If the image is generally in good shape, use a Radius of 0.5. If the edges are soft and syrupy, like the ones in Figure 12-7, use a Radius of 1.0. And if the edges are almost nonexistent, go with 2.0. Although the resolution of your image certainly factors into the equation, you generally don't want to go any lower than 0.5 or any higher than 2.0 (though 250 is the maximum).

✔ If you're using a whole number, you don't have to painstakingly type 1.0 or 2.0 into the Radius option box. A simple 1 or 2 will suffice.

✔ As with the Threshold option in the Dust & Scratches dialog box, the Unsharp Mask Threshold option determines how different two neighboring pixels must be to be considered an edge. (See Chapter 11 for a review of this concept.) The default value of 0 tells Elements to sharpen everything. By raising the value, you tell Elements not to sharpen low-contrast pixels.

The idea behind Threshold is great, but the implementation in Elements leaves something to be desired. The filter creates an abrupt transition between sharpened and ignored pixels, resulting in an unrealistic effect. Therefore, it's usually a good idea to leave Threshold set to 0.

Some sharpening scenarios

Figure 12-10 demonstrates the effects of several different Amount and Radius values on the same detail to which the piddly little Sharpen More command was applied in Figure 12-8. Throughout Figure 12-10, the Threshold value is 0.

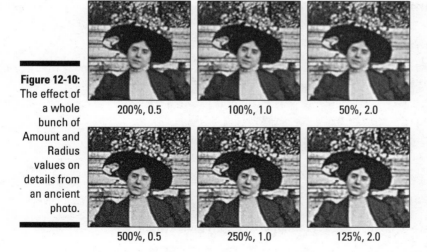

200%, 0.5   100%, 1.0   50%, 2.0

500%, 0.5   250%, 1.0   125%, 2.0

Figure 12-10: The effect of a whole bunch of Amount and Radius values on details from an ancient photo.

Figure 12-10 is organized into two rows. In the first image in the top row, the Amount value is 200% and the Radius is 0.5. Then the Amount value was halved and the Radius value was doubled in each of the next two images. Though the effect is similar from one image to the next, you can see that the right image has thicker edges than the left image. The differences are subtle; you may have to look closely. Put on your glasses (where applicable).

The bottom row of the figure features more pronounced sharpening effects. The first image in the bottom row has Amount and Radius values of 500% and 0.5. Then the Amount value was progressively halved, and the Radius value was progressively doubled. Notice that the edges in the right image are thicker, and the left image contains more artifacts (those little flecks in the jacket and hat).

After experimenting with a few different settings, the best setting seems to be an Amount of 250% and a Radius of 1.0. Figure 12-11 shows the final image sharpened with these settings.

One unfortunate byproduct of sharpening is that it can bring out digital *noise* in your image; rather than a creamy blue sky, you can get more of a blue sandpapery effect. The new Reduce Noise filter (located in the Noise category of the filters) can go a long way towards eliminating this problem. Just adjust the Strength slider to set the amount of smoothness, and increase the Preserve Details amount to bring back any smoothed-over details. If your image noise includes random pixels of vastly out-of-place colors, increase the Reduce Color Noise slider. Be careful: If Reduce Noise is abused, your subjects can take on a waxy, plastic appearance. But used properly, this filter is just the trick for silencing digital noise.

Figure 12-11:
The image from Figure 12-7 sharpened with an Amount value of 250% and a Radius value of 1.0.

Blurring Adds Depth

If you want to make a portion of your image blurry instead of sharp, you can apply one of the commands from the Blur category of the filters. Right off the bat, you quick thinkers are thinking, "Blurry? Why would I want my image to be blurry?" You're thinking of blurry as the enemy of sharp. But blurry and sharp can go hand in hand in the same image. The sharp details are in the foreground, and the blurry stuff goes in the background.

Take Figure 12-12, for example. In this image, the background was selected and blurred. The scene becomes a little more intimate, as though the background were far, far away. It also has the effect of making the foreground characters seem more in focus than ever.

The first two commands in the Blur category — Blur and Blur More — are the Dumb and Dumber of the blur filters. Like their Sharpen and Sharpen More counterparts, they produce predefined effects that never seem to be quite what you're looking for.

Figure 12-12: Blurring the background as well as a small tip of the foreground (bottom right) brings the family up close and personal.

The new Average filter, available in the Blur submenu of the filters, averages the colors of pixels. Apply it to an entire image, and you end up with a wall of solid gray. Whee. It's more useful when applied to selections, but frankly, even then it's not that useful. Feel free to ignore it, and instead sample the Blur filters that are — alphabetically speaking — *below* Average.

The filter that offers the powers you need to do the job is Gaussian Blur. The filter is named after Karl Friedrich Gauss, a dusty old German mathematician who's even older than the photograph from Figure 12-7. When you choose Gaussian Blur, the Radius value determines the number of pixels that get mixed together at a time. You can go as high as 250.0, but generally any value over 10.0 enters the realm of the legally blind. In Figure 12-12, the background was blurred with a Radius value of 4.0.

Gaussian Blur is an important part of Elements' toolkit. But of all the tools and filters we looked at in this chapter, the most valuable to you will be the Unsharp Mask filter. It's not a miracle worker — you can't take an image that's blurred beyond recognition and expect Unsharp Mask to pull details from it. But on soft-to-slightly blurry photos, it's the deal. Unsharp Mask is without question one of the top ten most important tools that Elements puts at your disposal. In fact, let's really go out on a limb: There's probably not a digital image out there that wouldn't benefit (or that hasn't already benefited) from being given a working over with Unsharp Mask.

So the next time you're in a movie theater and the screen goes all blurry because the projectionist is making out with his girlfriend and not paying attention to his job, lean your head back and scream at the top of your lungs: "Unsharp Mask! Unsharp Mask!" You'll feel better, and you'll suddenly find you have a lot of empty seats around you in the theater. Isn't digital imaging a wonderful thing?

Chapter 13

The Rainbow Correction

Here's a common scenario for you: You get some pictures or slides back from the photo developer — we're talking regular photos here, not the digital kind — and one of them catches your eye. The color is great, the composition is fantastic, everyone's smiling; it ranks among the best pictures you've ever shot. It's not 100 percent perfect, but you figure you can correct the few glitches with Photoshop Elements.

So you scan the image, open it up, and your heart sinks to the pit of your stomach. The image is dark, colorless, and generally a big, fat disappointment. The snapshot from the photo developer looks far better than this murky mess on-screen.

In a perfect world, this would never happen. But scanning is an imperfect process, and even if your scanner isn't one of those $50 "bargains," seeing a scanned photo on-screen for the first time can be discouraging.

Take Color Plate 10, for example. When viewed in a slide projector, the original slide looked something like the example in the bottom right, but when it was scanned and opened in Elements, the image appeared as shown in the upper left. If you run into a similar problem, never fear — you have cause to be optimistic. The colors may not look like much now, but chances are good that you have enough colors to get by. Although it may be hard to believe, your image very likely contains a few million colors; it's just that they're all squished toward the dark end of the spectrum. Your job is to bring these colors back to life.

We accomplished that very feat in the bottom-right image of Color Plate 10 with one Elements command: Levels. In fact, Levels and the Color Variations command are just about all you need when it comes to correcting bad scans. You don't need painting or editing tools, selection outlines, or colors added to the image. Color-correction commands merely stretch the existing colors in the image across the spectrum.

Elements offers many such commands, but you need only a few of these to do the job. In this chapter, you'll see how these miracle commands work. You'll also find out how to use adjustment layers, which let you do some of your color correcting on an independent layer, thereby providing you with extra flexibility and safety.

Color-Correcting Quickly

Photoshop Elements has a handful of fast color-correction commands designed to improve your image without any fuss on your part. These commands can be found in the Enhance menu, and they're available also in the Quick Fix mode, discussed in Chapter 12. These "instant" color-correction commands are definitely worth a try. Sometimes they do a great job, and if they make your image worse, they're easy enough to undo. Color Plate 10 shows what happens when four of these commands are applied to a dark, discolored scan of a slide.

Granted, not all images are in such bad shape, and different images will respond better to one command than another. As the lower-left image in Color Plate 10 shows, Auto Color Correction did better than Auto Levels, Auto Contrast, or Auto Smart Fix at lightening up the image and removing the color cast. However, we were still able to do a better job by hand using the more complex Levels command, as shown in the lower-right image. We'll fully explore Levels later in this chapter, but first let's take a look at the Levels command's not-so-trusty sidekick, Auto Levels.

Auto Levels

Auto Levels is sort of like that weird uncle you basically like, but you're not quite sure you can trust. Choose Enhance⇨Auto Levels or press Ctrl+Shift+L (⌘+Shift+L on the Mac) to automatically correct the contrast of an image. (You'll also find Auto Levels in the Quick Fix mode.) For example, Figure 13-1 shows a typical low-contrast image composed entirely of cheerless grays. The inset squares show the lightest and darkest colors in the image as well as some sample shades in between. With the Auto Levels command, Elements automatically makes the lightest gray white and the darkest gray black and stretches out the colors in between. Figure 13-2 shows the result.

Figure 13-1: What a dismal scene: Come to this gas station and get your tank filled with depression. The Grim Reaper will change your oil.

Figure 13-2: The Auto Levels command brings out some strong blacks and whites, but the grays remain dark and dreary. (And the autos don't look any more level than they did already.)

Unfortunately, Auto Levels doesn't always do the trick. Figure 13-2, for example, contains strong blacks and whites, but the grays appear overly dark (as witnessed by the shades in the inset squares). Furthermore, although it's not an issue in a black-and-white image like this one, Auto Levels has been known to introduce color casts to images. Auto Levels works its preset routine on each color channel individually, and this can potentially tint the entire image an off color, known in the biz as a *color cast.* Although the Levels command lets you adjust individual color channels, it also lets you adjust the channels as a whole. We cover the command in detail later in this chapter, in the section "Leveling the Contrast Field."

Further image enhancements

The Enhance menu has a few other fast and easy color-correction commands, and also some that skirt along the edges of slow and difficult. We'll look at Levels and Color Variations at length later in the chapter; for now let's concentrate on the others.

Auto Smart Fix

New to Elements 3.0, the Enhance menu's Auto Smart Fix command (Ctrl+M; ⌘+M on the Mac) promises to correct your colors, improve your shadows, and highlight your details, all in a single mouse click. As with all commands that start with the word *Auto,* sometimes it works well, sometimes it doesn't. If you feel it doesn't, try its cousin, Enhance menu's Adjust Smart Fix (Ctrl+Shift+M; ⌘+Shift+M on the Mac). This command gives you a Fix Amount slider to adjust the Smart Fix from a totally moronic 0 percent to an Einstein-level 200 percent.

For a truly smart fix, try Levels and Color Variations, described later in this chapter.

Auto Contrast

Avoid using Auto Contrast (Enhance⇨Auto Contrast). Stick with correcting contrast in an image by using the Auto Levels command — or better yet, use Levels, which gives you control.

Auto Color Correction

This command takes an image's midtones into consideration as it corrects the image. More often than not, Auto Color Correction gives more satisfactory results than any of the other one-shot commands. Definitely give it a try; if you don't like the results, simply undo and try Levels and Color Variations.

Shadows/Highlights

The functionality of the old Adjust Backlighting and Fill Flash commands has been rolled into the new Shadows/Highlights command. Located in the Adjust Lighting submenu, this command is designed to easily compensate for common photographic lighting problems. You probably have more than a few photos where the subjects in the foreground are in the shadows, yet the background behind them is extremely bright. (You guessed it: The flash didn't go off.) The Lighten Shadows slider can help bring out details in the shadowy foreground, whereas the Darken Highlights slider can lower the brightness of the sunny background. (Bear in mind that Elements has no idea what the foreground and background of the image are; it just looks at the brightness values of the pixels.) When you darken highlights and lighten shadows, you tend to push the entire image toward midtones; the Midtone Contrast slider can restore a bit of contrast to the image. Color Plate 11 shows a before-and-after view of an image that benefits greatly from the Shadows/Highlights command.

Brightness/Contrast

The Brightness/Contrast command (Enhance⇨Adjust Lighting⇨Brightness/ Contrast) is utterly and completely worthless. Seriously. If you've never used it, don't start. If you have used it, stop — you're hurting your images. You can improve brightness and contrast in plenty of other ways, the Levels command being foremost among them.

Remove Color Cast

Using the Remove Color Cast command (Enhance⇨Adjust Color⇨Remove Color Cast) is a breeze. Just select the command and use the eyedropper tool to click on an area in your image that should be devoid of color — white, black, or gray. Remove Color Cast will perform the necessary correction to drain the clicked area of color, adjusting the entire image accordingly. This command either works, as in Color Plate 13, or it doesn't. Whether or not it works depends on your image. It's certainly possible that your image may not contain any areas that ought to be white or black; in that case, move on to Color Variations as a color-cast correction tool.

Adjust Hue/Saturation

The Adjust Hue/Saturation command (Enhance⇨Adjust Color⇨Adjust Hue/ Saturation) is powerful for changing color and color intensity. The Hue slider rotates the color in your image around the color spectrum. Small adjustments can correct color casts, whereas large adjustments can create strange effects. Keep an eye on the rainbow-colored bars at the bottom of the dialog box; the top bar represents the colors of your image, and the bottom bar represents the hue shift. For example, crank the slider until the yellow in the bottom bar is below the red in the top bar, and you'll see that red objects in your image have taken on a yellow hue. The Saturation slider increases or decreases the intensity of colors, and the Lightness slider changes the overall brightness. Selecting the Colorize check box gives your image one overall tone, useful for creating sepia effects.

One of the most useful functions of Adjust Hue/Saturation is to desaturate only certain colors in an image. For instance, photos taken with some digital cameras tend to have oversaturated reds. That's where the Edit menu at the top of the dialog box comes into play. If you choose Reds from the Edit menu, changes you make with the Hue/Saturation controls will affect only the red hues in your image.

With a specific color range selected in the Edit menu, you can also adjust the range of affected colors with the eyedroppers and the Range controls, labeled in Figure 13-3. You can click the left eyedropper in your image to isolate a color, click the middle eyedropper to add a color to the range, and click the right eyedropper to subtract colors from the range. As you do so, you'll see the Range and Fuzziness controls move between the two rainbow bars. You can also drag these controls around to alter the range of affected colors. The area between the two range controls represents the color range you're isolating. The areas on either side of the range, bracketed by the triangular sliders, represent the fuzziness, affecting how far outside the range of isolated colors you want your changes to spread.

If that preceding paragraph has you scratching your head, don't worry about it. You'll probably never have to use these controls. If you need to isolate a range of colors, one of the six choices under the command's Edit menu should suffice.

 Although Adjust Hue/Saturation is a powerful, useful tool, you should never choose the Adjust Hue/Saturation command. "Why?" we hope you're asking. "Well," we answer, "because Hue/Saturation is available as an adjustment layer!" And for the straight dope on adjustment layers, see the section "Fiddling with Adjustment Layers," later in this chapter.

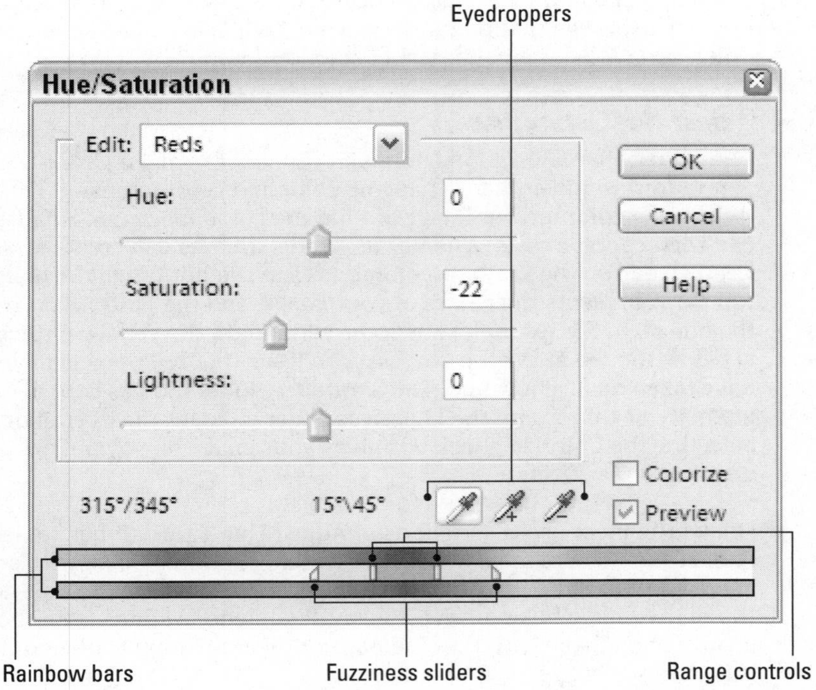

Eyedroppers

Figure 13-3:
The Adjust
Hue/
Saturation
command
lets you
make global
or selective
changes to
the colors in
your image.

Hue/Saturation

Edit: Reds

Hue: 0

Saturation: -22

Lightness: 0

OK

Cancel

Help

315°/345°   15°\45°

Colorize
Preview

Rainbow bars   Fuzziness sliders   Range controls

Remove Color

The Remove Color command (Enhance⇨Adjust Color⇨Remove Color) is just the thing for draining the color from a single layer or selected area and leaving it black and white. But if you want to convert an entire image to grayscale, choose Image⇨Mode⇨Grayscale instead (and see Chapter 5 for details).

Replacing Colors

Up to now, this chapter has dealt with color-correction commands that are designed to make your images look more like real life. But the Replace Color command and the new color replacement tool approach the concept of color "correction" from a slightly different angle — more like "That red ribbon I won really *should* have been blue!" Replace Color excels at isolating a single color in an image and turning it into a different color; at its core, it's a close cousin to Adjust Hue/Saturation. And if you used the previous version of Elements, you'll see that the color replacement tool is closely related to the old red eye brush.

The Replace Color command

To apply Replace Color, choose Enhance⇨Adjust Color⇨Replace Color. The Replace Color dialog box appears, as nobly depicted in Figure 13-4. The dialog box is divided into two parts: Selection and Replacement.

To use the Replace Color command, do the following:

1. **Apply Replace Color to your entire image or to a selection.**

   If an area of color in your image is similar to the one you want to replace, it may be a good idea to draw a rough selection around your target area. For more on selections, see Chapter 9.

2. **Click the Image radio button.**

   The image or the selected portion appears in the preview.

3. **With the eyedropper tool, click in your target area in the preview or in the image window.**

4. **Switch to the Selection radio button.**

   You should see the results of your selection in the preview window in white. Black areas in the Selection preview are totally unselected, white areas are completely selected, and gray areas are partially selected.

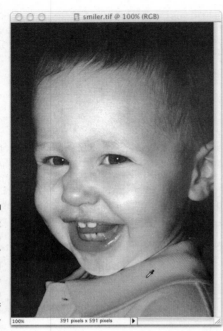

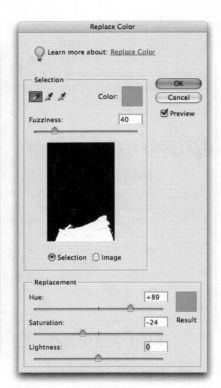

Figure 13-4:
The Replace
Color
command
can isolate
and replace
an area of
color in your
image.

5. **Adjust your selection with the add eyedropper, the subtract eyedropper, and the Fuzziness slider.**

   The add and subtract eyedroppers add to and take away from the targeted color area. The Fuzziness slider expands or contracts your selection. Higher Fuzziness values select more colors, and lower values select fewer colors. If you make an arbitrary change to the color using the Replacement sliders, you'll be able to see the selection in the image window as well. This can help you judge the quality of your selection.

   You can also click the new Color swatch to adjust the selected color using the Color Picker.

6. **When you're happy with your selection, change the color using the Replacement sliders.**

   You can adjust the hue (the "color" of the color), saturation (the richness of the color), and lightness (how light or dark the color is). The Sample swatch shows you the resultant color.

7. **When you're happy, click OK.**

   The color of the selected area is replaced with your new color. Color Plate 12 fittingly provides an example in living color.

Replace Color uses a sophisticated selection method that yields results that equal or surpass those of any of the standard selection tools. It's also a versatile command; as noted in Chapter 11, Replace Color can be a more powerful alternative to the red eye removal tool. Just draw a selection around your subject's eyes, apply Replace Color, select the red glow, and change its saturation and lightness.

The color replacement tool

Basically, the color replacement tool works by taking a color sample from the area in which you first click and then applying your foreground color to any area that matches your sample. If you were to use it to eliminate red eye, for example, you'd set your foreground color to near black, click in the middle of the red glow, and paint away. Here's a rundown of the controls available in the tool options bar:

- **Brush:** This pop-up palette lets you set the diameter and hardness of your brush, plus a few other options. These are covered at length in Chapter 15 in the section "Making your own brush."

- **Mode:** This menu tells the tool how to combine the newly painted pixels with the ones you're painting over. The default setting, Color, is almost always the best choice.

- **Sampling:** This option helps Elements decide what color you want to replace. Continuous causes the tool to keep sampling colors nonstop while you paint instead of changing only the color you first clicked on. A better choice is Once, which lets you change only the color upon which you first clicked. The final choice, Background Swatch, selects the designated background color as the color to be replaced. Generally, stick with Once.

- **Limits:** So you have Mode set to Color and Sampling set to Once, and you click in the middle of a glowing red eye and paint it away. What happens if — without releasing the mouse button — you drag over to the other eye to correct it as well? With Contiguous selected, the other eye won't be corrected, because the second pool of red isn't adjacent to the first. With Discontiguous selected, the other eye will get corrected.

- **Tolerance:** This slider determines how close a color has to be to the color of the pixel you clicked for it to be affected by the color replacement tool. Low values mean the color needs to be close; higher values mean that the tool will change a broader range of color.

- **Anti-aliased:** This allows for soft edges. Definitely turn it on.

As with Elements' red eye brush, the results you get with the color replacement tool vary from image to image. Getting the tool to work only where you want can be tricky; you're probably better off mastering the less-intuitive but more-powerful Replace Color command. Still, by all means give the color replacement tool a shot.

Fiddling with Adjustment Layers

Adjustment layers are really great. They operate just like the layers discussed in Chapter 10, except that you use them expressly to apply color-correction commands. By default, an *adjustment layer* applies the chosen color correction to every layer beneath it. However, you can always turn off the visibility of an adjustment layer or just delete it entirely, either way restoring your image to its original condition. Adjustment layers are often referred to as *non-destructive,* meaning that they don't permanently change the pixels in your original image; they float just above the pixels, making them look better. It's like having your cake and eating it too.

It's a shame, then, that Elements gives you only three truly useful commands that are available as adjustment layers: Levels, Hue/Saturation, and the sometimes useful Photo Filters, which we look at in the upcoming section "The Photo Filters." The other choices include Brightness/Contrast (boo, hiss) and a handful of commands also available in the Filter⇨Adjustments submenu that are handy when you need them, but that probably won't be too often.

Sharing space with adjustment layers are fill layers. You can use *fill layers* to add a layer of solid color, a gradient, or a pattern. Other than the masking abilities that fill layers share with adjustment layers (see the upcoming Technical Stuff icon), there's really nothing you can do with fill layers that you can't do just by selecting an ordinary layer and filling it with color. Fill layers have nothing to do with color correction, but for convenience's sake we take a look at them here, too.

Using adjustment and fill layers

As touched on earlier, adjustment and fill layers offer several advantages over ordinary layers:

- By default, the color correction of adjustment layers affects all the layers that lie beneath it in the Layers palette. Applying an ordinary color-correction command affects only the active layer.

- You can create as many different adjustment layers as you want. So, if you want a few layers to use just one color correction and the rest of the image to use another as well, just create two adjustment layers. You can also create as many fill layers as you want.

✔ Because the color correction exists on its own layer, you can experiment freely without fear of damaging the image. If, at some point, you decide that you don't like the effects of the color correction, you can edit the adjustment layer or just delete it and start fresh. You can also edit or delete fill layers.

✔ You can blend adjustment and fill layers with the other layers using the opacity and blending mode settings in the Layers palette, just as you can with any layer. (More on blending modes in Chapter 14.) These features give you even more control over how your image appears.

To create an adjustment layer, do the following:

1. **In the Layers palette, click the layer that you want to color correct.**

   When you create an adjustment layer, Elements places it directly on top of the active layer in the Layers palette. This adjustment affects the layer or layers underneath, depending on whether you turn on the Group with Previous Layer check box as mentioned in the next step.

   If you select a portion of your image before creating the adjustment layer, the color correction affects only the selected area across all underlying layers.

2. **Choose Layer⇨New Adjustment Layer and then select your desired adjustment from the submenu.**

   To follow along with the example, choose Levels. The New Layer dialog box appears. Here's a field guide to your options: If you want to give your adjustment layer a specific name, enter the name into the top option box. Skip the Mode and Opacity drop-down menus; if you want, you can change these settings later in the Layers palette. For now, skip the Group with Previous Layer check box. We'll look at this a little later in the chapter.

3. **Press Enter (Return on the Mac).**

   Elements adds the adjustment layer to the Layers palette and displays the Levels dialog box, which is explained in the next section.

Creating a fill layer is just as easy. Simply choose Layer⇨New Fill Layer and then choose Solid color, Gradient, or Pattern from the submenu.

You can also click the create adjustment layer icon in the Layers palette and select an option from the menu. This bypasses the New Layer dialog box, unless you hold down the Alt or Option key as you click the icon.

You may be wondering what that extra thumbnail shown in Figure 13-5 is; here's a brief explanation. Elements adds a *layer mask* to every adjustment or fill layer. In short, layer masks are like pieces of clear acetate that hover over the layer. You paint on them to selectively hide or display the adjustment or fill effect. Black pixels on the layer mask hide, white pixels show, and any gray colors in-between display or hide in varying degrees of transparency. In other words, to display the full-strength adjustment or fill over the image, leave the layer mask white (the default). To remove the adjustment or fill over the image, paint the mask with black. To partially display the adjustment, paint the mask with gray. To isolate only one portion of an image, leave it white and paint the rest of the layer mask black. The brush and gradient tools work best for layer masks.

The easiest way to paint on the layer mask is by Alt+Shift-clicking (Option+Shift-clicking on the Mac) on the layer mask thumbnail. If you've ever used the selection brush in Mask mode, this should now look familiar to you. As you then start to paint with black or gray in the image window, you'll see a pink overlay appear on the image. Where things are darkest pink, the layer mask is totally blocking the effect of the adjustment layer. Where things look normal, there's little or no blocking going on. You can also Alt-click (Option-click on the Mac) to view just the mask in grayscale without the underlying image. Shift-click the layer mask thumbnail to turn off the effects of the mask temporarily. Performing either of those commands again will set things back to normal.

In many ways an adjustment or fill layer works just like any other layer in the Layers palette. You can vary the effects of the adjustment by playing with the Opacity slider and blending modes; you can move the layer up or down in the Layers palette to affect different layers; and you can merge the layer with an underlying layer to permanently fuse the color correction or fill to the image. (You can't, however, merge an adjustment or fill layer with another adjustment or fill layer.)

If you want to change the settings for an adjustment or fill layer, just double-click the adjustment or fill layer icon in the Layers palette. You can also select the adjustment or fill layer and choose Layer⇨Layer Content Options. Elements redisplays the appropriate dialog box so you can modify the settings. To delete the adjustment or fill layer, drag it to the trash icon in the Layers palette.

To change the type of your adjustment or fill layer, choose Layer⇨Change Layer Content and select the new type of adjustment or fill you want.

You can flip back and forth between a view of your corrected image and your uncorrected image by clicking the eyeball icon next to the adjustment layer name in the Layers palette. When the eyeball is present, the layer is visible, showing you the color-corrected image. When the eyeball is hidden, so is the layer, giving you a "before" view of your image. You can do the same with fill layers.

New fill or adjustment layer

Clipping group icon   Fill layer

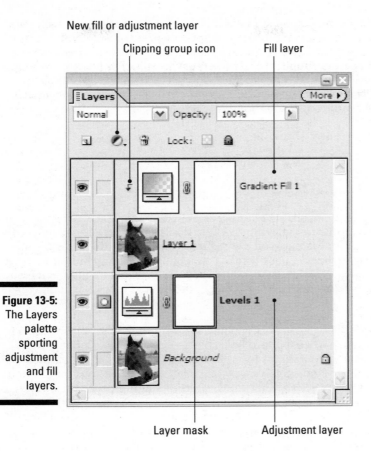

Figure 13-5:
The Layers
palette
sporting
adjustment
and fill
layers.

Layer mask   Adjustment layer

Let's have a brief explanation of the Group with Previous Layer option we told you to skip earlier. If you check this box in the New Layer dialog box, the adjustment or fill layer will affect only the pixels of the immediately underlying layer. Any layers below that will be unaffected. This technique is referred to in Elements' higher circles as a clipping group. In a *clipping group,* multiple layers are combined into a group, with the lowest layer in the group masking the others. You can create clipping groups also with regular layers. You can create a clipping group not only by selecting the Group with Previous Layer option in the New Layer dialog box, but also by selecting the adjustment or fill layer in the Layers palette and choosing Layer⇨Group with Previous or pressing Ctrl+G (⌘+G on the Mac). Or simply press the Alt key (Option key on the Mac) and click the horizontal line between the two layers. Notice that when you hold down the Alt or Option key, your cursor icon changes to an arrow with two circles. After you click, a small down-pointing arrow appears on the top layer (refer to Figure 13-5). To remove the clipping group, simply Alt-click (Option-click on the Mac) again or choose Layer⇨Ungroup or press Ctrl+Shift+G (⌘+Shift+G on the Mac).

Adjustment layers are so powerful and flexible, we'll crawl out on a limb and say you should absolutely *never* use the Levels and Adjust Hue/Saturation commands, but rather apply these commands as adjustment layers. True, most file formats don't support adjustment layers, but if you want to end up with a flat JPEG of an image, it's still a good idea to keep a layered PSD file around as a backup. Why make a permanent change to your original image when you may want to tweak it differently later?

Adjustment layers, in a word, rule.

The Photo Filters

The Photo Filters are available not only as adjustment layers, but also by choosing Filter⇨Adjustments⇨Photo Filter. Photo Filters are based on the filters that photographers place on their cameras to correct the color balance of their photos. Sunlight generally takes on a bluish cast, and indoor lighting often produces shades of reds and yellows. A photographer's filter can compensate for this before the picture is taken; the Photo Filters can compensate after the fact.

The Photo Filter dialog box gives you just a few options. The two Warming filters are good to use when a photo has a bluish cast, and the Cooling filters are a good choice to counteract the yellows of indoor lighting. The other choices in the Filter menu give you a wide array of color options for different effects. You can also click the Color radio button and then click the swatch to choose your own filter color from the Color Picker. The Density slider adjusts the intensity of the filter, and the Preserve Luminosity check box will keep the brightness values in your image the same after the filter is applied.

If you have a lot of experience with photography, you'll probably warm up to the Photo Filters quickly. They provide excellent simulations of their real-life counterparts. And because they're available as adjustment layers (Did we mention how much we like adjustment layers?), you can remove their effect at any time — something you definitely can't do in a photo taken with a real-world filter.

Color-Correcting Correctly

As we mentioned at the beginning of this chapter, Levels and Color Variations are pretty much the only commands you need when color correcting images. Sure, give the others a try. But sooner or later, you'll run into a problem image that just won't respond to the one-shot-wonder commands. That's where Levels and Color Variations come in. Although Color Variations is fairly intuitive, Levels is somewhat intimidating. Don't worry — that's why we're here.

Leveling the Contrast Field

Levels is one of the most essential functions in Elements. In fact, if an image displays any of the following symptoms, you can correct it with Levels:

- The image is murky, without strong lights and darks, like the one in Figure 13-1.
- The image has a color cast, like the one in Color Plate 10.
- The image is too light.
- The image is too dark.
- The image is gaining weight, losing hair, and developing bags under its eyes.

Whoops, that last item sneaked in by mistake. If an image gains weight, loses hair, and develops baggy eyes, you have to send it on a three-week cruise in the Caribbean. And tell it to stop writing computer books.

Making friends with the Levels dialog box

To apply the Levels command, you can create a new adjustment layer, as recommended in the preceding section, or choose Enhance⇨Adjust Lighting⇨ Levels, or press Ctrl+L (⌘+L on the Mac). Whichever method you use, the dialog box shown in Figure 13-6 appears.

Histogram

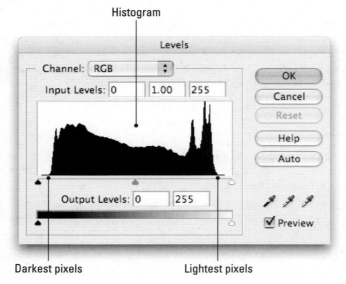

Figure 13-6:
The complicated-looking Levels dialog box contains many options that you don't need to worry about.

Darkest pixels   Lightest pixels

Luckily, you usually don't need to address all the options that inhabit this dialog box. So, before you break into a cold sweat or shriek at the top of your lungs (or do whatever it is you do when you see terrifying sights like Figure 13-6), let's try to distinguish the important options in this dialog box from the stuff you won't use very often:

- ✔ The options in the Channel menu let you adjust one color channel in a full-color image independently of the other channels. (This is proof-positive that those red, green, and blue color channels we told you about in Chapter 5 are really there.) These options are helpful if you know what you're doing, but they're generally not that important. We took full advantage of the three color channels to correct the image in Color Plate 10 with Levels, but you can remove color casts in other, easier ways, such as with Color Variations.

- ✔ The three Input Levels option boxes control the settings of the darkest, medium, and lightest pixels in your image, in that order. These options are important, which is why we cover them thoroughly in the next section.

- ✔ That black birthmark in the middle of the dialog box is called a *histogram*. It shows you how the colors in your image are currently distributed. It also rates the Seal of Importance.

- ✔ The slider bar directly below the histogram provides three triangles, one each for the darkest, medium, and lightest pixels in your image. These triangles correspond to the Input Levels option boxes and are the most important options of all.

- ✔ The Output Levels option boxes and the accompanying slider bar let you make the darkest colors lighter and the lightest colors darker, which is usually the opposite of what you want to do. Mark these options Not Particularly Important on your screen with a grease pencil. (Just kidding.)

- ✔ The OK and Cancel buttons are as important as always. One applies your changes, the other doesn't. No prizes for guessing which does what.

- ✔ The new Reset button restores things to the way they were when you entered the dialog box. Very helpful.

- ✔ Clicking the Auto button is exactly like applying Auto Levels. The only time you might want to use this button is if you want to apply the Auto Levels command as an adjustment layer.

- ✔ The three eyedropper icons let you click colors in your image to make them black, medium gray, or white. Steer clear of these icons except to stamp them Not Important, Ditto, and Doubly So.

- ✔ The Preview check box lets you view the effect of your edits in the image window. It's very important that you turn this option on.

The Histogram palette

So you find you love looking at histograms, and you want more, more, more? You're in luck! The new Histogram palette (choose Window⇨Histogram) is now available as a constant reminder of the beauty and wonder that is the histogram. Actually, the Histogram palette, seen in Figure 13-7, is pretty danged useful. The Channel menu lets you view each color channel individually or the RGB composite as a whole. You can also get a reading on the image's luminosity values, or choose Color for a spectacular full-color display.

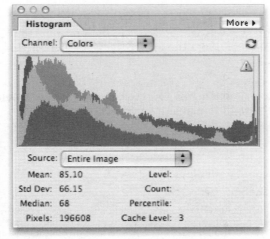

Figure 13-7:
The magnificent new Histogram palette.

The Source menu lets you view the histogram for the entire image or a selected layer. Or you can click an adjustment layer in the Layers palette, choose Adjustment Composite from the Source menu, and see the histogram for the layers being affected by the selected adjustment layer. By default, the Histogram palette shows an approximation of the correct histogram so that it can display faster, but if you click the recycling icon in the upper-right corner of the palette, the Histogram will recalculate to display an exact map of your image's levels.

Brightness and contrast as they should be

The histogram from the Levels command seen in Figure 13-6 is a graph of the color in the uncorrected image in Figure 13-8. The graph is organized from darkest colors on the left to lightest colors on the right. The peaks and valleys in the histogram show the color distribution. If the darkest colors were black, the histogram would start on the far-left edge of the slider bar. If the lightest colors were white, it would continue to the far-right edge. But as it is, the left and right edges taper off into flatlands. This means that the darkest and lightest pixels in the image are not as dark or light as they could be.

If some of that information went a little over your head, not to worry. Some folks like graphs, but other folks see a graph, think they're in a board meeting, and start to nod off. Either way, remember that the histogram is provided for your reference only. All that matters is how you adjust the slider triangles below the histogram:

✔ To make the darkest pixels black, drag the left slider triangle to the right so that it rests directly under the beginning of the first hill in the histogram. Figure 13-9 shows the dragged triangle and its effect on the image.

✔ To make the lightest pixels white, drag the right triangle to the left so that it lines up directly under the end of the last hill in the histogram, as in Figure 13-10.

✔ The most important triangle is the middle one. Called the *gamma point,* this triangle lets you change the brightness of the medium colors in your image. Drag to the right to make the medium colors darker. But more likely, you want to drag to the left to make the medium colors lighter, as demonstrated in Figure 13-11.

Figure 13-8:
This placid scene is simply awaiting an application of Levels.

Figure 13-9:
Dragging the first triangle affects the darkest pixels in the image.

Figure 13-10:
The image lightens when the white triangle is dragged to the left.

Input Levels: 18 1.31 233

Figure 13-11:
Dragging
the middle
triangle
brings out
the detail in
an image.

The values in the three option boxes above the histogram are updated as you drag the slider triangles. The left and right values are measured in color levels. Just like the RGB values in the Color Picker — where you define colors (see Chapter 5) — 0 is black and 255 is white. So if the left value is 18, as it is in Figures 13-9 through 13-11, any pixel colored with a level of 18 or darker becomes black. And if that explanation already has your mind reeling, trying to understand the workings of the gamma value — the middle one — would no doubt make your head explode. The point is, a gamma value of more than 1 lightens the medium colors; a value less than 1 darkens them.

Bear in mind that you can tweak these values for each color channel individually using the Channel menu, just as we did in Color Plate 10. But if you want to see the effect of the Levels command when applied to the combined RGB channels, you need look no further than Color Plate 13. We followed up Levels with the Remove Color Cast command, which in this case worked very well in eliminating the image's color cast.

Take the time to master Levels. It's bound to be good for any image.

If you notice a loss of color in your image after you apply the Levels command, don't worry. You can get that color back by using the Color Variations command, discussed next.

Variations on a Color Scheme

One negative effect of manipulating the brightness levels in an image is that it can weaken some of the colors, particularly if you lighten the medium colors by dragging the gamma point in the Levels dialog box to the left. To bring the colors back to their original intensity, choose Enhance⇨Adjust Color⇨Color Variations.

Although Elements has a dedicated Remove Color Cast command, the Color Variations command is generally more reliable in curing color casts, in which one color is particularly prominent in the image. A photograph shot outdoors, for example, may be overly blue; one shot in an X-rated motel room may be a shade heavy in the reds. Whatever color predominates your image, the Color Variations command can tone it down with elegance and ease. But first we'll examine how Color Variations can boost the colors in a Levels-corrected image.

Turning plain old color into Technicolor

To bolster the intensity of colors in your image — for what it's worth, color intensity is called *saturation* in image-editing vernacular — follow these pleasant steps:

1. **Choose Enhance⇨Adjust Color⇨Color Variations.**

   The enormous Color Variations dialog box erupts onto your screen, filled with a bunch of small previews of your image.

2. **Select the Saturation radio button, in the lower-left corner of the dialog box.**

   Most of the small preview images disappear. Only four remain, as shown in Figure 13-12. The two previews at the bottom of the dialog box represent different color intensities. The top two larger previews show the image as it appeared before you chose the Color Variations command and how it looks now, subject to the changes in the Color Variations dialog box.

3. **Drag the slider in the lower-left corner to the left.**

   This slider controls the extent of the changes made in the Color Variations dialog box. If you drag the triangle to the right, the changes become more drastic; drag it to the left, and they become more gradual. The setting is reflected in the previews at the bottom of the dialog box. The changes become more subtle as you drag to the left, and therefore the two previews at the bottom begin to resemble each other more and more.

   Because color intensity is a sensitive function in Elements, it's best to set the slider pretty far over to the left so that you can make gentle, incremental changes.

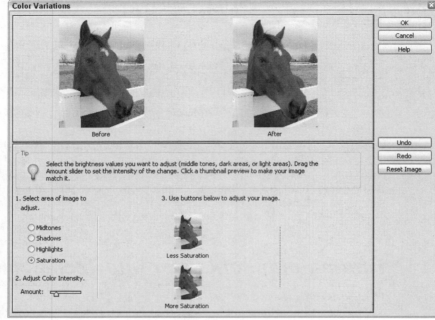

Figure 13-12:
Click the
More
Saturation
preview to
boost the
intensity of
the colors in
an image.

4. To increase color intensity, click the preview labeled More Saturation.

Clicking once increases the intensity by a small amount, owing to the slider bar setting. To add more intensity, click again. Each time you click, the After preview at the top of the dialog box updates to reflect your latest change.

If at any time you want to reset the After preview to the original image, click the Reset Image button or just click the Before preview.

5. When you're satisfied with the increased color intensity, press Enter (Return on the Mac).

Elements applies your settings to the original image, just as they were shown in the After preview. No surprises with this dialog box.

Changes you make using the Color Variations dialog box affect only the active layer. Unfortunately, you can't apply the Color Variations command using an adjustment layer as you can with the Levels and Hue/Saturation commands. For this reason, Hue/Saturation is arguably a better choice for increasing depleted saturation in an image; because you can use it on an adjustment layer, your changes won't be permanent. Then again, some people greatly prefer Color Variations' preview-clicking approach. Either way, Elements can satisfy.

Color Plate 14 gives you some idea of the various changes that Color Variations can make to your image.

Casting away bad colors

To remove a color cast using Color Variations, here's what you do:

1. **Choose Enhance⇨Adjust Color⇨Color Variations.**

   The Color Variations dialog box takes over your screen.

2. **Select the Midtones radio button, in the lower-left corner of the dialog box.**

   This option lets you edit the medium colors in your image. (You can likewise edit the dark or light colors by selecting Shadows or Highlights, but it's best to start with the Midtones because that's usually the principal source of the problem.)

   After you select Midtones, the bottom portion of the dialog box fills with eight previews, as shown in Figure 13-13. The six previews on the left let you shift the colors in the image toward or away from the three color channels in Elements — red, green, or blue. The two previews on the right let you lighten and darken the image. But because they're less capable than the gamma point control in the Levels dialog box, you can feel free to ignore them.

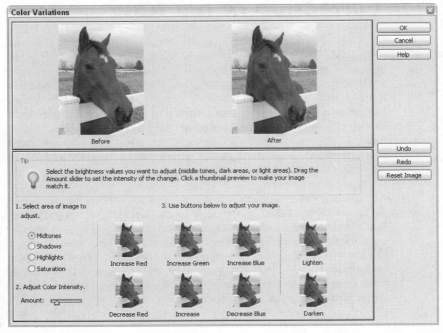

Figure 13-13: Click the Increase Blue preview to add blue in an image. Click Decrease Red to subtract red. You get the idea.

3. **Drag the slider in the lower-left corner to the left.**

   As with saturation earlier, it's best to adjust the colors in small increments.

4. **Click one of the Increase or Decrease previews to shift the colors in the image toward or away from a particular color.**

   Again, Color Plate 14 can give you another look at how clicking the previews can affect your image.

5. **If you go too far toward one color, don't panic.**

   You can do one of several things if you think your image is going to pot. If that last click of Increase Red really messed things up, click Decrease Red or simply click the Undo button. If you then decide things weren't so bad after all, click Increase Red again or click the Redo button. If you've made a total mess of your image, click the Before preview or click the Reset Image button.

Not only does Elements present you with variations on the colors in your image, it also gives you variations on ways to correct your screw-ups. You've gotta love an application like that.

Color Correcting in the Raw

Oh, stop blushing. We're talking about color correcting in the new Camera Raw dialog box. If you don't know what that is, allow us to explain. You see, after you snap a picture with your digital camera, the camera itself performs a whole bunch of operations designed to make the image look better. It's as if a tiny little person with a tiny little computer running a tiny little version of Elements is inside your camera, trying to make your pictures look better before you ever see them. To digital imaging professionals, this is not good news. Every improvement comes at some sort of cost to the image, and the real pros want to be able to work with an image exactly as their very expensive camera first saw it.

And so, on high-end and some midrange cameras, rather than taking JPEGs or TIFFs, users can take Camera Raw format images, which preserve all the original data info without any interference from the tiny guy in the camera. When you open a Camera Raw image in Elements, the enormous dialog box shown in Figure 13-14 appears. The dialog box contains a large preview, a histogram, and a bunch of controls that let *you* be the tiny guy in the camera, tweaking your image's colors before it gets sampled down to 16 or 8 bits per channel when you open it fully in Elements.

Figure 13-14:
This dialog box provides a smooth transition from the high-end Camera Raw format to the world of Elements.

Here's a quick rundown on the controls:

- ✓ **Depth:** Below the image preview is the Depth menu; set this to 8 Bits/Channel so that you'll have full access to the tools in Elements.

- ✓ **Settings:** Below the histogram, choose Selected Image from the Settings menu if you've opened this image before in Camera Raw and want to apply the same settings. Choose Camera Default to apply the settings for your make and model of camera from Camera Raw's database of camera profiles. Previous Conversion applies the settings from the last image you opened in Camera Raw that came from the same camera.

- ✓ **White Balance:** As Shot is the best choice if your camera preserves white balance info in the image's metadata. If not, or if you have no idea what that means, choose Auto.

- ✓ **Temperature:** Drag to the left to cool the image with blue; drag to the right to heat up the image with yellow.

- ✓ **Tint:** Drag to the left to tint the image green; drag to the right to *tint-a* magenta.

- ✓ **Exposure, Shadows, Brightness,** and **Contrast:** The Auto check boxes are safe bets, but adjust the sliders if you don't like what you see.

- ✓ **Saturation:** Drag to the right to increase the intensity of the colors.

- ✓ **Sharpness:** Leave this alone, and sharpen with Unsharp Mask after you fully open the image in Elements.

- ✓ **Luminance Smoothing:** This can reduce grayscale noise in an image, but use it very sparingly.

- ✓ **Color Noise Reduction:** This reduces color noise in the image; again, use a light touch.

After you click OK, Camera Raw calculates its settings and the image opens like normal in Elements. Note, however, that the image is actually a new file generated by the Camera Raw dialog box; your original Camera Raw image remains untouched.

If your digital camera doesn't take Camera Raw images, you'll never even see the Camera Raw dialog box. But if you have the right kind of camera, the next time you use this special format, you won't have to feel entirely raw yourself.

Part IV
Unreality Programming

The 5th Wave · By Rich Tennant

Jeez—that's impressive! Let's see that airbrush effect again.

In this part . . .

Thomas Alva Edison supposedly once said "Genius is 1 percent inspiration and 99 percent perspiration." (Unfortunately there's no record of him actually saying this, because he hadn't invented the phonograph at the time.) Although this quote brings to mind visions of sweat dripping down Mr. Edison's neck and into open light bulb sockets, he does have a point. A brilliant idea is nothing without the hours of back-breaking hard labor necessary to bring it to fruition.

Then again, Edison never used Photoshop Elements. (Recently unearthed evidence shows he never got beyond MacPaint 1.0.) With Elements, it's so easy to get the flashes of genius out of your head and on to the screen that it completely throws Edison's inspiration/perspiration equation out of whack. We're talking 90/10 . . . maybe 85/15 at the *most*. The previous parts of this book deal with enhancing the reality in your images; this part throws reality out the window and lets your imagination run wild. From painting and drawing to applying drop shadows and bevels, from adding text to stretching faces like Silly Putty — it's all here. We also look at some automated features that Elements offers; these amazing commands push the inspiration/perspiration equation to about 99/1.

But first, you have to perspire just a teeny bit while we help you master these powerful tools. Feel free to rip the pages from this book one by one as you finish reading them and use them to mop your fevered brow. We'll be proud to know that we've provided you with such absorbing literature.

Chapter 14

Startling Style

Come on, admit it. You're so ready for this chapter, you can taste it. Already, as you were working through this book, mischievous little ideas began to pop into your head. Maybe you were using the clone stamp tool to get rid of some dust specks in the sky, and you thought, "Gee, you know, this clone stamp tool is doing such a good job, that I guess — in theory — I could keep using this tool . . . to completely clone away my brother's head!"

Or maybe you were using the Replace Color command to gently tweak the color of your Uncle Waldo's cardigan sweater, and the thought occurred to you, "Well, gee whiz, this Replace Color command is doing such a nice job on Uncle Waldo's sweater, that I guess — in theory — I could use it to turn his head a virulent shade of screaming purple!"

Don't feel bad. It's perfectly normal to come to the realization that the image-correction tools in Elements can be not only used, but also abused. In truth, Elements has a host of other tools designed to let you inject images with your own personal sense of style — no matter how funky, bizarre, or downright perverse that sense of style may be. Some of these tools, such as the layer styles, you'll probably want to use every day. Others, such as blending modes, are useful for special effects. And still others, such as the Liquify command, are more-or-less digital torture devices, letting you vent your aggressions against your foes by pushing around a few pixels.

Add these tools to your Elements arsenal and you'll be able to not only make your images look more real than life, but also infuse that life with your personal sense of style.

Using Layer Styles to Shine and Shadow

If you want to create a dimensional-looking Web button or imbue your text with a true sense of depth, layer styles are the place to be. Elements makes the application of effects such as drop shadows, glows, and bevels mere child's play with the layer styles available in the Styles and Effects palette. Layer styles can be applied to regular layers and text layers (see Chapter 17), but not to the background layer.

Layer styles are linked to the contents of a layer. If you edit the contents, the styles are updated automatically, which makes layer styles incredibly flexible. Here is a step-by-step guide to applying a layer style:

1. **Start with an object on an active layer.**

   With layer styles in the bevel, shadow, and glow categories, you'll see the best results if there's transparency around the edges of the object. Text on a text layer is a great place to start.

2. **In the Styles and Effects palette, choose Layer Styles.**

   By default, the Styles and Effects palette is in the palette bin. If your Styles and Effects palette is currently hidden, choose Window⇨Styles and Effects to display it.

3. **Choose a layer styles category from the second drop-down menu at the top of the palette.**

   If you know you want a drop shadow, for instance, choose that category.

4. **Click a layer style.**

   The style is immediately applied to your object.

We describe the various types of effects and their settings in the following list, yet a picture is worth a thousand words. See Figure 14-1 and Color Plate 15 for some examples.

- **Bevels:** Create a chiseled 3-D effect around the edge of the object.
- **Drop Shadows:** Apply a shadow behind the object, giving the illusion that your layer is floating above the layers beneath it. The Outline, Fill/Outline, and Neon Drop Shadows create strange, unrealistic effects.
- **Inner glows:** Cast a glow from the edges of the object to within the object.
- **Inner shadows:** These apply a shadow on the object itself. This creates the effect that the object has been "cut out" from the layer behind it. Try it, and you'll see what we mean.
- **Outer glows:** These create a glow or halo effect around the object.

Drop Shadow

Inner Shadow

Outer Glow

Inner Glow

✔ **Visibility:** These make the object itself translucent or invisible, while keeping the layer style visible.

✔ **Complex:** Fittingly named, these are premade styles with intricate combinations of layer styles, textures, and colors. You can even apply complex layer styles one on top of the other for yet more complexity.

✔ **Glass buttons:** Also fittingly named, these are premade styles that can turn your objects into a multitude of different-colored glass buttons.

✔ **Image effects:** These layer styles combine the current contents of your object with various effects, such as snow and fog. These styles are probably more useful on photographs than with text or objects drawn with the shape tools.

- ✔ **Patterns:** These fill your object with various interesting textures, such as asphalt, marble, and dry mud.

- ✔ **Photographic effects:** Obviously intended for use on photographs, these are primarily helpful for quickly giving your image a tint, such as sepia.

- ✔ **Wow chrome:** These make your object look like it's made out of shiny chrome.

- ✔ **Wow neon:** These stroke the edges of your object with neon tubing; each color comes in both an on and off state.

- ✔ **Wow plastic:** These are similar to glass buttons, but often with a drop shadow or an outer glow added.

In addition to just clicking the layer style in the Styles and Effects palette to apply it to the active layer, you can apply styles in a few other ways:

- ✔ Drag and drop the style from the Styles and Effects palette onto the desired layer in the Layers palette.

- ✔ Drag and drop the style from the Styles and Effects palette onto the desired object within the image window.

Here are some other handy things to know about layer styles:

- ✔ To remove all layer styles from a layer, choose Layer➪Layer Style➪Clear Layer Style. You can also right-click (Control-click on the Mac) the *f* in a circle icon in the Layers palette and choose Clear Layer Style.

- ✔ You can switch between thumbnail view and list view by choosing the desired view from the palette's More menu.

- ✔ You can copy and paste layer styles from one layer to another by choosing commands from the Layer➪Layer Style submenu.

- ✔ You can hide the layer styles for a layer by choosing Hide All Effects from the Layer➪Layer Style submenu. If you hide the layer styles for a layer, choose Layer➪Layer Style➪Show All Effects to reveal the layer styles again.

- ✔ You can globally scale up or down the layer styles applied to a layer by choosing Layer➪Layer Style➪Scale Effects. If you shrink your object by 50 percent, for example, choose Scale Effects and set the Scale option to 50 so that the layer style will remain proportional to the object.

So the high drop shadow is too high, and the low drop shadow isn't high enough? Don't despair: Tweak instead! Choose Layer➪Layer Style➪Style Settings or, easier still, just double-click the little *f* in a circle icon on the layer in the Layers palette. This opens the Style Settings dialog box, pictured in the rosy blush of its eternal youth in Figure 14-2.

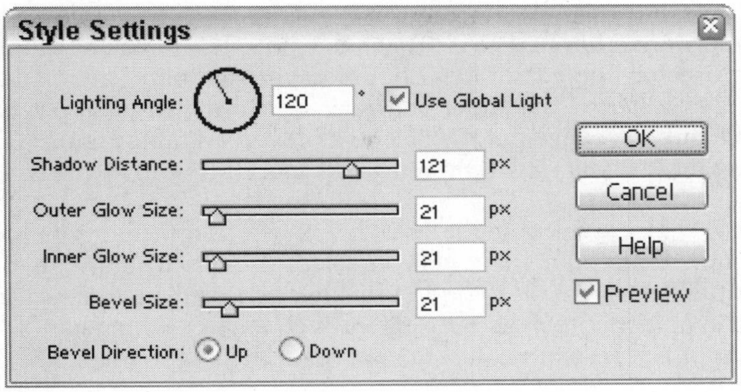

Figure 14-2:
The Style
Settings
dialog box
gives you
exacting
control over
certain
aspects of
layer styles.

Style Settings

Lighting Angle: 120 ° ☑ Use Global Light

Shadow Distance: 121 px

Outer Glow Size: 21 px

Inner Glow Size: 21 px

Bevel Size: 21 px

Bevel Direction: ⦿ Up ◯ Down

OK Cancel Help ☑ Preview

Here's the lowdown on the various controls contained therein:

- **Lighting Angle:** Determines the direction of the light source for bevels and shadows. Type a value in degrees — or just drag the circular dial to set the desired angle.

- **Use Global Light:** Checking this option keeps the Lighting Angle consistent for all layers in the same image. This is usually a very good thing, because it makes the various objects in an image seem to exist together in the same "room," so to speak. If this option is checked for all the layers in an image, making a Lighting Angle adjustment for one layer affects all the others.

- **Shadow Distance:** This sets the distance of the drop shadow from the object, and therefore creates the illusion of the object being closer or farther away from the layers beneath it. You can adjust the shadow's distance either by dragging the slider or by dragging the shadow itself in the image window. Notice that dragging the shadow can also affect the Lighting Angle for every layer for which Use Global Light is checked.

- **Outer Glow Size:** Affects the size of the outer glow.

- **Inner Glow Size:** Affects the size of the inner glow.

- **Bevel Size:** Affects the size of the bevel. (Boy, writing these books is easy!)

- **Bevel Direction:** Affects the direction of the . . . oh, okay, perhaps a bit more explanation is in order here. You can use Bevel Direction to make concave surfaces look convex, and vice versa. If the bevel is making your object look as though it's protruding from the image, switching the Bevel Direction to Down will make the object look as if it's recessed into the image.

A layer style is *live,* meaning that it updates itself as the contents of the layer change. For instance, the left image in Figure 14-3 shows a circle drawn with the elliptical marquee tool and filled, and then finished off with a Simple Sharp Inner Bevel layer style. If you then apply the Ripple filter to the circle, as shown in the middle image of Figure 14-3, the Ripple filter is theoretically applied *before* the layer style, meaning that the bevel applies itself to the rippled edges of the circle. If this isn't what you want — if, instead of a rippled circle with a bevel, you want a beveled circle that's been rippled — you have to simplify the layer before you apply the filter. Choose Layer⇨Simplify Layer. This will cause Elements to *rasterize,* or render, the layer style into just plain pixels. The layer style will look the same, but it will lose its "live," editable status. Then you can apply the filter at will. The right image of Figure 14-3 shows the result.

Layer styles also work splendidly well with the shape and type tools — so well, in fact, that you can apply layer styles directly from those tools' tool options bars. This enables you to quickly create dimensional-looking text and geometric objects (such as buttons for Web pages), which can be resized at will without any loss in quality. For more on the shape tools, see Chapter 15.

Figure 14-3:
A circle with a layer style applied (left); the same circle with the Ripple filter applied (middle); the first circle after first being simplified and then with the Ripple filter applied (right).

Tending Your Many Splendid Blends

A layer with a layer style applied is a layer proud of its individuality. "Look at me!" it fairly shouts. "I'm not like you other guys milling around in the Layers palette. I've got style, baby! Check out this bevel — am I cut, or what?"

But some layers pride themselves on working as a team, blending together to create an interesting cumulative effect. That's where blending modes can help. At its core, a *blending mode* is a mathematical formula for combining the pixels in two layers. It's possible to achieve some bizarre and beautiful effects with blending modes, but they can be hard to predict.

Before we dive into blending modes, let's look at a method of blending layers together that's the oldest trick in the book: changing opacity.

Fooling with layer opacity

One neat trick to try with a layer is to make it partially translucent by using the Opacity slider in the Layers palette. In Figure 14-4, for example, the fish was made partially translucent by setting the opacity to 70%. In the second example, he was made even more ghostly by lowering the opacity to 30%. To access the slider bar, click the right-pointing arrow to the right of the Opacity numeric setting.

Opacity: 70%

Opacity: 30%

Figure 14-4:
Hey, kids, it's Phantom Phish, star of Chapter 10, making a cameo appearance here to show off his translucent super-powers.

If a tool that doesn't have its own Opacity option in the tool options bar is selected, you can change the Opacity setting for a layer by pressing a number key. Press 9 for 90%, 8 for 80%, and so on, down to 1 for 10%. To return to 100%, press 0. You can also enter more specific Opacity values — such as 72 — by typing the digits quickly.

Keep in mind that the Opacity setting can't be changed for the background layer because nothing lies behind it. You'd be looking through the background into the void of digital space, a truly scary prospect. The same is true for the blending modes discussed in the next section.

Playing around with blending modes

Many of the options that appear in the blending mode menu in the upper-left corner of the Layers palette are the same ones we've seen in the Mode menu of the tool options bar for some of the editing tools (see Chapter 12). You have Darken, Lighten, Hue, and the rest of the gang. In the Layers palette, they're referred to as blending modes, and that's as good a name as any. You can also call them overlay modes or blend modes; some high-falutin' folks call them *calculations*. But just plain *modes* is fine for us regular faluters.

Here's a brief description of how the most important ones work:

- ✔ **Multiply** and **Screen:** Multiply burns the layer into the layers behind it, darkening all colors where they mix. Screen does the opposite, lightening the colors where they mix.

- ✔ **Difference:** The Difference mode creates a photo negative — or inversion — of the blended layers according to their colors. Where one of the layers is black, no inversion takes place. Where the layers are light, you find lots of inversion.

- ✔ **Overlay, Soft Light,** and **Hard Light:** These are similar options; that's why they're grouped in the blending mode menu. Overlay multiplies the dark colors and screens the light ones. Soft Light produces a more subtle effect. Hard Light is more dramatic than Soft Light and Overlay.

- ✔ **Color** and **Luminosity:** As with Multiply and Screen, the Color and Luminosity modes produce exactly opposite effects from each other. The Color mode blends the color of the layer with the detail from the underlying layers. Luminosity keeps the detail from the layer and mixes it with the colors of the underlying layers.

- ✔ **Color Dodge, Color Burn,** and **Exclusion:** For some other interesting effects, experiment with the Color Dodge, Color Burn, and Exclusion modes. These are subtly different from the Screen, Multiply, and Difference modes, respectively. Suppose that you have two layers, a background layer and layer 1. Color Dodge lightens the pixels in the background layer and infuses them with colors from layer 1. Color Burn darkens the pixels and infuses them with color. Exclusion turns all black pixels white, all white pixels black, and all medium colors gray.

- ✔ **Darken:** Similar to Multiply, this is another mode that can be useful. Suppose that you want to composite a scanned handwritten letter or sheet of music over an image. Obviously, you want only the handwriting or music notes to appear, and not the white paper, which would obscure the underlying pixels. By choosing Darken, only the dark pixels appear; the light area becomes transparent. Lighten does just the opposite — displays the light pixels and makes the dark pixels transparent.

For a look at some of what you can do with blending modes, check out Color Plate 17. Although this plate illustrates painting modes, discussed in the next chapter, the effects achieved are the same as with blending modes.

Those Funky Filters

So far in this book we've looked at filters that can make your images look better. But this doesn't even begin to scratch the surface where Elements' filters are concerned. In fact, you'll probably find more filters designed to make your images look weirder than to make them look better. But hey, it's all subjective, isn't it? One man's "freaky" is another man's "normal." Here are a few ideas for imbuing images with your own personal wacky style.

In a rare example of nonconformity, Adobe has given you three ways to access filters — the Filter menu, the Styles and Effects palette, and the Filter Gallery — but not all the filters are available in all places. The Filter Gallery only has filters that give an artistic look to your images. The Styles and Effects palette has almost all the filters but is missing a few. Only in the Filter menu will you have access to every single filter that comes with Elements.

Available only in the Filter menu, a handful of filters in the Adjustments category can do strange things to your image. In truth, you probably won't find them all that useful, but we might as well give them a quick look. So here goes:

- **Equalize:** The Equalize filter takes the brightest and darkest pixels from among the three color channels in the image and maps them to white and black. It then tries to evenly distribute the rest of the pixels between them in terms of brightness. This produces a higher-contrast image but isn't generally as effective as even Auto Levels.

- **Gradient Map:** The Gradient Map filter enables you to map any gradient to the grayscale values in your image. You can produce some interesting special effects with this filter.

- **Invert:** The Invert filter changes the color of every pixel to its opposite. White becomes black, blue becomes yellow, and so on. The result resembles a photographic negative, making Invert useful for special effects but not much else.

- **Posterize:** The Posterize filter limits each color channel to a specified number of brightness levels, redrawing your image with fields of solid color. Again, a nice effect, but not useful on a day-to-day basis.

- **Threshold:** The Threshold filter turns every pixel in your image either white or black, based on its brightness value according to a threshold you set. If you need it, there it is.

For info on the Photo Filter — which is actually useful — see Chapter 13.

Creating motion and puzzle pieces

In addition to Average, Blur, Blur More, and Gaussian Blur (discussed in Chapter 12), the filters' Blur category contains three filters exclusively for special effects: Motion Blur, Radial Blur, and Smart Blur. Of the three filters, Motion Blur is the filter you're most likely to use. When you choose Motion Blur, Elements displays the Motion Blur dialog box. The filter smears pixels at an angle and distance that you specify in the appropriately named option boxes. You can also drag the spoke inside the circle to change the Angle value, drag the slider to change the distance, or scrub (click and drag on) the words *Angle* and *Distance* to change the values.

For example, Figure 14-5 shows a couple of discrete applications of the Motion Blur filter. (To see this image without the Motion Blur filter, take a gander at Figure 12-7 in Chapter 12.) To blur the boy, we selected him, feathered the selection, and applied Motion Blur with an Angle value of 90° — straight up and down — and a Distance of 30 pixels. To blur his sister's arm — the one nearest her beaming brother — we used an Angle of 45° and a Distance of 6 pixels. As you can see, Distance values over 20 tend to smear the image into oblivion; smaller Distance values create subtle movement effects.

Figure 14-5:
Two unlikely
applications
of the
Motion Blur
filter.

Giving your images that gritty, streetwise look

Located quite logically in the Noise category of the filters is the Add Noise filter. Not to be confused with the as-yet-uncompleted Adenoids filter, Add Noise randomizes the colors of pixels. The result is a layer of grit that gives smooth images a textured appearance.

Apply Add Noise to display the Add Noise dialog box, shown in Figure 14-6. Here's how to use the options found therein:

✔ Drag the Amount slider triangle, click and drag to scrub the word *Amount,* or type a value between 0.10 and 400 to control how noisy the image gets. Low values permit a small amount of noise; high values permit more. Anything over 50 pretty much wipes out the original image.

✔ Select a Distribution option to control the color of noise. The Uniform option colors pixels with random variations of the shades it finds in the original image. The Gaussian option (which should be labeled High Contrast) colors pixels with more exaggerated light and dark shades. Gaussian produces an effect that's about twice as noisy as Uniform.

✔ The Monochromatic check box adds grayscale noise to full-color images. When you turn off the option, Elements adds all colors of noise. (The option has no effect on grayscale images except to shift the pixels around a little.)

Figure 14-6:
This filter adds "noise" to your image to give it a gritty texture.

Stamping your image in metal

Another intriguing and sometimes useful filter is Emboss, located in the Stylize category. This filter makes your image appear as though it were stamped in metal. The edges in the image appear in relief, and the other areas turn gray.

When you choose Emboss, Elements displays the dialog box shown in Figure 14-7. Here's the important stuff to know:

- ✔ How you set the Angle value doesn't matter. Feel free to drag the spoke on the circle until you get what you want, but don't expect big differences between one angle and another.

- ✔ Set the Height value to 1 or 2. Any value over 2 can impair detail.

- ✔ Okay, the Amount value is useful. Enter 50 for a subtle effect, 100 for a medium Emboss effect, and 200 for added drama. You can go as high as 500, but higher values make the contrast between blacks and whites too abrupt for most tastes.

TIP

After you've applied Emboss to an entire image once or twice, it gets a little old. Instead, you should apply it to selected areas.

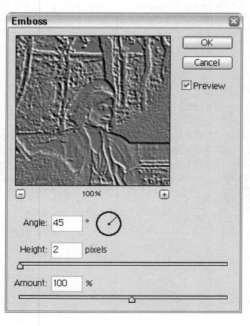

Figure 14-7: Use the Emboss filter to stamp images into sheets of metal (figuratively speaking, of course).

Here's how we achieved the thrilling mottled metal effect on the far right of Figure 14-8. We first selected the dark areas in the mother and son and applied the Emboss filter with an Angle of 45°, a Height of 2, and an Amount of 200%, as shown in the example on the far left. Then we blurred the selection using the Gaussian Blur filter set to a Radius of 2 pixels, as shown in the middle example. Finally, we applied Unsharp Mask with an Amount of 500% and a Radius of 2 pixels.

Emboss Gaussian Blur Unsharp Mask

Figure 14-8: After selecting the dark portions of the image, the selection was embossed (left), blurred (middle), and sharpened (right), creating a soft relief.

Your reaction may be, "Whoa, hold on a minute here. First you blur and then you sharpen? What kind of crazy logic is that?" Well, pretty sound logic, actually. After applying Gaussian Blur, the image turned overly gray, as you can see in the second example in the figure. Luckily, one of the properties of Unsharp Mask is that it increases the amount of contrast between dark and light pixels. So, to bring the blacks and whites back from the dead, we set the Radius value in the Unsharp Mask dialog box to the value we used in the Gaussian Blur dialog box — that is, 2.0. Using this value ensured that Unsharp Mask was able to correctly locate the blurred edges and boost their contrast. It's a great technique.

Merging colors in flaky images

The next two noteworthy filters — Facet and Median — average the colors of neighboring pixels to create areas of flat color. Both throw away detail, but they're great for smoothing out the imperfections in old, cruddy images such as the one that keeps popping up in this book.

Located in the Pixelate category, Facet is a single-shot filter that roams the image looking for areas of similarly colored pixels and then assigns the entire area a single color. Figure 14-9 shows the elder daughter from way back in Figure 12-7, before she was sharpened. The middle example shows Facet applied. See how the image is now divided into a bunch of globby areas? To make the image clearer, Unsharp Mask was applied to the far-right example, using an Amount value of 250% and a Radius value of 0.5.

Original   Facet   Unsharp Mask

Figure 14-9:
Starting with the original image (left), we applied the Facet filter (middle) and then reinforced the edges with Unsharp Mask (right).

Located in the Noise category, Median averages the colors of a certain number of neighboring pixels. To tell Elements that certain number, choose Median and type a value anywhere between 1 and 100 in the Radius option box.

Figure 14-10 shows the result of applying various Radius values to the elder daughter. The top row shows the effects of the Median command; the bottom row shows what happened when Unsharp Mask was applied to each image. Notice how higher values melt away more of the image's detail. A Radius value of 3 makes the image gooey indeed; any higher value is pure silliness.

You can use Facet and Median to blur background images, just as we did earlier with Gaussian Blur. Or you can combine them with the Add Noise and Emboss filters to create special effects.

Keep in mind that the real beauty of these more specialized filters is in combining them and applying them to small, selected portions of your image.

A number of filters in the Artistic, Brush Strokes, Sketch, and Texture categories can make your photographic image look hand painted. (All of these filters are available in the Filter Gallery.) Color Plate 16 shows examples of some of the most interesting filters.

Figure 14-10: The Median filter applied with three Radius settings (top row) and then sharpened (bottom row).

Median

Unsharp Mask

Making Taffy with the Liquify Filter

You thought Elements couldn't possibly give you any more ways to take your image out of the realm of reality, right? Well, hold on to your mouse, because the Liquify filter is in the house.

The Liquify filter lets you warp, twirl, pucker, and bloat your image — and more. It's enough to make a grown Elements user downright queasy! So take a deep breath and prepare to become "liquified":

1. **Open an image and decide whether you want to distort the entire image or just a portion.**

   You can use an area selected with one of the tools described in Chapter 9. Or you can use an entire layer (see Chapter 10). When you select an area, the unselected areas become *frozen,* or protected, from distortion. In Figure 14-11, the woman's head and a bit of the surrounding background were selected. She looks like she could use a good warping or two.

2. **Choose Filter➪Distort➪Liquify.**

   (You can find Liquify also in the Distort category of the Filters section of the Styles and Effects palette.) A huge dialog box appears, as shown in Figure 14-11. Note how a pinkish tint covers the nonselected area, similar to the Mask mode of the selection brush tool.

3. **In the top-right portion of the dialog box, select your desired brush size and pressure.**

   The Brush Size value controls how many pixels are affected at a time, and Brush Pressure controls the strength of the stroke. If you're using a graphics tablet, you also can turn on Stylus Pressure to make Elements adjust the Brush Pressure based on the amount of pressure you put on the drawing stylus.

Warp
Turbulence
Twirl clockwise
Twirl counter clockwise
Pucker
Bloat
Shift pixels
Reflection
Reconstruct
Zoom
Hand

Magnification menu

Figure 14-11:
The Liquify
dialog box is
where you
can distort
your image
into another
dimension of
reality.

4. **Adjust your view of the image with the zoom and hand tools.**

   And don't forget about the magnification menu, located in the bottom-left corner of the dialog box.

5. **And now, time for the fun stuff.**

   Use any one of the following tools to wreak havoc on your image. Check out the effects of each in Figure 14-12.

   - **Warp tool:** Pushes the pixels forward under your brush as you drag, creating a stretched effect. This tool gives the most taffy-like effect.

   - **Turbulence tool:** The turbulence tool distorts pixels in random directions as you drag. When you select this tool, you have access to the Turbulent Jitter tool option. Turbulent Jitter specifies the amount of random variation. The minimum value of 1 causes the turbulence tool to behave much like the warp tool.

   - **Twirl clockwise tool:** Rotates the pixels clockwise under your brush as you drag or hold down the mouse.

   - **Twirl counter clockwise tool:** Ditto the preceding, only in a counterclockwise direction.

   - **Pucker tool:** Moves the pixels toward the center of your brush as you drag or hold down the mouse, giving a kind of pinched look.

   - **Bloat tool:** The opposite of the pucker tool — moves pixels away from the center, creating a kind of spherical effect.

   - **Shift pixels tool:** Shifts pixels perpendicular to the direction you move the brush. (In Figure 14-12 the brush was dragged up; ditto for the reflection tool.)

- **Reflection tool:** Copies pixels from the area perpendicular to the direction you drag.

- **Reconstruct tool:** This is a sort of *nondistortion* tool, letting you restore selected areas of the image back towards the original state by painting over them.

6. **Click OK and show off your crazed masterpiece.**

The best advice for understanding the inner workings of the Liquify filter is play, play, play. If you have a few spare moments, open an image and do some freestyle reality altering of your own.

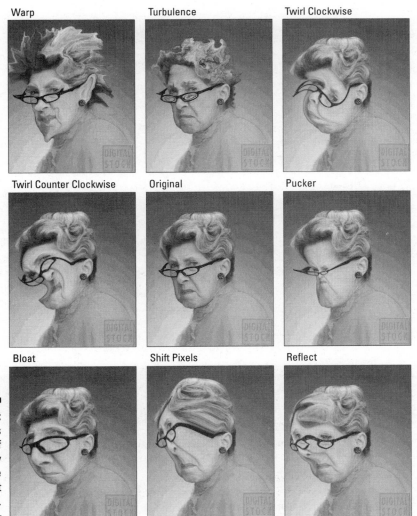

Figure 14-12:
The various effects of the Liquify filter can be downright terrifying.

Chapter 15

If a Picture Paints a Thousand Words . . . Then Shut Up and Paint

No, no, the title of this chapter isn't telling *you* to shut up. Heck, we're the ones using up all the words around here. But when it comes to painting, as a novice or casual Photoshop Elements user, you fall into one of two camps: artist or non-artist. Some people are so comfortable with a paintbrush that they feel as though they were born with the device. But a much larger group of Elements users falls into a camp that modern sociologists call "artistically challenged."

Take this quick test to determine where you fall:

✔ After doodling in the phone book, are you so horrified by the results that you rip out the page, pour ketchup on it, and feed it to your dog?

✔ When you're asked by someone to draw a map to your house, do you give them a blank piece of paper and try to assert that you live with a pack of polar bears in a snowstorm in the Arctic?

✔ Do you have recurring dreams in which you suddenly remember that today is the day your final project is due in the art class you've forgotten to attend all year? And as you attempt to quickly paint a lounging model, you notice that the model is fully clothed and you're the one who's naked?

If you answered "Yes" to any of these questions, you can safely assume that you belong to the non-artist camp. Whatever your level of artistic skill, though, a time will probably come when you'll want to rub the Elements painting tools against an image. But don't worry; the impressionist brush can make you look like you're an artist even if you aren't. And you can always use one of the several tools Elements provides for erasing your work. For that matter, the shape tools eliminate much of the need for an artistic hand anyway. So take a deep breath, and follow us.

Doodling with the Pencil and Brush

Here's the lowdown on Elements' two painting tools, the pencil and brush, as shown in Figure 15-1:

- **Pencil:** The pencil tool draws hard-edged lines of any thickness.
- **Brush:** The brush tool draws soft lines with slightly blurry edges to create more natural transitions.

Pencil tool —

Brush tool —

Figure 15-1: There's no reason to be afraid of the two Elements painting tools.

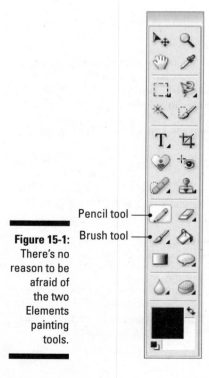

You can select the painting tools from the keyboard. Press B to select the brush, and N to select the pencil.

When you select the painting tools, Elements, by default, displays a cursor that matches the brush size exactly. If you press the Caps Lock key, however, the cursor changes to a crosshair cursor that can occasionally make it easier to see precisely what you're doing. The crosshair shows you the very center of the brush, regardless of how thick you've made it. (The upcoming section, "Switching the brush size," explains how to change brush sizes.) Press Caps Lock again to return to the brush-sized cursor.

If you prefer, you can make your painting tool cursors look like their icons: a little brush or little pencil. To make the cursor reflect the icon, press Ctrl+K (⌘+K on the Mac) to display the Preferences dialog box. Then choose Display & Cursors from the top menu or press Ctrl+3 (⌘+3 on Mac) to get to the cursor options. The Precise option gives you the Caps Lock crosshair full-time; select Standard from the Painting Cursors radio buttons and press Enter (Return on the Mac). Although they're kind of cute, these so-called "standard" cursors are the least helpful of all.

The painting tools are small, nonpoisonous, and good with children. So why not take them for a walk and see how you like them? To use the brush and pencil tools to create the friendly Mr. Sun image shown in Figure 15-3 (go ahead, flip forward to take a look), just follow these steps:

1. **Click the new icon in the shortcuts bar, choose File⇨New⇨Blank File, or press Ctrl+N (⌘+N on the Mac) to create a new canvas.**

   Elements displays a dialog box that asks what size to make the new canvas. The dialog box offers Width, Height, and Resolution options, as does the Image Size dialog box discussed in Chapter 4.

2. **Make the canvas about 400 pixels wide by 400 pixels tall.**

   Choose Pixels from the Width and Height drop-down menus, and enter **400** into each. Also, make sure the Color Mode drop-down menu is set to RGB Color, and that White is selected in the Background Contents menu.

3. **Press Enter (Return on the Mac).**

   The new empty canvas appears in a new window.

4. **Click the black and white icon at the bottom left of the toolbox or press the D key to set the foreground color to black.**

5. **Select the brush tool.**

   Click the brush icon in the toolbox or press the B key. That's *B* for *brush;* get it? Just make sure you get the brush and not one of its suitemates, the impressionist brush or the color replacement tool.

6. **Draw a circle in the middle of your new canvas.**

   A rude approximation of a circle is fine. Experts agree that a lumpy circle has more personality.

7. **Paint some rays coming off the circle.**

   Figure 15-2 shows more or less how your image should look so far, minus the face.

8. **Select the pencil tool.**

   To access the pencil from the keyboard, press N. That's *N* for . . . the third letter of *pencil.* Or maybe *nibble?*

9. **Draw a little face inside the sun.**

   Using the pencil, you get hard-edged lines, as shown in Figure 15-2.

10. **Switch back to the brush tool.**

    To do so, press B.

11. **Enable the brush's airbrush capabilities.**

    Click the airbrush icon in the tool options bar; it's the one that sort of looks like a knife with a squiggly line behind it.

12. **Change the foreground color to orange.**

    Click the foreground color icon to get the Color Picker. Use the color slider and the color field to get a nice orange, or enter 255 for R, 150 for G, and leave B at 0.

13. **Click and hold — without moving your mouse — inside the sun.**

    Notice that in Airbrush mode, the brush continuously pumps out paint. This is the unique capability of Airbrush mode; in Normal brush mode and with the pencil, after the tool is first clicked, it paints only when it's in motion.

14. **Paint some shading in the lower-right region of the sun.**

    Figure 15-3 shows a general idea. Airbrush mode is useful for shading images. Of course, the real sun can't possibly have a shadow, but it doesn't have a face either, so we can allow room for some personal expression here.

That's good enough for now. You may want to save this image, because we refer back to it later in this chapter. Then again, if something goes wrong and you don't save the sun, no biggie. You can always re-create it or experiment with a different image.

Figure 15-2:
A smiling sun, drawn with the brush and pencil tools.

Figure 15-3:
Use the brush's Airbrush mode to paint a highly unrealistic shadow on the sun.

Performing Special Painting-Tool Tricks

Dragging with a tool inside the image window is obviously the most common way to paint in Elements. But it's not the only way, as the following list makes clear:

✔ To create a straight line, click at one point in the image with the brush or pencil, and Shift+click at another. Elements automatically creates a straight line between the two points.

- ✔ To create a straight line that's exactly vertical or horizontal, click and hold with the brush or pencil, press and hold the Shift key, and then drag with the tool while the Shift key remains down. In other words, press Shift immediately after you click, and hold Shift throughout the length of the drag. If you release the Shift key while dragging, the line resumes its naturally free-form and wiggly ways.

- ✔ Alt+click (Option+click on the Mac) to get the eyedropper tool and lift a color from the image. Then drag to start painting with that color.

Choosing Your Brush

If the previous two sections covered everything about the painting tools, Elements would be a royal dud. But as we all know, Elements is not a dud — far from it — so there must be more to the painting tools than we've seen so far. (This is classic Sherlock Holmes-style deductive reasoning at work here. Element-ary, my dear Watson.)

You can modify the tools to a degree that no mechanical pencil or conventional paintbrush can match. For starters, you can change the size and shape of the tip of the tool, as explained in the next few sections. You can draw thick strokes one moment and then turn around and draw thin strokes the next, all with the same tool. This holds true of any tool that works like a brush, including the editing tools in Chapter 12. Plus, there are categories of brushes that spew forth eye-popping effects. And brushes are customizable, enabling you to tailor the presets to your whim and save the results for later use.

Switching the brush size

To change one brush for a different one, select the brush tool and click the arrow to the right of the long brush stroke icon in the tool options bar. Elements displays the brushes pop-up palette, shown in Figure 15-4, with the Default Brushes set currently active. Here you can find a total of 65 brushes, with some very unusual brushes toward the bottom of the pop-up palette.

The numbers to the left of the brush stroke icons represent the diameters of the brushes, in pixels. (In case that year of high-school geometry has altogether removed itself from your brain, diameter is merely the width of a circle measured from side to opposite side.) To change the brush, just click a brush stroke icon. Notice that the first six brushes have fairly hard edges, whereas the next twelve have a softer edge. These are followed by nine preset airbrushes, which have the softest edges of all. (Notice that when you select an airbrush preset, the airbrush icon automatically becomes selected in the tool options bar.) When you begin using the brush, the brushes pop-up palette puts itself back in its hiding place. You can also press Enter (Return on the Mac) or click the X in the upper-right corner to close the pop-up palette.

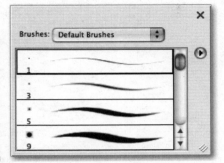

Figure 15-4: The brushes pop-up palette lets you switch one brush for another.

You can view the brushes palette in six ways: stroke thumbnail (the default), large and small thumbnails, text only, and large and small lists (a combo of text and thumbnails). To select any of these viewing options, access the brushes pop-up palette's drop-down menu by clicking the circle with the right-pointing arrow on the right side of the pop-up palette.

Right-click (Control+click on the Mac) on the canvas to display the brushes pop-up palette underneath your cursor. Select a different brush and continue painting. The pop-up palette then disappears.

The pencil and the editing tools (such as the smudge and sponge tools) all provide access to the brushes palette. However, bear in mind that the pencil tool draws a harsh, jagged line no matter which brush you select. Even the preset airbrushes produce jagged lines when used with the pencil.

Exploring the other brush sets

You'll find 13 sets of brushes available in Elements. All can be useful, but the special effect brushes are downright spectacular. To check them out, click the Brushes menu at the top of the brushes pop-up palette, and choose Special Effect Brushes. Click the first one (Azalea), set a nice bright foreground color and a contrasting background color, and drag your brush across an image.

Wow! The brush spits out a variety of differently colored, sized, and shaped flowers. This very nicely shows off the fact that a dynamic painting engine is lurking inside Elements, letting you easily achieve some amazing effects. We'll look at how to customize these brushes shortly, but for now we bet you'll want to spend a few minutes experimenting with these brushes, and painting masterworks like the one in Figure 15-5.

Making your own brush

A total of 328 preset brushes are in the combined 13 brush sets that come with Elements. How do we know that? We counted them all for you. You're welcome. Now, you may think that 328 brushes are enough to keep you happy well into your declining years. But rest assured, one day you'll want a brush size that's a little thicker than Option A and a little thinner than Option B. So you'll have to modify one or the other to come up with a custom brush of your own.

Changing the size of the brush is a simple affair; just use the Size control that appears to the right of the brushes pop-up palette icon in the tool options bar. You can click the arrow to access a slider; type a size; or just position your cursor over the word Size, click, and drag left and right to "scrub" your way to a new size. (You can scrub any numeric option in the tool options bar.)

To make other changes to the brush tool, click the more options brush icon on the far right of the tool options bar. In response to your click, Elements displays the More Options pop-up palette, shown in Figure 15-6.

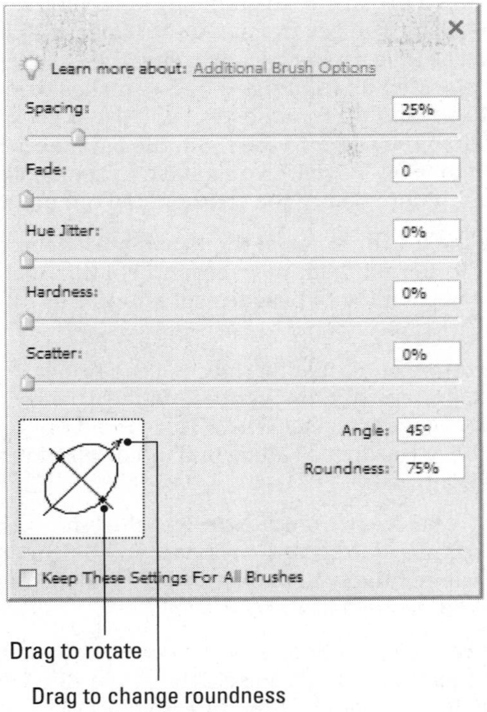

Learn more about: Additional Brush Options

Spacing: 25%

Fade: 0

Hue Jitter: 0%

Hardness: 0%

Scatter: 0%

Angle: 45°
Roundness: 75%

Keep These Settings For All Brushes

Figure 15-6:
The inner
workings of
a brush.

Drag to rotate

Drag to change roundness

Here's how you modify the brush:

- To understand the Spacing setting, go to the Default Brushes set and select the sixth one down, the Hard Round 19 pixels brush. Drag it across an open image. Now you would never know it from using a brush like this one, but Elements doesn't really paint a solid line when you drag a brush across an image. Instead, what it does is spit out a succession of shapes. With a basic brush like the one you just used, it spits out little circles, but they're packed so closely together that they look like a solid thick line. Go ahead and open the More Options pop-up palette, and increase the Spacing setting all the way up to 1000%. Now you'll see that the circle shapes are spaced much farther apart; in fact, the brush stroke icon in the tool options bar changes to reflect this. For general purposes, you'll want to leave the spacing option alone, but for brushes such as Azalea in the Special Effects Brushes set, you may well want to control exactly how far apart the flowers or shapes are spit out. That's what the Spacing control does.

The changes you just made to the Hard Round 19 pixels brush won't permanently change that brush; choose it again from the pop-up palette, and it will be back to normal. To save changes to brushes, see the upcoming section "Saving brushes."

✔ The Fade control makes a brush stroke gradually fade out over distance. Using Fade is a bit peculiar. The general default of 0 means that a brush stroke will never fade; as long as you keep wiggling the brush, paint will come out. However, one step up from there — 1 — makes the fade happen instantaneously. With a standard round brush, you'll just get one circle, and that's it. As you drag the slider to the right, the fade takes longer and longer, all the way up to 9999 — where you'd have to keep painting continuously for about a full minute before the stroke faded out entirely.

✔ The Hue Jitter value makes the color of the brush stroke fluctuate between the current foreground and background colors. Again, the Azalea brush in the Special Effects Brushes set shows this off to full effect.

✔ The Hardness value represents the blurriness of the brush. A value of 100% is hard, like the first six options in the Default Brushes set. Anything else is progressively fuzzier. The 12 feathered options in the Default Brushes set have Hardness values of 0%. The Hardness value isn't available for every brush.

✔ Scatter deals with how far away from the drag of the cursor the brush shapes are spaced. For standard round brushes, you'll probably want to keep this at 0%, but the relatively high Scatter value is one of the things that makes our beloved Azalea brush so special.

✔ Before we talk about the Angle option, which comes next, you need to understand how Roundness works. (You see, the Angle value doesn't have any effect unless you first change the Roundness value.) The Roundness option lets you make the brush oval instead of round. A value of 100% is circular; anything less results in a shape that is shorter than it is wide.

✔ If you want an oval brush to be taller than it is wide or some other variation on its present state, you can rotate it by changing the Angle value. A value of 90 degrees is a counterclockwise quarter-turn, 180 degrees is a half-turn, -90 degrees is a clockwise quarter-turn, and so on.

✔ You'll find it much easier to use the diagram in the lower-left corner of the dialog box to change the Angle and Roundness settings. Drag one of the two circular handles on either side of the circle to make the brush oval. To rotate the brush, drag the gray arrowhead or just click at the position where you want the arrow to point. The labels in Figure 15-6 tell the story.

✔ The Keep These Settings For All Brushes check box at the bottom of the More Options pop-up palette does just as it says; click the check box, and every brush you choose will adopt the current More Options brush settings. If you want to turn the settings back off (and we bet you eventually will), click again to deselect the check box.

If you're drawing with a digitizing tablet and stylus such as one made by Wacom, the new Tablet Options pop-up palette lets you determine which brush characteristics will be emphasized when you increase the pressure of the stylus on the tablet. You can choose size and opacity, plus three options from the More Options pop-up palette: hue jitter, scatter, and roundness.

Saving brushes

After you've edited your brush to perfection, the first step toward saving it is to click the circular button with the right-pointing arrow in the brushes pop-up palette and choose Save Brush from the top of the menu. Here you can give your brush a descriptive name. When you've done so, click OK. And there, at the bottom of the active set of brushes, you'll find your custom-made brush.

When you add a brush to a brush set, an asterisk appears before the set's name in the Brushes menu. This notifies you that the set has been changed. Should you want to use the menu to switch to another brush set, you'll first get a message asking whether you want to save your changes to the old set. Unless you reply in the affirmative, the brush you added will be lost forever.

So if you want to keep your brush around, click Yes (Save on the Mac). Accept the Untitled Brushes name, or give the brush set a new name if you want. But definitely save the set inside the suggested Brushes folder; that way, Elements will know where to find the brushes again.

Now, to access the brush set you just saved, you need to choose the Load Brushes command by clicking the circular button with the arrow on it in the brushes pop-up palette in the tool options bar. Choose the name of the set you saved, click Load, and the set appears again in the Brushes menu, complete with the brush you added.

Going nuts with the brushes palette

What we've seen so far would be plenty of brush options for an ordinary program. But Elements is no ordinary program. Elements is never satisfied to supply you with anything short of everything. You have to admire that in a program.

Here's what else Elements offers you, brush-wise:

- ✔ You can quickly change the brush size from the keyboard, without messing about with any controls in the tool options bar. Press the right bracket key ( ]) to increase the brush size; press the left bracket key ([ ) to decrease the brush size.

- ✔ To raise the hardness of a brush in 25 percent increments, press Shift+]. To lower the hardness, press Shift+[.

- ✔ To delete a brush from the pop-up palette, Alt+click (Option+click on the Mac) the brush. If you press the Alt (or Option) key, you get a miniature pair of scissors. That's how Elements tells you that you're ready to clip a brush into oblivion.

✔ The Edit➪Define Brush command gives you yet another way to create a custom brush. Just make a selection in an open image, choose Define Brush, and give your brush a name. Click OK, and the brush is added at the bottom of the currently active brush set. Using this technique, you can easily make a brush out of any object in an image, such as a letter of the alphabet or a person's face.

Exploring More Painting Options

Figure 15-7 shows the tool options bar that appears when the brush is active. We've looked at some of these controls, but here's how the other options work:

✔ The first icon on the far left is the tool identifier, which lets you know which tool is active. If you click the icon, you get a drop-down menu where you can reset the default options for the specific tool or do the same for all the tools.

Figure 15-7:
The brush tool options bar is headquarters for modifying the brush.

✔ The next set of icons lets you switch between the brush, the impressionist brush, and the color replacement tool, because these three tools share the same space in the toolbox.

✔ The Mode drop-down menu, available with the brush or pencil, provides access to a bunch of different painting modes that control how the foreground color applied by the tool mixes with the existing colors in the image. These modes function identically to the blending modes, which we describe in Chapter 14. You can perform fun tricks with some of the modes, as you find out in the next section.

✔ Available when you use the pencil or brush, the Opacity option controls the translucency of the foreground color you're applying. A setting of 100% ensures that the paint is opaque so that you can't see the colors underneath. (When you use a feathered brush, the edges are translucent even at 100%, but the center is opaque.) Any Opacity setting lower than 100% makes the brush translucent.

✔ If you can't quite see how the Opacity slider works, a visual depiction will make everything clear. Figure 15-8 shows four lines drawn with the brush, two using a standard brush and two using a feathered brush. In each case, one line is set to 100% Opacity, and the other line is set to 40%.

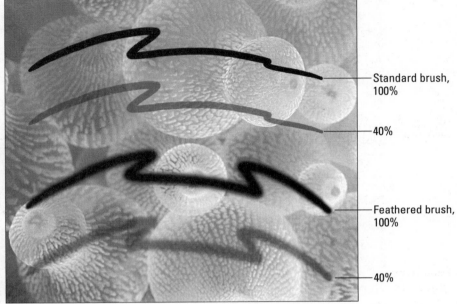

Standard brush, 100%

40%

Feathered brush, 100%

40%

Figure 15-8: Here's what it looks like when you paint over a sea anemone at different Opacity settings.

✔ Just as with a layer's opacity, you can change the Opacity value for tools in 10% increments by pressing a number key. As long as you have one of the painting tools selected, pressing 9 changes the setting to 90%, 8 changes it to 80%, and so on. Press the 0 key to change the setting back to 100%. If you want a more precise setting, say, 75%, just type the value quickly.

✔ The Auto Erase check box appears when you select the pencil tool. You can select this oddly named option to draw in the background color whenever you click or drag on a pixel painted in the foreground color. This option is useful for making touch-ups with the single-pixel brush — click to add the foreground color and click again to change it to the background color.

Experimenting with painting modes

If you read about blending modes in Chapter 14, you saw how they can be used to combine the colors of pixels in layers. Painting modes work in the same way, except that they combine the painted foreground color with whatever is underneath it. Color Plate 17 illustrates twelve painting modes, showing how the green foreground color interacts with a colorful background image. Here are a few specific effects you can achieve using painting modes.

For example, consider the sun image shown back in Figure 15-3. Suppose that you want to color the sun yellow and the sky blue. The problem is, if you try to color the sun and sky with one of the painting tools, you end up covering the face inside the sun with yellow and the rays outside the sun with blue. You can't correct the problem by lowering the Opacity value because doing that just results in washed-out colors, and you still obscure some of the sun's detail.

The solution is to select a painting mode. Choose Multiply from the Mode menu in the tool options bar. Miraculously, you can now paint both sky and sun without covering up the rays and the face. This is because the Multiply option darkens colors as though you had painted with watercolors. The Multiply option mixes the colors together to create darker colors.

Here are some additional painting modes and other information on this subject that you may find interesting:

- ✔ The Screen mode is the opposite of Multiply. Multiply mixes colors as though they were pigments, which is why the colors get darker. By contrast, Screen mixes colors as though they were lights, which is why they get lighter.

- ✔ The Overlay mode darkens dark colors and lightens light colors, resulting in a heightening of contrast.

- ✔ The Difference painting mode is the loopiest mode of them all and the most likely to surprise you. Through a mathematical process too complex to be explained within these humble pages, it creates a photonegative effect.

- ✔ You can also have some fun experimenting with Difference's cousin, Exclusion. It sends all blacks to white, all whites to black, and all medium colors to gray.

- ✔ Use the Color painting mode to colorize grayscale images or change the color of portions of RGB images.

- ✔ The Color Dodge and Color Burn painting modes offer an interesting new twist on the dodge and burn tools discussed in Chapter 12. In case you haven't discovered the dodge and burn tools yet, we'll mention that you drag with the dodge tool to lighten a portion of your image and drag with the burn tool to darken a portion of your image. If you paint with the Color Dodge mode, you can lighten your image and infuse it with color. Using Color Burn, you can darken and infuse with color. For example, to darken your image and give it a greenish tint, you paint with green using the Color Burn painting mode.

- ✔ To paint normally again, just select the Normal painting mode.

Shift+right-click (Shift+Control-click on the Mac) on your canvas with a painting tool to display a shortcut menu that provides access to the Edit Brush command and all the painting modes.

Six of the preceding painting modes — Multiply, Screen, Overlay, Difference, Color, and Normal — are super-useful, the kinds of modes you want to get to know on a first-name basis. Exclusion, Color Dodge, and Color Burn are also worth some attention. The others aren't nearly so useful. In fact, they're mostly boring and obscure. But who knows? Maybe you'll feel differently.

Elements 3.0 has a new painting mode called Hard Mix. It can give images a posterized, Andy Warhol-style look, but in general it belongs to the "boring and obscure" family of modes.

"Painting" with the impressionist brush

The impressionist brush allows you to paint in impressionistic swirls. Although it's not, strictly speaking, a paintbrush, we'll still refer to what the impressionist brush does as "painting," for lack of a better word.

Go ahead and open an image. Select the impressionist brush (which shares the same flyout menu in the toolbox as the brush tool) and just start moving it around on your image. You'll instantly get an idea of what the impressionist brush is all about. Color Plate 18 shows an image before and after a grueling workout with the impressionist brush. Pretty groovy, huh?

The performance of the impressionist brush depends on the settings in the tool options bar, pictured in Figure 15-9. Here are the options:

- **Mode:** This drop-down menu assigns a painting mode to the tool. See "Experimenting with painting modes," earlier in this chapter, for details.

- **Opacity:** Lower this value to create translucent strokes. To lower the Opacity from the keyboard, just press a number key any time the impressionist brush is active.

Figure 15-9: The tool options bar offers numerous settings for the impressionist brush.

Three more options are available in the More Options dialog box:

- **Style:** The impressionist brush paints with randomly generated corkscrews of color. You can decide the basic shapes of the corkscrews by choosing an option from the Style drop-down menu. Combine these options with different brush sizes to vary the detail conveyed by the impressionistic image.

- **Area:** This value defines the area covered by a single dollop of paint. Larger pixel values also mean that the brush lays down more strokes at a time; reduce the value for a sparser look.

- **Tolerance:** Change this value to give more or less tolerance to where the impressionist brush can paint within the image.

If impressionism interests you, experiment with this brush. If not, give this brush the slip. Although it's pretty nifty, it definitely falls under the heading of Whimsical Creative Tools to Play with When You're Not under a Deadline.

The Powers of the Eraser

What artist's toolbox would be complete without an eraser? Elements' toolbox wouldn't be complete without three erasers — the eraser tool, the background eraser tool, and the magic eraser tool.

To switch between the three eraser tools from the keyboard, press Shift+E.

Working with the regular ol' eraser tool

The eraser tool lets you erase in a couple of ways:

- If you drag with the eraser in an image that contains only a background layer, the tool paints in the background color, which is white by default. Technically this may be erasing, but it's really just painting in a different color. Who needs it?

- If your image contains more than one layer (we discuss layers in Chapter 10), the eraser works a little differently and becomes a lot more useful. If you drag the eraser on the background layer, the eraser paints in the background color, as usual. But on any other layer, the pixels you brush with the eraser become transparent, revealing pixels on underlying layers. (This assumes that the Lock Transparent Pixels option is deselected in the Layers palette. If you click the Lock Transparent Pixels option, the eraser paints on nontransparent areas in the background color.)

The eraser tool comes in three delicious eraser flavors. To switch flavors, choose an option from the Mode drop-down menu in the tool options bar. Two modes are named after painting tools — brush and pencil — and work exactly like these tools. This means that you can change the brush size and adjust the Opacity setting to make pixels only partially transparent in a layered image.

The third option, Block, changes the eraser to a square, hard-edged, fixed-size eraser. All the options in the tool options bar then become grayed out. The Block Eraser can be useful when you want to completely erase general areas, but you probably won't take it up very often.

Trying out the somewhat magic eraser

Of the background and magic erasers, the magic eraser is the easiest to use and the least capable. If you're familiar with the magic wand (see the section on using the magic wand in Chapter 9), the magic eraser is a cinch to use. The two tools operate identically, except that the wand selects and the eraser erases.

When you click a pixel with the magic eraser, Elements identifies a range of similarly colored pixels, just as it does with the magic wand. But instead of selecting the pixels, the magic eraser makes them transparent, as demonstrated in Figure 15-10. Bear in mind that in Elements, transparency requires a separate layer. So if the image is on the background layer, Elements automatically turns the background layer into a full-fledged layer, leaving nothing underneath: hence the checkerboard pattern shown in the second example in the figure — transparency with nothing underneath.

Notice in Figure 15-10 that the magic eraser deleted some of the blue sky, but not all of it. This is a function of the Tolerance value in the tool options bar. Just like the magic wand's Tolerance value, the magic eraser's Tolerance value determines how similar a neighboring color has to be to the clicked color to be made transparent. A higher value affects more colors; a lower value affects fewer colors. Therefore, if you want to erase a larger section of the sky in Figure 15-10, you can raise the Tolerance value and click again. (Remember, any change to the Tolerance value affects the next click you make; it does not affect the existing transparent area.)

The other options in the tool options bar work as follows:

- **Anti-aliased:** To create a soft fringe around the outline of your transparent area, leave this option turned on. If you prefer a hard edge — as when using a very low Tolerance value, for example — turn this check box off.

- **Contiguous:** When this is turned on, the magic eraser deletes only contiguous colors — that is, similar colors that touch each other. If you prefer to delete all pixels of a certain color regardless of their location, turn off the Contiguous check box.

✔ **Use All Layers:** When turned on, this check box tells Elements to factor in all visible layers when erasing pixels. The tool continues to erase pixels on the active layer only, but it erases them according to colors found across all layers.

✔ **Opacity:** Lower this value to make the erased pixels translucent instead of transparent. Low values result in more subtle effects than high ones.

For a more detailed description of these options as they affect the magic wand tool, read the section on using the magic wand in Chapter 9.

Figure 15-10: To delete a homogeneously colored background, such as the sky at top, click it with the magic eraser (bottom).

Using the more magical background eraser

The magic eraser is as simple to use as a hammer and every bit as indelicate. It pounds away pixels, leaving lots of color fringes and shredded edges in its wake. You may as well select an area with the magic wand and press the Backspace or Delete key. The effect is the same.

The more capable, more scrupulous tool is the background eraser. As demonstrated in Figure 15-11, the background eraser deletes background pixels as you drag over them. (Again, if the image is on the background layer, Elements floats the image to a new layer to accommodate the transparency.) The tool is intelligent enough to erase background pixels and retain foreground pixels provided — and here's the clincher — that you keep the cross in the center of the eraser cursor squarely centered on a background pixel. Move the cross over a foreground pixel, and the background eraser deletes foreground pixels as well. As Figure 15-12 demonstrates, it's the position of the cross that counts.

Figure 15-11:
Drag around the edge of an image with the background eraser to erase the background but leave the foreground intact.

To change the size of the background eraser, click the brush control in the tool options bar and adjust the diameter in the pop-up palette that appears. You can also use the bracket keys, [and], to make the brush size smaller or larger.

Figure 15-12:
Keep the cross of the background eraser cursor over the background you want to erase (top). If you inadvertently move the cross over the foreground, the fore-ground gets erased (bottom).

You can also modify the performance of the background eraser using the options in the tool options bar. Here are your options:

✔ **Limits:** By default, the background eraser deletes colors inside the cursor as long as they are contiguous with the color immediately under the cross. To erase all similarly colored pixels, whether contiguous or not, set the drop-down menu to Discontiguous.

✔ **Tolerance:** Raise the Tolerance value to erase more colors at a time; lower the value to erase fewer colors. Low Tolerance values are useful for erasing around tight and delicate details, such as hair.

Isn't Elements Just a Paint Program?

For those of you asking, "Isn't Elements just a paint program," perish the thought. Elements also includes shape tools, which are handy at drawing geometric objects to be used for things such as Web buttons. Shapes drawn with these tools are exceptions to the way things generally work in Elements because they're not pixel-based. The shape tools draw *vector objects,* which can be scaled to any size with no loss in quality. A vector triangle, for example, is a *mathematical description* of a triangle, rather than a grid of pixels that form the shape of a triangle. Because vectors are just mathematical descriptions, they can be scaled without any loss in quality.

Suppose that you take the brush tool and paint a red circle in Elements on a very small white canvas — say, roughly 20 pixels by 20 pixels. You'll have an image with some red pixels, some white pixels, and some pink pixels around the edge of the circle. If you then scale your canvas up to around 2000 pixels by 2000 pixels using the Image Size command, the pink edges of your circle will look very fuzzy. But use the ellipse shape tool to draw a circle on a 20-x-20 canvas, scale it up to 2000 by 2000, and the ellipse-drawn circle will look perfect, with razor-sharp edges. Understand the difference?

The new cookie cutter tool starts out like the custom shape tool, but true to its name, it chops a shape out of a preexisting layer and throws away the excess pixels like so much cookie dough. We'll visit this nifty new tool at the end of the chapter.

The shape tools

Six shape tools are available: the rectangle, rounded rectangle, ellipse, polygon, line, and custom shape tools. In addition, there's the shape selection tool, which we get to in a minute. To experiment with the shape tools, do the following:

1. **Select a shape tool from the toolbox.**

   The icon in the toolbox shaped like a "word balloon" is the custom shape tool and is visible by default. To access one of the other shape tools, click and hold your cursor on the visible shape tool, and a flyout menu will appear. Or just click the visible shape tool in the toolbox and then choose the specific shape tool you want from the tool options bar, as pictured in Figure 15-13. (If you've experimented with the shape tools at all before, go over to the shape tool on the very far left, click it, and choose reset tool before you follow along with us.)

2. **Drag with the tool to draw a shape on the canvas.**

   If you have the Layers palette open, you'll see that you just created a new layer. (It really helps to have the Layers palette open while you work with the shape tools.) By default, the color of the shape is the foreground color, but after drawing the shape, you can change the color by clicking the Color box in the tool options bar to display the Color Picker.

3. **Draw another shape.**

   You'll see that you've created another layer. This happened because the create new shape layer icon (labeled in Figure 15-13) is selected by default. Selecting one of the other four icons will keep the next shape you draw on the same layer. Each of the four icons has its own options for combining shapes on the same layer. See Figure 15-14 for a visual reference to the effects of the shape area icons.

4. **Click the undo icon in the shortcuts bar to undo the last shape you drew, click the add to shape area icon (labeled in Figure 15-13), and draw a shape again.**

   This time make sure your new shape overlaps the old one. Use the step backward icon again and experiment with the other three icons, drawing overlapping shapes. Lather, rinse, repeat.

Add to shape area   Subtract from shape area

Shape tools   Create new shape layer   Intersect shape areas

Figure 15-13: Reset   Geometry options   Exclude overlapping shape areas

The shape tool options bar provides a plethora of options.

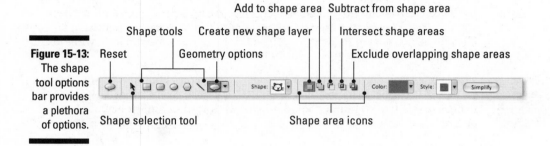

Shape selection tool   Shape area icons

Add   Subtract

Figure 15-14: The shape area icons specify how different shapes on the same layer interact with each other.

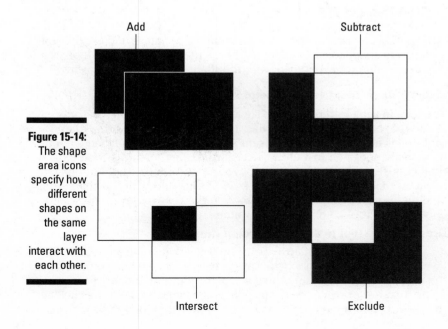

Intersect   Exclude

At the right end of the seven shape tools in the tool options bar, the drop-down menu gives you access to geometry options for the tools. The options here change depending on which tool is selected, but here's a rundown of all possible options:

- ✔ **Unconstrained:** Enables you to draw your shape freely, stretching or squashing it if you want, as you draw.

- ✔ **Square:** Enables you to draw a square with the rectangle and rounded rectangle tools.

- ✔ **Fixed Size:** Enables you to draw a shape with a set width and height.

- ✔ **Proportional:** Lets you draw a shape with a proportional ratio of width and height.

- ✔ **From Center:** This option enables you to draw from the center out, rather than from a corner.

- ✔ **Snap to Pixels:** Aligns the shape perfectly with the "pixel grid" of the image. This ensures that straight lines will always appear crisp.

- ✔ **Radius:** Sets the width of the polygon.

- ✔ **Smooth Corners:** Makes smooth polygon corners.

- ✔ **Star:** Enables the polygon tool to draw a star.

- ✔ **Indent Sides By:** Creates the spikes of a star when the polygon tool's Star option is selected. A larger value makes sharper and spikier points.

- ✔ **Smooth Indents:** Curves the sides of a star.

- ✔ **Circle:** Similar to the Square option, this constrains the ellipse tool to draw a perfect circle.

- ✔ **Arrowheads:** Enables you to specify the placement of the arrowhead, the shape of the arrowhead, and the concavity (or curvature) of the arrowhead for the line tool.

- ✔ **Defined Proportions:** The opposite of Unconstrained, this keeps you from distorting a custom shape as you draw it.

- ✔ **Defined Size:** Constrains drawing custom shapes to the size at which they were created.

Some tools have other options available in the tool options bar:

- ✔ **Radius:** Specifies the amount of curve on the corners of the rounded rectangle tool.

- ✔ **Sides:** Specifies the number of sides for the polygon tool.

- ✔ **Weight:** Specifies the thickness of the line.

✔ **Shape:** Gives you access to the Shape pop-up palette when using the custom shape tool. From here you can select a different shape to draw. Click the drop-down menu in the Shape pop-up palette to access 23 libraries of shapes, or choose All Elements Shapes to see the whole circus. The drop-down menu also lets you choose from several viewing options for the Shape pop-up palette.

The tool options bar also makes it easy to add layer styles, which we cover in Chapter 14. And the final tool in the tool options bar is the Simplify icon. No, the Simplify icon doesn't make all the confusing shape tools disappear. Clicking the Simplify icon rasterizes your shape layer. *Rasterizing* is the process of converting your vector shape to pixels, meaning the shape loses its special resizable status. However, simplifying is necessary if you want to add filters and effects to your shape.

The shape selection tool

If you're not happy with where you drew a shape, that's when the shape selection tool can come in handy. This tool (labeled in Figure 15-13) lets you click a shape and drag it to a new location, but it also has a few other tricks up its sleeve:

✔ After you've clicked a shape, go to Image⇨Transform Shape. This gives you access to four commands — Free Transform Shape, Skew, Distort, and Perspective — wherein you can distort your shape in any number of interesting ways.

✔ When you have more than one shape on a single layer, choosing the shape selection tool gives you access to the Combine icon in the tool options bar, which combines various shapes on a single layer into one complex shape.

The cookie cutter tool

The cookie cutter tool is a lot like the custom shape tool: same geometry options available in the tool options bar (located for the cookie cutter tool in the Shape Options menu), same vector shapes to choose from in the Shape pop-up palette. However, rather than creating a shape on a new layer like the custom shape tool does, the cookie cutter tool chops a shape out of a preexisting layer, just like a cookie cutter chops a gingerbread man out of rolled-out dough. The pixels that fall outside the shape get thrown away, leaving just the shape filled with the image.

The creative possibilities are endless. Figure 15-15 shows how the cookie cutter tool was used to create a contrasting winter/spring image.

Figure 15-15:
Starting with two contrasting layers (left), the cookie cutter tool was used on the top flowers layer to reveal parts of the underlying winter scene (right). We used the Tile 4 shape from the default shape library.

Here's how to use the tool:

1. **Make your initial choices in the tool options bar.**

   The most important choice you have to make is, naturally, the shape in the Shape pop-up palette that you want to cut out of your layer. You can also make choices in the Shape Options menu to influence the size and proportions of the shape; see the long bulleted list in the previous "The shape tools" section for details on these options.

   You can also choose whether you want the edges of your shape to ultimately be feathered (soft); if so, enter a pixel value in the Feather option. If you check the Crop check box, you'll not only chop your chosen shape out of the selected layer, but also cause the entire image to be cropped down to a size just large enough to contain the shape.

2. **Drag to draw your shape.**

   Make sure you have the correct layer selected in the Layers palette. If you draw your shape on the background, the background will be converted to a regular layer.

3. **Make size, rotation, and skewing adjustments as desired.**

   Notice that the mysterious transform tool is now active in the tool options bar; we discuss the transform tool in Chapter 10. Briefly, you can drag the square handles on the bounding box in the image window to resize the shape, or use the controls in the tool options bar to scale, rotate, and skew the shape. See the "Using the transform tool" section in Chapter 10 for the lowdown on these options.

4. **Click the commit icon.**

After you click commit, Elements chops the shape out of your layer. Unlike the custom shape tool, no vector outlines are left to be adjusted at a later time; your chopped layer is pure pixels.

If you change your mind about cookie-cutting your layer, you can always click the cancel icon instead. Chicken.

Chapter 16

Painting with the Digital Stencil

●●

In This Chapter

▶ Painting and editing inside a selection outline

▶ Using the paint bucket tool

▶ Using the Fill dialog box

▶ Applying different types of gradients

▶ Stroking a selection

●●

As Chapter 15 shows, Photoshop Elements has a whole mess of options for replicating the process of drawing or painting on a canvas. But have you ever spray painted using a stencil? In case you've never engaged in this riveting pastime, here's how it works:

1. **Hold the stencil up to the surface you want to paint.**

2. **Spray recklessly.**

When you take the stencil away, you discover a painted image that matches the shape of the stencil. It's the epitome of a no-brainer.

In Elements, you can use a selection outline in the same way. Just as a stencil isolates the area affected by the spray paint, a *selection outline* isolates the area affected by a paint or edit tool. You can also fill a selection outline with color or trace around the selection outline.

In this chapter you're going to discover every nuance of painting, filling, and tracing selections. Chapter 9 explains how to create and manipulate selection outlines; this chapter shows you some of the things you can do with them.

Painting within the Lines

If some portion of an image is selected, Elements treats all deselected areas as protected. You can use any paint or edit tool inside the selection without worrying about harming areas outside the selection.

This chapter utilizes an image of a jar in a nook, which has a certain austere beauty about it. If you want to get an idea of what the jar's contents looked like originally, check out Color Plate 19 (and ignore the rainbow-hued frame for now). The jar is such a lovely object that during the course of this chapter we will, or course, completely muck it up. To begin with, we painted the inside of the jar without harming the background. Here's how we did it:

1. **We selected the object.**

   This was the only step that took any work. We began by selecting the body of the jar with the elliptical marquee tool. If you're making a selection and have problems getting the marquee exactly on an object — it's hard to know where to start dragging so that it comes out right — just make sure that the marquee is approximately the right size, and then use the arrow keys to nudge the outline into position. You can reposition the selection outline on the image also by temporarily holding down the spacebar as you're dragging.

   After we selected the body to our satisfaction, we Shift+dragged with the lasso tool to incorporate the neck of the jar into the selection as well.

2. **We made the necessary modifications.**

   We blurred the selection outline a tad using Select⇨Feather, as explained in Chapter 9. If a selection outline isn't dead on, the Feather command helps to fudge the difference a little.

   We also pressed Ctrl+H (⌘+H on the Mac) to hide the selection after we made it. It's important to remember that a hidden selection is still active; pressing this keyboard shortcut or choosing View⇨Selection just makes those distracting marching ants invisible, so it's easier to see what you're doing.

3. **We painted and edited away.**

   And we had a lot of tools to choose from. Inside a selection, you can paint with the brush or pencil; edit with the smudge, focus, or toning tools; or clone with the clone stamp. Rest assured that the area outside the selection will remain as safeguarded from changes as the driven snow (or whatever the saying is).

In Figure 16-1, we painted the inside of the jar using a single tool — the brush — with a single brush size and only two colors, black and white. As a result, we transformed the jar into a kind of marble. Looks mighty keen, and not as much as a drop of paint is outside the lines, just as if we had used a jar-shaped stencil.

This stenciling feature is so all-fired handy that you'll frequently want to select an area before applying a paint or edit tool. The fact is, the selection tools are easier to control than the painting or editing tools, so you may as well take advantage of them.

Figure 16-1:
Using the brush, we painted the inside of the selected jar.

Dribbling Paint from a Bucket

Elements enables you to fill a selection with the foreground color, the background color, a pattern, or a gradual blend of colors called a *gradient*. But before we look at any of these eye-popping options, let's spend a moment kicking around the paint bucket tool, which is part selection tool and part fill tool. The paint bucket tool (it looks like a tilted bucket of paint) lets you fill an area of continuous color or a selected area by clicking the area.

In Figure 16-2, for example, we clicked the paint bucket tool on the row of broccoli in the jar with the foreground color set to white. Elements filled the broccoli with white, turning it into a rough facsimile of cauliflower.

To adjust the performance of the paint bucket, use the tool options bar, also shown in Figure 16-2. As with the magic wand tool, the Tolerance value determines how many pixels in your image the paint bucket affects. The only difference is that the paint bucket applies color instead of selecting pixels. You can also select the Anti-aliased check box to soften the edges of the filled area. (In Figure 16-2, the Tolerance value is 32 and Anti-aliased is turned on, as it is by default.)

Figure 16-2:
The paint
bucket fills a
continuous
area of
color with a
different
color.

Paint bucket tool

The problem with the paint bucket tool is that it's hard to get the Tolerance value just right. You usually end up undoing and then resetting the Tolerance value several times until you find the value that colors only the pixels that you want to color. Although the paint bucket is an okay tool for filling already selected areas, the results you get when you use it to fill a continuous area of color are just fair-to-middling. It's best to use the selection tools first, and then click with the paint bucket; that way you have more alternatives at your disposal.

You can select the paint bucket at any time simply by pressing K. (For "kick the bucket" — get it?)

Applying Color to Selection Innards

Although filling selection outlines is what the paint bucket does best, that doesn't mean it's the best way Elements gives you to fill a selection outline. So what is the best way? Read on:

✔ To fill a selection with the foreground color, press Alt+Backspace (Option+Delete on the Mac).

✔ To fill a selection with the background color, press Ctrl+Backspace (⌘+Delete on the Mac).

✔ Choose Edit➪Fill Selection to display the Fill dialog box, which gives you other options, such as filling the selection with translucent color or a pattern.

✔ Drag with the gradient tool to create a gradient (a gradual blend) between two or more colors.

Two of these options — Edit⇨Fill Selection and the gradient tool — require more discussion, which is why the rest of this chapter is so filled to the gills with text.

Doctoring the Fill

Choose Edit⇨Fill Selection to display the Fill Selection dialog box. The Use drop-down menu lets you specify the color with which you want to fill the selection or lets you choose the Pattern option. The Blending options let you mix the filled colors with the colors already inside the selection. We discuss all these options in more detail in this section. Note that filling works not only within a selection but also on an entire layer. If you don't have an active selection, you'll be able to choose Edit⇨Fill Layer instead, and the entire active layer will be filled. Figure 16-3 shows the Fill Layer dialog box; its controls are identical to those of the Fill Selection dialog box.

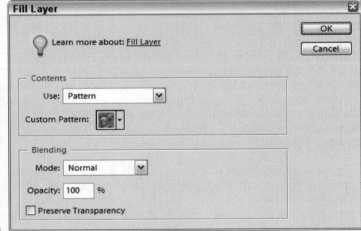

Figure 16-3:
Specify how you want to fill a layer by using the options in the Fill Layer dialog box.

You can also display a Fill dialog box by pressing Shift+Backspace (Shift+Delete on the Mac).

Selecting your stuffing

The most important part of the Fill Selection or the Fill Layer dialog box is the Use drop-down menu. Here you select the stuff you want to use to fill the selection or layer. The options are as follows:

- ✔ The Foreground Color option fills with the foreground color, and the Background Color option fills with the background color. We hope you're not surprised by this news.

- ✔ The next option, Pattern, fills with a repeating pattern. You can define a pattern by selecting a rectangular area and choosing Edit⇨Define Pattern from Selection. If you don't define a selection, Elements creates the pattern from the entire canvas. You can access the patterns you've created, along with a variety of preset patterns, with the Custom Pattern drop-down menu.

- ✔ The last three options — Black, 50% Gray, and White — fill with black, medium gray, and white, respectively. Again, no surprises.

Mixing colors the wrong way

You can enter a value for the Opacity option in the dialog box to mix the fill color or pattern with the colors in the selection or layer. You can also mix the fill and the selected color using the options in the Mode drop-down menu, which include Multiply, Screen, Difference, and other wacky blending modes (see Chapter 14).

Notice that we said you *can* do these things, not that you should. The truth is, you don't want to use the dialog box's Blending options to mix fills with selections. Why? Because the dialog box doesn't let you preview the effects of the Blending options. Even seasoned professionals have trouble predicting the exact repercussions of blending modes, and it's likely that you will, too. And, if you don't like what you get, you have to undo the operation and choose Edit⇨Fill Selection or Edit⇨Fill Layer all over again.

The better way to mix fills is to create a new layer, fill the selection on that layer, and experiment with the Opacity slider and blending mode options in the Layers palette. Naturally, you have no idea what this means if you haven't read the supremely insightful Chapters 10 and 14. Until you do, take this valuable advice and be content to ignore the Blending area of the Fill Selection or Fill Layer dialog box.

The Preserve Transparency check box comes into play when you're working on a layer other than the background layer, as discussed in Chapter 10. If the check box is turned on, only the opaque pixels in a selection are filled when you apply the Fill Selection or Fill Layer command — the transparent areas remain transparent. If the check box is turned off, the entire selection is filled. The option is dimmed if the Lock Transparent Pixels option in the Layers palette is turned on.

Gradients: The Ever-Changing Color Sea

The gradient tool lets you fill a selection with a fountain of colors. By default, the gradient blends from the foreground color to the background color.

But Elements can do more than create simple two-color blends. You can create custom gradients that blend a multitude of colors and vary from opaque to transparent throughout the blend. Elements has five gradient types: Linear, Radial, Angle, Reflected, and Diamond. And the tool options bar offers settings that enable you to play with blend modes, opacity, and color reversals.

Checking out the gradient tool

The following steps provide an insightful, probing introduction to the gradient tool:

1. **Select some portion of your image.**

   In Figure 16-4, we selected the jar again. Just love that jar. It's so pristine; it just begs to be messed up.

   If you don't select a portion of your image before using the gradient tool, Elements fills the entire image with the gradient. (Or, if you're working on a layer, as discussed in Chapter 10, the gradient fills the entire layer.)

Figure 16-4:
The vegetables inside the jar have been replaced with a black-to-white gradient.

Gradient tool

Gradient picker drop-down palette

2. **Select the gradient tool.**

   To do it quickly, just press the G key.

3. **In the options bar, select your desired gradient type.**

   You can choose from five different types, which we cover in just a bit.

4. **If it isn't selected already, select the foreground to background option (the first swatch) from the gradient picker drop-down palette in the tool options bar.**

   This choice will create a gradient that begins with the foreground color and ends with the background color.

5. **Set the foreground and background colors the way you want them.**

   This step is up to you. You can use black and white or select new colors with the eyedropper tool or the Color Picker. For the purposes of Figure 16-4, the colors are set to black and white.

6. **Begin dragging at the point where you want to set the foreground color.**

   In Figure 16-4, the drag began at the bottom of the jar.

7. **Release where you want to position the background color.**

   In this case, it was the top of the jar. The result is a black-to-white gradation.

If you Shift+drag with the gradient tool, Elements constrains the direction of your drag to a horizontal, vertical, or 45° diagonal angle.

Changing the way of the gradient

You can mess around with the performance of the gradient tool by accessing the settings in the tool options bar (refer to Figure 16-4).

The Opacity and Mode controls in the gradient tool options bar are best ignored. If you want to mix a gradation with the existing colors in a selection, create the gradation on a layer and select options in the Layers palette, as discussed in Chapter 14.

Choosing between the five gradient tools

As stated at the beginning of this section, Elements gives you five gradient choices (see Figure 16-5):

- **Linear:** Creates a gradient in which colors blend in a straight line.

- **Radial:** The colors blend in concentric circles, from the center outward.

  Note: In every example in Figure 16-5, the foreground color is black and the background color is white. Setting the lighter color to the foreground color when using the Radial option creates a glowing effect. If the foreground color is darker than its background compatriot, the gradation looks like a bottomless pit, as you can see from the radial gradient shown in Figure 16-5.

- **Angle:** Creates a conical gradation with the colors appearing clockwise.

- **Reflected:** If dragged from edge to edge of your selection, a reflected gradient acts like a linear gradient. If dragged from the interior to an edge of the selection, however, the gradient reflects back on itself.

- **Diamond:** As does the radial gradient, this tool creates concentric shapes — in this case, diamonds or squares, depending on the angle at which you drag.

Linear   Radial

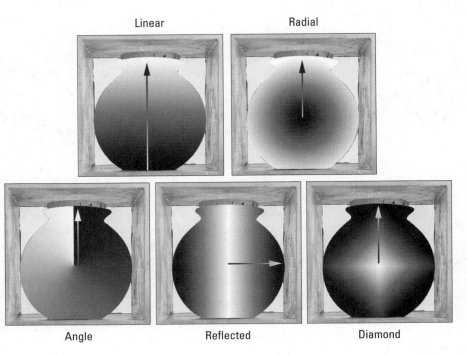

Figure 16-5:
The jar filled with five different gradient types — Linear, Radial, Angle, Reflected, and Diamond. The arrows indicate the direction that the mouse was dragged.

Angle   Reflected   Diamond

Choosing gradient options

The tool options bar has three check boxes to influence your gradient: Reverse, Dither, and Transparency. Here's a rundown of what these options do:

- **Reverse:** When the Reverse check box is checked, the gradient starts with the background color and ends with the foreground color. This option is useful for creating radial gradients while keeping the default colors intact.

- **Dither:** The Dither check box helps eliminate banding. *Banding* is distinct bands of color in a printed gradient — that's a bad thing in 9 out of 10 households. Leave the check box turned on unless you're feeling especially contrary and want to create a banding effect.

- **Transparency:** The Transparency check box is a little more complicated. Here's the scoop: Gradients can include areas that are partially or fully transparent. In other words, they fade from a solid color to a more transparent color. When the Transparency check box is turned off, Elements creates the gradient by using all opaque colors, ignoring the transparency information.

Selecting your colors

The gradient picker drop-down palette lets you change the way colors blend inside the gradation and select from a variety of prefab gradients. Your choices include:

- **Foreground to background:** By default, this option is selected. It blends between the foreground and background colors, as in the examples in Figure 16-5.

- **Foreground to transparent:** If you select this option, the gradient tool blends the foreground color into the original colors in the selection. The examples in Figure 16-6 were created with this option selected.

- **Remaining options:** The rest of the options in the gradient picker drop-down palette create a variety of factory-made gradients, some involving just a few colors and others blending a whole rainbow of colors.

- **Gradient libraries:** You also have at your disposal a vast array of gradient libraries, which have preset gradients that you can easily load for your painting pleasure. Simply click the arrow in the upper-right corner of the gradient picker palette to access the drop-down menu, and then scroll down to the bottom, where you'll find the various gradient libraries. Select one and it will replace your current gradient set.

When you select a gradient from the gradient picker palette, Elements displays the gradient in the gradient preview in the tool options bar.

Linear   Radial

Figure 16-6:
Here's the
jar filled
with a linear
and radial
gradient and
with the
Foreground
to
Transparent
option
selected.

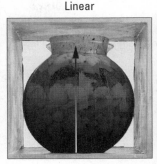 

Foreground to Transparent

If none of the existing gradients suits your taste, you can create a custom gradient, as in Color Plate 19. The next section explains the ins and outs of building your own gradients.

In the gradient picker palette, you can choose between viewing your gradients by thumbnails, text only, or a combination of both text and thumbnails. Click the right-pointing arrow in the upper-right corner of the palette to make your selection.

Becoming a gradient wizard

It's pretty easy to design a custom gradient if you just spend a few moments to dissect and understand the various parts of the Gradient Editor dialog box. Start by clicking the Edit button to the right of the gradient preview in the tool options bar. The Gradient Editor dialog box, shown in Figure 16-7, appears.

The Gradient Editor dialog box is complex, and chances are you won't use it much. But the following list introduces the dialog box and starts you off creating your own gradient:

✓ **Presets:** The palette at the top of the dialog box lists all the preset gradients — the same ones in the gradient picker drop-down palette in the tool options bar. From this palette, you select the gradient you want to use as a starting point for your custom gradient. It doesn't much matter which you choose; you can change it to your heart's content.

✓ **Gradient Type:** You can choose between gradients made with Solid colors and those created with Noise. Noise gradients randomize the colors of pixels and produce interesting yet unpredictable results.

✓ **Smoothness/Roughness:** This control varies with your choice of Gradient Type. Either way, drag the slider or type a value to determine how smoothly or roughly you'll blend one color into another color.

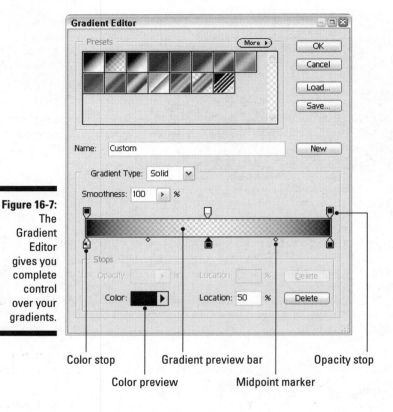

Figure 16-7:
The
Gradient
Editor
gives you
complete
control
over your
gradients.

Color stop   Gradient preview bar   Opacity stop

Color preview   Midpoint marker

The following options are available only when you select the Noise gradient type:

- **Color Model** and **color sliders:** Enable you to change the color model and limit the color range by moving the sliders, respectively.

- **Restrict Colors:** Keeps colors from becoming too saturated.

- **Add Transparency:** Enables you to incorporate transparency in your noise gradient.

- **Randomize:** Changes the colors in a noise gradient. Remember, it's a *random* process — every time you click you get a new set of colors. Better than watching reruns on TV.

Gradients can be saved and loaded just as swatches are, as discussed in Chapter 5. It's important to save your gradient to disk if you want to be able to use it again later.

To remove a gradient from the list, press Alt (Option on the Mac) and click the gradient. Note that your cursor turns into a scissors icon, signifying "delete."

Changing, adding, and deleting colors

When you select the Solid Gradient type, little house-shaped boxes, called *stops,* appear on either side of the gradient preview bar. There are color stops on the bottom and opacity stops on the top. You use these stops to change the colors, opacity, and location of colors in the gradient, as explained in the two upcoming sections.

To change one of the colors in the gradient, first check to see whether the roof on that color's color stop is black. A *black roof* indicates the active color stop — the color that will be affected by your changes. If the roof isn't black, click the color stop to make it active.

After you activate the color stop, you have one of three choices. One, you can click the color preview, which displays the Color Picker. Two, you can access the foreground or background color from the Color pop-up menu, located right next to the color preview. (If you use the foreground or background color, switching to the User Color option in the Color pop-up menu keeps the gradient from changing should you later switch the foreground or background color.) Three, you can use the eyedropper to click a color in your image or a color in the Color Swatches palette.

Here's some more stuff you need to know about playing with the colors in your gradient:

- ✔ To add a color to the gradient, click just below the gradient preview bar at the point where you want the color to appear. You get a new color stop icon representing the color.

- ✔ To remove a color from the gradient, drag its color stop down and away from the gradient preview bar.

- ✔ If you drag a color stop to the right or left, you can change the position of the color in the gradient. Suppose that you have a gradient that fades from black to white. If you want more black and less white, drag the black color stop toward the white stop.

- ✔ The little diamonds found above or below the gradient preview bar represent the midpoint between two colors or two opacity settings. Using the example of a black-to-white gradient again, the midpoint marks the spot at which the gradient contains equal amounts of black and white. To move a midpoint, just drag the diamond.

- ✔ The Location option shows the placement of the active color stop or midpoint marker. If you want to be terribly precise, you can type a value in the Location box, instead of dragging the icons, to position a color stop or midpoint marker.

    When a color stop is active, a value of 0% represents the very beginning of the gradient; 100% represents the very end. Midpoint values are always relative to the two color stops on either side of the midpoint. A value of 50% places the midpoint an equal distance from both color stops. The minimum and maximum midpoint values are 5% and 95%, respectively.

Changing the transparency

Elements lets you adjust the amount of opacity in a gradient. You can make a portion of the gradient fully opaque, completely transparent, or somewhere in between the two.

You change the transparency like you change the color: Click to select a stop and then adjust the Opacity amount in the Stops area of the Gradient Editor. Black stops represent opaque areas, white stops represent transparent areas, and gray stops represent everything in between. The gradient preview bar also shows you opaque areas in their actual colors and transparent areas in the gray-and-white checkerboard pattern.

You can add as many opacity stops as you want and set different Opacity values for each. To move an opacity stop, just drag it right or left. To delete a stop, drag it off the bar. To move a midpoint, drag it right or left.

Taking on Borders with the Stroke Dialog Box

EDIT ONLY WHEN IN EDITOR

The last item on this chapter's agenda is Edit⇨Stroke (Outline) Selection, a command that traces borders around a selection. When you choose this command, Elements displays the Stroke dialog box, shown in Figure 16-8.

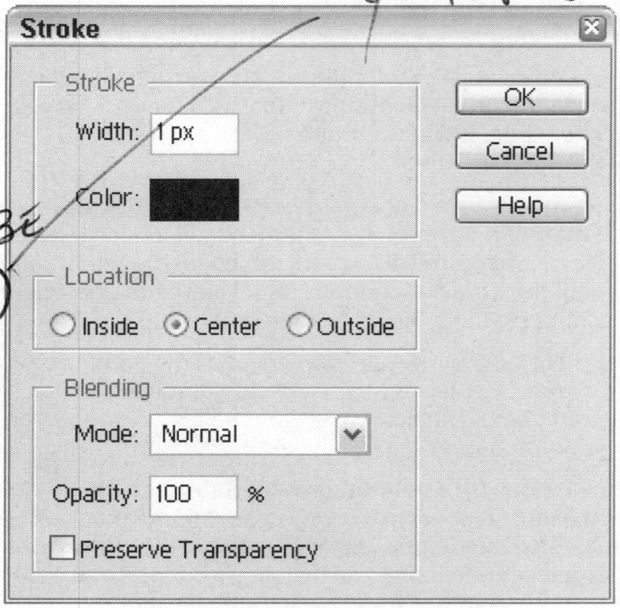

ALSO SEE (OR ESPECIALLY SEE)

STYLES AND EFFECTS

(WHICH MAY BE IN LAYERS?)

TRY SIMPLE SHARP

Yes, it is

Figure 16-8: Use the Stroke dialog box to draw a border around a selection.

Stroke

Stroke

Width: 1 px

Color: ▮

OK
Cancel
Help

Location

○ Inside   ● Center   ○ Outside

Blending

Mode: Normal ▾

Opacity: 100 %

☐ Preserve Transparency

In the Width option, type the thickness of the border you want. This value is measured in pixels, with a range from 1 to 250 pixels. You can, however, enter units other than pixels. For example, if you type **2 in**, Elements accepts it and converts the value from inches to an equivalent number of pixels.

In Figure 16-9, we placed a 16-pixel-wide black stroke around the selected jar. Then using the same selection, we placed an 8-pixel-wide white stroke on top of that. Slick, huh? (Oh, come on, say it is, even if it's just to make us feel better.)

Figure 16-9: The classic double-border effect, so in demand at today's finer jar emporiums.

You can also choose a color from the Stroke dialog box. Simply click the Color swatch, and you're transported to the Color Picker. No need to slap yourself on the head for not choosing the right color beforehand. Note that changing the color in the Stroke dialog box changes the foreground color as well.

How the border rides the track

The Location options in the Stroke dialog box determine how the border rides the selection outline. The border can cruise around fully inside or fully outside the selection, or it can sit astride (centered on) the selection. Why might you want to change this setting? Well, take another look at Figure 16-9. Suppose that instead of the white border being flanked on either side by black (both of which were created using the Center option), you want the borders to sit beside each other. If you select the Inside option, the white border appears inside the selection, and the black border appears inside the white border. If you select Outside, the white border traces the outside of the jar, and the black border extends even farther.

Actually, we don't recommend that you use the Outside option. It has a nasty habit of flattening the edges of curves. For the best results, stick with Inside or Center.

Mix your stroke after you press Enter (or Return)

Like the Blending and Opacity options in other dialog boxes, the ones in the Stroke dialog box don't provide you with a preview of how the effect will look when applied to your image. So, if you want to play with the blending modes or opacity of your stroke, ignore the options in the dialog box. Instead, create a new layer (as explained in Chapter 10) and do your selecting and stroking on that layer. You can then adjust the blending mode and opacity using the Layers palette (as discussed in Chapter 14).

On the off chance that you're curious about the Preserve Transparency check box, we'll tell you that it affects only images with layers. If you don't have any layers going, don't worry about it. (Again, we explain layers in Chapter 10.) The check box just ensures that the transparent portions of layers remain transparent.

We explore the Stroke dialog box more in Chapter 17, where we cast a penetrating gaze at the world of type in Elements. So keep reading if you're curious, or go ahead and take a breather if you need it. We promise not to go ahead without you.

Chapter 17

Type Righter

Chapter 9 leads you on a merry tour of the various tools and commands for selecting a part of your image. But that chapter skips one other type of selection outline that you can create in Photoshop Elements, and you'll never guess what it is. Not in a million years. Give up? The answer is *text*. That's right, Elements lets you build a selection outline out of numbers, vowels, consonants, and any other characters you can type from your keyboard. Selection outline text is one of the two kinds of text that Elements lets you create. You can also create regular text, which has the distinct advantage of remaining editable long after you create it.

In general, the Elements approach to text makes it an ideal program for subjecting large letters to special effects. The bigger your text, the better it looks. But you shouldn't mistake Elements for a word processor. Even though Elements deals with text admirably, it's still not the best choice for creating large chunks of text. Instead, use a word processor such as Microsoft Word or a desktop publishing program such as InDesign or QuarkXPress.

Working with the Type Tools

Elements gives you four type tools, two that create horizontal text and two that create vertical text. Each pair has a regular tool for creating normal text, and a mask tool that creates selection outlines. The vertical type and vertical type mask tools are great for Asian fonts, but for Roman letters they probably won't be very valuable to you. Therefore, we're going to pretty much ignore them for the rest of this chapter. Doing so will make it a lot easier to deal with the similarities and differences between the regular type tools and the type mask tools.

If you find that you do need vertical type, just remember that the vertical type tool behaves almost exactly like the horizontal type tool; ditto for the vertical type mask tool and the horizontal type mask tool. And anyway, after creating horizontal letters, it's a snap to switch them to vertical letters if you need to; the change orientation option (the control on the far right in the tool options bar) is there for just that purpose.

You can select the type tools by pressing the T key on your keyboard. (The icon for the tool even looks like the letter T, making this the only icon that serves as its own tool tip.) By default, pressing Shift-T cycles through the selection of various type tools. You can change this by deselecting the Use Shift Key for Tool Switch option in the General pane of Preferences; if you do so, pressing just T will cycle through the type tools.

Following is a briefing on the difference between the horizontal type tool (active in Figure 17-1) and the horizontal type mask tool:

- **The horizontal type tool** creates text on a new text layer (Chapter 10 explains layers in detail), which enables you to work with the text without worrying about touching the underlying image.

  You can come back and edit the text contents and attributes long after you've moved on to another part of the image by simply highlighting the text with the horizontal type tool. Although you can't use painting or editing tools on a text layer, you can make the text more or less translucent by adjusting the Opacity percentage in the Layers palette, and you can blend the text with the underlying layers using the blending modes drop-down menu.

- **The horizontal type mask tool** enables you to create your text as a selection outline. Until you decide to "commit" your text, you can work with selection outline text just as you would with regular text. Also, you can manipulate, edit, paint, and otherwise play with a type selection outline as you can with any other selection outline. And because the horizontal type mask tool works like any other selection tool, you can use it to add to or subtract from an existing selection outline (see Chapter 9). Note that after you click the commit icon in the tool options bar, you can't edit selection type as you can regular type created with the horizontal type tool.

So, which option do you use when? Most of the time, you'll want to use the horizontal type tool. If you want to retain true editability, this tool creates the text on its own layer. Otherwise, which option you use depends on the effect you're trying to create. If you want to create text outlines (such as those we show later in Figure 17-3), use the horizontal type mask tool and then stroke the selection outline using Edit⇨Stroke (Outline) Selection. See "Declaring Open Season on Type Selection Outlines" for more on using the horizontal type mask tool.

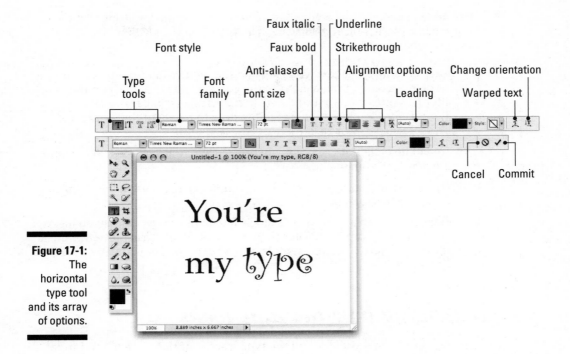

Figure 17-1:
The
horizontal
type tool
and its array
of options.

Putting Your Words On-Screen

Many similarities exist between using the horizontal type tool and the horizontal type mask tool. We focus first on the horizontal type tool, but if you want to create type selection outlines with the horizontal type mask tool, you should read this section, too, because we cover all the text formatting options here.

To type a few letters in Elements, select the horizontal type tool and click in the image. It doesn't really matter where you click, by the way. Elements creates a new layer and positions your text at the spot you click, but you can always move the text after you create it. You get a little blinking cursor (called an *insertion marker*) that you may be familiar with from working in other programs. After the insertion marker appears, you're free to type your text.

Typing what must be typed

Using the horizontal type tool creates what is known as a *text layer*. In the Layers palette, you'll notice a new layer with a capital letter T icon, indicating that the layer is indeed a text layer. The name of the text layer corresponds to the text you typed.

Here are a few more things you may need to know while inputting text on your canvas. We'll look at formatting a little later in the section "Changing how the type looks."

✔ After entering your text, you may find that you've made a mistake or two. To delete a letter, first make sure the correct layer is active and then click after the letter you want to delete and press Backspace (Delete on the Mac). To delete more than one letter, drag to highlight the letters and press Backspace (or Delete).

✔ To add text, click at the point where you want to insert the text and enter the new text from the keyboard.

✔ To replace text, drag over it with the cursor to highlight it and then start whacking those keys.

✔ Elements places all words on a single line in the image unless you insert a hard return by pressing Enter (Return on the Mac). To achieve the effect shown in Figure 17-1, for example, press Enter (or Return) between *You're* and *my type*.

Changing how the type looks

The tool options bar provides all the typographic options needed to format your text. These options control the typeface, the type size, the type color, the alignment, and all that other rigmarole. When all these characteristics get together in the same room, they're usually called *formatting attributes*. You can make additional enhancements to the appearance of your text after you return to the image window, but the formatting options let you set up the fundamental stuff.

Here are some things to keep in mind when exploring the type options:

✔ To change the attributes of your text, the horizontal type tool must be active. If you want to change only a portion of your text, highlight it with the tool. If you want to select all the text, highlight all of it or simply click the commit icon and keep that particular text layer selected in the Layers palette.

✔ If you know what you want, you can always establish your formatting attributes *before* you create your type. Who knows, you may get it exactly right the first time around with no need for further editing.

✔ You select a typeface from the font drop-down menu. Select a style from the font style drop-down menu. Type styles such as bold and italic (sometimes referred to as "oblique") appear in their own submenus.

✔ Enter the size of the text into the font size option box. The size value is measured in points (one point equals ½ inch), pixels, or millimeters, depending on your Type setting in the Units & Rulers panel of the Preferences dialog box.

✔ If you want to squash or stretch your text, switch over to the move tool and drag one of the squares on the bounding box that appears when the Show Bounding Box move tool option is active. You can then switch back to the horizontal type tool and, amazingly enough, the text is still editable. It's best, however, to use this option sparingly. Otherwise, you run the risk of totally destroying the appealing proportions of a type-face. Most typefaces have been designed by trained artists who spend their lives perfecting the shape and form of each letter. Not that you should feel guilty or anything.

✔ In case your font doesn't have a built-in bold or italic state, the type tool options bar gives you access to Faux Bold and Faux Italic. You can also choose to underline your text, or strike through it for that "pretend you can't read this" look.

✔ By default, the color that first appears in the color swatch in the tool options bar is the current foreground color. To change the color after you click your type tool but before you create the text, click the color swatch in the tool options bar and choose a new color. (If you need a basic color refresher, see Chapter 5.)

✔ Select an alignment option to determine whether multiple lines of text are aligned by their left edges, right edges, or centers.

✔ You can mix most formatting attributes within the same text layer, but alignment is one attribute that can't be mixed.

✔ If you press Enter or Return as you're using a type tool to break your type onto multiple lines, Elements 3.0 now lets you change the size of the space between lines, known as *leading* (pronounced "ledding"). By default, lead-ing will be set to Auto, meaning that Elements is automatically assigning a standard leading amount to your text (120% of the font size, if you're curi-ous). To increase or decrease the leading, select the lines in question and change the amount in the tool options bar's leading field.

A few options can be found not only in the tool options bar but also in the Type submenu of the Layer menu:

✔ **Horizontal/Vertical:** This text orientation option lets you switch hori-zontal text to vertical text, and vice versa.

✔ **Anti-aliasing:** You almost always want anti-aliasing on because if you don't, your text will have tiny jagged edges.

✔ **Warp Text:** This feature is so neat it deserves its own section. So read on.

Warping type into strange and unusual shapes

Warping text in Elements is a little bit like the feature known as path text, found in drawing programs such as Illustrator, Freehand, and CorelDraw. You can twist, push, and pull to create a variety of cool and crazy effects. Take a glance at Figure 17-2 to see a small sampling of these effects.

Figure 17-2:
You can warp type into a variety of interesting shapes.

Follow these easy steps to warp your very own text:

1. **Select the text layer in the Layers palette.**

2. **Select a type tool in the toolbox and click the warp text icon in the tool options bar. Or choose Layer⇨Type⇨Warp Text (any tool can be active to choose this).**

3. **In the Warp Text dialog box, choose a Style from the drop-down menu.**

4. **Play with the options.**

   Choose Horizontal or Vertical orientation for the selected style. Adjust the Bend value to apply more or less warping. Use the Distortion sliders to apply a perspective effect to the warp.

5. **If you're happy with your warp, click OK.**

   Simple instructions, we know, but in truth the secret to warping text is just playing around with the options. Setting the proper Style is the most important decision; the other options simply give you permutations based on the Style you choose. So choose a Style and start exploring. Luckily, it's such a fun command that you'll enjoy exploring it (imagine that)!

Editing the Text Layer

If you notice a misspelled word or some other typographical gaffe, select the offending text layer and drag over the text with the horizontal type tool to edit it. You can then edit the contents or any of the attributes. Provided you keep your file in the PSD, TIFF, or PDF formats, text layers are saved with the image, so you can revise the text at any time as long as you don't simplify the layer (see the section "Simplifying a Text Layer" for more info) or flatten the layers (see Chapter 10 for more on layers).

Here are some things you can do to a text layer and still have the text editable:

- ✔ You can reorder or duplicate the text layer in the Layers palette, just as you can with a regular layer. To move the layer in front of or behind another one, drag it up or down in the list of layers in the Layers palette. A black line shows where the layer will be inserted. To duplicate, drag the layer onto the create a new layer icon at the bottom of the Layers palette.

- ✔ You can lock text layers (see Chapter 10 for more on this feature).

- ✔ You can move or clone the text. Drag with the move tool to position the text. Alt+drag (Option+drag on the Mac) to clone the text. Note that Alt+dragging (Option+dragging on the Mac) creates another text layer.

- ✔ You can perform the transformation commands Free Transform and Skew, found in the Image menu under the Transform submenu. Distort and Perspective transformations aren't available to text layers.

- ✔ You can apply layer styles (see details in Chapter 14) to the text layer. Even after you apply the effect, if you change the type in any way (such as a different font or even a different word), the layer style magically updates to the changes.

- ✔ You can fill the type with the foreground or background color by using the fill keyboard shortcuts. Press Alt+Backspace (Option+Delete on the Mac) to fill with the foreground color. Press Ctrl+Backspace (⌘+Delete on the Mac) to fill with the background color. Note that the Edit➪Fill Layer menu command is grayed out — you can utilize only the keyboard shortcuts.

Here are three things you can't do to a text layer, unless you simplify the text layer and convert it to a regular layer (see more about this in the next section):

- ✔ You can't use any of the painting and editing tools. When you click the painting and editing tools on the text layer, you get an error message saying you must first simplify the type layer.

- ✔ You can't apply filters from the Filters palette.

- ✔ You can't apply effects from the Effects palette. Well, okay, technically you *can,* but the effect is going to automatically simplify the text for you anyway.

A text layer can't be created for images in Indexed color or Bitmap modes because these modes don't support layers of any kind — text or otherwise. Type created in these modes is treated like type created with the horizontal type mask tool; it gets applied to the background and can't be edited after it is committed. If you want type included in GIF images you're preparing for the Web, for example, be sure and wait until you finish compositing your layers and editing your type to convert the image to indexed color.

If you decide you don't want the text layer any longer, delete it by dragging the layer to the trash icon at the bottom of the Layers palette (for help, see Chapter 10). You can also click the layer in the Layers palette and then click the trash icon.

Simplifying a Text Layer

To apply a filter or paint on a text layer, you must first do what Elements calls simplifying the layer. *Simplifying* is just a simpler word for *rasterizing;* it means to convert the text layer into a regular layer containing just pixels. To simplify a text layer, choose Layer➪Simplify Layer. After simplifying, the type looks the same; however, you can no longer edit the text. (Notice that the T icon isn't there anymore in the Layers palette.) So, a word of advice — be sure the text is exactly the way you want it before you simplify the text layer, because editing capabilities go down the drain. (You could, of course, also just duplicate the text layer by dragging it to the create a new layer icon in the Layers palette. Then turn off the visibility for one copy by clicking the visibility eyeball for that layer in the Layers palette, and simplify the other copy. That way you have a backup — perfect for when you feel you're not quite ready to make a commitment.)

Declaring Open Season on Type Selection Outlines

Almost all the previous formatting information applies also to type created with the horizontal type mask tool. The big difference is that after you click that commit icon, press the Enter key on the numeric keypad, or select another tool, you can't edit your text any longer.

The first thing you may notice when you click with the horizontal type mask tool is the appearance of a funky pink overlay. And as you type, your letters will appear transparent, as if they were cut out of the pink overlay. This is Elements' way of telling you that you're creating a kind of mask, where parts of the layer are masked off and can't be affected by editing. (And when you think about it, that's exactly what you do when you make any kind of selection.) When you click the commit icon in the tool options bar or just switch to another tool, the overlay disappears and the familiar marching ants of the selection appear. (See Chapter 9 for more on selections.) Now that your newly created selection outline type is there inside your image, you can do all kinds of things with it, including the following:

✔ To move a text selection outline, drag with one of the selection tools or press the arrow keys to nudge the selection outline this way or that.

✔ To move or clone the text selection, use the same techniques you use to move or clone any other selection (refer to Chapters 9 and 10). Drag with the move tool to move the text; Alt+drag (Option+drag on the Mac) to clone the text.

In other words, selections that you create with the type selection option work just like any other selection.

✔ You can paint inside the text. After you paint inside the letters, you can use the edit tools to smear the colors, blur them, lighten them, and so on.

✔ You can fill the text with the foreground color by pressing Alt+Backspace (Option+Delete on the Mac). To fill the text with the background color, press Ctrl+Backspace (⌘+Delete on the Mac). To fill the text with a blend of colors, just drag across the text with the gradient tool. It couldn't be easier.

✔ You can apply a border around your type by choosing Edit➪Stroke.

✔ Before you fill or stroke a selection outline, be sure that your text is positioned where you want it. You can't move the stroked text after you create it without leaving a hole on your layer. Ditto with any other painting or editing commands you apply to a text selection outline. That's

> why it's a good idea to create a new layer before you make your text selection outline; it enables you to move the text without affecting the underlying image.
>
> ✔ If you want to delete text that was created with the horizontal type mask tool — and you didn't create that text on its own layer — you need to undo your steps. Use the Undo History palette (see Chapter 8) to bring your image back to its pretext appearance.

The following steps tell you how to create genuine outline type, like the stuff shown in Figure 17-3. You can see through the interiors of the letters, and you can make the borders as thick as you please. What more could you ask from life?

1. **Create a new layer.**

   You don't have to put your text on its own layer, but doing so makes it simpler to edit the text later if necessary. To create a layer, click the create a new layer icon in the Layers palette, as discussed in Chapter 10.

2. **Select the horizontal type mask tool in the toolbox.**

3. **Set the formatting attributes in the tool options bar.**

4. **Click with the tool on your canvas.**

   Type away and then press Enter *on the numeric keypad* (not the main Enter key in Windows) or click the commit icon in the tool options bar. Then move the text selection outline into the desired position by dragging it or nudging it with the arrow keys.

5. **Set the foreground color to white.**

   You can do this quickly by pressing D to get black and white and then X to swap them.

6. **Make sure that the Lock Transparent Pixels check box in the Layers palette is deselected.**

   In the next step, you apply a stroke to the center of your selection outline (that is, with half the stroke appearing on the inside of the outline and half appearing on the outside). If the Lock Transparent Pixels check box is selected, Elements doesn't let you paint on the layer.

7. **Choose Edit⇨Stroke (Outline) Selection, select the Center option, and enter 12 as the Width value.**

   After making your selections in the Stroke dialog box, press Enter (Return on the Mac). You now have a 12-pixel thick, white outline around your type. Depending on the size of your type, you may need to enter a value other than 12.

8. **Make black or some other dark color the foreground color.**

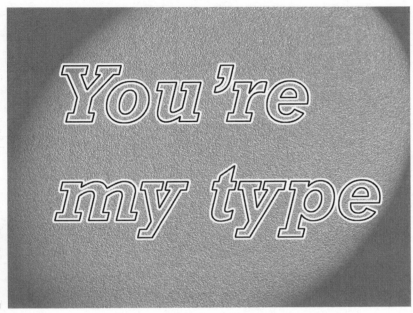

Figure 17-3:
Outline type
created the
correct way.

9. **Choose Edit⇨Stroke (Outline) Selection and enter** 4 **as the Width value. Leave the Location at Center.**

   Then press Enter (Return on the Mac). Congratulations! You get the effect shown in Figure 17-3. If you created your text on a layer, as recommended back in Step 1, you can use the move tool to reposition the text if needed. You can also play with the blending modes and opacity control in the Layers palette to change how the text blends with the underlying image.

Although this stroking effect is pretty cool, it pales in comparison to what can be achieved with a text layer created using the horizontal type tool and layer styles. Text layers and layer styles go hand in hand. After you've applied an inner bevel and drop shadow to a text layer, you probably won't ever be satisfied with plain ordinary flat text again. And don't forget that even with a layer style applied, text layers are still completely editable. Although why anyone would need to go back and edit his or her text is a compleet mistery.

Chapter 18

Can Photoshop Elements Do *That?*

● ●

In This Chapter

▶ Pulling off special effects

▶ Processing a bunch of files

▶ Converting a multipage PDF file

▶ Animating GIFs

▶ Putting it together with Photomerge

▶ Attaching a file to e-mail

▶ Making slide shows

▶ Creating a contact sheet

▶ Wrapping up a Picture Package

▶ Making a Web Photo Gallery

● ●

*O*rganizing the many different functions of Photoshop Elements into the chapters of this book was like trying to herd a couple thousand weasels into 17 different pens, making sure they were all correctly sorted by gender, birth weight, IQ, religious persuasion, cholesterol level, and batting average. After a prolonged tussle, a great deal of squirming and wriggling, and much yanking from one pen and plopping down into another, things looked pretty good. Panting, exhausted, we turned around — and saw a few more danged weasels in the corner. These guys seemed to defy any classification. They were rebels. They refused to be pigeonholed — *weaselholed* — by The Man.

And so this, the 18th chapter, contains the weasels that wouldn't go into the 17 other pens.

On reflection though, it became clear that these weasels all had something in common: They all dealt with *automation*. The automation in most of these weasels — okay, these *features* — works just as you'd expect: You tell Elements what to do, say "Go!", and then sit back while Elements does it. And with one feature, animated GIFs, the automation comes after the fact: After the animated GIF is loaded in a Web user's browser, the animation plays back automatically.

Another thing these functions have in common: They're probably the most amazing stuff that Elements has to offer. Up to now, Elements has been a hands-on application, and necessarily so. Now it's time to sit back and watch. Prop your feet up. Take off your shoes. And put a pillow on your chest so you won't bruise your chin when your jaw drops open in amazement. This is the stuff that makes you say: "Can Photoshop Elements do *that?*"

We start this chapter with amazing things that work pretty much the same on the Mac and in Windows. Then we branch off into functions that are implemented differently depending on which computer platform you're using. So just look for those "Windows" and "Mac" icons, and you'll be just fine.

Taking on the Effects

An *effect,* in Elements' terminology, is a series of commands — combining filters and layer styles with more mundane stuff such as Filling and Image Sizing — prebuilt and prerecorded for your use. As with the Blur More and Sharpen More filters, effects are one-shot wonders — you just apply them, and if you don't like the result, too bad. No tweaking is allowed (at least, not until after the fact).

Applying effects from the Styles and Effects palette is identical to applying filters from the same palette. You have three options:

✔ Click the desired effect to select it, and then choose Apply from the Styles and Effects palette's More menu.

✔ Double-click the desired effect.

✔ Drag the desired effect from the Effects palette into the image window.

Four categories of effects (or five if you count All) are available:

✔ **Frames:** As you may expect, these effects can create a frame around your image. Some Frame effects will operate only if an existing selection is active. As you saw in Chapter 9, the Vignette effect is quite attractive. Drop Shadow Frame would be a great choice for creating Web images where the Web page's background color was white. And Photo Corners is nice for that retro look.

✔ **Image effects:** These are a mixed bag. They perform a variety of different creative processes on your image and work with selected parts of images or entire layers. Fluorescent Chalk and Quadrant Colors perform their magic on the entire layer, regardless of whether there's an active selection. If you want the color in your image to gradually fade out to black and white, Horizontal Color Fade and Vertical Color Fade were

made for you. As an alternative, you can also use the Color Fade —
Horizontal and Color Fade — Vertical layer styles (in the Image Effects
category) to achieve the same effect.

✔ **Text effects:** Probably the most useful of the effects. They require a text
layer to work, so first create your text with the horizontal or vertical
type tool (see Chapter 17 for more information). The three Outline effects
can be a bit blocky, but the other eight options are quite attractive. Use
Brushed Metal to give your text a shiny look or Water Reflection to reflect
your text in a photo of a body of water, as seen in Figure 18-1. Note that
these effects automatically simplify your layer (see Chapter 17), so make
sure you've finished editing your text before you apply one of the text
effects.

✔ **Textures:** You can create solid fields of different surfaces, from Bricks to
Molten Lead to Sandpaper. The Ink Blots, Marbled Glass, Sunset, and
Wood-Pine effects can work on only the entire layer, regardless of whether
there's an active selection or not. To see the Textures effects in action,
turn back to the color pages in the book. Many of the backgrounds behind
the color plates are rendered from Textures.

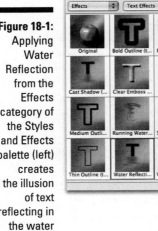

Figure 18-1:
Applying
Water
Reflection
from the
Effects
category of
the Styles
and Effects
palette (left)
creates
the illusion
of text
reflecting in
the water
(right).

Processing Multiple Files

If you have a whole bunch of different images that must conform in terms of file format and image size, the Process Multiple Files command is just the ticket. Based on Elements' old Batch command, this new version also lets you add Quick Fix image adjustments and labels to the images. All you have to do is tell Elements where the files are, what you want the common file format to be, what changes you want to make, and where to save the files. Click OK, and Process Multiple Files does the rest.

Here's the step-by-step game plan:

1. **Choose File⇨Process Multiple Files.**

   The command is also available from the File Browser; on the Mac it's under the Automate menu, and in Windows it's under the File menu. However you access it, the Process Multiple Files dialog box appears, as shown in Figure 18-2.

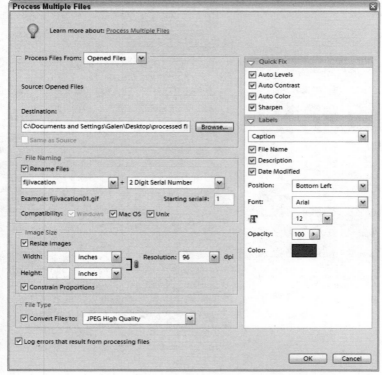

Figure 18-2: In the Process Multiple Files dialog box, you can tell Elements everything it needs to know to make changes to your files.

2. **Use the Process Files From drop-down list to locate the images that you want to process.**

   Choose Folder if the images are already grouped in a folder somewhere on your hard drive. Then click the Source option's Browse button, navigate to the correct folder, select it, and click Choose. If you have other folders containing images in your Source folder and you want to process those too, click the Include All Subfolders check box.

   Choose Import if you want to get the pictures from a scanner, a digital camera, or a PDF file. Choose your source in the From pop-up menu. When you click OK after choosing your other settings, Elements will take you to another dialog box, depending on the type of device and plug-ins you have installed. If you've chosen PDF file, you'll be asked to locate the file and then be given a chance to preview the images to be extracted from the PDF file.

   Choose Opened Files if you want to process all currently opened files in Elements. Choose File Browser if you want to process files from the current folder in File Browser. If thumbnails are selected in the browser, only those selected images will be processed; otherwise, all the photos inside the current folder will be processed.

3. **Specify where you want the files to be saved.**

   After clicking the Browse button in the Destination section and navigating to the appropriate place on your hard drive, you may want to take the opportunity to click the new folder button and save the batch-processed images in their own folder. If you check the Same as Source check box, the processed files will overwrite the originals unless you use the File Naming controls to give the processed versions different names.

4. **Specify a File Naming convention.**

   If you want the files you're saving to have different names from the source files, click the Rename Files check box. You can then choose two variables for creating the names of your files. The three "document name" options retain or change the capitalization of the name currently assigned to the file. Alternatively, you can click and type a name of your own in one of the option fields. You can also append today's date or sequential strings of numbers and letters.

   For instance, let's say that you have a folder containing a few dozen photos of your family's vacation in Fiji, and you want the photos to be named fijivacation01.jpg, fijivacation02.jpg, and so on. Click and type fijivacation in the first field, and then choose 2 Digit Serial Number in the second field. Note that you're required to include a document name, serial number, or serial letter choice when you process your files; otherwise, you'd end up giving all your files the same name — a big impossibility in computer terms.

   If these images are destined for the Web, it's a good idea to make sure all three Compatibility check boxes are checked.

5. **Choose whether you want to change the image size or resolution.**

   Turn on the Resize Images check box and enter the desired width, height, and resolution in the appropriate fields (see Chapter 4 for info about these options). Make sure the Constrain Proportions check box is activated to ensure that images of varying sizes won't get squashed or stretched.

6. **Choose your desired file format in the File Type drop-down menu.**

   You have Elements' usual long list of possibilities.

7. **Turn on any Quick Fix options.**

   You can apply Auto Levels, Auto Contrast, Auto Color, and Sharpen. Just be sure that all the photos you're processing actually suffer from the same problems before you use these options.

8. **Add text to your images as desired.**

   Under the Labels options, you can choose in the top menu to add either captions or watermarks to the processed images. The Watermark option lets you enter text directly into the Custom Text field, which prints by default at 50 percent opacity (though you can change this). The Caption option draws upon up to three sources for creating the caption; it can use the filename, the date the image was modified, and the image's Description.

   You can add a description to an image by choosing File⇨File Info and then typing in the Description field. Mac users can add descriptions also by editing the IPTC Metadata in the File Browser (see Chapter 3). If Windows users have added a caption to the image in Elements' Organizer component (see Chapter 6), this caption gets saved as the image's description.

   You can specify a position, font, font size, opacity, and color for the watermark or caption using the controls at the bottom of the Labels panel.

9. **Click the OK button, and sit back while Elements automatically processes the images according to your guidelines.**

Converting a Multipage PDF File

If you have a multipage PDF file and you need to open all the pages in Elements, it can be a drag to repeatedly open the file and choose a single page at a time to open. The File⇨Automation Tools⇨Multi-page PDF to PSD command can convert the PDF file into a folder of individual PSD files, each page in its own individual file.

Select the PDF file you want to convert by clicking the Choose button. The Page Range option lets you convert the entire document or a consecutive group of pages. The Output Options let you choose a resolution, color mode, and whether you want Elements to anti-alias the resulting PSD files (recommended for maximum image smoothness). And finally, the Destination options let you choose a destination folder for your PSD files and choose a Base Name for the files; the files will have names such as document0001.psd, document0002.psd, and so on. Click OK and let Elements go nuts!

Creating an Animated GIF

So you're tired of still, static images. You want excitement. Life. Movement. You're in luck, because Elements is an amazing tool for creating still images and not too shabby at animation either! Animated GIFs have been enlivening Web pages for quite a few years now, and Elements' Save for Web command makes creating them a breeze.

Chapter 10 mentions that Elements' layers work similarly to traditional cel animation. Indeed, the Layers palette holds the key for creating animated GIFs as well. Elements programs an animated GIF to display the different layers of the Layers palette in sequence, from bottom to top. If you plan your file correctly, so that each layer represents a point in time immediately after the layer below it, it's easy to build an animation in this way.

We explain this feature by walking you through the creation of an actual animated GIF. We're going to create the effect of the word *motion* moving across the document and stopping in the center. While we'll actually move the word across the image (or *frame,* as they say in the movie biz) progressively layer by layer, we'll also add the Motion Blur filter to heighten the effect.

1. **Create a document.**

   We set ours to a width of 600 pixels, a height of 100 pixels, and a background of White.

2. **Type the word** motion **in the image with the horizontal type tool.**

   Choose a highly contrasting color, such as black.

3. **Simplify the layer.**

   Choose Layer⇨Simplify Layer. This is necessary for when you apply the Motion Blur filter.

4. **Duplicate the layer seven times.**

   We dragged the motion layer onto the create new layer icon seven times, as shown in the top-left image in Figure 18-3.

5. **Apply the Motion Blur filter to the bottom motion layer.**

   The Motion Blur filter is in the Blur section of the filters. Keep the angle set to 0 degrees, and set the distance to 70 pixels.

Figure 18-3:
A carefully
built file
consisting
of many
layers (top
left) is
converted to
an animated
GIF using
Elements'
Save for
Web
command.
The frames
from the
final
animation
appear on
the right.

6. **Apply the Motion Blur filter to each of the motion layers except the top copy, decreasing the Distance setting as you move up the layer stack.**

   We gave the first copy above the original a Distance setting of 60, the next copy up a Distance of 50, and so on. You can press Ctrl+Alt+F (⌘+Option+F on the Mac) to reapply the filter with access to the dialog box. Don't apply the filter to the top copy.

7. **Select the move tool and move the bottom motion layer to the left until only the very rightmost portion of the blurred text is showing. Move the layer above it to the left, but not quite as far. Keep moving up the stack, moving the layers progressively less far to the left, so that the next-to-the-top layer is barely moved at all. Leave the top layer where it is.**

   After you select the move tool, you can use the left arrow key to nudge the layer to the left without moving it vertically. You can also add the

Shift key to the left arrow key to move the layer in 10-pixel increments. You'll probably need to turn on and off the visibility of layers to better see what you're doing.

8. **Choose File⇨Save for Web.**

   The Save for Web dialog box appears. Adjust your GIF settings as desired (see Chapter 7 for details). To fill the transparent areas in the motion layers with white, set the Matte color to White. Click the Animation check box; this gives you access to the Animation controls at the bottom right of the dialog box.

   If you want the animation to play over and over, click the Loop check box. The Frame Delay setting determines how long in seconds each frame displays on-screen before the next frame replaces it. For this animation, 0.1 or 0.2 is a good setting.

   You can view the frames by clicking the VCR-style buttons in the Animation section of the dialog box (see the bottom-left image in Figure 18-3). The far-left and far-right buttons take you to the beginning and end of the animation, respectively. The second button takes you back one frame, and the third button takes you forward one frame.

   If you want to preview the animation in real time, choose a browser in the Preview In menu below the image preview. The browser will open and play the animation. If you didn't set the animation to loop, you can click the Refresh or Reload button in the browser to watch it again.

9. **Click OK in the Save for Web dialog box.**

   The image on the right in Figure 18-3 shows the nine frames that make up the final animation from the empty background layer to the top motion layer copy.

Creating Panoramic Pictures with Photomerge

What Photomerge does is simple in premise: If you shoot a group of photos, each capturing a section of a larger scene, Photomerge can automatically stitch them together into one big panoramic shot. And we do mean automatically; if the images are ideally framed, there's almost no work necessary on your part.

The effectiveness of Photomerge depends largely on the suitability of the photos you're trying to unite. Images need to overlap, but not too much; Adobe recommends an overlap of between 30 and 50 percent. But be aware that too much overlap can cause just as many problems as not enough overlap. The best advice is to overshoot, taking more photos than you'll need, with large areas of overlap, and then remove the unnecessary ones when you're working in the Photomerge dialog box.

Although Photomerge can correct for rotational problems between images shot with a handheld camera, working with a tripod yields the best results. If your camera has automatic exposure compensation, your results will improve if you can turn it off. If you're shooting a building with an expanse of sky behind it, the visible parts of the building will appear much darker in shots predominantly filled with sky. Photomerge can somewhat compensate for the difference in exposure, but turning off automatic exposure is still a good idea. And finally, remember that Photomerge compositions don't have to be exclusively horizontal in nature; vertical shots of tall objects such as buildings work well too.

It may be a good idea to use Image Size to reduce the pixel dimensions of the photos you'll be using before applying Photomerge. If you're trying to merge six photos taken in a horizontal line, and each image is 2,000 pixels wide, your final panorama will be somewhere in the neighborhood of 8,000 pixels after the areas of overlap are considered. That's a very big image, and if you don't have enough RAM, Photomerge may not be able to handle it.

If you want to reduce the size of your images, choose Image⇨Resize⇨Image Size. Make sure both Constrain Proportions and Resample Image are checked, with Bicubic or Bicubic Sharper chosen in the Resample Image menu. Set a Width or Height menu to Percent, and enter a smaller percentage, such as 75 or even 50. Click OK. You may want to choose the Save As command and save the image in a different location if you want to keep your original higher-resolution image around. Repeat this process for all the images you want to merge, taking care to resize them all by the same percentage value.

You could also resize the files using the Process Multiple Files command, as described earlier in this chapter.

Now then. Here's how to use the Photomerge command:

1. **Choose File⇨New⇨Photomerge Panorama.**

   The first Photomerge dialog box appears. Any opened images are already in the list.

2. **Click the Browse button to add additional photos you want to merge.**

   You can Shift+click images to select a group. When you've selected all the images you need, click Open. The images are added to the list. If you made any mistakes in selecting images, you can click an image's name in the list and click the Remove button.

3. **When you've selected your images, click OK.**

The magic begins. You can watch Photomerge opening each of your images, and then apparently combining them all into a very long document. What's it doing? Who knows? But it's fun to watch.

You may have to wait a few minutes, depending on the number and size of the images involved, but eventually the main Photomerge dialog box appears, as seen in Figure 18-4. You'll see Elements' best effort at assembling the photos in the large window. If it's encountered problems and can't even guess where to place some of the images, those images will be in the long horizontal box at the top of the window.

Photomerge has a Navigator window, similar to the Elements Navigator palette, which lets you zoom in and out on your image by clicking the buttons on either side of the slider or by dragging the slider itself. You can also reposition the view box to center on the portion of the composition you need to see. The move view tool (in the upper-left grouping of tools) doesn't need to be fingerprinted for us to know that it's our old buddy the hand tool in disguise; you can even press H to switch to it or hold down the spacebar to temporarily access it, and use it to drag the composition within the large window. The zoom tool (Z) is also available for your zooming pleasure.

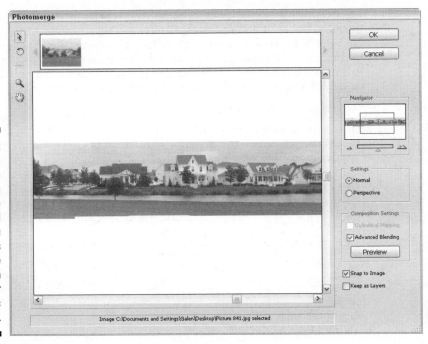

Figure 18-4: The workspace of the Photomerge command gives you lots of ways to tweak the construction of your panoramic shot.

4. **If you want to place images from the top portion of the dialog box into the composition, click them with the default select image tool (A) and drag them into the large window.**

   As you drag, the image will turn translucent so that it's easier to see how it might overlap with the other images. The Snap to Image check box can also be deselected if you don't want Photomerge to try to help you place the image by snapping it to areas of similar pixel content. You can also rearrange images in the large window with the select image tool, in case Photomerge didn't do a good job of placing them. If an image you're trying to place needs to be rotated, click the rotate image tool (second from the top in the upper-left group of tools) or press R and drag to rotate the image.

5. **Adjust the perspective of the composition if desired.**

   Adjusting perspective can help solve distortion problems in your composition. The wider your composition is, the more dramatic these problems can be. However, the composition can also be too wide for perspective correction to be effective.

   To adjust the perspective, first select the Perspective radio button in the Settings section of the dialog box. Then select the set vanishing point tool (third from the top in the upper-left group of tools) or press V, and click an image in your composition. You'll typically want to click the centermost image. If you're having trouble telling where one image stops and the next one starts, hold down the Alt key (Option on the Mac). A red outline will appear around the border of each image as you pass over it with the tool. The image containing the vanishing point, however, will have a light blue border instead of a red one.

6. **Adjust the Composition Settings.**

   One problem that perspective can introduce to your composition is the bow-tie effect, where the overall composition is stretched tall on the edges and squeezed in the middle. When available, turning on Cylindrical Mapping can help untie the bow-tie effect. Advanced Blending helps correct problems resulting from different exposures in adjacent images. The effects of the Composition Settings are visible only in Preview mode; click the Preview button to see Cylindrical Mapping and Advanced Blending. Click Exit Preview to leave the preview.

7. **Adjust any final settings, and click OK.**

   The new Keep as Layers check box will keep each individual image in Photomerge as its own separate layer, in case you want to do any hands-on adjusting after the fact. Just be aware that the multiple layers result in a much bigger file size.

   When you click OK, Elements works a little more magic, and then your finished panorama appears on-screen. You'll probably want to crop the image to eliminate areas where the transparency shows around the stitched photos.

Although it's neat that Elements can automatically construct a panoramic image from a series of individual images, with almost no work on your part, why can't it also perform the necessary cropping automatically? Gee, what a slacker.

GOOD STUFF!

For adding frames to emailed images or emailing slide shows

Attaching a File to E-Mail

So you want to share your Elements masterpiece with the world? Elements would like nothing more! That's why Attach to Email is one of many ways Elements gives you to share your photos.

Here's how to do it in Windows:

1. **Either in Editor or in Organizer, choose File➪Attach to Email.**

   Elements switches to the Organizer component if necessary and opens the dialog box shown in Figure 18-5.

2. **Specify the images you wish to e-mail.**

   Any selected images are already loaded in the Items section of the dialog box. Clicking the Add button takes you to the Add Photos dialog box, where you can choose other images to affix to the e-mail. If you make a mistake and add a wrong photo, select a thumbnail in the Items section of the dialog box and click the trash can icon to detach the photo.

3. **Choose the people you want to send the e-mail to.**

   To quickly specify a person, click the Add Recipient button and enter the person's first and last name and e-mail address. However, the Edit Contacts button should key you in to the fact that Elements maintains a contact book for you. Click the button to view the contact book.

Figure 18-5: Why waste words? Attach a photo to your e-mail and show folks what mere words can't describe.

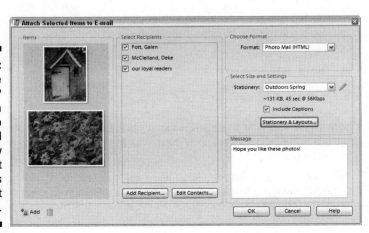

Here you can double-click an existing contact to add additional information, click New Contact to add additional people, or click New Group to create helpful groupings of people you can e-mail all at once.

4. **Select a format and appropriate settings for the e-mail.**

There are three formats to choose from:

- **Photo Mail:** This option embeds the photo or photos right in the e-mail. It also gives you access to Organizer's fabulous built-in stationery options, with tons of choices for adding frames and creative backgrounds to your e-mailed photos. Click the Stationery & Layouts button, and then choose a style from the list in the Stationery & Layouts Wizard that appears. Click the Next Step button, and you'll be presented with choices for items such as background color, layouts, and fonts. Then click Done to exit the wizard, and you'll be back in the Attach to Email dialog box.

- **Simple Slide Show (PDF):** This option attaches a PDF file to your e-mail. The PDF contains a slide show of your photos; the recipient needs Adobe Reader to be able to view the slide show. You can choose how big you want your photos to appear with the Size menu; if you don't see a size you like, click the Customize button to edit Organizer's preferences for e-mailing files.

- **Individual Attachments:** This option simply adds the photos to your e-mail as attachments. As with the Simple Slide Show option, you can use the Size menu to specify the size for your images, or create a size of your own by clicking the Customize button.

5. **Enter a message.**

This is the message that will appear in the e-mail.

6. **Click OK.**

Elements fires up your e-mail program and creates the e-mail you specified. Happily, you'll have a chance to view the e-mail before you send it, so you'll be able to change the Subject line from the default "You have received photos from Adobe Photoshop Elements" to something a little more personal.

7. **Click Send, and you're finished!**

Here's how to attach a file to an e-mail on the Mac:

1. **Choose File⇨Attach to Email, or just click the icon in the shortcuts bar — it's the one with the envelope in front of the earth.**

If your image is already a JPEG and is of sufficiently small file size and pixel dimensions, your e-mail program will automatically fire up, and an unaddressed, outgoing e-mail file will open with your image already attached. If the photo is too big or not a JPEG, a warning message appears.

2. **If you receive a warning message, you can click Send As Is to go ahead and attach your file to an e-mail, or click Auto Convert.**

   If you get a message that your image is large and you click Auto Convert, Elements changes the pixel dimensions of your image as necessary so that either the width or height is 1200 pixels. If you get a message that your image is not a JPEG and you click AutoConvert, Elements saves your image as a JPEG. In either case, you can click Send As Is to preserve your image in its current state. After you've dealt with any warning messages, Elements attaches your file to an unaddressed, outgoing e-mail. We recommend clicking Auto Convert if necessary; the reduced file size makes the image download faster, and the JPEG file format means that the recipient can definitely open the file after it has downloaded.

Projecting a Slide Show

When folks got back from vacation in the olden days, they'd invite all their friends and neighbors over and drag out the projector to bore everyone with a slide show. Well, things have really changed. Now in the 21st century, we can bore people with *digital* slide shows! Actually, if your slide show is boring, it must have something to do with your photos, because Elements gives you some pretty exciting tools for the job.

Creating a PDF slide show

The Windows version of Elements gives you two choices for creating slide shows: a simple PDF slide show or a more complex custom slide show. Here's how to create a simple PDF slide show in Windows:

1. **Either in Editor or in Organizer, click the Create button in the short-cuts bar.**

   The Creation Setup dialog box pictured in Figure 18-6 appears.

2. **Click OK to choose the default creation type, Slide Show.**

3. **In the next screen, choose Simple Slide Show from the list on the left, and then click OK.**

4. **Add and arrange the photos for the slide show.**

   Click the Add Photos button to choose the photos you want to appear in your slide show from the Add Photos dialog box. When you've placed check marks next to the photos you want to add, click Add Selected Photos, and then click OK. Next, drag the photos around in the thumbnail preview window to arrange them in the order in which you want them to appear. When a thumbnail is selected, you can click the Use

Photo Again button to make a photo appear twice in the slide show or click Remove Photo to exclude it.

5. **Choose your slide show options.**

   Elements gives you lots of flashy ways to make the transition from photo to photo. The default Random Transition setting is a great way to preview them all and add a note of unpredictability to the proceedings. You can also determine how long you want each photo to display, whether you want the slide show to loop back to the beginning again after it reaches the end, and whether you want to view your slide show immediately upon saving it.

6. **Set your photo options.**

   In the final set of options, you can determine the size of the images in your slide show and the level of quality for saving the images. Because a PDF slide show is going to be viewed on a computer screen, it's probably best not to go larger that 1024 x 768. But you can choose Custom from the Photo Size menu if you want, and enter whatever size you like. You'll also need to set a quality level for the image compression using the Quality slider.

7. **After you've made your choices, save your slide show.**

   Click Save. Navigate to the location where you want to save your PDF slide show, name it, and click Save again. You'll receive a message telling you that your slide show was successfully created; click OK. If you choose [LB1]to view your slide show immediately after creating it, enjoy the show!

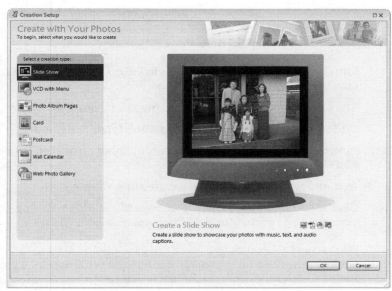

Figure 18-6:
The Creation Setup dialog box is Organizer's first step along the path to many different and exciting Creations.

Here's how to create a PDF slide show on the Mac:

1. **Choose File⇨Automation Tools⇨PDF Slide Show.**

2. **Choose the files you want to include in your slide show:**

   • If the images you want to include in your slide show are already open in Elements, click the Add Open Files check box to automatically include them.

   • Otherwise, click the Browse button and locate your files with the resulting Open dialog box. If you accidentally add the wrong file, select it in the list and click the Remove button.

3. **Choose your output options.**

   If you just want to turn your images into a multipage PDF document, click the Multi-Page Document radio button. But we'll bet that's not what you want. So click the Slide Show radio button instead, and turn on the View PDF after Saving check box if desired.

4. **Set your Slide Show Options.**

   The Slide Show Options give you control over a few aspects of the presentation. If the Advance Every _ Seconds check box is active, you can enter the number of seconds that you want each image to be displayed before the next image takes over. If the check box is unchecked, each image in your slide show will stay on-screen until you click the mouse. If you want the slide show to endlessly repeat, click the Loop After Last Page check box. And the neatest part of a PDF slide show is the transition from slide to slide. You can choose from a large number of transitions; set it to Random Transition if you like being pleasantly surprised. When you've made your choices, click OK.

As long as the computer on which you'll be viewing the presentation has Adobe Reader (a free download is available from www.acrobat.com), you're in good shape. Just double-click the PDF file and enjoy the show!

Creating a custom slide show in Windows

Here's how to make a custom slide show in Windows:

1. **Either in Editor or in Organizer, click the Create button in the shortcuts bar.**

   The Creation Setup dialog box appears.

2. **Click OK to choose the default creation type, Slide Show.**

3. **In the next screen, choose Custom Slide Show from the list on the left, and click OK.**

   The dialog box shown in Figure 18-7 appears.

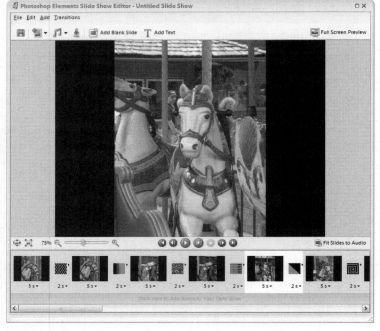

Figure 18-7:
The Slide
Show Editor
lets you
write,
record,
arrange,
produce,
and edit a
slide show
of epic
proportions.

4. **Add images, audio, and text.**

   Here's your chance to be a real auteur. Custom Slide Show offers a nearly
   overwhelming variety of options. Here are some of the things you can do:

   • Click the Add Photos button below the dialog box's menu to add
     images from Organizer or a specific folder.

   • Click the adjacent Add Audio button to specify an audio track to
     play as the soundtrack for your slide show.

   • Click the adjacent microphone button to add or edit any audio cap-
     tions you may have recorded for specific images to the slide show's
     soundtrack.

   • Click the Add Blank Slide button to enter a solid field of color
     (black by default) into the slide show.

   • Click the Add Text button to superimpose text over the selected
     slide or blank slide.

5. **Assemble the slide show.**

   The wide horizontal strip at the bottom of the dialog box is the area
   where you arrange your slides and set transitions for them. Click a
   thumbnail and drag it to a different location to change the order of the

slides. Click the small black down-pointing arrow below the thumbnail to set a duration for the image to display in the slide show.

Between the image thumbnails are gray squares that represent the transitions. Click the square to choose a specific transition from the many options, and use the menu below the transition square to set a duration for the transition.

A handy feature for synchronizing the slide show to the soundtrack is the Fit Slides to Audio button. Clicking this button automatically adjusts the durations of slides and transitions so that the length of the slide show matches the length of the soundtrack. If you've added audio files and want to adjust the soundtrack itself, double-clicking below the thumbnail strip takes you to the Edit Slide Show Audio dialog box. Here you can import, arrange, and reorder the audio files you want to play as the soundtrack.

You can use the VCR-style controls below the large preview window to preview your slide show as you develop it. To the left of the VCR-style icons are controls for adjusting the size of the preview. In the upper-right corner of the dialog box, the Full Screen Preview button offers a full screen display of your masterpiece in progress.

6. **Save the slide show.**

   Click the floppy disk icon or choose File⇨Save to save your slide show to disk. Make sure you give it a descriptive name; custom slide shows are so much fun to make and view that you'll probably be creating a lot of them.

If you want to watch your slide show as a Windows Media video file, choose File⇨Output as WMV, pop some popcorn, and enjoy the movie!

Creating and Printing a Contact Sheet

Elements can create a digital version of a traditional contact sheet. This feature takes a group of images, creates thumbnails, and arranges them on a single page. It's good for record-keeping because it enables you to catalog large quantities of files. It's also useful for merely checking out a big batch of images.

Here are the steps for creating and printing a contact sheet in Windows:

1. **In Editor, choose File⇨Print Multiple Photos. In Organizer, choose File⇨Print.**

   Either way, the dialog box shown in Figure 18-8 appears.

2. **Choose the images you want to print on the contact sheet.**

   Any selected images will already be added to the panel on the left. You can click the Add button at the bottom of the panel to add more images. Click the trash can icon to delete any images you accidentally added.

3. **Make sure your printer is selected in the Select Printer dialog box.**

4. **Choose Contact Sheet from the Select Type of Print menu.**

5. **Edit the layout of your contact sheet.**

   The major decision you have to make is how many columns you want on your contact sheet. Use the conveniently-named Columns option to set the number of columns. As the preview clearly shows, this option affects the size of the thumbnail images. If you need more than one contact sheet to hold your images, you can view a preview of each page by clicking the buttons below the large page preview. You can also click the Add a Text Label check boxes to add dates, captions, filenames, and page numbers to your contact sheet.

   If you want to switch to a wider-than-it-is-tall (landscape) orientation for your paper, click the Page Setup button at the bottom of the dialog box.

6. **When you're finished, just click Print, and let your printer take it from here.**

Figure 18-8: To print a contact sheet in Windows, this is the place to be.

Here's how to print a contact sheet on the Mac:

1. **Choose File⇨Contact Sheet II.**

   The command is available also in the File Browser's Automate menu. Either way, the Contact Sheet II dialog box appears.

2. **In the Source Images section, specify the images you want to print.**

   You can select a folder of images (click Choose to specify the folder), all open images, or the currently selected images in the File Browser.

3. **In the Document section, specify the size and resolution of the contact sheet.**

   If you're unsure about what resolution to specify, see Chapter 4 for details.

   If you deselect the Flatten All Layers check box, your finished file will contain each image on its own layer and each caption on its own editable text layer. This can be helpful if you want to tweak the layout or rename the files, but otherwise it just balloons the file size. However, even if you do check Flatten All Layers, your finished document will have two layers: a background layer and a layer with all the thumbnails and captions on it.

4. **Specify a color mode: RGB Color or Grayscale.**

   For information on color modes, see Chapter 5.

5. **In the Thumbnails section, specify the order and the number of columns and rows for your layout.**

   The Place menu lets you determine whether you want your thumbnails to proceed vertically or horizontally across the page. The preview on the right side of the dialog box gives you a rough idea of how your contact sheet will appear. If the number of rows and columns you've specified isn't sufficient to hold all the images you've chosen, you'll see an indication of this fact under the preview. In this case, Contact Sheet II will generate a file for each page needed.

   The Use Auto-Spacing check box usually yields good results, but you can deselect it and enter your own spacing in the Vertical and Horizontal options. The Rotate for Best Fit check box will rotate thumbnails as needed so that they fit optimally on the contact sheet.

6. **Decide whether you want to use the Filename As a Caption option for your images.**

   If so, specify the font and font size.

7. **Press Return or click OK.**

   An automated process opens, copies, pastes, resizes, and positions each file. When the process is complete, you should see one or more files, similar to what is shown in Figure 18-9.

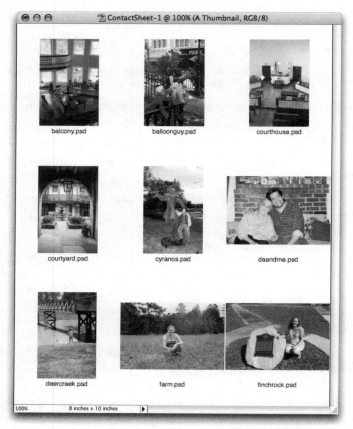

Figure 18-9:
Contact
sheets can
provide
a good
method for
cataloging
a large
quantity of
images.

Creating and Printing a Picture Package

Another feature that may come in handy is Picture Package, which lets you fill a page with multiple copies of multiple images, if you want. The images are scaled to common print sizes, such as 5 x 7, 4 x 5, and wallet snapshots. Whether you're a professional photographer or just want to print some pictures of the kids for Grandma, Picture Package does it all.

Here's how to create a Picture Package in Windows:

1. **In Editor, choose File⇨Print Multiple Photos. In Organizer, choose File⇨Print.**

2. **Choose the image or images you want in the picture package.**

   Any selected images are already added to the panel on the left. To add more images, click the Add button at the bottom of the panel. Click the trash can icon to delete any images you accidentally added.

3. **Make sure your printer is selected in the Select Printer dialog box.**

4. **In the Select Type of Print menu, choose Picture Package.**

5. **Edit the layout of your picture package.**

The first step is to use the Select a Layout menu to choose how many images will print on the page and at what size. If you're using multiple photos, you can click the One Photo Per Page check box to devote an entire page to each photo.

After you've chosen your layout, you can drag thumbnails from the column on the left directly into the middle preview window to determine precisely where each photo should be placed. You can also drag thumbnails within the preview to rearrange the placement of the photos.

You can also add frames in the Select a Frame menu. If you're creating a multipage picture package, the frame you select will print around every photo on every page, so choose wisely!

6. **When you have your picture package the way you want it, just click Print.**

Here's how to create a Picture Package on the Mac:

1. **Choose File⇨Picture Package.**

You can also choose Picture Package from the File Browser's Automate menu.

2. **Specify the images you want to include in your layout.**

The File and Folder options let you click the Choose button to navigate to the desired file or folder of files. You can also choose all Open Files, only the Frontmost Document from the open files, or Selected Images from the File Browser.

3. **Choose your desired document settings.**

Start by choosing a Page Size appropriate for your paper and printer. Then choose a layout in the Layout menu. For an idea of what the layout will look like, check out the large preview area on the right. Choose an appropriate resolution and color mode (see Chapters 4 and 5, respectively, for more on these topics). As with the Contact Sheet feature, deselect Flatten All Layers if you want to be able to easily tweak your layout by hand after the Picture Package command is finished.

4. **Choose a label for each image, if you want.**

If you've entered a copyright, a caption, an author, or a title for your images in the File⇨File Info command, you can utilize that information in the Content menu here. But we'll bet you haven't. You can cancel out of the Picture Package command and do so, or better yet, use the name of the file or some custom text as a label. You can type the custom text in the provided field. Select a font, font size, color, and opacity level. Then decide where you want the text to appear in the image. Be warned that

Centered does indeed put the text smack in the center of your image; one of the other choices will put it in a corner, which is probably what you had in mind. You can also rotate the text as needed; a little trial and error will probably be required for you to figure out the appropriate settings.

5. **Select other images for inclusion in your Picture Package, as desired.**

   You can click any image in that layout and replace it with a different file. Just use the resulting Select an Image File dialog box to locate the file.

6. **Press Return or click OK.**

   An automated process opens, copies, pastes, and positions each file. When the process is complete, you should see a file similar to the one in Figure 18-10.

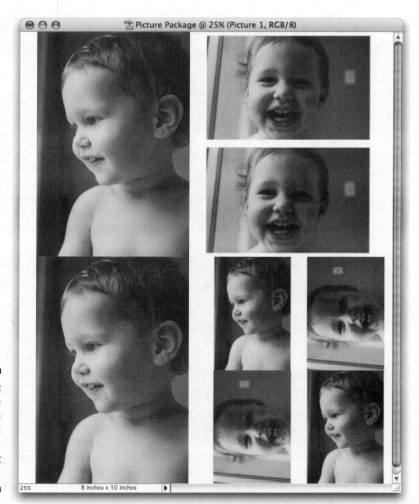

Figure 18-10:
The Picture Package command can give you instant octuplets.

Creating a Web Photo Gallery

A Web photo gallery assembles a folder of images into a Web site, complete with HTML pages and JPEG images. You specify the name of your page, the size of the thumbnails, and the size and compression of the larger gallery images. The result is a slick Web site that the whole world can admire.

Here's how to create a Web Photo Gallery in Windows:

1. **In Editor or Organizer, click the Create button in the shortcuts bar.**

2. **Choose Web Photo Gallery from the list on the left of the Creation Setup dialog box, and then click OK.**

3. **Select the photos you want to use in your Web Photo Gallery.**

   You can click the Add button to add photos to the column on the left. If you add a photo accidentally, select it and click the Remove button to delete it.

4. **Choose a style for the gallery.**

   You can choose from 33 presets. Many have themes that make them appropriate only for specific types of photos, but the Classic, Horizontal, Simple, and Vertical Frame choices are good for any occasion.

5. **Create a banner for your Web pages.**

   This information will appear on the Web pages you create. You can enter a title, a subtitle, and an e-mail address, as well as choose a font for this information. The e-mail address on the final Web page will be hyperlinked, so that clicking it will fire up an e-mail program on the viewer's computer and create a blank e-mail to send to that e-mail address.

6. **Specify options for the thumbnail images.**

   You can choose from four size options in the Thumbnail Size menu. You can also include a caption for each thumbnail, displaying the thumbnail's filename, caption, and date.

7. **Specify options for the large photos.**

   If you're working with high-resolution images, you'll want to turn on the Resize Photos check box so that the images will be made small enough to display on the average computer monitor. The Large preset is a pretty good place to start, but feel free to experiment with the size and Photo Quality options, as well. As with the thumbnails, you can display the image's filename, caption, and date under the photo.

8. **Specify the custom colors you want to use.**

   You can specify the color of the background, banner section, and text. Not all options are available for all gallery styles.

9. **Specify where you want to save the gallery.**

   Click the Browse button in the Destination section to navigate to a spot to save the files and folders that the Web Photo Gallery will create. You'll probably want to create a new folder to hold these items.

10. **Click the Save button at the bottom of the dialog box.**

    Elements churns out all the thumbnails, images, and HTML code necessary, and then displays the interactive result in a window for you to enjoy (see Figure 18-11).

Here's how to create a Web Photo Gallery on the Mac. To begin, choose File⇨ Create Web Photo Gallery or choose Web Photo Gallery from the File Browser's Automate menu. Following are the various options involved in creating a gallery:

- ✓ **Choose a style:** You can display the various styles in the tiny preview thumbnail in the dialog box.

- ✓ **Enter an e-mail address:** If you want a clickable e-mail address to appear on your Web page, enter it in the Email field.

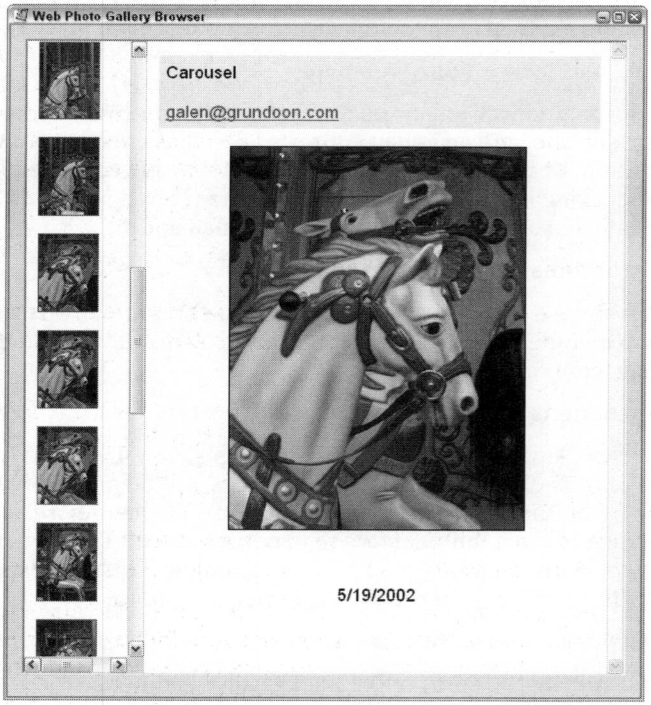

Figure 18-11: Immediately after creating a Web Photo Gallery, Elements displays a window where you can try out your interactive gallery before sharing it with the world.

Web Photo Gallery Browser

Carousel

galen@grundoon.com

5/19/2002

In the Source Images section, you can specify the images you want to use in your online gallery. If you want to use all the images in a certain folder, select Folder from the Use menu and click the Choose button to navigate to the folder. The other Use menu choices let you create your Web gallery from all open files, or from images selected in the File Browser. After you've specified the images you want to use, click the Destination button to choose a location for saving all the files that will constitute your online gallery.

Elements gives you many Options from which to choose, although not all gallery styles use all options. Here's a look at the six categories:

- ✔ **General:** Unless you know you need a specific choice of extension, either .htm or .html should work fine for you. UTF 8 encoding helps compatibility when your Web site is viewed on older operating systems, but is generally not necessary. You can also choose to preserve the metadata for your images when they are converted to JPEGs.

- ✔ **Banner:** The Site Name appears in the browser's title bar, as well as on the page itself. You can also enter the photographer's name, contact info, and a date if you want that information to appear on the site. And finally, you can specify a font and font size for this information.

- ✔ **Large Images:** These options establish the settings for the large images (the image that loads when the user clicks a thumbnail). If you want to resize your images, you can quickly choose from Small, Medium, or Large settings, or enter your own Custom pixel amount. The Constrain option determines how that pixel amount will be used. If you choose Width, all large images will have a width of the specified pixel amount; likewise for Height. Choosing Both makes Elements resize the larger of the height or width to the specified pixel amount for each image.

  You can set your desired JPEG compression level with the JPEG Quality menu or the File Size slider. Border Size lets you specify the size of the border around each image, if you want one.

  You can specify a title for each image using the filename or information you've entered in the File⇨File Info command. And finally, you can choose a font and font size.

- ✔ **Thumbnails:** The options here mirror those found for Large Images, with one exception. You can specify the number of columns and rows for displaying your thumbnails. It's important to know the number of images you're using to determine the appropriate settings here.

- ✔ **Custom Colors:** This option enables you to choose colors for all the various components of your Web page. Not all styles use custom colors.

- ✔ **Security:** These options mirror the Label options for the Mac Picture Package command (see "Creating and Printing a Picture Package," earlier in this chapter). They embed text in the pixels of your image, thereby making people less likely to download the images from your site and use them for their own nefarious purposes.

After you click OK, Elements does a little work on its own and then displays the Web page in your Web browser. Elements saves the HTML file and the JPEG images in your Destination folder. Color Plate 20 shows the Spot Light style.

And that, friends, brings this chapter to a close. Lots of other nifty automated options are available in the Windows version of Elements, such as creating the wall calendar shown in Color Plate 21. To explore these, just click that Create button in the shortcuts bar in Editor or Organizer, and check out the choices. Happily, using the Creation Setup dialog box is such a gentle, easy-to-understand, and fun process that we know you'll be in good hands when you explore the other options on your own.

Part V
The Part of Tens

The 5th Wave   By Rich Tennant

"...and here's me with Cindy Crawford. And this is me with Madonna and Celine Dion..."

In this part . . .

. . . we say goodbye, but not before we take a last, loving look at Photoshop Elements from a different angle. You've made it this far with us, as we've painstakingly sifted through the enormous mountain of Elements features and functions. You've gone from "What's a pixel?" to creating animated GIFs to liven up your Web site. Just getting through each tool and command has taken us a few hundred pages (sixteen of them in color), but you did it. So what's left?

We start this final part with a chapter on ten important techniques to remember, all of them dealing with easily forgotten keyboard shortcuts. From there, we wrap up the book with a look at ten things you *can't* do with Elements, but you can do with Elements' almighty ancestor, Adobe Photoshop.

Catch the common thread? Both of the following chapters center on the number ten. Hence the title of this part of the book: The Part of Tens. Why tens? Well, we could tell you tales of Little Indians, fingers and toes, or Woodmen (okay, we guess that last one doesn't count), but those would be nothing more than tales. The Part of Tens is the Part of Tens because it's a *For Dummies* tradition, that's why. And to break with tradition, we'd have to be dummies indeed.

Chapter 19

Ten Shortcuts to Commit to Long-Term Memory

*P*rofessor, poet, and Pulitzer Prize-winning author Odell Shepard once said, "A man's memory is what he forgets with." No doubt Odell — or Odie, as his friends called him — was talking about that feeling you get (usually when you're in bed, trying to sleep) that you've forgotten something that's pretty much going to send your life spinning into a state of absolute chaos. This feeling is commonly known as the Odie Syndrome.

Well, we can't help you with every aspect of your life, but we can help you with Photoshop Elements. Suppose, for example, that you wake up at 2 a.m. with the dreaded suspicion that you've forgotten an important Elements shortcut. You figure that you'll have to give up on your technological pursuits and take up beet farming. But thanks to this chapter, people like you can live happy and productive lives again because these pages contain the most important Elements shortcuts. For Windows users, these apply to the Editor component of Elements. For everyone, a few minutes of reading will restore order in your life.

The following tips don't begin to address all the many Elements shortcuts. For some additional timesavers, be sure to check out (or rip out) the Cheat Sheet at the front of this book.

Hiding Selection Outlines

Ctrl+H (⌘+H on the Mac)

After you've selected part of your image, this shortcut makes those distracting marching ants turn temporarily invisible, making it easier to see what's going on in your image. Don't confuse this with deselecting your selection; with the ants hidden, you can still edit only the part of your image that's selected. This is probably the most useful shortcut of all. Remember it!

Displaying and Hiding the Palette Bin

F7

To display and hide the screen-hogging palette bin, press F7.

Changing an Option Box Value

Up arrow, down arrow

Activate the option box and use the up or down arrow key to raise or lower the value by a small amount, usually 1. Press Shift+↑ or Shift+↓ to multiply the raising or lowering by a factor of 10. Then press Enter (Return on the Mac) to accept the new value.

Scrolling and Zooming

Spacebar

Press the spacebar to temporarily access the hand tool. Spacebar+drag scrolls the image.

Ctrl+spacebar and Alt+spacebar (⌘+spacebar and Option+spacebar on the Mac)

To get to the zoom in cursor, press Ctrl+spacebar (⌘+spacebar on the Mac). Pressing Alt+spacebar (Option+spacebar on the Mac) gets you the zoom out cursor. This means that you can magnify the image at any time by Ctrl+spacebar+clicking (⌘+spacebar+clicking on the Mac). To zoom out, Alt+spacebar+click (Option+spacebar+click on the Mac). You can also Ctrl+spacebar+drag (⌘+spacebar+drag on the Mac) to marquee an area and magnify it so that it takes up the entire image window.

Ctrl++ (plus) and Ctrl+– (minus) (⌘++ and ⌘+– on the Mac)

Another way to magnify or reduce the image is to press Ctrl++ (plus sign) (⌘++ on the Mac) to zoom in or Ctrl+– (minus sign) (⌘+– on the Mac) to zoom out.

Changing the Brush Size

Right bracket (])

Press] (right bracket) to increase the brush size in the following increments: 1-pixel increments up to a size 10 pixel brush, 10-pixel increments up to a size 100 pixel brush, 25 pixels up to a size 200 pixel brush, 50 pixels up to a size 300 pixel brush, and 100 pixels up to a size 2500 pixel brush.

Left bracket ([)

Press [(left bracket) to decrease the brush size by the same increments listed in the preceding section.

Shift+[and Shift+]

For the round and fuzzy round brushes, Shift+[(left bracket) reduces the hardness of a brush in 25 percent increments. Shift+] (right bracket) increases the hardness in 25 percent increments.

Creating Straight Lines

Shift+click

To create a straight line with any of the painting or editing tools, click at one end of the line and Shift+click at the other. Elements connects the two points with a straight line.

Click with polygonal lasso and Alt+click (Option+click on the Mac) with regular lasso and magnetic lasso

The polygonal lasso creates straight-sided selections; you just click to set the first point in your selection and keep clicking to create additional points.

When working with the regular lasso tool, you can temporarily switch to the polygonal lasso by Alt+clicking (Option+clicking on the Mac). Alt+click (Option+click on the Mac) to set the first point in the selection and keep Alt+clicking (Option+clicking on the Mac) until you finish the desired outline.

When working with the magnetic lasso, press Alt (Option on the Mac) and click with the mouse to get the polygonal lasso. Release the Alt key (Option on the Mac), click, and then drag to reset to the magnetic lasso.

However, don't use this approach when you want to add to or subtract from an existing selection. When you have an active selection, pressing Alt (Option on the Mac) subtracts from the selection instead of switching you between lasso tools. So use the actual polygonal lasso tool to add or subtract straight-sided areas from a selection.

Adding to, Subtracting from, and Reselecting Selection Outlines

Shift+drag and Shift+click

To select an additional area of your image without deselecting the part that is currently selected, Shift+drag around the new area with a lasso or marquee tool or Shift+click with the magic wand.

Alt+drag and Alt+click (Option+drag and Option+click on the Mac)

To deselect an area of the selection, Alt+drag (Option+drag on the Mac) around it with a lasso or marquee tool or Alt+click (Option+click on the Mac) with the magic wand.

Shift+Alt+drag and Shift+Alt+click (Shift+Option+drag and Shift+Option+click on the Mac)

To retain the intersection of the existing selection and the new outline you draw with a lasso or marquee tool, Shift+Alt+drag (Shift+Option+drag on the Mac) with the tool. To retain an area of continuous color inside a selection, Shift+Alt+click (Shift+Option+click on the Mac) with the magic wand.

Ctrl+Shift+D (⌘+Shift+D on the Mac)

To reselect your last selection (even if you've painted or done some other activity since selecting), press Ctrl+Shift+D (⌘+Shift+D on the Mac).

Moving, Nudging, and Cloning

The shortcuts in this section work with most tools active.

Ctrl (⌘ on the Mac)

To move selections and layers, use the move tool. To temporarily access the move tool when any tool is active, press and hold Ctrl (⌘ on the Mac).

Arrow

To nudge a selection 1 pixel, press Ctrl (⌘ on the Mac) and an arrow key.

Shift+arrow

To nudge a selection 10 pixels, press Ctrl+Shift (⌘+Shift on the Mac) with an arrow key.

Alt+drag, Alt+arrow, and Shift+Alt+arrow (Option+drag, Option+arrow, and Shift+Option+arrow on the Mac)

To clone a selection and move the clone, Alt+drag (Option+drag on the Mac) the selection with the move tool. You can also press Alt (Option on the Mac) with an arrow key to clone a selection and nudge it 1 pixel. Press Shift+Alt+ arrow key (Shift+Option+arrow key on the Mac) to clone and nudge 10 pixels.

With most other tools, you can accomplish the same cloning feats by pressing and holding the Ctrl key (⌘ on the Mac) with the other keys. Pressing Ctrl (⌘ on the Mac) usually accesses the move tool, remember?

Drag with a selection tool

To move a selection outline without moving anything inside the selection, just drag it with a marquee tool, lasso tool, or the magic wand. You can also press the arrow key or Shift+arrow key to nudge the selection outline in 1-pixel and 10-pixel increments, respectively. This works with any tool except the move, crop, and type tools.

Ctrl (⌘) with a shape tool

Pressing Ctrl (⌘ on the Mac) with any of the shape tools displays the shape selection tool.

Filling a Selection

Ctrl+Backspace (⌘+Delete on the Mac)

To fill a selection with the background color, press Ctrl+Backspace. If the selection exists on the background layer, you can also press just Backspace to accomplish the same thing. However, if the selection is on a layer, pressing Backspace empties the selection instead of filling it. So, pressing Ctrl+Backspace instead of Backspace to fill your selections is a good idea. Mac users, substitute the Delete key for the Backspace key . . . but you probably already knew that by now.

Alt+Backspace (Option+Delete on the Mac)

To fill any selection with the foreground color, press Alt+Backspace. Mac users should press Option+Delete.

Shift+Backspace (Shift+Delete on the Mac)

Press Shift+Backspace to display the Fill dialog box, which lets you fill a selection with all kinds of stuff. Mac users should substitute Delete for Backspace.

Stepping through the Undo History Palette

Ctrl+Z and Ctrl+Y (⌘+Z and ⌘+Y on the Mac)

To undo one history state at a time, press Ctrl+Z (⌘+Z on the Mac). To redo one state at a time, press Ctrl+Y (⌘+Y on the Mac). You can change these shortcuts in the General panel of Preferences.

Chapter 20

Ten Reasons Why You Might Want to Upgrade to Photoshop Someday

· ·

· ·

*B*y this late stage in the book, we'd certainly like to think you're so pleased with Photoshop Elements — and your newfound skills in using it — that the thought of all other image-editing applications has completely faded from your memory. But one image editor will probably never be driven from your mind by Photoshop Elements — and that's Photoshop itself. We've already told you that, in Elements, you have the majority of Photoshop's power for a tiny fraction of its price. But still, you might be wondering, "What exactly am I missing?"

That's the purpose of this chapter: to give you a good idea of how the power of Elements is extended in Photoshop. This chapter is by no means designed to make you want to spend hundreds of dollars on new software. You have a great thing in Elements, and unless you plan on making a living creating graphics, Elements is probably the only program you'll ever need. But Photoshop does have some amazing and useful features, and we thought you might be curious about them. So after a good deal of deliberation, here are the ten reasons why you might want to upgrade to Photoshop someday.

The Layer Comps Palette

Have you ever wished you could save the Undo History palette's history log along with an image just in case you ever want to undo a change you made? If so, you'd love Photoshop CS's new Layer Comps palette. As you adjust your layers' position, visibility, and layer styles, the Layer Comps palette can take "snapshots" of the image at any point in time. Later, you can recall these snapshots instantly, letting you make before-and-after comparisons with a single mouse click. The palette is a great tool for presenting clients with variations on a particular design scheme. "Do you like the text here . . . *or here?*" "Do you like the hat on the dog . . . or should we *get rid of it entirely?*" Layer comps can't save all the changes you might make to an image, but they're a big help for designers with fussy clients. See Figure 20-1.

Figure 20-1:
Photoshop CS's new Layer Comps palette records changes in the composition of your layered image and lets you compare these saved states with the click of a button.

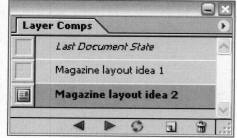

The Channels Palette

We've talked about color channels in this book, but when using Photoshop Elements, you have to more or less take our word that they exist. Channels do pop up in the Levels command and the Histogram palette, but by and large they're a phantom presence. Not so in Photoshop, which actually has a

Channels palette that lets you view and edit each color channel individually. You also can directly edit *alpha channels,* which control transparency in images. The fact that channels are a tangible, easily viewable presence in Photoshop makes it much easier to be in complete control of every pixel in your images. Figure 20-2 features the Channels palette showing off our next top ten Photoshop feature.

Figure 20-2: Photoshop's Channels palette presents conclusive evidence that color channels exist. Here the Channels palette is displaying the channels for an image in CMYK color mode.

CMYK Color Mode

Just as RGB color mode rules when viewing images on-screen, CMYK color mode rules on paper. As Color Plate 2 illustrates, cyan (C), magenta (M), and yellow (Y) inks absorb different portions of the spectrum of light and bounce back other portions to your eyes. Black ink (K) is also added because in the imperfect real world, cyan, magenta, and yellow inks combine to produce a muddy brown, not black. Because Photoshop is a vital tool for preparing images for print, Adobe lets you work directly with your images in CMYK color mode, as shown in Figure 20-2. Combine the CMYK mode with Photoshop's advanced color management capabilities, and it becomes a lot easier to ensure that your fussy client's teal and mauve logo will be the precise shades of teal and mauve when it comes back from the printer.

The Brushes Palette

Photoshop's Brushes palette gives you incredible power when creating brushes. As shown in Figure 20-3, the Brushes palette gives you advanced control over features such as scattering, texture, jitter, and noise. Elements is generous where brushes are concerned, but as is frequently the case, Photoshop gives you more power and control.

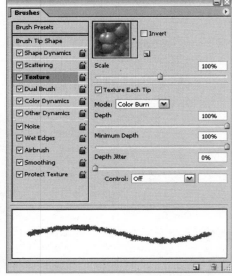

Figure 20-3:
The Brushes palette lets you tweak your custom brushes to suit your whim.

Following the Paths

Elements gives you a small sampling of paths with the shape tools (see Chapter 15). Photoshop, however, gives you a host of tools for drawing your own vector-based paths, as seen in Figure 20-4.

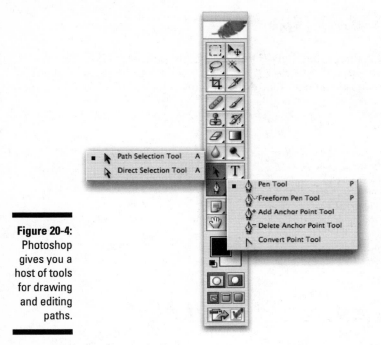

Figure 20-4:
Photoshop
gives you a
host of tools
for drawing
and editing
paths.

Photoshop uses *bezier* tools for drawing vector paths, which enable you to create shapes by clicking anchor points and dragging control handles. It takes a while to master the bezier tools, but after you do, you can draw any shape imaginable. After you've drawn a path, you can then convert it into a selection or manage it with the Paths palette.

Eyeing Those Curves

If you thought Levels was an intimidating command, get a load of Curves! True, the Curves command makes using Levels seem positively intuitive, but it can accomplish things that Levels simply can't. By clicking to add points to a line and dragging the points around the graph shown in Figure 20-5, you create a curve that can be used to give you unparalleled control over the brightness levels in your image.

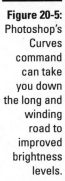

Figure 20-5: Photoshop's Curves command can take you down the long and winding road to improved brightness levels.

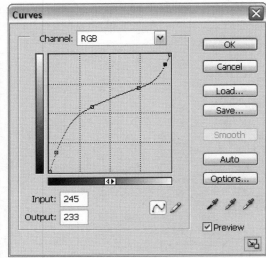

Lights . . . Camera . . . Actions

If you think the Process Multiple Files feature in Elements (see Chapter 18) is the coolest thing since sliced bread, Photoshop's actions are definitely for you. Processing multiple files lets you take a bunch of images and automatically convert them so that they have the same file type, image size, resolution, and naming convention. Actions let you take a bunch of files and do almost *anything* to them. Just set up a new action, click the record button in the Actions palette (see Figure 20-6), and then go to town on your image. You can change the image size, apply filters, make selections and fill them, create text layers — almost any operation you can perform in Photoshop, you can record with the Actions palette. And from there, you can perform that sequence of commands on another image with a click of the play button.

Photoshop also comes with prerecorded actions, but that's no big deal because Elements has prerecorded actions too. "How can Elements have prerecorded actions when it doesn't have an Actions palette?" we hear you ask. Well, Elements' effects are nothing more than a set of prerecorded actions given a new name and a nice tidy Styles and Effects palette to live in. You can't record your own effects, but they should give you some idea of the awesome time-saving powers of actions.

Figure 20-6:
The VCR-style controls at the bottom of Photoshop's Actions palette let you record and play back a sequence of image-editing operations.

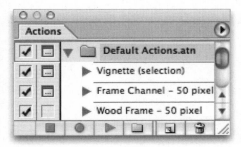

Being an Art Historian

Whereas the Undo History palette in Elements lets you travel back in time and reverse mistakes, Photoshop's History palette also gives you the option of sending only *portions* of your image backward in time. The history brush (see Figure 20-7) lets you paint from a previous history state of your image onto the current state. You could, for instance, apply an artistic filter to your image and then paint from the previous nonfiltered state of your image onto the filtered state, in effect erasing the filter from wherever you paint. Likewise, the art history brush (also in Figure 20-7) packs the whirlin', twirlin' power of Elements' impressionist brush with the history brush's time-traveling capabilities, making for a truly creative experience.

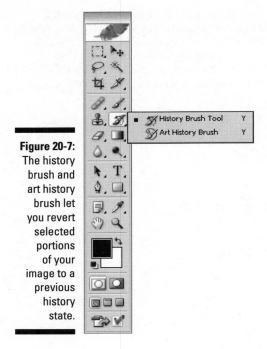

Figure 20-7:
The history
brush and
art history
brush let
you revert
selected
portions
of your
image to a
previous
history
state.

Photoshop Speaks!

Okay, this one is truly weird. But if you're passing an image along to be
reviewed by a co-worker or client, it's understandable that you might want to
also give them a note about the image, saying something like "Do you like this
font?" or "Should I remove this zit from the model's nose?" The notes tool lets
you click and add a virtual yellow sticky note to your image. Of course, it
doesn't actually meld into the pixels in the image, but it sort of floats above
the surface as a little icon that viewers can click to see your comments (see
Figure 20-8).

But that's nothing compared to the audio annotation tool. Click the audio
annotation tool on your image, and you actually get a chance to record a
spoken message that will be embedded in the image. The audio message
appears on the image as a little speaker icon; you can double-click the icon to

play back the message. Although this certainly could be a useful tool for passing comments along with an image, we'd like to propose an alternative use for this multimedia tool: recording mood music to be listened to while your work of art is viewed. Sure, you did a great job of cleaning up that spaghetti picture for the Italian restaurant's ad campaign — but wouldn't it be even more effective if the restaurant owners could listen to *That's Amore* while they're reviewing your work on-screen? We think so.

Audio Annotation icon

Notes icon

Figure 20-8:
Audio annotations and notes mean that your Photo-shop work doesn't necessarily have to speak for itself.

A Little Help to Get Your ImageReady

And finally, one last thing you'll get if you upgrade from Elements to Photoshop is . . . an additional application! Adobe ImageReady is installed along with Photoshop on your hard drive. ImageReady bears a strong resemblance to Photoshop (see Figure 20-9) but is tailored for creating Web graphics. In fact, Elements inherits its animated GIF-making capabilities (see Chapter 18) not from Photoshop but from ImageReady.

Other Web features that ImageReady can handle include roll-over Web buttons that change as a Web surfer's cursor moves over them, and image maps that let you assign different Web links to various portions of a graphic.

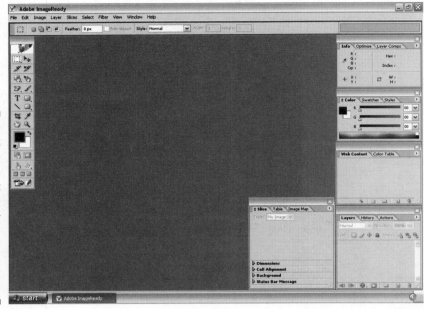

Figure 20-9:
The Image-
Ready
interface
looks a lot
like Photo-
shop —
which looks
a lot like
Elements,
come to
think of it.

Index

• *D* •

• Q •

• R •

BUSINESS, CAREERS & PERSONAL FINANCE

0-7645-5307-0

0-7645-5331-3 *†

Also available:
- Accounting For Dummies †
  0-7645-5314-3
- Business Plans Kit For Dummies †
  0-7645-5365-8
- Cover Letters For Dummies
  0-7645-5224-4
- Frugal Living For Dummies
  0-7645-5403-4
- Leadership For Dummies
  0-7645-5176-0
- Managing For Dummies
  0-7645-1771-6

- Marketing For Dummies
  0-7645-5600-2
- Personal Finance For Dummies *
  0-7645-2590-5
- Project Management For Dummies
  0-7645-5283-X
- Resumes For Dummies †
  0-7645-5471-9
- Selling For Dummies
  0-7645-5363-1
- Small Business Kit For Dummies *†
  0-7645-5093-4

HOME & BUSINESS COMPUTER BASICS

0-7645-4074-2

0-7645-3758-X

Also available:
- ACT! 6 For Dummies
  0-7645-2645-6
- iLife '04 All-in-One Desk Reference
  For Dummies
  0-7645-7347-0
- iPAQ For Dummies
  0-7645-6769-1
- Mac OS X Panther Timesaving
  Techniques For Dummies
  0-7645-5812-9
- Macs For Dummies
  0-7645-5656-8

- Microsoft Money 2004 For Dummies
  0-7645-4195-1
- Office 2003 All-in-One Desk Reference
  For Dummies
  0-7645-3883-7
- Outlook 2003 For Dummies
  0-7645-3759-8
- PCs For Dummies
  0-7645-4074-2
- TiVo For Dummies
  0-7645-6923-6
- Upgrading and Fixing PCs For Dummies
  0-7645-1665-5
- Windows XP Timesaving Techniques
  For Dummies
  0-7645-3748-2

FOOD, HOME, GARDEN, HOBBIES, MUSIC & PETS

0-7645-5295-3

0-7645-5232-5

Also available:
- Bass Guitar For Dummies
  0-7645-2487-9
- Diabetes Cookbook For Dummies
  0-7645-5230-9
- Gardening For Dummies *
  0-7645-5130-2
- Guitar For Dummies
  0-7645-5106-X
- Holiday Decorating For Dummies
  0-7645-2570-0
- Home Improvement All-in-One
  For Dummies
  0-7645-5680-0

- Knitting For Dummies
  0-7645-5395-X
- Piano For Dummies
  0-7645-5105-1
- Puppies For Dummies
  0-7645-5255-4
- Scrapbooking For Dummies
  0-7645-7208-3
- Senior Dogs For Dummies
  0-7645-5818-8
- Singing For Dummies
  0-7645-2475-5
- 30-Minute Meals For Dummies
  0-7645-2589-1

INTERNET & DIGITAL MEDIA

0-7645-1664-7

0-7645-6924-4

Also available:
- 2005 Online Shopping Directory
  For Dummies
  0-7645-7495-7
- CD & DVD Recording For Dummies
  0-7645-5956-7
- eBay For Dummies
  0-7645-5654-1
- Fighting Spam For Dummies
  0-7645-5965-6
- Genealogy Online For Dummies
  0-7645-5964-8
- Google For Dummies
  0-7645-4420-9

- Home Recording For Musicians
  For Dummies
  0-7645-1634-5
- The Internet For Dummies
  0-7645-4173-0
- iPod & iTunes For Dummies
  0-7645-7772-7
- Preventing Identity Theft For Dummies
  0-7645-7336-5
- Pro Tools All-in-One Desk Reference
  For Dummies
  0-7645-5714-9
- Roxio Easy Media Creator For Dummies
  0-7645-7131-1

* Separate Canadian edition also available

† Separate U.K. edition also available

Available wherever books are sold. For more information or to order direct: U.S. customers visit www.dummies.com or call 1-877-762-2974.
U.K. customers visit www.wileyeurope.com or call 0800 243407. Canadian customers visit www.wiley.ca or call 1-800-567-4797.

SPORTS, FITNESS, PARENTING, RELIGION & SPIRITUALITY

0-7645-5146-9

0-7645-5418-2

Also available:

- Adoption For Dummies
  0-7645-5488-3
- Basketball For Dummies
  0-7645-5248-1
- The Bible For Dummies
  0-7645-5296-1
- Buddhism For Dummies
  0-7645-5359-3
- Catholicism For Dummies
  0-7645-5391-7
- Hockey For Dummies
  0-7645-5228-7

- Judaism For Dummies
  0-7645-5299-6
- Martial Arts For Dummies
  0-7645-5358-5
- Pilates For Dummies
  0-7645-5397-6
- Religion For Dummies
  0-7645-5264-3
- Teaching Kids to Read For Dummies
  0-7645-4043-2
- Weight Training For Dummies
  0-7645-5168-X
- Yoga For Dummies
  0-7645-5117-5

TRAVEL

0-7645-5438-7

0-7645-5453-0

Also available:

- Alaska For Dummies
  0-7645-1761-9
- Arizona For Dummies
  0-7645-6938-4
- Cancún and the Yucatán For Dummies
  0-7645-2437-2
- Cruise Vacations For Dummies
  0-7645-6941-4
- Europe For Dummies
  0-7645-5456-5
- Ireland For Dummies
  0-7645-5455-7

- Las Vegas For Dummies
  0-7645-5448-4
- London For Dummies
  0-7645-4277-X
- New York City For Dummies
  0-7645-6945-7
- Paris For Dummies
  0-7645-5494-8
- RV Vacations For Dummies
  0-7645-5443-3
- Walt Disney World & Orlando For Dummies
  0-7645-6943-0

GRAPHICS, DESIGN & WEB DEVELOPMENT

0-7645-4345-8

0-7645-5589-8

Also available:

- Adobe Acrobat 6 PDF For Dummies
  0-7645-3760-1
- Building a Web Site For Dummies
  0-7645-7144-3
- Dreamweaver MX 2004 For Dummies
  0-7645-4342-3
- FrontPage 2003 For Dummies
  0-7645-3882-9
- HTML 4 For Dummies
  0-7645-1995-6
- Illustrator cs For Dummies
  0-7645-4084-X

- Macromedia Flash MX 2004 For Dummies
  0-7645-4358-X
- Photoshop 7 All-in-One Desk Reference For Dummies
  0-7645-1667-1
- Photoshop cs Timesaving Techniques For Dummies
  0-7645-6782-9
- PHP 5 For Dummies
  0-7645-4166-8
- PowerPoint 2003 For Dummies
  0-7645-3908-6
- QuarkXPress 6 For Dummies
  0-7645-2593-X

NETWORKING, SECURITY, PROGRAMMING & DATABASES

0-7645-6852-3

0-7645-5784-X

Also available:

- A+ Certification For Dummies
  0-7645-4187-0
- Access 2003 All-in-One Desk Reference For Dummies
  0-7645-3988-4
- Beginning Programming For Dummies
  0-7645-4997-9
- C For Dummies
  0-7645-7068-4
- Firewalls For Dummies
  0-7645-4048-3
- Home Networking For Dummies
  0-7645-42796

- Network Security For Dummies
  0-7645-1679-5
- Networking For Dummies
  0-7645-1677-9
- TCP/IP For Dummies
  0-7645-1760-0
- VBA For Dummies
  0-7645-3989-2
- Wireless All In-One Desk Reference For Dummies
  0-7645-7496-5
- Wireless Home Networking For Dummies
  0-7645-3910-8